To
JERRY

CONTENTS

FOREWORD

By Martha E. Williams

Public access to online databases was initiated in the early 1970s when the National Library of Medicine, Mead Data Central, DIALOG, and SDC initiated their search services. At that time online searching was rather an elitist activity and very few librarians were active searchers. Today we have hundreds of online search services and online searching is commonplace at least among information specialists and reference librarians in information centers and libraries. These searchers, often called intermediaries, however, are not the only ones searching databases. End users are entering the marketplace though not in as great numbers as the producers and vendors had hoped. The papers included in this book are directed toward intermediary searchers though end users should also find them helpful.

The database industry has shifted from the formative stages in the 1970s to the current status of having enough maturity and size to merit being called an industry. The database industry continually grows and changes, thereby creating a challenging environment for the searchers.

For the past twenty years I have monitored the database industry and for the past ten years I have monitored the online database industry in the information center/library market.* Issues in this market are the subject of Carol Tenopir's book. The online database industry is the background against which database searching takes place. The database industry underlies database searching: it provides the resources and the limits for searching. Searchers can only access data that is contained in databases and their searches are constrained by the capabilities and features of the software (both mainframe and microcomputer) for search preparation, for database search and retrieval, and for post-processing search results.

There are now some 4,500 publicly available databases. In the late 1960s there were only about a dozen, in 1975 there were 301, in 1983 (the year in which Carol started writing the "Online Databases" columns which make up a good portion of this book) there were about 1,800—a respectable number from which searchers could make their selections. In 1988 there were 4,200, and now there are more than 4,500.

There are many metrics one can use for evaluating the size and success of the database industry. The size of the available collection of databases is one, the number of producers is another, and the number of sites processing databases for customers is yet another. In 1975 the 301 publicly available databases were produced by 200 database producers and were processed (both in the batch mode and online) by 105 organizations that offered services to the public. In 1988 the 4,200 databases were produced by 1,733 producers, and services were provided by approximately 750 processors. This represents significant growth for the industry and increased complexity for the searchers.

The numbers of databases, producers, and processors, however, by themselves do not mean much in business terms. The existence of databases is not enough to create an industry. They must be used and users must pay for the use, otherwise the databases cannot remain in existence. There are real and substantial costs associated with database development and maintenance, and with the provision of the search services online. These costs must be recovered by the producers and online vendors through user charges or there can be no industry.

---

*This discussion, in fact, will present some of the data I have gathered for my own book *Information Market Indicators: Information Center/Library Market*, issue no. 23 (Monticello, Ill.: Information Market Indicators Inc., 1989) and "The State of Databases Today," my foreword to *Computer-Readable Databases*, edited by K. Y. Marcaccio, J. A. DeMaggio, and M. E. Williams (Detroit, Mich.: Gale Research, 1989).

While this book focuses mainly on a half-decade time period I will look back ten years to show the growth of the online word-oriented database search activity and its concomitant financial support of the database industry. In 1978 the expenditures for online database searching in the information center/library market were about $40 million. By 1983 they were $173 million and by 1987 they were $386 million. From the beginning to the end of the ten-year period the growth was nearly tenfold. The *amount* of growth in the early years was not as great as in the last five years of the period. The *rate* of increase was larger in the early years because the base was relatively small.

Over the same ten-year period usage increased from 780,000 connect hours to 3,020,000 hours, and the number of searches (one query against one database) increased from 2.7 million per year to 26.5 million per year. Expenditures increased nearly tenfold. (This refers to expenditures of the whole market where increasing numbers of organizations entered the market; undoubtedly expenditures within the average user organization also increased though not drastically.) Usage increased nearly fourfold, and the number of searches increased nearly tenfold though searches are now of shorter duration. Connect hours increased at a slower rate than did expenditures, presumably because of both baud rate and price increases. In the early years most searching was conducted at 300 baud; communications baud rates of 1200 and 2400 are now common (with the overall effective average probably being 1800).

The average cost per search has varied over the ten years, going up and down several times. In 1978 it was approximately $14.80. The low occurred in 1979 and 1980 with $12.50, the high in 1986 with $17.50, and in 1987 it dropped back to $14.60. The dollar cost per search is slightly lower than it was ten years earlier, however; the searches are of shorter duration. If one were to take into consideration the Consumer Price Index (CPI) adjustment, the average cost per search would be considerably lower than it was ten years ago. Users are getting more for their search dollar than ever before.

Since the initiation of her column "Online Databases" in *Library Journal*, Carol Tenopir has been chronicling database searching for the library community. It is against the database industry backdrop just described that she has written. The many types of databases, search systems, and pricing schedules are the milieu within which the searchers operate. It is from the point of view of database searching that Carol has looked at the searchers (chapter 1), the resources (chapters 3, 4, 5, 6, and 9), evaluation and analysis of the resources (chapters 7 and 8), and the industry (chapter 10).

Searchers may be professional searchers or end users. When she discusses the training required and the characteristics of good searchers she is talking about professional searchers, but they are not the only searchers. For quite some time the industry has been in pursuit of the elusive end user. The number of end-user passwords assigned by vendor services has grown dramatically in the past five years but I suspect that the volume of use of word-oriented databases by those end users is not very large. The number of passwords is a very misleading metric. The number of passwords assigned is probably ten times the number of passwords that are used at least two hours per month; many are not used for even one hour per year. Thus, while the number of end-user passwords is on the increase, end-user use of the word-oriented databases is still not a large fraction of the total use of those databases. The intermediary is still foremost.

The resources involved in database searching include hardware, software, databases, and aids or tools for locating and selecting databases, developing search strategies, and the like. Carol's treatment of hardware includes the use of microcomputers for searching databases and downloading data. She discusses software for micros and the selection of software for in-house database searching as well as software interfaces to external databases on vendor systems. Database resources are of several types and are available and searchable on several media. Carol covers not only the more traditional databases but also full-text databases and recent events relative to CD-ROM databases.

Searchers need to evaluate the resources and tools of their trade. Chapter 4 deals with evaluation of microcomputer software for library retrieval, and chapters 7 and 8 treat evaluation of database coverage, the literature cited, database structures, database design, access points, and, of course, the systems for searching the databases. Database searching is not done in a vacuum or without aids and so Carol has discussed a set of aids for keeping up-to-date, identifying and selecting databases, and for developing search strategies. Carol concludes with a chapter on the database industry, which is where I began.

MARTHA E. WILLIAMS
University of Illinois
at Urbana-Champaign

PREFACE

Issues in Online Database Searching is Number 1 in my new Database Searching Series for Libraries Unlimited. This first volume illustrates my personal perspective on many of the major issues that are important to the professional online searcher in the library environment. It includes mostly short articles written by me over the last ten years on many different topics. Several of these topics will be covered in depth in later volumes by other experts who have agreed to write original contributions for this series.

The book is arranged in ten chapters, each representing an issue that I feel is of interest or concern to today's database professionals. As I looked over my writings in the database field for the past ten years, certain topics emerged over and over again. This made it easy to organize the articles by topic. Some of the topics are of special personal interest (e.g., full-text databases, in-house databases), but almost all the topics are of continuing concern to some degree to every "online librarian."

Most of the articles in this book were originally published in my "Online Databases" column in *Library Journal*. I began writing that monthly column in February 1983 and have written over sixty columns as of 1989. For several years I have been asked by many people to collect and reprint my columns in a single volume. I considered taking the easy way out—just reprinting all of the columns in a chronological arrangement—but decided that would not best serve the reader. In a chronological arrangement articles on the same or similar topics would be scattered, because I purposely try to scatter my coverage of topics throughout the *Library Journal* issues and because I usually update "hot" topics every year or two. Instead, I decided on the broad subject arrangement that brings together similar columns and updates. This arrangement made it easier to be selective. Not every *Library Journal* "Online Databases" column is reprinted here: some were simply too out-of-date to reprint without extensive updating; others were judged not to be of lasting value. It also made it easier to include some of my lengthier articles that were originally published in other journals in the library and information science field, including *Information Technology and Libraries*, *Microcomputers for Information Management*, *Online*, and *Online Review*. Only those articles that were authored by me alone are included; coauthored articles are omitted. For those who might be trying to track down a *Library Journal* column that is not included here or to find an article for which I had a coauthor, a complete chronological list of my publications is given in the Appendix.

Many of the original articles selected for this volume still include a certain amount of time-sensitive information such as prices, addresses, etc. I have brought this information as up to date as possible. Admittedly, prices and addresses will change again with time, but as of December 1988 this information is current. That means some of the articles here are not just reprints, they are updated versions of the original articles. Chapter introductions note those that have been updated extensively.

Many of the articles report research results or discuss issues and trends. The perspective at the time those articles were written is important to their content; therefore they were not updated after the benefits of hindsight: most of these articles are reprinted exactly. Most of the articles in Chapter 10, for example, discuss issues and trends in the database industry, not specific software packages or online systems.

As you read these articles you will notice inconsistencies in spelling and word forms of certain words or phrases. Sometimes it is *inhouse*, other times *in-house* or even *in house*; likewise, *end user*, *full text*, *free text*, *front end*, *laser disk*, etc., appear in several different forms. Sometimes the variation is due to editorial policies of the journals that originally published the articles; sometimes it is because my preference for a particular form changed over time. Only *online* and *database* have been widely accepted as single words in the database searching world. Only time and user acceptance (and not, I suspect, the rules of English grammar) will determine the final common usage of these phrases. My thanks (and apologies) to my English-teacher proofreader (and sister), Kathryn Tenopir Remkiewicz.

A volume such as this represents much of the work of my professional life to date, at least on topics relating to databases. I owe thanks to more people than I can acknowledge. I especially want to thank the people most responsible for helping shape my ideas and for getting my work into print: Martha E. Williams, Professor at the University of Illinois Coordinated Science Laboratory and Editor of *Online Review*; John N. Berry III, Editor-in-Chief of *Library Journal*; and Gerald W. Lundeen, Professor at the School of Library and Information Studies, University of Hawaii and my coauthor on many articles about in-house databases. I also want to thank the members of my indexing class at the University of Hawaii at Manoa School of Library and Information Studies who prepared the index as a class project: James Adamson, Ah Win, Nancy Allerston, Mary Bailey, Patricia Butson, Nand Dayal, Wallace Grant, Aung Gyi, Keiko Hassler, Soon Young Kim, Christine Orrall, and Fred Roecker.

CHAPTER

1

INTERMEDIARY SEARCHERS

Intermediaries—people who do database searches for other people—have been the mainstay of online use since online searching began. Librarians and other information professionals have served as online intermediaries for their clients for almost twenty years and are still an important part of online services.

The process of meeting someone else's information needs presents unique challenges. Intermediaries must possess skills that range from good reference interview techniques, to the ability to estimate costs, to searching in the most cost-effective manner possible. Intermediaries face the challenge of having to search many different databases, frequently on topics for which they have no expertise. They must translate the information needs of a client into a formal search strategy statement. They have to be knowledgeable about online sources, CD-ROM sources, and printed sources, and be able to judge which best fits the information need of a particular client. They have to be able to balance costs of electronic information sources with the benefits of different media and different databases.

These unique challenges and the need for these unique skills form the basis for many of the articles in this book. The professional intermediary is the primary audience for all of the articles.

This first chapter focuses specifically on the persona of the professional searcher. The first article reviews recent research that has attempted to discover what makes a good searcher, particularly what makes a good intermediary searcher. Personality traits, intelligence, and experience with databases or online searching have all been examined in an attempt to identify the traits of good searchers. "Good" has been defined in various quantitative and qualitative ways. Besides being of personal interest to current searchers, the reasoning goes that if specific background experience or character traits can be linked to successful searching, educators could do better career counseling and would-be searchers could perhaps work to maximize their experience in the identified areas. As of the late 1980s, however, there is yet no definitive answer to the question "what makes a good searcher?" Speculation abounds and the issue offers a fruitful area for research.

The second article in this chapter switches to more objective and readily identifiable characteristics of searchers without tackling the difficult definition of "good." "Online Professionals" analyzes the first (1984) edition of the *Marquis Who's Who Directory of Online Professionals*. The directory and corresponding online database were created in part with input from questionnaires sent to members of several information-related professional groups. Within the obvious limitations of who is included in the directory and how the information was gathered, analyzing the directory paints a picture of the professional online searchers of today. In addition to information that describes the workplace and personal characteristics of searchers, the directory reports information about the online systems and databases that professional searchers use most often.

Learning how to search and then honing those skills and keeping up with new developments are important to an intermediary's professional life. "In-House Training and Staff Development" outlines various levels of staff education and training for online searching. Libraries that offer intermediary searches have a responsibility to their clientele and to their staff to provide continuing educational activities for all levels of personnel. Some programming possibilities are presented.

The decisions that searchers within the library environment must make are outlined in "Decision Making by Reference Librarians." In this age when online, CD-ROM, and printed reference materials are all available, the reference librarian must continually make decisions about which form or format to access. These decisions are made at the collection development level and again at the reference question level after collection decisions have been made. The decisions that all intermediaries have to make impact the work environment and the ability of their clients to access the best sources of information.

A short essay on the future needs of education for database searching concludes this chapter. "Online Education: Planning for the Future" is the only article in the chapter that was originally published in a source other than my *Library Journal* column. It was written for the tenth anniversary issue of *Online* magazine in 1987. The essay is written from my perspective as a teacher in a master's program in library and information science. Many of the issues raised in this essay are covered in more detail from other perspectives in later chapters. Laser disks (a.k.a. CD-ROM), end users, full-text databases, and intermediary computer software such as gateways and front ends are all briefly introduced as influencing elements in the education of online professionals. Each of these issues is covered in a separate chapter of this book.

WHAT MAKES A GOOD ONLINE SEARCHER?*

Every online intermediary, online services manager, and online educator has an intuitive feel for what traits distinguish a good online searcher. By observing good (and poor) intermediary searchers in action, it is clear that not everyone is able to search with equal ease or success. Why is it some people seem to take to searching naturally, while for others it is always difficult? In the last few years, several researchers have attempted to supplement intuition with data in answering this. Although the research is not definitive, coupled with observation and intuition it may eventually help to let us draw a profile of a good online searcher.

INTUITION

Many people have expressed their opinion on what they believe are the traits of a good searcher:

- enthusiasm for the job and for the process of online searching;
- good verbal communication skills and patience with people (important in the reference interview);
- self-esteem (confidence in his/her ability to interact with equipment, to make decisions on whether or not a search is appropriate);
- creativity (the ability to see and try different approaches to a problem);
- courage and the ability to make quick decisions (to change strategies while online);
- logical and analytical way of thinking (the ability to separate concepts, look at problems by their component parts, and proceed in a stepwise fashion);
- memory for details (of command languages, database structure, formats, etc.);
- intelligence;
- spelling, grammar, and typing skills;

- subject-area knowledge (particularly important in highly specialized or complex subject areas);
- an organized mind (the ability to gather all information required and go through the many steps required in the search process);
- willingness to grow (to keep up with system enhancements, learn details of databases, and refine strategy skills);
- willingness to share knowledge with others; and
- experience with online systems and printed indexes.

One could argue that a person who possesses all of these traits should be good at anything! Certainly an argument can be made that a good reference librarian possesses most of these characteristics, whether or not he/she uses online tools. Do these characteristics stand up to systematic testing?

WHAT IS "GOOD"?

The first question to ask is what makes a searcher good, or at least better than another? To answer this in a controlled setting, most studies rely on comparing results of a series of searches by several searchers. In order to compare searchers' success, researchers have had to set some definitions of good search results, defining good in several ways.

One way is to test the results of each search by the standard measurements of *precision* and *recall*. Precision measures what percentage of the citations retrieved in a search are relevant to the request. (It assumes, of course, that the requester or searcher can judge that an article will be relevant to their request.)

Recall attempts to measure what percentage of the citations in a database that are relevant to a given query were actually retrieved in a given search. Recall is more difficult to measure because, unless the researcher examines every single citation in a database, they can never be sure they have identified all relevant documents. In experimental situations,

---

*Reprinted from *Library Journal* Mar. 15, 1987. Copyright © 1987 by Reed Publishing, USA, Div. of Reed Holdings, Inc.

researchers often settle for "relative recall"; that is, after several searchers conduct the same online search, the pool of all the citations retrieved is used to form the 100 percent recall set. Each individual's results can then be compared to the total set.

Other objective measures commonly used to define good searching:

- the number of search statements entered for a given query (to measure efficiency);

- the cost of the search, including online time and citation printing charges (to measure unit cost per relevant document, also called cost effectiveness); and

- error rate (e.g., errors in Boolean logic, command syntax, etc.).

These objective measures are assumed to reflect the less obvious components of searcher quality such as a searcher's reference interview technique or database knowledge. They are considered easier to control and more accurate than subjective measures such as asking patrons if they are satisfied with a completed search or having expert searchers judge quality of search strategies.

These various objective and subjective measures have been used in studies to attempt to see if good searchers possess certain identifiable characteristics: experience with online systems and databases; scholastic aptitude; personality traits and creativity; and cognitive style.

EXPERIENCE

Intermediaries would like to think that the more experience searchers have, the better they will search. Research has not completely borne this out.

Fenichel[1] used DIALOG's ONTAP ERIC database to study searchers with different levels of experience on both the online system and the database. Her results showed that experience contributed only to some success factors and that "compared to the experienced subjects, the novices performed surprisingly well. Although, as a group, they searched more slowly than the experienced subjects, made more errors, and scored lower on most (but not all) outcome measures, the differences were not as great as might be expected."

Moderately experienced searchers, with ERIC experience, on the average performed the most cost-effective searches (perhaps because most of them are academic librarians from libraries that charge for searches). The most experienced searchers on an average achieved highest recall, but precision was no better than novice scores. Other studies have found similar results. Fenichel found considerable differences in search strategy among individuals, regardless of search experience: a wide variety in the number of commands entered, terms used, and time connected. Fenichel concluded that "this individual variability may be the overriding factor in online searching behavior."

SCHOLASTIC APTITUDE

Intelligence is difficult to measure, but there are some factors that can be used as indirect measures of intelligence as it relates to academic success. GRE scores of library school student subjects were used by Bellardo,[2] while Borgman[3] looked at the high school GPA and SAT scores of her undergraduate subjects.

Bellardo found that GRE scores can be used to a limited extent to predict online search performance. She cautions however, that "although it was the general tendency for better searchers to have higher GRE scores ... there were some students with low GRE scores who performed quite well. Individuals with low GREs who are especially motivated or interested in searching therefore should not necessarily be discouraged from pursuing training. They ... are more likely to experience difficulty in the learning process."

Borgman found that science/engineering majors generally were more successful in their early encounters with an online system than were humanities/social science majors. In a later study, Borgman found that engineering majors also score higher in certain measures of scholastic aptitude such as high school GPA and SAT scores.

CREATIVITY AND PERSONALITY

Both creativity and personality traits are difficult to judge objectively. Standardized tests have been developed which, although sometimes criticized, are generally accepted as broad measures of a person's creative tendencies and personality traits. Bellardo used the *Khatena-Torrance Creative Perception Inventory* to measure creativity. She used the *Interpersonal Disposition Inventory*, which measures traits associated with masculinity and femininity, to assess personality.

Bellardo found no traits that were conclusively associated with good searching. Clusters of traits such as assertiveness, self-confidence, dominance, and risk taking, and another including openness, warmth, sensitivity, and compassion, were not found to predict search performance within the limitations of the study. Artistry (especially literary) and traits of preferring to work alone, analytical and critical thinking, and liking to deal with theoretical and complex concerns had a slight association with recall scores.

COGNITIVE STYLE

Standard tests of cognitive style have been used by several online researchers. If good searchers share cognitive styles, such tests might be useful for predicting who will be successful. Cognitive style research, though ongoing, is as yet inconclusive.

The "Learning Styles Inventory" (LSI) measures individual preferences for different styles of learning. Woelfl[4] found that experienced MEDLINE searchers are most often convergers (those who focus on specific problems, use hypo-thetico-deductive reasoning, and do best when there is a single correct answer).

The second most frequent type are assimilators (those who are strong in inductive reasoning, theoretical models, and logic). Borgman found that engineering majors tend to be convergers, while a majority of English majors fall at the opposite end of the spectrum (divergers, or those whose primary strengths are imagination, creativity, and open-ended questions). A later study by Logan and Woelfl[5] found that novice library school student searchers tended to be divergers.

Another study[6] found that items retrieved by searchers who favored an abstract-conceptualization learning style had the greatest chance of being relevant, while items retrieved by concrete-experience learners had the least chance. This study also found that searchers with higher language abilities, as demonstrated by the "Remote Associates Test," are better searchers, regardless of the topic of the search. People who scored higher on a "Symbolic Reasoning Test" and had higher mathematical scores are poorer searchers.

CONCLUSION

Any conclusions must be taken cautiously. This research is at the beginning stages; much of it is done with a small number of subjects or searches and uses small databases. Broad conclusions are based on averaging individual searchers' results. There will always be individual exceptions to any generalization.

REFERENCES

[1]Fenichel, Carol. *Online Information Retrieval: Identification of Measures That Discriminate Among Users with Different Levels and Types of Experience*. Ph.D. dissertation, Drexel Univ., 1979. Available from University Microfilms International (UMI). Summarized in: Fenichel, Carol, "Online Searching: Measures That Discriminate Among Users with Different Types of Experience," *Journal of the American Society for Information Science*, January 1981, p. 23-32.

[2]Bellardo, Trudi. *Some Attributes of Online Search Intermediaries That Relate to Search Outcome*. Ph.D. dissertation, Drexel Univ., 1984. Available from UMI. Summarized in: Bellardo, Trudi, "An Investigation of Online Searcher Traits and Their Relationship to Search Outcome," *Journal of the American Society for Information Science*, July 1985, p. 240-251.

[3]Borgman, Christine. *The User's Mental Model of an Information Retrieval System: Effects on Performance*. Ph.D. dissertation, Stanford Univ., 1984. Available from UMI; and Borgman, Christine, "Individual Differences in the use of Information Retrieval Systems: a Pilot Study," *ASIS 86*, Proceedings of the 49th Annual Meeting of the American Society for Information Science, Learned Information, 1986, p. 20-31.

[4]Woelfl, Nancy. *Individual Differences in Online Search Behavior: the Effect of Learning Styles and Cognitive Abilities on Process and Outcome*. Ph.D. dissertation, Case Western Reserve Univ., 1984. Dissertation Abstracts International, Ann Arbor, Mich.

[5]Logan, E. L. & Nancy Woelfl, "Individual Differences in Online Searching Behavior of Novice Searchers," *ASIS 86*, Proceedings of the 49th Annual Meeting of the American Society for Information Science. Learned Information, 1986, p. 163-166.

[6]Trivison, Donna & others, "Effectiveness and Efficiency of Searchers in Online Searching," *ASIS 86*, Proceedings of the 49th Annual Meeting of the American Society for Information Science, Learned Information, 1986, p. 341-349. ∎

ONLINE PROFESSIONALS*

Did you ever wonder who, besides librarians, does online searching for a living? Where are these online professionals employed? How many hours per month do they search and on what systems? These questions and others can be answered in part by the new Marquis Who's Who *Directory of Online Professionals* and corresponding PRO-Files database on DIALOG.

Last year Marquis mailed over 100,000 requests for biographical information to people on the mailing lists of online producers, vendors, periodicals, relevant professional associations, and online user groups. Many of you probably received several of these mailings because, as Marquis admits, there is considerable duplication among the lists. Marquis estimates the actual size of the online industry to be between 25,000 and 45,000 people.

BIOGRAPHIES OF 6000 SEARCHERS

Roughly 6000 online searchers responded, providing detailed biographical information including their: name; current position; current online function; online experience; systems currently used; hours of searching per month; library type (if any); equipment used; databases frequently used; database subject expertise; consulting experience; speaking experience; electronic mail systems used; birth information; education; career history; career-related activities; professional memberships; creative works; and address and telephone numbers.

In addition, Marquis identified notable people in the field who must be included in the directory whether or not they responded to the mailing. The Marquis staff researched these approximately 400 biographies.

As in all Marquis Who's Who publications, the biographee-provided information is accepted as it is submitted without verification. Conclusions about the online profession drawn from the directory must of course keep the editorial policies and response to the mailings in mind. Only 6148 names out of an estimated field of 25,000-45,000 are included. Inclusion primarily depends on a searcher's motivation to respond to a commercial mailing. One of the advantages the database has over the printed directory, however, is that errors can be corrected and new names can be added in a much more timely fashion. The PRO-Files database will be updated quarterly and Marquis will include corrections submitted by the biographees and newly submitted profiles in each update. There will probably be many additions and corrections to the first update this spring, as searchers see the printed directory and online database for the first time.

The printed directory will be updated biannually. In August 1985 galley proofs of the current sketches will be sent to all biographees for correction and updating. At the same time, new entries will be identified through another mailing campaign.

Quarterly updates will make the online version a more valuable product than the printed directory. Another advantage of the online version is the ability to search any field or combination of fields to create statistical profiles of the biographees. Educational degrees and current position can be combined to find out how many searchers in the Marquis Directory have the masters in library science but work outside libraries. Hours per month spent on searching can be combined with years of online experience or current job function or even online systems used most frequently to begin to build a profile of searchers and searching habits. Within the limitations of the directory contents, many interesting combinations will help reveal characteristics of the people in this industry.

SEARCHER CREDENTIALS

All 6,148 entries in the first edition were available for searching in the PRO-Files database (file 235 on DIALOG) as of January 1985. Before the database was completed, Marquis generated statistics of online professionals using about two-thirds of the records. This test file is believed to be characteristic of the entire database and answers some of the questions I posed earlier.

Of the biographees in the test file, only 32 percent hold a masters degree in library science (46 percent attended library school). Nearly three-quarters of the biographees belong to a library or information-related professional organization, however, with the Special Libraries Association, American Library Association, and the American Society for Information Science heading the list. (This high percentage of professional affiliation may be because the mailing lists of these and other professional organizations were among the sources used to get biographical submissions.)

WHERE THEY WORK

More searchers work in the private sector than anywhere else (45 percent), followed by the academic sector (33 percent), government (14 percent), and all other (eight percent). Many of these private sector employees are not librarians, for only 19 percent of the respondents work in special/corporate libraries. College libraries employ 28 percent of the total biographees, but public libraries account for only three percent of the online professionals in the directory. Approximately 65 percent of the biographees work in some kind of library.

Not only are there fewer public library searchers (contained within the "other" employment sector category) than private company searchers, on the average the public library searchers spend less time online each month. Of the private sector searchers 26 percent search more than 20 hours per month as compared to 17 percent of the "other" sector searchers. In government, 26 percent of the searchers are also

*Reprinted from *Library Journal* Feb. 15, 1985. Copyright © 1985 by Reed Publishing, USA, Div. of Reed Holdings, Inc.

heavy users and 17 percent of the academic sector searchers search more than 20 hours per month.

A majority of the Who's Who online professionals have between two and nine years of experience in the field (38 percent have two to five years, 28 percent have six to nine). Because online searching has been widespread for only a little over a decade, it is not surprising that only 11 percent of the biographees have over 10 years of experience in the field.

In connection with the experience figures, almost three-quarters (72 percent) of the online professionals are between the ages of 25 and 44. Since the average age of MLS students is usually older than the average college student, it would be interesting to also look at the number of years since their last college degree in addition to the age of searchers. Fifty-eight percent of the online professionals are women. The test file biographees came from 46 different countries, although the data collection method favored the United States and other English speaking countries.

THE MOST POPULAR SYSTEMS

In addition to the personal profiles of searchers, the Marquis database provides information on the systems and databases most frequently used by the respondents. DIALOG is the most heavily used system by far, with 80 percent of the respondents using it. Over 50 systems in all are used by the biographees with just 20 of these used by five percent or more of the searchers and only 10 used by 10 percent or more. After DIALOG with 80 percent use, BRS is next most popular with 37 percent of the searchers using it, followed by SDC Orbit with 35 percent, OCLC with 26 percent, NLM with 20 percent, NEXIS with 13 percent, and Dow Jones News/Retrieval with 12 percent. In the top 20 systems are the consumer information services The Source and CompuServe and bibliographic systems such as Pergamon Infoline, Chem Abstracts, DOE Recon, and the European Space Agency.

Many online professionals do not limit their searching to a single system. The directory shows that 42 percent of DIALOG users also access BRS and 41 percent also access SDC Orbit, while 20 percent access all three systems. OCLC is used by 27 percent of DIALOG users, 20 percent use NLM, 16 percent use NEXIS, and seven percent also use Dow Jones News/Retrieval. In keeping with DIALOG's popularity, 90 percent of BRS users, 95 percent of SDC Orbit users, and 82 percent of NLM users also search DIALOG.

Although a large majority search DIALOG, these online professionals come from diverse subject backgrounds and search a variety of subject areas. No one subject is searched by a majority, with 30 percent searching business topics, 25 percent searching medicine, and 20 percent searching sci/tech topics. Between 10 and 18 percent of the online professionals listed search (in order): education, chemistry, social sciences,

information science, life science, current affairs, psychology, computer science, and law.

Information about hardware used, baud rate, and electronic mail systems used was also solicited in the questionnaire. This type of information is probably already out of date since expert predictions in the industry have anticipated a major shift in 1984 and 1985 to searching with microcomputers with 1,200 baud modems. Tracing the changes over time in these areas would be interesting, but unfortunately because the burden of updating the information in a biography is on the biographee, many changes won't be reflected.

In the first edition of the directory and database, 69 percent of the respondents still searched using a dumb terminal. The remaining 31 percent were not asked if they used a microcomputer or just a smart terminal. Only a small number (18 percent) of the test file respondents used an electronic mail system. Of those, most used either ONTYME (offered through CLASS—the Cooperative Library Agency for Systems and Services) or the BRS electronic mail service. Since DIALOG now has an electronic mail system, I am sure these figures are already outdated.

When searching the PRO-Files database, as when searching the Marquis Who's Who database, it is necessary to check the database documentation and DIALOG blue sheet. The database is highly structured, with each item of information about a person in a separate field specified by a unique additional index prefix.

The contents of each field make extensive use of abbreviations, not all of which are obvious. "Info Mgr" means information manager in the Current Online Function field, "spl-assn/soc" is the library type for association or society special libraries, "profl jours" indicates publications in professional journals, etc. The abbreviations make sense in a printed directory by serving to keep the book to a manageable size, but they are often a hindrance to searching in an online file.

There are also typographical errors in the first edition that can be overlooked in the printed directory but that will pose searching problems in the online file. In this first edition, the typographical errors may be as high as one percent of the total characters. The first quarterly online update should improve that figure in the database. Because of the additional indexes, use of abbreviations, and typographical errors, extra care in search strategy formulation is required.

Online directories such as this one have potential far beyond their printed equivalents. Many more questions about searchers and searching can be answered in the PRO-Files database by combining fields in different ways. The printed directory is limited to geographic, subject expertise, and online function indexes. The online PRO-Files database provides a fascinating picture of the online professionals included in the Marquis *Directory of Online Professionals*. Initially the PRO-Files database contains only the online professionals. Other directories of professional groups will eventually be included in PRO-Files corresponding to other Marquis directories underway. ∎

IN-HOUSE TRAINING & STAFF DEVELOPMENT*

Staff development and in-house training of any type are considered luxuries in many libraries. Such programs are more important than ever, however, with continuing expansion of the library's role, developments with new technologies, and the growth, developments, and changes in online database searching.

In the area of online database searching, in-house programs can help to supplement vendor workshops and keep searchers up-to-date with new systems or services. These programs can be used to train new searchers or give experienced ones a chance to upgrade their skills. A good program can help to acquaint all library staff with the powers or limitations of online searching and with commercially available databases. This month's column will examine different levels of in-house programs, discuss various methods tried by some libraries, and look at some inexpensive alternatives that can be managed even by libraries with very small budgets. In-house programs need not be just for large libraries or those with unlimited budgets.

Depending on the size of staff, budget, administrative commitment to staff development, and geographic location of the library, different levels of intensity or involvement with online search training might be adopted. The three most common levels found in libraries are: 1) general staff orientation programs; 2) searcher updating and skills improvement; and 3) basic search training. Some libraries offer all of these levels; others choose those that best fit their circumstances and needs.

GENERAL STAFF ORIENTATION

Even in a small library—or especially in a small library—most librarians recognize the importance of keeping all workers apprised of services offered by the library. Formal programs that introduce online search services to all staff levels from volunteers to management can improve staff morale, alleviate fears, and ultimately improve the online search service.

Such programs can be planned when search services are newly introduced in a library, but should be repeated from time to time for new employees and to keep older employees who are not directly involved with online searching aware of new developments.

The content of such a program will vary with the individual situation and background of personnel, but generally will include:

- definitions of online searching, online systems, and databases;

- an overview of what databases are available and those that will most likely be accessed in the library;

- an overview of what systems are available and those that will be accessed in the library;

- an explanation of the necessary equipment, documentation, and training necessary to begin searching;

- a basic introduction to the search process, including the role of telecommunications, query languages, and database characteristics;

- an outline of the search strategy development process;

- an explanation of how search request forms and presearch interviews are used;

- specific decisions made in the library regarding staffing, pricing and use policies, equipment, etc.

By budgeting as little as $10, a short demonstration can wrap up the program and will help make all of the above clear to even the most inexperienced participant.

The total time required to attend such a program need not be long; times ranging from one hour to half a day have been successful. The preparation time required is, of course, much greater. Time will need to be allotted in the schedule of the searcher or search coordinator doing the sessions.

Except for very small libraries, it is best to have the searcher (or searchers) at the individual library prepare and present the orientation session. Other options are possible, however. It is common for a central office of a library system or network to prepare the session for presentation to all system libraries. Alternatively, a group of libraries can divide the topics to be covered and produce a cooperative session. This may require staff travel to a central location or the presentors giving the same program many times, conditions that are not always feasible. Other options include asking a guest speaker from a search system, a local college or university, or a library that has more search experience to present the general information while the staff of the host library presents local policies and decisions. Introductory films, slides, and videotapes are available, but are less personal and can be used as supplementary material.

A nice benefit of taking the time to plan this first level of program is the use of the program to introduce the library board, community, or faculty and administration to the online search services thus creating more visibility for the library as well as fulfilling its educational role.

SEARCHER UPDATING

The second level of in-house training programs (the second most widely used by libraries) may be called current awareness, intermediate searching, or online refresher, but their primary purpose is to keep searchers and other staff members up-to-date. Where the audience of the first level of programs included at least the entire library staff and perhaps other interested parties, the current awareness program has a narrower focus. In a large institution, the focus could just be on online searchers. Advanced search tips and techniques,

*Reprinted from *Library Journal* May 1, 1984. Copyright © 1984 by Reed Publishing, USA, Div. of Reed Holdings, Inc.

databases on specific topics, and upgrading search skills have all been a part of these in-house programs in libraries. They can be organized by a searching coordinator who either teaches the sessions or finds staff members and outside experts for various topics. A committee can substitute for the coordinator's role. When such programs are done in-house, the time commitment by other staff need not be great and costs can be kept low.

Online practice is a useful component of refresher sessions. The chance to try out different strategies for the same topic or discuss the approaches of others to a question helps refine search skills. Online practice requires a budget, however, and adequate time may be impossible for some libraries. Low cost options include using such things as DIALOG's Online Training and Practice (ONTAP) files at $15 per hour plus telecommunications, limiting practice to the relatively inexpensive ERIC databases, or using the free time often available for new databases. (Locally-produced search simulation systems or computer-assisted instruction programs are other options that have been reported in the literature. Such systems require initial programming and start-up costs that are beyond the grasp of most libraries. They may become more widespread in the future, however.) In lieu of individual practice time, participants can work out search strategy options together and try them online as a group.

Level two staff development for searchers is often done through an online user group. In a large academic library or system, this can be composed of all searchers and other reference librarians. In a small institution, a consortium of several libraries can arrange periodic refresher programs. This type of program is also widely offered through professional societies and vendors. Inconvenient meeting times, fees, or the inability to get time off may limit the number of searchers who can participate in such opportunities. By planning such programs in-house, meeting times can be varied so all appropriate staff members are able to attend and the programs can be tailored to individual situations.

Refresher programs should not always be limited to online searchers. All library staff members will benefit from finding out about new databases and new trends in the online world. Programs on the proliferation of nonbibliographic databases, database copyright issues, possibilities of end-user searching, changes in database pricing, etc. affect all library employees. One hour programs (in some places held at noon in the lunchroom) are usually sufficient to help staff members keep up on developments in the online world and on how these developments may affect them.

BASIC SEARCH TRAINING

The first two program levels are both primarily in-service staff development programs to make everyone in a library feel a part of library operations as well as in control of technology by being aware of its powers, limitations, and new developments. In-house training programs that provide basic instruction in online searching are less common, in part because they are expensive and require a high level of expertise to be done well, and in part because there are other alternatives for learning. A survey by M. Murphy shows that vendors train the majority of new searchers. Library school courses, professional conferences, or workshops are also used.

Still, Murphy's survey found that many searchers are self-taught or are tutored by colleagues. These people may be too far from training sites, unable to pay the tuition fees, or simply would rather work at their own pace. A formal in-house basic training program offered within an individual library or by a consortium of libraries solves several of these problems. It has the advantage of allowing instructors and students to continue to work together after the course is over so the learning process does not end when the class does. It can provide a collegial atmosphere and sense of accomplishment for students and instructors alike. Programs and examples can be tailored to the unique library and schedules can be designed to accommodate all staff members.

In-house training is not inexpensive or easy, however. Sufficient online time must be budgeted; materials must be prepared; the staff doing the instructing will require extensive time for lesson planning. Vendors now do most of the training because they do it well. If inexperienced searchers are training new searchers, errors and inefficiences can be passed on perpetually. The ideal training situation is, therefore, probably a combination of vendor and in-house training. If a library has the facilities to host a vendor's basic training session, it can earn free registrations. In an area where there are enough interested paying participants, this can be a way to cut vendor training costs. After the vendor training, an in-house session run by experienced searchers or a search coordinator can reinforce new skills and provide continuity.

In-house training and staff development programs for online searching deserve a closer look in these times of change and limited budgets. They should not be dismissed as too expensive or too difficult since there are many different program options. Such programs will provide a return on a library's investment of time and money by cutting travel costs, developing a more knowledgeable staff, improving in-library communications, and, most importantly, ultimately improving service.

BIBLIOGRAPHY

Caruso, Elaine. "TRAINER," *Online* 5, January 1981, p. 36-38.

Gershenfeld, Nancy J. "In-House Online Training of the Information Specialist: a Program to Meet the Needs and Capabilities of the individual Searcher," *Proceedings of the 1981 National Online Meeting*, 1981, p. 117-21.

Hudnut, Sophie K. "Educating the Online Searcher: The Database Vendor's Viewpoint," *Proceedings of the Online '81 Conference*, 1981, p. 1-6.

Jackson, William J. "How to Train Experienced Searchers to Use Another System," *Online* 6, May 1982, p. 27-35.

Kennedy, Sue. "Online Training: Patterns, Preferences, Predictions," *Proceedings of the Online '81 Conference*, 1981, p. 125-28.

Murphy, Marcy. *On-Line Services in Some Academic, Public and Special Libraries.* Univ. of Illinois, Graduate School of Library and Information Science, Occasional Paper Number 151, November 1981.

Saunders, Marian L. "Educating the Online User: The Role of the In-House Coordinator," *Proceedings of the Online '81 Conference*, 1981, p. 273-78.

Tedd, Lucy. "Teaching Aids Developed and Used for Education and Training for Online Searching," *Online Review* 5, June 1981, p. 205-16.

Tenopir, Carol. "An In-House Training Program for Online Searchers," *Online* 6, May 1982, p. 20-26.

Triolo, Victor A. & John J. Regazzi. "Continuing Education in On-Line Searching: An Instructional Module for Special Librarians," *Special Libraries* 69, May 1978, p. 189-200. ■

DECISION MAKING BY REFERENCE LIBRARIANS*

Technology provides choices for reference materials and reference services that were not possible ten or even five years ago. Having choices means an increased need for decision making by reference librarians, and the decisions that are made will impact reference services, staff, and patrons. I was recently asked by the organizers of the New Mexico State Library Reference Training Institute to come up with some guidelines (besides costs) for choosing among alternatives for reference materials, and to outline some of the effects of adding technological reference sources to a library.

THE WAY IT STANDS NOW

Although online searching and CD-ROM are used widely in academic research and special libraries, a 1987 survey by OCLC showed that only 17 percent of OCLC-member public libraries and 24 percent of college libraries were using CD-ROM ("1987 OCLC Compact Disk Study," *Laser-disk Professional*, May 1988, p. 44-49). Online use, as well, is still not widespread in public and school libraries. The OCLC survey found that many libraries were planning to make more use of technology in their reference services in the near future. All libraries, whether they are currently using online or CD-ROM or just planning for the future, will need to keep up with new products and developments. The need to choose the most appropriate technology and to make decisions is a continuous one.

The current biggest contenders by far for your reference dollar are online databases, locally held databases (especially CD-ROM), and printed materials. Online databases may be provided by intermediaries using the full online systems such as DIALOG, BRS, Medlars, etc., or with end user search services using end user systems such as BRS/After Dark, front-end software such as Wilsearch, or gateways such as EasyNet. (See my column, "Four Options for End User Searching," *LJ*, July 1986, p. 56-57.) CD-ROM and print are used by both patrons and staff.

Decision making happens at two levels: 1) the collection development level for overall policy and purchasing decisions; and 2) the reference question level for choosing the most appropriate technology for a particular user or question.

Online, CD-ROM, and print have their own unique advantages. Each is better for certain circumstances, questions, or users.

WHEN TO CHOOSE ONLINE DATABASES

Online databases should be used to expand the coverage and scope of the reference collection. They allow a library to access reference materials they would not otherwise have. Depending on the size and clientele, most libraries have print subscriptions to certain standard tools such as *Readers' Guide*, *Psychological Abstracts*, *Books in Print*, etc. These libraries probably do not subscribe to print versions of all the highly specialized tools. There are over 5000 publicly available databases today, nearly 1000 on the online systems most used by libraries. It makes sense to access these online in the rare times they are needed.

In addition to the somewhat esoteric sources, online provides access to sources you may not be able to afford in print such as *Chemical Abstracts*, *Beilstein*, or *Social Science Citation Index*. Online is often the most cost-effective medium for seldom-used materials because most online databases are pay-as-you-use. You don't have to encumber the full price of a reference source that may be used only once a week or once a month or once a year. When a source is needed it can be accessed online, often for as little as $5-$15 for ready reference.

Online databases are a logical choice when currency is important. In most cases the online version will be the most current published resource available. Some wire services on DIALOG are updated every 15 minutes. Dow Jones News Retrieval updates stock prices throughout the day. Other bibliographic, directory, or full-text databases are updated daily, weekly, or monthly. Full texts of wire services, magazines, and newspapers are an especially good choice for school or public libraries that may have limited collections but do a lot of current event searching. Through systems like CompuServe or The Source, wire services can be accessed relatively inexpensively.

A final reason to choose online databases is to answer reference questions that can't be readily answered by any other means. Complex questions that require a combination of several factors are quickly and easily answered online by an intermediary but would require a tedious and time-consuming search in printed works. "I'd like to know what's been written by Canadian researchers in the last ten years about effects of acid rain on trout populations in Canadian streams"; "How many software companies in San Francisco employ more than 50 people?"; and "Can you help me find an article I read last year or the year before in some magazine like *Time* or *Newsweek* that had a title something like 'How To Become a Millionaire Before You're Thirty'?" are all much easier to do online.

WHEN TO CHOOSE CD-ROM

Online databases are not the answer for all reference work. Choosing from among the approximately 200 CD-ROM databases available today is a good option for some libraries and for some uses.

Because CD-ROM allows unlimited use of a work once it is purchased or leased, it makes sense to use CD-ROM for those databases that will get heavy use in your library. In a library with a lot of business searching, for example, the CD-ROM version of ABI/INFORM from UMI will be a popular addition to the library. Information Access Company's InfoTrac products are heavily used in general reference situations. Medline from one of many CD-ROM vendors is a smart addition to a medical library.

Like online, many CD-ROM products offer the advantage of increased subject access to information by allowing complex combinations of terms. The capabilities and ease of use vary widely, though, so the reference librarian must look closely at the software that comes with a CD database. CD-ROM databases are much faster than searching the equivalent tool in print for all but the simplest questions.

CD-ROM products have proven to be very popular with patrons. Response has been overwhelmingly positive in almost every library that has offered CD-ROM searching. CD-ROM makes it easy to offer end user search services because you don't have to keep track of online time or worry about security of passwords. Librarians and users can spend more time learning and browsing without an online "meter" running. Most users like database searching and almost always seem to prefer it to print, but they don't like to be rushed.

A final reason to select CD-ROM is if telecommunications links are a problem. If you are in a rural or remote area far from a major city you may have to dial a long distance number to reach the nearest telecommunications node, adding to the cost of the online search. If local phone systems are unreliable you may experience unacceptable downtime. CD-ROM is not dependent on outside phone systems that are out of your control.

WHEN TO CHOOSE PRINT

There are still times when printed reference books are the best choice. They are usually the most straightforward to use and require less initial training. Adding a technological

reference source to the library requires time by the library staff to learn how to use the new medium and to teach others. Books have little downtime or mechanical failures.

Printed reference works are very good and fast for answering one-dimensional reference questions: "What pharmaceutical company manufactures Valium?" or "Help me find five recent magazine articles on drug testing" or "What is the boiling point of rubbing alcohol?"

If you need pictures or other illustrations, books are still the best option with 1988 technology. This won't always be true, but today the print version of an encyclopedia article on Hawaii includes photographs, charts, drawings, etc. The online and most CD-ROM versions have only text.

ADMINISTRATIVE IMPACTS

Technology impacts library service both positively and negatively. Decision making can be tedious and involves a certain amount of stress. When one decision is made it seems to lead to many more. What is the appropriate technology for a particular reference title? What end user or intermediary service will be offered? What option or options will be selected for end user searching? If a title is available in more than one format, how much should be duplicated? Decisions must be made at all of these levels and by everyone in the library, especially administrators, collection development librarians, and reference librarians.

Adding technology is often expensive, so it calls for creative financing. Few libraries can afford everything they want or need. Charging user fees is one method chosen by libraries (in spite of the American Library Association's clear policies to the contrary), but there are other ways. Librarians are beginning to report successful creative ways to finance technologies (e.g., dropping little-used print subscriptions, writing grant proposals to pay for start-up costs, getting local corporations to sponsor a CD-ROM workstation and index).

Almost every decision that is made involves changes that affect people. For example, if an end user search service is started using a system such as BRS/After Dark, reference departments must be staffed during evening and weekend hours. CD-ROM workstations require hardware troubleshooters and people who can help new users with the mechanical as well as the intellectual process of searching. Technologies mean the need for a commitment to staff development and continuing education.

INTERPERSONAL IMPACTS

Experience has shown that the image of the librarian almost always changes for the better when online searching or CD-ROM searching is added to reference services. The status of the librarian improves in users' minds and the library as a whole is viewed as a more progressive place.

In addition, the training role of the librarian is increased as many users require one-on-one help from reference staff to learn how to use the new system. Unlike training to use print sources, however, technology requires an emphasis on hardware and software as well as content. This may make some librarians uncomfortable or insecure about their own abilities to deal with the new automated sources. Again, a commitment to staff training together with time to learn before public access begins is essential.

Some libraries experience a staff split between "computerphobes" and "techies." While most people probably fall somewhere in the middle, there are those who want nothing to do with automated reference sources and others who discover latent talents and don't want to do anything else. An understanding administration, good staff relationships, and the willingness to let people proceed at their own pace are needed to smooth the transition.

INTELLECTUAL IMPACTS

Sometimes the thrill of a new technology blinds us and the patrons to the content of the reference source that is being provided by the technology. We need to make sure that librarians and users understand the difference between the medium (CD-ROM) and the content (ERIC).

It is fashionable to blur the difference among sources— providing an "answer machine" or "magic computer." Librarians know that there really are differences among databases and must guide the user to the most appropriate source no matter the technology. We need to select technological tools with the same care we select printed tools. Junk on a computer is still junk.

In addition to evaluation of the content, librarians must now be software evaluators as well. With a dozen or so versions of Medline and six or so versions of ERIC on CD-ROM, it is up to the librarians to decide which one is easiest to use or most powerful or most appropriate for their users.

The choices offered by technological reference sources require so many decisions that it may at times seem overwhelming. But, on the whole, the choices that force us to make decisions and the corresponding impact of technology on reference work are positive. Technology offers choices for better access to information, choices for better services to users, and choices for more enjoyable research and library use. ■

ONLINE EDUCATION
Planning for the Future*

In the last decade, schools of library and information science have recognized the important role they play in educating online intermediaries. A survey in 1982[1] found at that time 76% of all schools accredited by the American Library Association included online searching in their curriculum. In 1988 that percent is certainly higher.

Most of these courses to date have concentrated on the mechanics of "how to search" one or more online systems. They extend traditional reference classes by providing the future intermediary with searching skills and with knowledge of machine readable reference materials.

As online education and training in graduate schools enters the next decade, more classes will need to go beyond the "how-to-search" phase. Students will need to be prepared to participate fully in many aspects of the information industry, including database creation, search software design, marketing, online training, and system design, as well as intermediary searching. It is no longer sufficient to teach just search commands and database contents.

The major developments that are changing online education in library schools include:

- the introduction of new database formats (e.g., laserdisk)

- the proliferation of online services and databases produced in many different countries

- the increasing role of the end-user searcher in addition to the intermediary searcher

- the growth in the number of full-text databases

- the growing reliance on "computer intermediary" software (e.g., front ends, gateways).

While these developments are undoubtedly topics of discussion in every online searching course, the next decade will see them go beyond discussion to shape online education in library schools. Some of the necessary emphases in course content are discussed below.

FUTURE ROLES

The introduction of different database formats such as laserdisks and floppy disks in addition to online access emphasizes the role of the information professional as evaluator. Students will need to concentrate on evaluation skills to be able to determine which of several database formats is appropriate in a given situation. Skills in systematically applying criteria such as cost, durability, compatibility, quality, ease of use, etc. will become more important than how to search one particular database or online system.

The economics of database production and how it impacts library budgets is important for every future librarian. These economics are no longer a matter of just comparing online use with print subscriptions. Implied is a familiarity with optical and magnetic technologies and the ability to use problem solving skills to assess the relative value. Knowledge

*Reprinted from *Online* Jan. 1987. Copyright © 1987 by Online, Inc.

of database design and creation is also important for all students as there is a growing demand for people who are knowledgeable in the creation of in-house databases.

The proliferation of systems and databases emphasizes the ability to select appropriate systems. Fundamental too is an understanding of the decisions that must be made by each segment of the database industry. Students need to understand the costs and procedures of database design and production. They need to know how editorial decisions are made and the problems of keeping costs low and quality high. They need to know how decisions made by producers affect users and how they can exert influence on decisions.

The increasing role of the end-user searcher is changing the emphasis in online education from just training intermediaries. The information professional as instructor becomes more important as students learn to assist end-users in doing their own searching. Even as intermediaries, students may face more knowledgeable and demanding clients. New issues of ethics and liability arise as new relationships develop.

Marketing knowledge is important both for students who will be working for database producers or online services and for those who become searchers. Identification of potential markets and the best ways to reach them are skills that all information professionals must cultivate.

End-users are expected to be the primary users of full-text databases. An increase in full text means that librarians must learn to judge when purchase of a book or journal in electronic form is advantageous for users and when print might be best. Technical knowledge is important for the future full-text database creator. An understanding of conversion technologies, hardware approaches to databases, text retrieval research, and full-text database design will help students design as well as search full-text databases.

Finally, changes in education will come from the increased emphasis on software design. Some information professionals are involved in creating front end software. Even those who are not programmers may be involved with writing specifications or evaluation and testing. Thorough knowledge of information seeking behavior, artificial intelligence and expert systems, and the theoretical foundations of information retrieval is required for all of these students. A better understanding of different ways of retrieving information, including the research in new search algorithms, will help students to become leaders in software design.

A recurring question among educators is how do we fit all of this new knowledge into the same one or two year curriculum? One answer may be specialization, with students selecting a course of study as database experts. These experts would be prepared for jobs with database producers, online systems, other information firms, or libraries. A more likely solution for many schools in the immediate future will be the incorporation of much of this information into existing classes with the addition of one or two new electives and prerequisite skills.

The curriculum of many schools of library and information science is evolving and responding to current and anticipated future changes in the online industry. In the next decade more schools must approach their database curriculum as more than a how-to-search reference skill and prepare students for all aspects of the information industry.

REFERENCES

[1]Stephen P. Harter and Carol H. Fenichel, "Online Searching in Library Education," *Journal of Education for Librarianship* 23 Summer 1982: 3-22. ∎

CHAPTER

2

END USERS AND SYSTEMS
FOR END USERS

In addition to intermediary searchers, the human elements in the search process are the clients for whom the search is conducted and the so-called "end users"—people who do their own searches. Lots of people in the database industry don't like the term "end user" and have consequently called people who do their own searches other things such as "direct users" or "primary searchers." Like it or not, the term "end user" seems to have stuck and I have used it fairly consistently throughout this chapter.

The people an intermediary calls end users do not of course call themselves that. The term is used by online professionals to distinguish their intermediary services from services that allow users to search for themselves. Since the target audience for all of my writings is the information professional, my discussions of end users or the online systems marketed to end users are directed at people who are viewing end-user searching as one phenomenon within the broader world of online services. End-user searching, as an issue for intermediaries and its impact on the information industry, is often my focus.

"Online Searching in the Popular Literature," the first article in this chapter, is an analysis of how online searching is described in general-interest periodicals. I attempt to explore how others see us or see online searching as reflected in articles aimed at the people we would call end users. Although the articles discussed in this 1984 article are no longer the most current mass-market articles about online searching, I suspect many of the general traits of the literature remain the same. The accuracy and reliability of the articles varies considerably, as does the portrayal of libraries or other traditional sources of intermediary searches. Librarians have had little input into the general market literature.

"Why Don't More People Use Databases?" is a view of the end-user market from the perspective of people in the database industry. It explores some reasons why the end-user market has not grown as quickly as anticipated and offers some brief solutions. Many online vendors and database producers began courting the end-user market in the hopes of augmenting a fairly saturated intermediary market, but without knowing much about their potential new users.

"Systems for End Users: Are There End Users for the Systems?" continues this look at market predictions and market trends. Intermediaries are a known market to online vendors and to database producers, but end users are a new and often hard-to-identify market (actually many markets). New products and systems are being developed that target end users, either in general or in special-interest target groups. The great potentials of end-user searching tempered by the great marketing difficulties are related by several representatives of the database industry in this and the preceding article. Some vendors or producers seem to be learning how to reach the end-user market by trial-and-error marketing tactics. The information about specific systems in this article had to be updated extensively, a necessity that illustrates the unsettled nature of the end-user market.

All of the concerns about end user markets may be solved in the future when the students who are currently in high school or junior high school are in the work force. Teaching online searching in schools as part of the research/writing experience is taking hold in many parts of the country. "Online Searching in Schools" describes some of the efforts to bring online into the school environment and some of the many options open to teachers and school librarians in doing so. A longer version of this article was published in two parts in April and May 1986 in *The Computing Teacher*.

Next in this chapter I turn to end-user search services within the general library environment. "Four Options for End User Searching" is an overview of options for providing alternative search services. Mentioned here are end-user search systems, front-end software packages, gateway services, and locally held databases. All of these are covered elsewhere in more detail; in this article they are described only in brief as ways for a library to offer end-user searching.

The details of several end user options are given in the final articles in this chapter. "DIALOG's Knowledge Index and BRS/After Dark" was one of the first published comparative reviews of these two systems. At the time it was written (January 1983, published March 1, 1983) Knowledge Index and BRS/After Dark were both brand new. The idea of systems designed for and marketed to end users both intrigued and frightened us. Intermediaries could only speculate on the impact these systems would have on their online search services. Now, six years later, both systems are widely accepted and improved. They are used by end users and intermediaries alike, more frequently because of their low online costs, I suspect, than for their simplified searching. I made few changes to the original article because I wanted to retain the fresh perspective of looking at these systems for the first time. Only the factual information such as costs has been updated.

"The EasyNet Gateway" describes one of the best examples of the intelligent gateway option for end-user searching. Like Knowledge Index and BRS/After Dark, EasyNet is going strong now several years after its inauguration. It has won acclaim and awards, including the EUSIDIC European Database Product of the Year Award in 1987. EasyNet can be used within a library context for end-user search services or by anyone who has a microcomputer and modem (or dumb terminal).

ONLINE SEARCHING IN THE POPULAR LITERATURE*

Popular magazines have discovered online databases in the last few years. Many are publishing articles aimed at home computer users to introduce them to online database searching. Others target specific professional groups to describe the benefits of database access on personal computers for their professional development. Libraries report an increasing number of inquiries from patrons who have seen advertisements or articles about databases. The inquiries range from confusion about what databases can do to inquiries asking which is the "best" online system.

Unfortunately, the readability, accuracy, and overall quality of articles in the popular press vary tremendously. Of the dozens I have read, only a handful are accurate and clear.

Diodato's article in the May 1984 *Online* (p. 24-30) provides an extensive bibliography of popular magazine articles about databases from 1980 through 1983. He includes articles that discuss all types of database systems including CompuServe or the Source, Dow Jones News/Retrieval, DIALOG, BRS, and Orbit. Forty of the 55 articles concern the Source or CompuServe.

REPLACEMENTS FOR LIBRARIES

Although Diodato does not individually review each of the articles, he offers an interesting analysis of the articles as a group. Especially disturbing in most of the articles Diodato examined is their failure to mention the role of libraries or search intermediaries. Most articles fail to mention libraries at all; those that do mention them often tout databases as replacements for libraries.

Popular articles also tend to exaggerate the benefits of online database searching without providing any comparison of systems, search strategy development, or search techniques for difficult searches. Many articles never define databases (or do so inaccurately referring, for example, to DIALOG as a database). Many never make it clear that bibliographic databases only supply references or abstracts to articles. Most do not include sample searches.

Intermediaries can provide a valuable service by recommending the popular articles that best convey accurate information. I reread many articles, judging them by Diodato's criteria. Then I compiled a list of the best articles that discuss research systems such as DIALOG or BRS, excluding those that discuss only consumer services such as CompuServe or the Source.

OVERVIEW ARTICLES

General articles that clearly explain online searching, online systems, and databases are the hardest to find. The overview article, more than any other type, exaggerates, makes factual errors, and provides a limited amount of information.

One well-written overview article for the home searcher is "Online: a Smorgasbord of Services" by Steven K. Roberts in the November 1983 issue of *Today* (p. 24-29, 48). Roberts does a good job of defining databases by separating them into three categories: full text, bibliographic, and "just the facts." For each category, he gives sample databases, the online vendors that make the databases available, and search strategy hints. Potential problems are mentioned throughout this balanced and realistic article.

---

*Reprinted from *Library Journal* Dec. 1984. Copyright © 1984 by Reed Publishing, USA, Div. of Reed Holdings, Inc.

Unlike many overviewers, Roberts emphasizes that "there is more to using on-line services than buying a terminal and signing a contract with a vendor." He mentions the inconsistencies among databases and the problems of keeping up with many different databases. The company librarian and other intermediaries are mentioned as viable alternatives to doing it yourself (but to Roberts the "competence" that allows an intermediary to really "draw you out" is "rare" and "expensive").

"Online: a Smorgasbord of Services" is the second of two *Today* articles by Roberts. The first, "On-Line Information Retrieval: a New Business Tool," in the October 1983 issue (p. 14-20, 48), targets a business audience. In it, Roberts defines online systems, discusses the advantages of searching, and tackles such issues as pricing. It is unusual to find a popular magazine article that discusses the fee vs. free issue in libraries. Roberts even quotes the 1977 ALA policy on fees.

"On-Line Information Retrieval" discusses other issues as well, including gateway software, full text databases, the growth of data communications networks, and copyright. After the initial focus on business, this article assumes a more general tone. It is recommended for potential end users, although I prefer the second *Today* article for its more specific information and straightforward style.

Unfortunately, *Today*, a magazine for CompuServe users, may not be widely available in libraries although it has a wider appeal. In 1984, the title became *Online Today*, and is available from CompuServe Inc., 5000 Arlington Centre Blvd., P.O. Box 20212, Columbus, OH 43220. As an alternative, there is an acceptable article by Roberts in the December 1981 issue of *Byte* ("Online Information Retrieval: Promise and Problems," p. 452-61).

SPECIFIC SYSTEMS

It is easier to find well-written popular articles that focus on a specific search system — *if* the system you are interested in is DIALOG. Besides the consumer information systems such as CompuServe, popular articles mostly focus on DIALOG, occasionally mentioning BRS and, even less often, Orbit.

One excellent one is Jeremy Joan Hewes' "DIALOG: The Ultimate On-Line Library" in the September 1983 issue of *PC World* (p. 74-88). Hewes includes almost everything I look for in a popular article. In addition to a short history of DIALOG, there are accurate definitions of online systems and databases, price information, discussions of search strategy, and hints for better searching. Public libraries are mentioned as search service providers, as are information brokers. Several sample searches are shown and annotated. Unlike most articles, this one explains Boolean logic using Venn diagrams.

Hewes manages to instill excitement about online searching, while cautioning that the DIALOG training, study of the manuals, and searching experience are necessary to become a good searcher. I like Hewes' tips for better searching, especially her first and second: "learn to think like a librarian" and "plan your search strategy in advance."

Knowledge Index is mentioned as a low-cost alternative to the full DIALOG system. BRS and BRS/After Dark are discussed only as DIALOG's competition. The short portion on BRS is not as well-researched as the rest and seems to be an afterthought.

In addition to the Hewes article, Stan Miastkowski's "Information Unlimited: The DIALOG Information Retrieval Service" in the June 1981 issue of *Byte* (p. 88-108) provides a good introduction to DIALOG. Miastkowski includes definitions of systems and databases, plus a short history of DIALOG, followed by a discussion of search strategy development, price information, and a tutorial of DIALOG commands. Librarians are mentioned as the primary users of DIALOG (but their potential role in helping users with difficult searches is not).

The Miastkowski article was written before Knowledge Index began and it does not discuss BRS or Orbit. DIALOG is differentiated from consumer information systems, however, and its primary purpose of "finding references to information" is emphasized. The strongest feature of Miastkowski is the clearly labeled sample searches. All DIALOG commands are labeled in the context of a search, including Expand and Search/Save. Another nice feature is extended information on selected databases.

The Hewes and Miastkowski articles stand out as two of the best articles on DIALOG searching and on reference systems as a whole in the popular press. The more recent article, "Researching On Line With DIALOG," in the August 1984 issue of *Business Software* (p. 60-64) is tempting because it provides a tutorial on DIALOG commands, defines databases and systems, gives information on costs, shows a sample search, and discusses search strategy. It contains some errors, however, including the claim that DIALOG has 340 separate databases and an incorrect use of internal truncation. The article makes no mention of bibliographic databases, librarians or search intermediaries, or of Knowledge Index. The Hewes and Miastkowski articles, although older, are more accurate, better written, and more complete.

TARGET AUDIENCES

Many of the best articles on online searching are aimed at a specific end user target audience rather than at the general user. There are too many articles in too many specialty magazines to review in detail, but several have a wide appeal.

The target group for articles on online searches in business is a large one. In addition to the articles by Stephen Roberts in *Today* mentioned above, Howard Karten's two-part overview in *Management Technology* "Getting Smart: Public Databases" (August 1983, p. 49-53) and "Getting Smart: Public Databases II" (September 1983, p. 34-39) is a good introduction for the business community. Karten defines online systems and databases, differentiates between bibliographic, full text, and directory databases, and talks about problems with search strategy development. These two articles emphasize business databases on DIALOG and the Dow Jones News/Retrieval Service, but other databases and systems are mentioned.

The corporate library is recommended as a source for online searches. Karten describes his failures as well as his successes with searching (but probably could have had more successes if he had taken his own advice and asked the corporate librarian for help).

More good online searching articles are written for medical professionals than for any other group. Two new journals about computers and medicine have included overview articles. Articles written by librarians such as "Your Computer Puts the Literature At Your Fingertips" by Gretchen V. Naisawald, in the 1983 "Premiere Issue" of *MEDCOMP* (p. 34-39) and "The Library Connection—Information Retrieval" by Priscilla Mayden and Carol Tenopir in the July/August 1984 issue of *Update: Computers in Medicine* (p. 24-37) introduce health science professionals to online searching on their home computers. Naisawald points out that home computer systems such as BRS/After Dark and Knowledge Index are relatively easy to use but do not include all of the databases available on the full systems. She defines databases and systems, gives sample search strategies, and provides general information on several vendors. An especially nice feature is a chart that shows which systems include medical databases.

Dwight R. Tousignaut's "Online Literature Retrieval Systems: How To Get Started" in the February 1983 *American Journal of Hospital Pharmacy* (p. 230-239) is a good explanation of how to begin online searching with clearly labeled sample searches.

THE LIBRARY ROLE

Among the many articles in the popular literature there are several that provide accurate and interesting descriptions of online searching for the home computer user. Any library can begin to take a role in end user searching by recommending them. The next easy step is providing the latest information on databases and systems and distributing information on the hardware and software requirements for going online (DIALOG, BRS, Orbit, and NLM all provide fact sheets for searching with a microcomputer). Assisting new users with search strategy development, problem searching, and even online training logically follows. ■

WHY DON'T MORE PEOPLE USE DATABASES?*

I spent much of this summer away from the online world. I didn't go to conferences or read many online magazines. For almost two months I didn't touch a terminal, didn't turn on a microcomputer, and didn't see a modem. I did visit libraries in different parts of the United States and United Kingdom (without telling anyone I was a librarian) and I talked to many different kinds of people. It struck me how little of an impact online information sources have yet to make in most people's lives and work. A vast majority of library users never use online services. Even many microcomputer owners have only a vague idea of what online has to offer. After 15 years, ours is still a relatively unknown service and the issues that seem so important to our workday lives are unheard of to a vast majority of people.

Since we are so close to online searching so much of the time, I think it is valuable to step back at times and examine why more people are not database users. Several speakers at the National Online Meeting in New York this May took this approach and discussed various barriers to widespread use of databases.

MYTHS, REALITIES

Leroy Cook, a private investigator and online end user, spoke from the perspective of an outsider looking into the online industry in "The View from the Bullseye." He discovered the value of online information retrieval when he purchased a personal computer and began looking for something worthwhile to do with it.

Cook is excited by the potential of online, but can't understand the lack of interest. "Why isn't the whole population fighting like shoppers at a clearance sale for what you, the online industry, have to offer?" He told the audience that "you have the equivalent of the industrial revolution and most of the world could care less." Cook went on to discuss some of the obstacles to success.

Steve Arnold of Data Courier, Inc., in "End Users: Old Myths and New Realities," discussed "some of the myths [that arose] when end users, we thought, lurked behind every office door" and the causes for differing realities. The perspective of the information broker was delivered by Reva Basch of Information on Demand, who spoke about the characteristics and expectations of "The Electronic Client," someone who requests searches or documents through electronic messages.

REACHING THE CUSTOMERS

The most obvious reason why people don't use databases is because they don't know about them. Reaching the many potential customers who are as yet uninformed about online searching is where most of the effort in the online industry is being spent. The expectation of many in the industry is that if people know what online searching can offer they will become users.

The difficulty of reaching a vast and nebulous clientele is being realized, so "vertical marketing" has become the buzzword in the industry. Vertical marketing identifies discrete segments of users that have similar needs and characteristics. Not all segments in the population need what online databases have to offer, but certain segments have a high potential. Products are developed, packaged, and promoted specifically for each of these segments. Ideally, once people in a targeted segment learn about online searching they will become users. This does not always happen, however, because of several barriers to use.

OBSTACLE #1: HARDWARE

Hardware is the first obstacle. The basic necessity of purchasing a computer or terminal is cited by Cook as a major limitation on the number of users. Arnold noted that "the [personal computer] market is soft because end users aren't able to use the machines easily and effectively." Personal computers are still best suited to the "person intrigued by technology." The microcomputer market has not lived up to original predictions because almost all of it is difficult for a novice to use. Purchase is still approached from the hardware perspective rather than the applications perspective.

Most online intermediaries or producers don't get very involved with hardware. The initial connection to an online host is often difficult and the hardware salesperson is generally not qualified to offer much help. Lack of standards makes it difficult to upgrade or change hardware.

Telecommunications hardware also sometimes poses problems. Valerie Noble, manager of the business library at the Upjohn Company, wrote to me about her inability to use end user software at her company. "They won't work on our ROLM digital phone system. Internal technical personnel have been troubleshooting all of our discs, to no avail. And, to date, no vendor has offered any solutions. The result: potential service we cannot fulfill."

OBSTACLE #2: SOFTWARE

The second obstacle is software, both at the user's end of the database and the vendor's end. For the user, neither communications software nor front-end software can yet be considered user friendly. It can be time consuming and frustrating to install a communications package, as many of us have experienced. After years of complaints, documentation is still notoriously inadequate. Once installed, packages often have illogical commands or inconsistent requirements.

At the vendor's end, query languages are often cryptic, confusing, and inconsistent, especially to the infrequent user. Arnold complained of this inconsistency from the end user's point of view. "For every function which is made easy, new ones come along which are hard to master.... Nothing seems to strike a comfortable balance between hard and easy; it is either one or the other." He pointed out that to inexperienced users "the fact remains that logging on successfully, selecting an online service, searching and retrieving the appropriate information, reading it, shaping and interpreting it, and preparing the data in a form suitable for a customer's use are difficult tasks."

Cook is especially bothered by the lack of consistency in "terms, symbols, and prompts" among various online systems. To the potential end user the differences are major but are seemingly solvable. He complained, however, that when he mentions this to members of the online industry, standardization is dismissed as impossible.

To Cook, standardization is "not only possible, it's inevitable.... Words, symbols, and prompts are not technically

required to be anything except what someone arbitrarily decides they will be. There are a lot of us who would like to use your services, and we would even pay money to do so. We don't have the time or the resources, however, to totally reeducate ourselves every time we change a piece of hardware or software. The unnecessary proliferation of terms, symbols, and prompts standing between the end users and your databases limits your potential market to a tiny fraction of what it might otherwise be."

According to Arnold, "if anything, the principal vendors of online information look less similar today than they did five years ago." In addition, the databases are not standard in terms of structure, abbreviations, and quality. "With more and more organizations becoming database producers, the customer has a bewildering job to determine which database in a general topic area is useful. Trying to evaluate the quality of one database with another is a near impossible task. Consistency is farther away today than it was in 1981." The necessity of learning "the idiosyncratic structures of each database," in addition to the host systems, is often too much to expect. Front-end software or gateways are not yet sophisticated enough to solve these problems completely.

OBSTACLE #3: EXPECTATIONS

A third barrier is unrealized expectations. Arnold points out that "generally speaking, end users have not found online information retrieval the godsend the online industry's hype promised. Timesharing vendors, software companies, manufacturers, database producers, and other companies have overpromised what information can actually deliver."

Basch deals with "technophile" clients who are very comfortable with computers but often have little experience with research. They assume "that *everything* is available online—all subjects, all types of material, going back to the invention of moveable type.... They also expect full-text retrieval as a matter of course, and are often skeptical about the utility of abstracts. Personal computer hobbyists, especially, who have read about the wonders of database searching, must be told that not all publications are indexed online, and that coverage generally begins with the early 1970s, at best. There's a noticeable letdown when we inform them that all or part of their project will be tackled manually."

Unfortunately, the expectations that microcomputers and access to online information in the workplace would substantially increase productivity are yet to be realized. Arnold told the audience that "sadly, in 1986 it is quite difficult to equate the PC's presence with increased revenues and greater profitability." Using the manual sources in a library can still sometimes yield better results at a lower cost with less frustration.

THE PROBLEM OF COST

Related to overexpectations is cost. Prime-time costs for databases, in general, keep going up. Costs are often too high for the casual user. In the business community, Arnold believes that users are becoming more price sensitive because "companies are spending more money on PCs, software, and online information. Costs to the organization have probably increased. This puts greater pressure upon the online user to keep costs down."

At the same time, special non-prime-time discounts and reduced prices for special services have started. Most of us see these lower prices as positive, but Arnold warned that they have served to devalue information to a clientele that "does not have the ability to understand the value of information." Often the lower-priced special services are the first exposure to online databases for end users. Arnold fears it is difficult to raise prices or expect users to pay higher prices for other services once they have been made so low.

SOLUTIONS

Many in the information industry are working on solutions to overcome these barriers. Others continue to believe that better marketing alone will vastly increase the number of online users. Librarians have an important role to play with the information industry. We can continue to work actively on the development of standards for online systems and database structures. We can help vendors develop better software by sharing our expertise and criticisms with software developers. (Or as some have done, become software developers ourselves.) We can encourage fair pricing schemes that allow increased access to information while maintaining the value and quality of that information. We need also to find a way to communicate with hardware developers and dealers so they can be better informed of the needs of database users and of online applications.

Proceedings of the 1986 National Online Meeting are available for $50 from: Learned Information, Inc., 143 Old Marlton Pike, Medford, NJ 08055. ■

SYSTEMS FOR END USERS
Are There End Users for the Systems?*

The Sixth National Online Meeting held in New York this spring provided information on many topics of interest to online searchers. One topic—software and systems for easing end user searching—dominated the discussions, exhibits, contributed paper sessions, and the keynote speech. The potential of a large market for online databases is intriguing to database producers and to intermediaries.

The keynote speech by Martha Williams and the opening panel discussion which followed it focused on software or systems for end users. User friendly substitutes for system manuals and documentation attempt to make the commands or quirks of the host system "transparent" to the user.

Williams pointed out that the proliferation of online hosts combined with their attempts to penetrate the end user market make such transparent systems necessary. The terminology used to differentiate different types of transparent systems may be confusing, however. Williams differentiated between the various terms commonly in use.

User friendly *front-ends* are software packages that stand between the user and the target system. Front-ends can aid the novice searcher who does not know the host system command language by replacing commands with a simple series of menu choices. The menu choices are then translated into the appropriate system commands by the front-end software. Although front-ends remove some of the interactive power of online searching, they provide a good way to overcome initial hesitation to online searching. A well known example of a front-end is *In-Search* (now called *Pro-Search*) for DIALOG searching.

Intermediary systems replace the human intermediary searcher in some ways. Typically, a series of menu prompts guides the user through the search negotiation process. They include help with word stems, Boolean combinations, and unique features of specific databases. Williams defined intermediary systems as those that are database specific or limited to a family of related databases. They are often designed by the database producer to encourage wider use of their databases. Examples are Disclosure Inc.'s *MicroDisclosure* and Information Access Company's *SearchHelper*.

Gateway systems allow users to connect to any of several host systems by passing the user from a single gateway computer through telecommunications lines to various online vendors. The gateway eliminates the need for remembering different network procedures, memorizing logon protocols, and having personal accounts with each of the systems. Some include a front-end procedure that simplifies online searching on multiple systems. *INET* in Canada and *Easynet* are examples of gateway systems.

Williams emphasized the positive and negative sides of transparent systems. On the positive side, they decrease the time and cost spent online, decrease the need for intermediaries for simple searches, decrease the cost of keeping up with documentation and systems, and decrease the amount of keyboarding required. On the negative side, they remove some beneficial differences among different online vendors, decrease search power, increase the distance between users and online vendors, and increase the distance between users and intermediaries.

Still, Williams and many others believe that transparent systems "are a must if we are going to reach large numbers of users."

EASYNET

Occasional searchers will perhaps be more interested in the gateway system *Easynet* (described in my January 1, 1985 column, p. 62-63). A user dials the *Easynet* computer which in turn switches him to an appropriate database on one of seven host systems. Subjects are indicated to the system by responding to a series of menu screens. The user then inputs words or phrases to search and *Easynet* translates the input into the command language and requirements of the host system accessed (including truncation, field tags, etc.). The switching and translating are transparent to the user.

If no hits are retrieved in a search there is no cost to the user; *Easynet* charges to enter the system as well as for each database used. Charges can be billed to an institutional account or to a personal credit card.

To help with search strategy formulation *Easynet* has a 24 hours a day "SOS" service. When a user types "SOS" while connected to *Easynet* a search specialist comes online to offer expert interactive help in search strategy formulation or database selection. This personal intermediary service is available at no cost. Write to *Easynet*, Telebase Systems, Inc., 763 W. Lancaster, Bryn Mawr, PA 19010.

IS THERE AN END USER MARKET?

Designers of transparent systems such as these assume there is a vast untapped market of end users who are now discouraged from using databases because the systems are too complicated to use. While information professionals are excited about the many new and innovative interfaces appearing, one can ask if this vast end user market actually exists today.

Some creators of databases and front-end systems related lessons they had learned from experience in the past year in attempting to tape the end user market. They learned that the *potential* of an end user market is great, that good transparent systems are necessary if this potential is to be tapped, but that most of the people in this potential market don't yet realize they need access to databases.

Stephen Arnold of Data Courier Inc. discussed his company's attempts to conduct seminars for end users. They found that "end users don't know that they are end users" and "information consumers are tough to locate." Marketing to these people is expensive because no one really knows who the potential users are. Data Courier discovered that often the corporate personnel who were the target of promotion campaigns passed the information on to intermediaries and that intermediaries were the ones who came to the seminars aimed at end users. Data Courier learned the hard way "to never forget the intermediary and corporate library." Intermediaries are the ones who not only know the value of databases, but know who the likely end users are.

Intermediaries can indirectly help the end user by helping the database producers identify this market and target materials for them. They can help by passing on well-written information about databases or online systems and let potential users know the value of databases that meet their particular information needs.

Barbara Newlin of Menlo Corporation described the creation and growing pains of *Pro-Search*, Menlo's front-end software package. *In-Search* was introduced in 1984 as a front-end to make DIALOG searching easier for end users. They soon found that many people did not understand what DIALOG was, that: "*In-Search* was ahead of its time, that Menlo had come too early to a job that was too big for any one company. The end user market had not yet generated a groundswell demand for online information. People wouldn't buy *In-Search* until they could understand why online information was important to them, why it was worth paying for, and, finally, how *In-Search* simplified the search and retrieval process. The effort to educate its market had nearly exhausted Menlo's resources."

The unexpected high costs of marketing and unrealized end user market, together with the problems of keeping up with the many changes in the DIALOG system, led Menlo Corporation to cut their sales and marketing staff and instead focus on new product development. They realized that an established market that was of limited size (intermediaries) is more profitable than a market that is theoretically unlimited but is now only potential (end users). Consequently, Menlo redirected their efforts to create a front-end package for professional searchers. This product (*Pro-Search*) is now available from Personal Bibliographic Software for the IBM-PC and Macintosh. In addition to serving as a communications package and front-end access to BRS and DIALOG, *Pro-Search* allows searching in the native command mode of the systems and produces accounting reports. For more information contact: PBS, P.O. Box 4250, Ann Arbor, MI 48106.

Phil Williams, Userlink Systems Ltd., described some things that are needed to attract end users in great numbers to online searching. The most important of these is informing people how the information in databases can help them in their jobs. Marketing efforts by database producers are certainly one way to achieve this, but based on the experience of Data Courier, the efforts and input of intermediaries may be even more crucial at this early stage.

Awareness and education are not enough, however, according to Williams. Practical problems must be overcome, including: making it easy to initiate contact with an online system or multiple systems, devising simple and consistent charging schemes, and making all systems accessible from a multi-purpose microcomputer work station. Intellectual barriers to wide spread end user searching include the need for: assistance with search formulation (automatic or human), assistance with database selection, tutorial assistance in formulating the initial search, and assistance in revising and improving the search.

Intermediaries who have introduced end user searching in their organizations or communities report enthusiasm for searching once the need for information is perceived and the search process mastered (mastery takes less time but is still required when a gateway or front-end is used). The role of the information professional in this process—in generating initial enthusiasm and in translating this enthusiasm into searching skills—should not be underestimated. The database and software producers who candidly reported their experiences recognized that important contribution.

As Barbara Newlin summed up the *In-Search* experience:

> Even given a product as well-designed, well-reviewed, and well-marketed as In-Search, end users will not storm the computer stores and turn themselves into DIALOG searchers.... The curious and adventurous among them may do a DIALOG search from time to time, but they will not (and cannot) duplicate what we do as information professionals.... When they find out about databases and come looking for gurus, we'll be there.

Intermediaries of course need not wait for end users to somehow find out about databases and "come looking." We can play an active role in informing and educating the people in our communities and organizations.

Proceedings of the Sixth National Online Meeting (1985) are available for $50 from: Learned Information Inc., 143 Old Marlton Pike, Medford, NJ 08055. ■

ONLINE SEARCHING IN SCHOOLS*

Many school librarians have hesitated to introduce students to online searching because they believe the costs are too high or feel it would interfere with learning manual reference skills. An increasing number of high school librarians, and even those in intermediate and elementary schools, are recognizing the value of online searching for students. Vendors are also providing low-cost options to help make online searching feasible in schools.

Ann Lathrop, library coordinator, San Mateo County Office of Education, compiled information about online searching in schools, in what will be a first comprehensive list of schools that provide it. Some of the most active programs are discussed below.

Since 1976 senior high school students at the Montgomery County Public School System (Md.), a pioneer in online searching, have had access to *DIALOG* searches to supplement their manual information gathering. Initially students submitted search requests to the Professional Library where searches were done by a librarian without the student present. Later selected school media specialists and student assistants were trained to do online searches for students in their high schools. Now *DIALOG* searches are incorporated into the library skills program.

Students learn database construction, search strategy, choosing appropriate databases, and accessing information online. The most frequently used databases are *Magazine Index*, *Medline*, and *ERIC*. Students do online searches only after they have exhausted all manual sources (see Pruitt, Ellen & Karen Dowling, "Searching for Current Information Online ... How High School Library Media Centers in Montgomery County, Maryland, Are Solving an Information Problem Using *DIALOG*," *Online*, March 1985, p. 47-60).

According to Anne Caputo, program coordinator for *DIALOG*'s educational program, Radnor High School (Pa.), another pacesetter, was the first high school in the nation to establish a *DIALOG* educational account. All ninth-grade honors students are required to learn about online searching before passing to the next grade.

Cypress-Fairbanks School District (Texas) introduced *DIALOG* searching in a variety of classes and created its own curricular material and manuals.

High schools offering online searching on systems such as *DIALOG* include: Princeton HS; Bellarmine College Preparatory HS, San Jose, Cal.; St. Thomas Aquinas HS, Ft. Lauderdale, Fla.; and Lexington School for the Deaf, Jackson Heights, N.Y. (see Bev Smith, "Student Searchers: Are They Out There? *Information Today*, March 1984, p. 1-2, 32-33). Caputo estimates that high schools hold 20 to 25 percent of *DIALOG*'s educational/instructional passwords.

Much of the online searching in schools is experimental. Lucy Anne Wozny ("Online Bibliographic Searching and Student Use of Information: An Innovative Approach," *School Library Media Quarterly*, Fall 1982, p. 35-42) describes an experiment in which ninth-grade honors students at Radnor High were introduced to *DIALOG* searching as one way to gather sources for a research paper on energy. After they defined and narrowed their search topics through a manual search, they were introduced to online searching. After the library media specialist assisted with search strategy refinement, each student chose a database and performed the search. Since energy was the topic students used only four databases (*Energyline*, *Enviroline*, *Magazine Index*, and *Historical Abstracts*).

Probably because their school library did not have them, most students (81 percent) did not include in their bibliographies the references they retrieved online. (Only five percent of the total references in the student bibliographies were retrieved online.) Wozny feels that online searching provided other benefits, however. The search process made students aware of the variety of materials available and forced them to think logically and to develop search strategy skills.

In "An Introduction to Online Bibliographic Searching for High School Students: A Successful Approach" (*Educational Technology*, June 1984, p. 39-41), Kathleen Craver and Lee Ounanian report on a study of college-bound seniors who used *DIALOG* to find information on debate topics. After

---

manual searching to refine their topics, the students were introduced to the principles of online searching. Debate groups selected an appropriate database, formulated a search strategy, and observed a search on their topic. (Students did not do their own searching.) A post-test showed that students understood online searching and almost all expressed their approval of the online searching curriculum unit.

BRS offered bibliographic support services for ACCESS-86, a New Jersey project in classroom data communication which provides technical assistance, training, and curriculum development for either public or private schools, grades eight through college, that plan to offer online searching. *BRS* training will be incorporated into the project that also includes computer skills and data communication principles.

Some intermediate and upper elementary schools are also beginning to introduce online searching to students. Caputo says that only a handful of intermediate schools are now using *DIALOG*, but that number will probably increase. Many school libraries, especially in elementary and middle schools, feel their students do not need to access such sophisticated systems as *DIALOG*. An alternative is the consumer information online services such as *The Source* and *CompuServe*. As Suzan Prince ("Information at Your Fingertips: How One School Is Making It Happen," *Electronic Learning*, September/October 1981, p. 38-40, 63) and William Martin ("Touring an Informational Wonderland," *Classroom Computer Learning*, February 1984, p. 52-60) point out, both *The Source* and *CompuServe* have been widely used at all grade levels.

Both systems provide access to newswire services, some periodicals, the *Academic American Encyclopedia*, and bulletin boards. They also have features like CB simulators, electronic shopping, travel planning, quizzes on academic subjects, and remote computing. The *Academic American Encyclopedia* database is most often accessed by students of this age. Wire services are used for current events. Despite limited search powers, *The Source* and *CompuServe* provide a simple introduction to online information and can cost less than research databases.

DIALOG, *BRS*, and *Wilsonline* are all now actively seeking the school library market. According to Anne Caputo, high schools, intermediate schools, and the upper grades of elementary schools are among *DIALOG*'s top priorities. Each of these major online systems mentioned above offers low-cost options to make online searching feasible for schools.

DIALOG has offered an educational discount program for instructional purposes since the early 1970s. Almost all graduate schools of library and information science take advantage of this program and *DIALOG* has turned to other professional schools and the high school and elementary school market.

For about $15 per hour, instructional plan users can access almost all of the *DIALOG* databases (the Chemical Abstracts Databases are notable exceptions) and use most of the *DIALOG* search features. (No offline prints, SDIs, or permanent saves are allowed.) Most of the high schools mentioned above use the *DIALOG* plan.

In the fall of 1986 *DIALOG* introduced an even more attractive option for secondary and upper elementary grades. Curriculum materials aimed specifically at schools have been developed and are being tested at six school sites. They include a teacher's guide, masters for overhead transparencies, and sample exercises and will be sold with passwords that are good for a preset amount of online time. The price is low enough to make online searching attractive to many schools. Curriculum materials are also being developed for targeted professional schools (such as business, medical, and law) and the library school lab workbook was revised.

The new high school and elementary school option will access *Knowledge Index*, *DIALOG*'s simplified search service aimed at end-users which provides access to only a subset of *DIALOG*'s more than 300 databases. It includes the databases thought to be of most interest to students (e.g., *ERIC*, *Magazine Index*, *National Newspaper Index*, *Medline*). Regular users of *Knowledge Index* can access it only after 6 p.m. or on weekends but the school option will be available during regular school hours.

For more information about DIALOG school programs contact: Anne Caputo, Program Coordinator, DIALOG Information Services, 1901 N. Moore St., #809, Arlington, VA 22209.

BRS also has a long-standing instructional plan available to all grade levels. For a total charge of $15 per hour *BRS Instructor* provides access to almost all of the *BRS* databases (including, as of late 1985, *Magazine Index* and *National Newspaper Index*). *BRS Instructor* comes with a workbook, transparency masters, and *BRS* database information.

For educational professionals *BRS* offers *BRS Educator* (formerly *BRS Colleague/Education*) which allows the choice of the *BRS* command-driven system or their simpler menu-driven system. The one-time set-up fee of $75 includes a user's manual, and online charges start at $12 per hour. Some databases of interest to educators are available only on *BRS*. *Resources in Computer Education* (*RICE*) contains information on school applications of microcomputers and specific information about software and *School Practices Information File* contains descriptions of all types of educational programs.

WILSONLINE, the H. W. Wilson Company's online search service, carries the *Readers' Guide to Periodical Literature*, the print version of which is relied upon by school libraries for student's manual searching. (All other Wilson products are also on *WILSONLINE*.) The cost of *WILSONLINE* access depends on how much online time you buy and whether your library subscribes to the corresponding print index. Subscribers to the print *Readers' Guide* who do not buy a specific number of online hours pay $35 per hour to use the *Readers' Guide Database*.

Only relatively current information is available online. *Readers' Guide* contains citations to literature from January 1983 to the present, *Education Index* from September 1983 forward. *WILSONLINE* is updated twice weekly, however, so current information is almost immediately available.

WILSONLINE also offers an instructional program with all Wilson databases available for $15 per hour, with a *WILSONLINE* tutorial and the user's manual available. Of particular interest to schools is Wilson's menu-driven software interface called *WILSEARCH*, for use with IBM PCs and Apples, which helps users formulate search strategies and select databases. *WILSEARCH* then connects to the *WILSONLINE* system and executes the search. The yearly licensing fee is $150 for *WILSEARCH*, with reduced prices for multiple copies. The additional charge for every search (every group of ten references retrieved) goes from $1 per search, if you commit to 2000 searches per year, to $5 if you do not take the prepaid subscription.

An alternative to online access for schools is to purchase search software and subsets of some databases on floppy disk. The best subsets for school use are *ERIC Microsearch* and *Microcomputer Index on Disk* (*MIND*), both of which serve as simulation tools to teach searching before allowing students to access full databases online (see my "Database Subsets," *LJ*, May 15, 1985, p. 42-43) for more detail.

BENEFITS OF ONLINE SEARCHING

Researchers and school librarians have found that students derive many benefits beyond just finding articles or reports for research projects from the online searching experience. Students learn research and problem-solving skills and use logical thinking processes to develop search strategies and work with the librarian to refine their questions for a computer search. The major online systems require knowledge of set theory and Boolean logic.

Awareness of the wide variety of electronic information sources opens up new worlds of information for the students. Schools using online searching find that students do not rely solely on articles from the popular literature. Even when they do not access the complete document found in a bibliographic search, students are made aware of the potential value of government documents, research reports, conference proceedings, and specialized journals.

School librarians and classroom teachers cooperate in most online searching experiences, leading to closer ties between the library and classroom. Finally, as Anne Caputo pointed out in her "Online Goes to School: Instruction and Use of Online Systems in Secondary and Elementary Education" (in *Proceedings of the Sixth National Online Meeting*. Medford, NJ: Learned Information, 1985, p. 85-90) students *enjoy* online searching and discover that research can be a pleasurable experience. ∎

FOUR OPTIONS FOR END USER SEARCHING*

For libraries that want to offer end user searching, four options (end user search systems, front-end software, gateway services, local databases on floppy diskettes or optical discs) are summarized below.

Access to an online system designed specifically for end user searching is the option chosen so far by most academic or public libraries. (For a bibliography and list of libraries see: Richard V. Janke, "Online After Six: End User Searching Comes of Age," *Online*, November 1984, p. 15-29.)

END USER SYSTEMS

The two most popular systems are *BRS/Afterdark* (BRS Information Technologies Inc., 1200 Route 7, Latham, NY 12100) and DIALOG's *Knowledge Index* (DIALOG Information Services Inc., 3460 Hillview Ave., Palo Alto, CA 94304). Both systems provide access to a limited number of the most popular databases that are available on the parent system. *BRS/Afterdark* offers 88 databases including bibliographic and many full text in a variety of subject areas. *Knowledge Index* offers 58 databases, including many on business, computers, news, and science and technology.

Both systems are available only after 6 p.m. local time or on weekends, but the connect-hour rates are considerably lower than the parent systems. *BRS/Afterdark* charges between $6 and $31 per hour with a $12 monthly minimum and a one-time $75 fee. All *Knowledge Index* databases are $24 per hour with no monthly minimum and a $35 per hour start-up fee that includes two hours of search time. Both systems offer direct and credit card billing.

BRS/Afterdark uses a simple menu-driven interface that allows even inexperienced users to search. *Knowledge Index* uses a simplified version of DIALOG's command language so reading the manual or some instruction is needed.

These systems offer several advantages: the relatively wide range of databases available (there will be some material of interest to most library users); and the library staff is often familiar with the databases because they are the same as on the parent systems. Cost advantages are: either a microcomputer or a dumb terminal can be used to search; like the parent BRS and DIALOG systems, the library or user pays only for the time spent online, so start-up and ongoing costs may be relatively low.

There are several disadvantages to choosing this option. Only a small portion of the databases on the parent systems are available. Also, library staff often will need to help users select databases and formulate searches. Instruction in Boolean logic seems to be particularly important. The connect-hour pricing option is more difficult to budget and may not be attractive to high-volume users. Telephone lines are needed and the quality of the connection will vary. Finally, the restricted hours of access may require staffing changes and limit which users can take advantage of the service.

Users of the regular *BRS/Search* system can also search with menus instead of commands by requesting "MENUS" instead of a database name.

*Reprinted from *Library Journal* July 1986. Copyright © 1986 by Reed Publishing, USA, Div. of Reed Holdings, Inc.

The end user system option is popular, especially as an extension of existing online reference service. It is particularly popular in academic libraries which traditionally have evening-hour service and are familiar with the full DIALOG and BRS.

FRONT-END SOFTWARE

Another end user option is to purchase microcomputer software that makes it easier to search the full online systems. Good front-end software allows searches to be formulated off-line and assists with such things as database choice, term selection, and Boolean logic. The software then connects to the desired host system and uploads the stored search. Once the search is run, most software allows the users to make modifications and download the search results.

Some of the best front-end packages for end user searching are: *Sci-Mate Searcher*, *Pro-Search*, and *WILSEARCH*, all available for the IBM PC and some other computers.

The *Sci-Mate Searcher* from ISI helps with searching BRS, DIALOG, NLM, SDC ORBIT, and Questel. It provides menu-driven search strategy development and includes information such as field tags for selected databases on each host. The biggest advantage of *Sci-Mate Searcher* is that it is one part of a three-part system. Downloaded searches may be transferred to the *Sci-Mate Manager* to create in-house databases and to the *Sci-Mate Editor* to create formated bibliographies. The *Sci-Mate* package is especially good for special libraries or for academic faculty when personal files and reformatting are important. [The Institute for Scientific Information (ISI) no longer supports Sci-Mate.]

Pro-Search, a front end for searching BRS and DIALOG, includes information about most DIALOG and BRS databases and assists search strategy development. It is a visually attractive package that makes good use of windows, function keys, and help screens.

Personal Bibliographic Software, Inc. (PBS) acquired *Pro-Search* this year from Menlo Corporation. The package is now marketed in a "Searcher's Tool Kit" with the PBS *Pro-Cite* and *Biblio-links* packages that can be used to download and create formatted bibliographies. Like *Sci-Mate*, *Pro-Search* is good for special and academic libraries, especially when reformatting is desired. *Pro-Search* alone is now $495, or all three packages may be purchased for $995 (PBS, P.O. Box 4250, Ann Arbor, MI 48106).

WILSEARCH provides simplified access to the *WILSONLINE* system, including search strategy development, automatic logon, and downloading results. *WILSEARCH* automatically disconnects from *WILSONLINE* after downloading results; the connection must be made again if a search is to be modified.

Unlike the other two packages mentioned, the purchase of *WILSEARCH* provides the option of prepaid search time. Prepayment plans vary with a maximum of $2000 that will buy 2000 searches, each retrieving up to ten references. If a library does not prepay, searches of up to ten references cost $5 each. There is no charge if no references are retrieved. An annual software licensing fee of $150 is also required. *WILSEARCH* is especially good for school libraries, general public libraries, or undergraduate libraries where Wilson indexes are heavily used and precise, low-cost searches are desired (H. W. Wilson Company, 950 University Ave., Bronx, NY 10452).

The main advantage of using a front end is that all of the databases on the host system are accessible. Some packages offer access to more than one host. Front-end programs are useful for intermediary searchers and end users. Despite the initial cost, online connect time will be reduced, saving money in the long run. In addition, several of the packages interface with other software that allows editing of downloaded records or creation of in-house files.

Disadvantages include the need to have microcomputer and telecommunications links. Libraries that have used these packages report that most users need help formulating queries and interacting with the software. At first, most users do not find them simple to use. Databases are charged at the regular connect-hour rate and the library must get accounts with all systems to be accessed.

GATEWAY SERVICES

Gateway services connect a user through a host computer to the computers of one or more online vendors. The most valuable gateways for end user searching also serve as front ends by adding many of the search-assistance features offered by microcomputer front-end packages.

The gateway service most appropriate for end user search services in public or academic libraries is *EASYNET*, which can be accessed with either a microcomputer or a dumb terminal. When a user dials 800-EASYNET or selects *EASYNET* from CompuServe menus, they are connected to the *EASYNET* system which helps with search strategy development and database selection. *EASYNET* then connects to one of over 700 databases on 13 systems.

Cost is $8 per search for up to ten citations on one database, plus a surcharge for some databases (no charge if no citations are retrieved). *EASYNET* has direct or credit card billing (EASYNET, 134 N. Narberth Ave., Narberth, PA 19072).

The main advantage of a gateway is the ability to access many databases on many online systems. With *EASYNET*, the library does not need accounts with the different online systems. Charges are made only when a search is done and citations are retrieved. Start-up costs are low.

Disadvantages, as with all remote online services, include the need for telecommunications access and unpredictable costs that vary with the amount of use. At a minimum of $8 per search, the cost of a simple search may be higher on *EASYNET* than through other options. A gateway service such as *EASYNET* is a good end user option for public libraries that want low start-up costs, have a variety of types of users, and need access to different types of databases and vendors.

LOCAL DATABASES

The final option for end user searching is to house the database system in the library. In-house, local databases are available from a variety of database producers in several formats (see my columns, May 15, 1985, p. 42-43 and March 1, 1986, p. 68-69, for more details). Although magnetic tape versions of databases for loading on a local mainframe have long been available from database producers, they are not cost effective or practical for most libraries. New subsets of databases for use with a microcomputer are practical for almost all libraries. Subsets of several hundred records are sold on floppy disks for such databases as *BIOSIS*, *ERIC*, *Microcomputer Index*, and *Medline*.

Much larger complete databases or subsets of databases are available on compact optical discs (CD-ROM). Now available or planned soon are: Information Access Company's *InfoTrac*; *ERIC*, *PsycLit*, *AV-Online*, *PAIS*, *LISA*, and many others from SilverPlatter; *ERIC*, *NTIS*, and many others from MEDLINE DIALOG: *Dissertation Abstracts* and others from UMI/DATA COURIER; and most of the H. W. Wilson databases.

The main advantage of locally held databases is the set subscription price. Libraries can budget for these services as they do for journals. No matter how much the database is used, the price remains the same (unless an additional microcomputer work station is added). Libraries that do not want to charge patrons for end user searching will find this option attractive. Another advantage is these systems do not use telecommunications, so access is not dependent on host system hours or poor local telephone connections.

A disadvantage is that locally held databases are less frequently updated than online databases. Discs are only updated monthly, quarterly, or annually, so current information is often inaccessible. Another disadvantage, especially for small libraries, is the cost. Database subscription fees and hardware costs must be paid annually whether or not the system is heavily used. Libraries must be commited up front to the price of the product, each typically costing several thousand dollars per year, so these databases may replace subscriptions to expensive print indexes rather than online databases.

A final disadvantage is that most of the databases do not use the same search software. Library users must thus switch search tactics for different databases and the library may need to set up separate microcomputer workstations for each.

Still, the in-house database option holds great promise for end user searching in many types of libraries. Libraries that have heavy use of one or two indexes will find this option particularly attractive. ∎

DIALOG'S KNOWLEDGE INDEX AND BRS/AFTER DARK
Database Searching on Personal Computers*

"Your own university library online at home" promises the advertisement for the new BRS/After Dark service. Access to "one of the largest information storehouses available anywhere," says the DIALOG Knowledge Index manual. BRS/After Dark and DIALOG's Knowledge Index are new services being marketed to microcomputer owners to allow them to have access to databases at low rates during evening hours. Potentially, these services could mean the beginning of a new direction in online searching because access is from the home rather than through the library. No intermediary is needed because both have developed simplified query languages. The systems are similar in intended audience and potential impact, yet there are some differences between them.

The user of DIALOG's Knowledge Index chooses the general subject of the databases he or she is interested in searching and then is given a choice of databases to choose from within the section. Until January only the News section offered more than one database (Newsearch and National Newspaper Index), but additional databases are to be added to other sections. Users can choose from nine subject sections: Agriculture information (AGRICOLA), Business information (ABI/INFORM), Computers and Electronics (INSPEC), Corporate News (Standards & Poor's News), Education (ERIC), Engineering (Engineering Literature Index), Government Publications (GPO Publications Reference File), Magazines (Magazine Index), Medicine (MEDLINE), News and Psychology (PSYCINFO).

Four pages of information on each database are included in the *Knowledge Index Manual*. These information sheets contain much of the descriptive information found on DIALOG blue-sheets, but they also include some tutorial information and hints on searching for both subject concepts and nonsubject concepts in that database.

SUBJECT FOCUS

A "Subject Guide to Knowledge Index," an appendix in the *Manual*, helps the user select the appropriate subject section. Individual databases are not given in the subject guide; instead it focuses on subject sections. This appendix is a useful addition because DIALINDEX (DIALOG's online subject guide) is not available to Knowledge Index users. The focus on subject sections is curious, in that there is only one database in each subject section. When additional databases are added to a subject section, the user will be left with a choice within the section but will get no more help from the system.

Like Knowledge Index, BRS/After Dark emphasizes subject categories first rather than individual databases. After

*Reprinted from *Library Journal* Mar. 1, 1983. Copyright © 1983 by Reed Publishing, USA, Div. of Reed Holdings, Inc.

Dark users could choose among six subject categories as of January 1983: science and medicine databases, social science and humanities databases, and energy and environmental databases. Only the section on reference databases contains a single database (*Books in Print*). Several databases are available in most of the categories. Once the subject category choice is made, the user is asked to select an individual database.

SELECTING A DATABASE

When librarians approach an online search they generally use their knowledge of individual databases and choose the database or databases they feel are most appropriate for a topic. Online tools such as DIALINDEX and BRS's CROSS Index help this process, which is becoming increasingly difficult as more and more databases become available.

Knowledge Index and After Dark attempt to downplay distinction among databases and instead emphasize subject categories. This is, of course, necessary when the user has little familiarity with individual databases, their printed counterparts, or the differences among them. The information sheets in the manuals do cover idiosyncrasies of each database, but when more databases are added to the subject sections I wonder how an inexperienced user will know how to choose among them.

We all wish at times that we could ignore differences among databases, but because they are created by different publishers, these differences do exist. Coverage, accuracy, and quality of information varies from database to database, and librarians spend a great deal of time keeping up with these variations. Ignoring characteristics of individual databases is likely to result in less than optimal searches. Most likely, the typical Knowledge Index or After Dark user will not know enough about comparative quality among databases to know if his search results could have been improved.

SEARCHING "KNOWLEDGE INDEX"

The query languages of both systems are designed to simplify the search process, but they have quite different approaches. Knowledge Index, like DIALOG's regular search system, has the user input commands and Boolean expressions after a prompt sign (a question mark). The Knowledge Index query language is slightly different from that of regular DIALOG, however, and many features are not offered. "Find" is used instead of "select"; "recap" is used instead of "display sets"; "display" is the only option for looking at search results, etc. Terms or set numbers can be combined with the "find" command and the appropriate logical operator(s), but only a single set number is given for each "find" command entered (like "select," without the "select steps" option). If a typographical or logical error is made on input the entire expression must thus be reentered.

"Expand," the command which shows a portion of the alphabetical indexes, is the same as in the regular DIALOG, as is truncation (called a wild card character in Knowledge Index). Online ordering of documents is also the same as for all DIALOG users. The Knowledge Index version of the

"begin" command uses the first four letters of the subject section rather than a database number. If there is more than one database in a section, the user is then asked to choose the database to be searched.

Knowledge Index provides a scaled-down version of the DIALOG software, offering only those features necessary for basic searching without confusing the novice searcher with advanced commands. Distinctions among parts of the basic index (titles, descriptors, etc.) are not made in searching, but additional non-subject indexes can be searched. The manual discusses searching by journal title and author and it does a good job of explaining the problems with inconsistent handling of these fields by different databases and offers appropriate search strategy solutions. (Here the distinction among databases is noted!)

One of the most frustrating features of the DIALOG system for new users is the necessity of memorizing eight different output formats. Knowledge Index has simplified this by giving a choice of short, medium, or long displays of citations. Because Knowledge Index searchers are assumed to be using microcomputer screens, more than one citation at a time cannot be displayed without resetting the vertical screen size to zero (thus telling the system to ignore vertical screen size and print continuously). Offline printouts are not possible.

When I had novice searchers sit down at the terminal with only a summary of the Knowledge Index commands they were able to conduct simple searches within a few minutes. The excellent *Knowledge Index Manual* helped them deal with more difficult searches with its clear explanations and many sample searches. The *Manual* provides help with the modification of unsatisfactory search results and addresses some of the differences among databases and, thus, is an invaluable aid. Knowledge Index cannot be searched without at least the summary of commands.

SEARCHING "AFTER DARK"

BRS/After Dark takes a different approach to searching. After Dark is a menu-driven system that leads the user through a series of choices. Ideally, if the user knows how to log on, it should be possible to search without studying any commands and without consulting the user manual.

After a series of three menu steps, the user reaches the database of choice and can enter the terms to be searched. The command "S" is entered to continue searching, the command "P" causes the first citation of the results of the last search statement to be displayed in full format. Subsequent carriage returns with no other command will display additional citations in turn. As with Knowledge Index, no offline printing is allowed. In complex searches or multi-term searches I found that entering "S", carriage return, waiting for the search prompt, then entering the search terms, took longer than using the "find" command in Knowledge Index. The After Dark menu-driven system gets very tedious very quickly, even to relatively inexperienced searchers, although it is possible to circumvent some of the levels.

A menu system allows the user to search without studying the manual, but it can be frustrating if the user runs into trouble. I tried entering "help" at several levels of the menu and got little help at all. At the database level when I was trying to search for an author, the system responded to my "help" plea with a list of choices available in the system—"type S to continue searching, P to print first item, M to return to the master menu," etc. At other levels "help" brought such responses as "Invalid selection. Please try again." Admittedly, turning to the manual at this point probably would have answered my questions, but any menu-driven system that purports to allow novices to search without training should have available useful and appropriate help messages.

COMPARISONS

Both After Dark and Knowledge Index have greatly simplified word proximity searching. Instead of entering a special word proximity character ("adj" or "(w)") for multi-word subjects, the user merely inputs the phrase normally with blanks between the words. The search software automatically assumes an adjacency character and searches free text for the terms in all basic index fields. This feature greatly simplifies searching if simple adjacency is sufficient. Users do not have the full power of the parent services, including specifying that terms fall within several words of each other, in the same field or sentence as each other, or within a certain specified field such as title or descriptors. As with other features of these systems, the word adjacency feature succeeds at making simple searching very easy, but ignores some of the complexities of searching that inexperienced searchers often find necessary in order to get satisfactory results.

After Dark offers a wider selection of databases than does Knowledge Index at the present time. Its search system is less powerful, however, with such disturbing features as the inability to see frequency counts for all terms entered in a single search statement. Modification of an unsuccessful search strategy is easier in DIALOG because frequency counts for all terms are displayed, although the "steps" option for each term is not offered. No one really knows yet whether menu-driven software or command-drive is preferable for most novice users. To find out, we will need both experience and research.

A major advantage of the BRS/After Dark service is that in the near future it promises to be much more than just a citation search service. It will offer its users a choice of functions, including a microcomputer software order service, electronic mail service, and "swap shop." These kinds of services are available on other personal computer database services such as The Source and Compuserve and should make BRS competitive with such services. DIALOG's International Software Database allows online ordering of microcomputer software. This valuable service would probably be popular with Knowledge Index users. Full-service systems are what personal computer users will come to expect in the future.

These services offer the personal computer owner a chance to locate citations to literature at home and order the desired articles online (to be mailed later). The number of home computers, although growing rapidly, is still small. The cost of microcomputer plus the online search fees and costs of document delivery ensure that, for the present, many people will not be able to afford such services at home. Will the library or search service agencies thus serve those who cannot afford to search for themselves or who don't want to take the time?

THE POTENTIAL

The full potential of such systems will not be reached until the full text of the desired document is also available in machine-readable form and data transmission rates decrease significantly. At the present most database search specialists would agree that to conduct effective searches of indexing and abstracting databases requires familiarity with the search system software, skill in search strategy and knowledge of databases available. BRS/After Dark and DIALOG Knowledge Index eliminate the need for the first of these by simplifying the search process. They attempt to eliminate the last by grouping databases into subject categories. While these systems simplify the search process, they do not compensate for the lack of skill and knowledge of the user. Searching is indeed simpler from the user's standpoint, but the power of the systems is diminished and the complexities of searching are merely masked by ignoring them.

I have no doubt that end user searching will some day replace searching by a trained intermediary. Before this happens, however, the systems must progress to the point that they are able to provide the interpretation and understanding now provided by a human intermediary. Artificial intelligence and knowledge based systems are not yet this sophisticated, but they must be before novice users will be able to achieve search results equivalent to what a trained searcher can now offer. ■

THE EASYNET GATEWAY*

EasyNet, the gateway system to multiple online vendors, has elicited excitement among information professionals since it debuted in 1984. EasyNet had several things that made it especially attractive from the beginning: credit card billing at each use so no contract was needed; an 800 telephone number so there were no extra telecommunications charges; the ability to access many different vendors without learning different search protocols or without signing contracts; the ability to access the system with either a dumb terminal or microcomputer; the system's capability of choosing appropriate databases for novice users; and the credibility of sponsorship by the National Federation of Abstracting and Information Services (NFAIS).

In the last two years, EasyNet has continued to make modifications and enhancements. Librarians who haven't looked at EasyNet since its debut may want to give it another look now, either for end user searching or as a supplement to their own searching.

VENDORS

EasyNet can connect a user to any of 13 online vendors that together provide access to 900 databases. In addition to the original seven well-known vendors (DIALOG, BRS, Orbit, Newsnet, VU/TEXT, Pergamon, and Financial Data Services Questel), EasyNet now connects with some systems that many users would not have access to otherwise: ADP Network Service; Datastar (Switzerland), Datatimes (United States), SINORG (formerly G. Cam Serveur); WILSONLINE, and PROFILE Information. With these systems, EasyNet has available many Canadian, British, and French news, legal, and business databases. There are many full-text as well as statistical and bibliographic files.

A searcher might not use many of the available databases enough to warrant accessing them directly, but using EasyNet as a gateway allows occasional access without learning each system's commands or contracting with each vendor. A library or individual that uses a system regularly would still want to go directly to that vendor. But for the occasional question requiring access to different databases, going through EasyNet is a simple solution. On EasyNet you may directly select the database you wish to search or allow the system to help you select one as you answer a series of questions about your topic.

THE EASYNET SYSTEM

To access EasyNet, a user may have either a dumb terminal, a microcomputer with modem and communications software or Telex machine. Since the EasyNet computer does all of the search assistance and switching to the different vendors, you don't need to purchase any special equipment or front-end software.

EasyNet is available in all states by dialing 800-EASY-NET. Optionally, access can be made via packet networks (Telenet, Tymnet, and CompuServe).

Once you have logged onto EasyNet you may choose EasyNet I, EasyNet II, or EasyNet III. EasyNet I leads the user through a series of diagnostic questions, resulting eventually in the system selecting an appropriate database. Not all databases are available through this automatic service. Most times the system selects one of the major databases on BRS or DIALOG. EasyNet II lets the user select any of the 900 databases directly. EasyNet III permits interactive searching through common language.

EasyNet makes the connection to the online vendor, translates the search query into the appropriate format and syntax, and reports the results. Although system commands and field labels are supplied by EasyNet, searchers are expected to enter correct Boolean operators, including parentheses, and to eliminate stop words. An online Help gives examples of all of these, but if the user does not read the examples and gets an unsatisfactory search, EasyNet attempts no automatic diagnosis.

The system does provide an "SOS" service. At any time during a search session (24 hours a day) a user may type SOS and receive online help from a search specialist at the other end. According to an EasyNet spokesperson, the most common types of problems via SOS are searching in an appropriate database, using stop words in a search statement, or entering incorrect Boolean operators.

Once a search is run on a host system, EasyNet downloads the first ten records, logs off, and presents the ten citations to the searcher. If a searcher wants to see more than ten, EasyNet must log back on to the host and run the search over. If the searcher chooses to see abstracts or full text instead of just citations, EasyNet has to once again log back on and rerun the search.

COSTS

Automatic logging off and on keeps the costs to EasyNet low. Costs to the searcher are based on citations received plus connect time. The costs are generally low but they can mount up quickly if more than ten citations are desired, if abstracts are requested, or if the database has a surcharge.

If the credit card billing option is chosen, no prior contract with EasyNet is required. Users simply dial the number and enter their American Express, Visa, or Master-Card number when prompted by the system. The credit card option has no start-up costs or ongoing charges; the user is billed just for the online session.

A basic search retrieving up to ten references costs $10 plus 35¢ per minute teleconnect charge. The next ten cost an additional $8. Abstracts cost $2 each. Some databases have a surcharge but EasyNet does not charge if no documents are

---

*Reprinted from *Library Journal* Nov. 1, 1986. Copyright © 1986 by Reed Publishing, USA, Div. of Reed Holdings, Inc.

retrieved. I did one author search on the *Sci-Search* database that retrieved 12 citations. To see the first ten cost $10 plus a $5 surcharge and approximately $1 connect time. I requested three abstracts at $2 each. To see the next two citations (one of which turned out to be a duplicate record) cost another $8 plus $5 plus about 40¢ connect time. This simple search cost over $33. Another more complex search on *Management Contents* cost only a little over $10 because I was satisfied with ten records and there was no surcharge.

LIBRARY OPTIONS

Some public libraries have chosen the credit card option as an easy way to offer adult end users access to database searching without the library having the hassles of passwords or record keeping.

A better option for most libraries is to subscribe to one of EasyNet's special options. For public or academic libraries, the Public Access Database System is an attractive option. For an annual subscription fee of $550 the library gets $100 in introductory searches, ten passwords, charge-back billing, plus a variety of user aids. A nice feature is the ability to create customized welcome screens. Searches that retrieve references are billed at $5 each plus 20¢ per minute with prepayment discounts available of up to ten percent.

Special libraries may want to become full commercial subscribers. For $600 per year EasyNet supplies ten passwords, charge-back billing, $150 worth of initial searches, the ability to create customized screens, user aids, and a 20 percent discount if the subscriber dials EasyNet via his or her own long distance service. Prepayment discounts of 5-18 percent are available to full commercial subscribers.

An especially attractive feature for large special libraries is the ability to customize the system to integrate EasyNet with an organization's in-house databases or electronic mail system. Small special libraries might choose the $100 per year single-password subscription with fewer special features.

School libraries may select a special Secondary Schools subscription program. Seventy databases have been selected that will be of most interest in secondary schools. A special version of the "reference interview" menus that lead to the database choice is geared to the secondary student.

In this subscription option, one search is defined as five citations plus one abstract or full-text article *or* two no-hit searches. Passwords work for a single search only, with a cost

for each of $3.50. The annual subscription rate is $250 plus the single-session passwords purchased in blocks of 100. The newest option for libraries, Direct Connect, allows EasyNet to be accessed through the library's Online Public Access Catalog.

ALANET

Librarians might choose to access EasyNet another way. ALA has joined forces with EasyNet's parent company, Telebase Systems, to offer EasyNet access through Alanet. The new service, Alanet Plus, allows Alanet users to connect to EasyNet and to a selection of ALA databases and newsletters with no additional subscription or password required.

Like the regular EasyNet service, Alanet Plus has two levels of service: 1) where a series of menus leads the system to select the database to be accessed, or 2) where the user directly selects the database.

The arrangement with ALA is not the first such special access arrangement made by Telebase Systems. Access to EasyNet is also available through CompuServe as IQuest, Western Union as InfoMaster, and ten other sponsoring agencies.

EVALUATION

EasyNet isn't perfect. Costs can mount up if you are not careful and the system does not automatically help if no hits are retrieved. The system does try to overcome these problems by warning about surcharges, abstract costs, etc., and by offering instantaneous SOS help.

EasyNet is attractive for end user searching in the library. The system is easy to use and many unique library options allow for a customized service. For information professionals EasyNet is one way to search seldom-used online vendors or databases without an up-front commitment of time or money. For more information about EasyNet contact: EasyNet, Telebase Systems Inc., 763 W. Lancaster, Bryn Mawr, PA 19010; 215-526-2800. For more information about Alanet Plus contact: Joel M. Lee, Alanet, American Library Association, 50 E. Huron St., Chicago, IL 60611; 312-944-6780. A recent article is Mick O'Leary's "EasyNet Revisited: Pushing the Online Frontier," *Online* 12 (5) (Sept. 1988), p. 22-30. ■

3

MICROCOMPUTERS
FOR ONLINE SEARCHING

Chapter 3 turns the focus away from the people who search to the hardware and software used for searching. When the microcomputer became widely used for online searching beginning in the early 1980s, it began to have profound impacts on many aspects of online searching. A dumb terminal was merely a conduit to online systems—the intermediary had the knowledge and skill at one end, the online host had the information and software to search it at the other. The terminal just got the intermediary and the host together and contributed nothing to the search process.

While a microcomputer can be used just as a telecommunications device like a dumb terminal, it offers possibilities not available before. It has made searching available to end users (mostly microcomputer owners at first, now often through the library) with friendlier front-end interfaces. It has allowed searchers to formulate search strategy offline and upload stored searches, so the actual online time is minimized. It has allowed downloading of search results with subsequent editing (post-processing) or the transferring of records into in-house databases. Software to accomplish all of these things and to optimize online searching has proliferated in the last few years.

The impacts brought about by the microcomputer are certainly felt by searchers and end users, but also by database producers and online hosts. Database producers worry about the effects on database integrity of widespread downloading and both producers and hosts are concerned about revenues that may be lost if in-house databases replace repeated online searches. This chapter explores some of these issues as well as the mechanics of online searching with a microcomputer. (Impacts are covered again in Chapter 10. Software for in-house databases is treated in Chapter 4.)

Although the information in the first article in this chapter ("Online Searching with a Microcomputer") may now be old hat to many online searchers, it still contains information of value for new searchers. Since this article is basically a factual overview of hardware requirements for searching remote online databases, prices and specific information have been brought up to date as much as possible.

One of the biggest issues generated by searching with a microcomputer instead of with a dumb terminal is downloading, discussed in the second article. The concerns and issues presented in "Online Searching with a Microcomputer: Downloading Issues" are still current. As larger storage capacities become common on microcomputers and as faster baud rates are available for online searching, widespread downloading becomes even more of a possibility. No clear-cut legal ruling guides us yet and database producers have not arrived at a consensus as to what the best policy is for them. In the original version of this downloading article (published in *Microcomputers for Information Management*) there was a final section labeled "Effects of Downloading." This section discussed two main effects: changes in database pricing structures and the availability for purchase of subsets of databases for in-house use. I left this information out of the revised version because the specific details were out of date. Pricing policies have undergone even more changes in the last few years and database subsets have taken on new importance with the proliferation of CD-ROM. Each effect is covered in more detail and is brought up to date in subsequent chapters. Pricing policies are covered in Chapter 10 and database subsets, especially CD-ROM, are discussed in Chapter 5.

Online searching with a microcomputer relies on good software; online searchers now find themselves spending a lot of their time learning about new packages and comparing features. "Software for Online Searching" describes some representative packages of different types: a front end to search a single online host; a front end that accesses two hosts, and the post-processing functions of a database package. Addresses and prices have been updated.

The final article describes "An Interface for Self-Service Searching" developed under grant at the University of Illinois. The program typifies what many librarians consider a futuristic ideal. End users are able through one microcomputer and one software interface to search the university's online public access catalog, to search remote databases on BRS, BRS/After Dark, or DIALOG, and (eventually) to search locally held periodical databases on CD-ROM or magnetic tape. The interface makes the searching process seem relatively simple and the switching is transparent to the user. The University of Illinois interface is an example of the real power of a microcomputer for database searching in a library environment. When the power of front-end user-friendly software is coupled to a local mainframe with local communications links and to remote systems through telephone lines, the scope of database searching takes on new dimensions. Such systems will become commonplace in universities in the next decade.

ONLINE SEARCHING WITH A MICROCOMPUTER*

By the end of 1985 more than half of all search intermediaries switched to using microcomputers instead of dumb terminals for online searching. Many of you have already made the switch. This column is for those who are contemplating the move to a microcomputer and need some basic information.

BENEFITS

If your current terminal needs replacing or if you are in the market for an additional terminal, in most cases it makes more sense to purchase a microcomputer. For very little more money, the microcomputer is much more cost-effective because it can be used for other purposes such as word processing, administrative support functions, and library record keeping. For small libraries that do not conduct online searches all day, this multiple use capability is especially attractive. Currently many new micro models are almost as portable as the smallest dumb terminal (although the smaller computers are often not as comfortable as larger computers for functions such as long hours of word processing).

Searching with a microcomputer may allow you to spend less total time online and derive more benefits from your online time. With proper software, a microcomputer allows you to:

- automate the log-on protocols to the telecommunications networks and host systems,
- store initial search strategies and then upload them to the host system,
- capture search results on disk (download) for later printing,
- reformat captured searches to eliminate duplicates or to create custom formatted bibliographies,

- create in-house databases of database subsets, and finally,
- make use of powerful database access software that will allow you to do such things as search more than one system using a single set of commands.

HARDWARE & SOFTWARE REQUIRED

Computer store personnel seem to be more knowledgeable about online communications now than they were two or three years ago, but it is still good to have a clear idea of your requirements before approaching a retail store. The basic requirements are simple but there are many options within each:

1. A microcomputer with a) an Electronics Industry Association standard RS232C serial port (to allow connection of a modem) and, b) at least one floppy disk drive. In many micros, the serial port is built in; in others (notably Apples and IBM PCs) you must purchase a communications card with a serial port.

2. You will need a modem. Some microcomputers come with built-in internal modems (e.g., Radio Shack Model 102 and Kaypro 4). Others allow you to purchase an internal modem contained on a plug-in circuit board (an alternative to buying the communications card and separate modem for Apples and IBM PCs). External modems can be either direct connect or acoustic coupler. Most everyone is familiar with the old rabbit ears acoustic coupler. They are still OK, but direct-connect modems are more reliable, allow more functions, and are now comparable in price.

---

*Reprinted from *Library Journal* Mar. 15, 1985. Copyright © 1985 by Reed Publishing, USA, Div. of Reed Holdings, Inc.

3. If you have an external modem, you will need an RS232C cable to connect your modem to your microcomputer serial port.

4. Communications software you will need is discussed in more detail below.

5. A printer is optional but highly desirable.

MORE ABOUT MODEMS

As mentioned above, there are many options when it comes to buying a modem. Your modem should be purchased at the same time or after you purchase the computer and communications software, because it must be compatible with each. Some communications software is made to work best with certain types of modems. For example, the *PC-Talk III* package for IBM PCs is configured for the Hayes Smartmodem (or for Hayes compatible modems). It must be reconfigured to work with other modems. *Remember II*, a package for the Apple IIe, works only with the internal Hayes Micromodem IIe.

The modem can be either 300 or 1200 baud, or for some systems 2400 baud, with 1200 baud more cost effective in the long run with online systems that charge by connect hour. A 300 baud external modem generally sells for between $100 and $300, a 1200 baud modem for between $250 and $600. The 2400 baud modems are now on the market for approximately $800; 9600 baud modems for use over voice grade telephone lines are also on the market. But the major online systems do not yet support 2400 baud searching. Look for this to change in the near future with developments such as Dialog's own telecommunications network, DIALNET.

The modem should allow both full duplex and half duplex modes and communicate in an asynchronous mode. Except for software compatibility, the brand of modem doesn't generally matter as long as it meets industry standards. The 300 baud modems must be compatible with the standard Bell 103 modem, 1200 baud with the Bell 212A modem or Racal-Vadic 3400 series. Also it is generally safer to purchase any equipment at a store where you can go back for help or with problems rather than through the mail. If you purchase a direct connect external modem, you must have a modular phone jack so the modem can be plugged directly into the wall.

Modems for online searching need only the "originate" capability because generally you are initiating all of the calls. If for other functions you will ever want to have someone call your computer (patron access of an in-house database for example), you will also need an answer capability. Originate-answer modems are becoming the standard, however, and there seems to be little cost difference between originate only and originate-answer modems.

Other optional but desirable modem features include: the ability to do both touch tone and pulse code dialing; automatic dialing; and automatic redial of last number.

COMMUNICATIONS SOFTWARE

There is a wide variation in the capabilities, sophistication, and cost of communications software suitable for online searching. Some do little more than turn your microcomputer into a terminal (terminal emulators), others offer enhancements to the search process. You will want to reread "Mason on Micros" in the October 1, 1983 *LJ*, p. 1855-57, for more on "Communications Software." Sources of communications software are listed at the end of this column. Important basic features to look for in communications software include:

- ASCII code transmission (American Standard Code for Information Interchange);

- compatibility with hardware and modem;

- ability to specify at least 300 and 1200 baud rate and full or half duplex;

- asynchronous mode;

- break key emulator (most microcomputers don't have a break key);

- ability to redefine other keys;

- downloading capability (often called receiving or capturing);

- uploading capability;

- ability to access the communications software command mode without logging off from the host system;

- control of printer;

- ability to store telephone numbers and passwords;

- automatic log-on using the stored numbers and passwords; and

- automatic redial feature if lines are busy.

Prices for packages offering these basic features range from free to approximately $200. Some of the free or nearly free software is surprisingly good, although you won't get glossy manuals or fancy packaging. Most of these free packages are available through local user groups (or check guides such as Glossbrenner's *How To Get Free Software* for alternative sources). I have used Modem-7 for CP/M systems and *PC-Talk III* for IBM PCs and find both to be good. *PC-Talk III* is "freeware"—you may freely copy it, but the author asks you to send $35 if you like the program.

Database access programs are the sophisticated end of communications programs. They simplify the search process by translating user input into the host system command language in addition to serving as a terminal emulator. If you invest in a database access program, make sure it has all of the basic communications features in addition to the more advanced features these programs offer. Database access software packages and their features are covered in more detail in my October 1, 1984 *LJ* column (p. 1828-29).

COSTS

Total costs to begin searching with a microcomputer vary considerably, but it is reasonable to anticipate an initial investment of between $1500 and $3500 because you will want to have enough computing power to do other things with your micro. Listed in the Table are the three hardware configurations we use at the University of Hawaii with approximate costs in today's [1985] market. There are of course many other possible configurations.

TABLE

	Approximate cost
1. Kaypro 10 (CP/M portable computer)	$ 1000
Dot Matrix Printer and parallel cable	$ 300 - $ 500
1200 baud Hayes Smartmodem (or Hayes compatible)	$ 300 - $ 500
Serial cable for modem	$ 30 - $ 60
Communications software	$ 00 - $ 200
(We use *Modem 7*, a public domain free package)	
2. IBM-PC	$ 2000 - $ 3000
Dot Matrix Printer and parallel cable	$ 300 - $ 500
2400 baud Hayes Smartmodem (or Hayes compatible)	$ 300 - $ 500
Serial cable for modem	$ 30 - $ 75
Communications software	$ 00 - $ 200
(We use *DIALOGLINK* AND *SMARTCOM II*)	
3. Apple IIe	$ 1200 - $ 2000
Dot Matrix Printer and parallel cable	$ 300 - $ 500
300 baud Hayes Micromodem IIe (plug-in circuit board)	$ 250 - $ 330
Instead of above can purchase: modem	$ 100 - $ 500
and Serial communications card with cable	$ 60 - $ 100
Communications software	$ 00 - $ 200
(We use *SMARTCOM* with the plug-in board, a public domain package.)	

SELECTED SOFTWARE SOURCES

These all provide selection criteria as well as directories to specific packages:

Barden, William J., "Smart Terminals: New Software and Hardware To Simplify Data Communications," *Popular Computing*, August 1982, p. 117-121.

Bernstein, Amy, "Software Survey: More Power, Speedy Protocols," *Business Computer Systems*, November 1984, p. 81 + . Includes comparison chart of many commercially available communications programs.

Bruman, Janet L. *Communications Software for Microcomputers*. San Jose, CA: CLASS, January 1983. Also available from ERIC ED234740. Discusses things to look for in communications software. The directory provides only program name, producer, computer, and price with no evaluation. Short bibliography.

Glossbrenner, Alfred. *How To Buy Software*. St. Martin's, 1984. Chapter 17, "How To Buy Communications Programs," includes a useful checklist. This is not a software directory but a guide to selection criteria.

Glossbrenner, Alfred. *How To Get Free Software*. St. Martin's, 1984. Communications software is spread throughout the book, but there is an index. This book may give you more information than you want. Evaluative comments on specific programs are given as well as how to get the programs.

Miastkowski, Stan & George Stewart, "Modems: Hooking Your Computer to the World, Part II, Software Communications," *Popular Computing*, December 1982, p. 111-118.

Software Vendor Directory. Norcross, GA: Hayes Microcomputer Products, 1982. Software compatible with Hayes modems.

Whole Earth Software Catalog. Quantum Pr./Doubleday, 1984. Twenty pages on telecommunicating includes descriptions of some online systems and books as well as software. Not comprehensive but has critical comments.

ARTICLES ABOUT MODEMS

Austin, Sandy, "Modem Survey: Faster Rates and Lower Prices," *Business Computer Systems*, November 1984, p. 80-106.

Gabel, David, "Modems," *Personal Computing*, January 1985, p. 109-119. Excellent, up-to-date buyers guide.

_____. "Modem Mistakes You Don't Have To Make," *Personal Computing*, June 1984, p. 120-134.

Miastkowski, Stan, "Modems: Hooking Your Computer to the World," *Popular Computing*, November 1982, p. 88-104.

The, Lee, "Data Communications: a Buyer's Guide to Modems and Software," *Personal Computing*, March 1983, p. 96-128.

Veit, Stanley & David Gabel, "Modems: Your Line to the World," *Personal Computing*, September 1981, p. 90-102.

FLIERS AVAILABLE FOR FREE

Making the DIALOG Connection. DIALOG, 3460 Hillview Avenue, Palo Alto, CA 94304.

Terminal Access to the NLM Databases. Office of Inquiries and Publications Management, National Library of Medicine, 8600 Rockville Pike, Bethesda, MD 20209. ■

ONLINE SEARCHING WITH A MICROCOMPUTER
Downloading Issues*

INTRODUCTION

Of all the benefits that microcomputers bring to online searching, the capability of downloading search results is probably the most exciting and the most controversial. Downloading (or data capture) in the context of online database searching is the capturing onto magnetic media of the records retrieved in a search. Today this generally means capturing the results from searching on a vendor's mainframe system onto a disk on your microcomputer. With the proper software, these records can then be edited, reformatted, or merged into a locally held database. Downloading increases the potential for enhancing search results, for increasing the use of retrieved information, *and* for violating copyright or contract law. This article explores the issues surrounding these potentials. Hardware and software requirements for downloading are covered in the article by Fenichel in this issue.

Fran Spigai (1983), in a presentation at the Online 1983 Meeting in Chicago, cited three factors that she predicted would lead to an increase in downloading in 1984 and 1985. These factors are:

1. *Higher access speeds to online databases.* 1200-bps transmission (and now 2400-bps) allow large numbers of records to be captured at a reasonable cost. Few of the large online vendors as yet charge extra for higher transmission speeds.

2. *Increased storage capacity.* Hard disk drives on microcomputers allowing storage of 10-40 million characters are now readily available at relatively affordable costs. This dramatic increase in storage capacity on low-cost computers makes inhouse databases of downloaded records feasible.

3. *Software developments.* Many communications packages are available at costs from free to approximately $100. In addition to simple communications packages, there are now software packages that enhance the search process, that facilitate searching and downloading on one or more online systems, and that link downloaded records to search and retrieval programs.

As Spigai predicted, all of these factors are present in today's online searching world. Downloading has become an accepted benefit for online searchers who use a microcomputer and an accepted problem for the publishers who produce the databases.

TYPES OF DOWNLOADING

Searchers download online search results for several reasons. A primary reason so far, and the reason that is least objectionable to database publishers, is to print search results at a different time. If your printer is slower than your modem, it is less costly to download search results to disk, log off from the host system, then print the search results. The disk file can then be erased.

Related to this use is downloading for the purposes of editing search results before printing. Editing may be as minor as correcting erroneous characters caused by line noise or correcting typographical errors in a database. More extensive editing may be done to delete duplicate citations or merge and sort citations from multi-database searches, to add information such as a local call number, to add clearer field tags, or to delete confusing fields. Some organizations may need to edit search results to meet a standard bibliographic format.

*Reprinted from *Microcomputers for Information Management* April 1985. Copyright © 1985 by Ablex Publishing Corporation.

These uses provide nicer output, but are generally done for a single user or one-time use only. Of more concern to database producers is what is described by Spigai (1983) as "downusing" rather than downloading just for cosmetic purposes. Downusing implies reusing the downloaded information—thus depriving producers of revenues from subsequent use of their data. With increased storage capacities for microcomputers and better information retrieval software on the market, this increasingly means creating an inhouse database on a topic of continuing interest that can be searched and re-searched at no additional online cost. Inhouse databases are especially attractive in special libraries where subject interests may be narrowly defined and a specific group of users needs continuing access to information on their subjects.

Another extended use of downloaded information is of even greater concern to database producers. This involves editing downloaded results in different ways for different audiences and reselling the information. Producers are concerned about loss of integrity of their data as well as loss of revenues.

DOWNLOADING STUDIES

How widespread are each of these levels of downloading? No one knows for sure because online vendors cannot tell whether an online user is downloading or merely searching and printing results on paper. Some recent studies attempted to discover the scope of downloading by surveying various members of the online community.

Judy Burnham of the office of the United States Trade Representative, Washington, D.C., reported on a "modest survey of users, producers, and vendors to ascertain their views on downloading and re-use of online records" (Spigai, 1983, p. 279) at the June 1983 Special Libraries Association Meeting.

Of the 90 online users who responded, 80% felt downloading should be allowed. Approximately 50% did not have the necessary equipment to download, however. Of the 20% that were currently using microcomputers for searching and downloading, over half indicated they did not reuse downloaded information. An additional 10% of the respondents planned on having the capability to download in the near future (Tenopir, 1984).

In the summer of 1983 the Information Industry Association (IIA) Downloading Subcommittee surveyed online search vendors and database producers in preparation for writing a position paper on downloading. Only 57 valid responses from 300 questionnaires were received. Fifteen percent of the respondents felt enough people were downloading for it to be a serious issue, but 43% felt that by 1984 downloading would be widespread enough to be an issue. More than 50% of the database producers felt downloading will eventually have a positive effect on revenues (revealing perhaps their anticipated changes in pricing policies).

Over 72% of the vendors and producers had received requests from users for permission to download and/or reuse records. Almost 75% of these requests indicated the downloaded information would be used inhouse only, with 26% requesting permission to commercially resell it. Most producers granted permission, some did not, and some simply did not reply to the requests because they had not yet formulated downloading policies. Over half of the producers reported that their organizations had devoted time to developing downloading policies, with 33% offering downloading as a separate product or service. Only 11% of the companies distribute software for downloading, but almost all of them are aware of commercial products to facilitate downloading.

Most database producers who responded to the IIA study believe online vendors cannot even monitor the practice. This inability to either control or monitor downloading has led many database producers to change pricing structures or to formulate downloading policies. These are discussed later in this article.

The most ambitious study of downloading was completed in 1984 by Cuadra Associates Inc. According to Judith Wanger of Cuadra Associates,

> the purpose of the study, entitled *Downloading Online Databases: Policy and Pricing Strategies*, was to develop data that could help database producers and online services to decide what policies they should establish for the downloading and re-use of their data—for their own protection and for the benefit of users. (Wanger, 1983, p. 45)

A representative sample of 625 users and 150 suppliers were surveyed via questionnaires and interviews. Users of 12 different online database services were involved, including users of "reference, library cataloging, numeric, full text, and combinations of these classes of database services" (Wanger, 1983). In addition, the study reviews the literature on downloading, analyzes existing policy statements, summarizes policy and pricing options for database producers and online services, and provides recommendations.

Thirty-seven percent of the users surveyed admitted downloading. They cited a variety of purposes, including editing searches before local printing, temporary retention, permanent retention for inhouse databases, and resale. Seventy-seven percent downloaded for temporary use only, 41% for editing and reformatting, 32% for limited reuse, and 19% for re-searching ("Downloading: Windfall or Pitfall?" 1984).

Only 25% of the respondents cited "no present need" as the reason for not downloading; the major reason given was lack of suitable hardware or software. The Cuadra study concluded that 60% of users would solve these hardware and software problems within six months to one year, indicating that downloading is probably now much more widespread.

All of these studies look at the status of downloading in 1983 and draw conclusions for 1984 and 1985. Where these studies are leading was suggested by Spigai at the Online 1984 Meeting in San Francisco in October 1984. She described the various studies as the second stage in the six stages of downloading.

- Stage 1 (Early 1982): The phenomenon emerges, paranoia and confusion follow.

- Stage 2 (1983): Study of the phenomenon—what is it? how big? is it friendly or hostile? what do we do?

- Stage 3 (1984): The first policies emerge to control prices.

- Stage 4 (1985): Education of the marketplace to policies.

- Stage 5 (1985-1986): Marketplace reaction to policies and pricing.

- Stage 6 (1987): Policies are reshaped as a result of marketplace reaction and later we settle into a few price models or structures (Spigai, 1984).

As a reaction to downloading, database producers are reexamining copyright law, initiating downloading policies, formulating new pricing structures, and introducing some new products. If Spigai is correct, these will continue to emerge and be reshaped for the next few years as producers strive to obtain a fair price for their information and protect the validity and integrity of the data they provide.

LEGAL ISSUES WITH DOWNLOADING

Copyright

Downloaders run the risk of two violations—violating their contract with the database vendor or database producer, and violating the U.S. Copyright Revision Act of 1976. Although databases are not explicitly mentioned in the 1976 law and no court has yet ruled on the legality or illegality of downloading, copyright lawyers have stated that databases are protected just as printed works are protected (Warrick, 1984). It is clear that downloading an entire database violates copyright (see the Final Report of the National Commission on New Technological Uses of Copyrighted Works [CONTU]), but it is less clear whether the more common practice of downloading only selected parts of a database violates copyright. Still, the copyright provisions for works in public domain, compilations, derivative works, and original works all seem to apply to databases (Miller, 1983).

Public domain material—information created or collected by the federal government—is not copyrightable. Also excluded are non-creative works, which, according to Miller (1983), include commonly available data and most elements in a cataloging record. Works that incorporate such data are copyrightable, however, because collecting, organizing, and arranging data allows it to be copyrighted as a compilation (Osborne, 1985). A work consisting of editorial revisions, annotations, elaborations, or other modifications which, as a whole, represent an original work of authorship, is a copyrightable "derivative work" (United States Code, 1976).

The organization of public domain information is what is copyrighted, not the bits of data themselves, but only a single copyright notice needs to be published on the database. Since it is difficult for a database user to tell which data may come from public domain sources and which are original contributions, "the user has little choice but to respect the copyrights claimed in the compilation" (Miller, 1983, p. 204). Unfortunately, cases in court on copyright infringement of compilations or derivative works have reached inconsistent conclusions. Clearly database producer-added abstracts, classification numbers, descriptors, codes, etc., are copyrightable, but the amount of originality necessary to be added to the rest of the work is less clear. Warrick (1984) states "whether a particular judge would find the downloading of a large number of public domain facts to be an infringement becomes a test almost of the individual preferences of the judge ..." (p. 63).

The majority of numeric, directory, and bibliographic databases fall under the compilation or derivative work provisions. Original works, which includes most full text databases, are clearly copyrightable. The doctrine of fair use becomes important when downloading parts of such original works. Fair use attempts to limit restrictions on the free flow of information, especially for research or reference purposes, without creating a negative economic impact on the copyrighted work (Greguras, 1981). Determination of fair use takes into account the following factors:

1. the purpose and character of the use

2. the nature of the copyrighted work

3. the amount and substantiality of the portion used in relation to the copyrighted work as a whole

4. the effect of the use upon the potential market for or value of the copyrighted work (Greguras, 1981, p. 6)

Copyrighted works may be fairly used for purposes such as criticism, comment, news reporting, teaching (including multiple copies for classroom use), scholarship, or research without infringing copyright (United States Code, 1976). Publicly accessible libraries and their patrons are allowed to do small-scale, non-systematic, not-for-profit copying. It is not yet known whether routine downloading would be considered systematic, and therefore in violation (Warrick, 1984).

If fair use is used as a defense in a copyright infringement suit, the burden of proof is normally on the defendant, although in the Betamax case (Universal City Studios v. Sony Corp. of America) the plaintiffs were required to prove the defendant's actions were not fair use (Greguras, 1981).

Because so many databases are composed of non-copyrightable data and the copyright law is open to a wide variety of interpretations, many database producers have chosen to rely on contract law instead. When users sign a contract with an online vendor, they agree to follow the stated provisions of that contract, including database-specific provisions on downloading. Going beyond the vendor contract, some database producers are adding specific downloading policies to be negotiated directly between the user and the database producer.

Contract Provisions and Policies

At the 1983 National Online Meeting, Carlos Cuadra mentioned that five years ago when one broker asked 33 database producers for permission to download for the purposes of reformatting, 7 said yes, 1 said no, and 25 did not reply. Some did not reply because they had not yet formulated a downloading policy, some because they had not yet faced the then just-emerging issue.

Now, seven years later, not all database producers yet have downloading policies, but some have formulated them. Specific downloading policies are written statements that tell the user "precisely what he can do and what the database producer will consider a violation. The database producer will be able to prove to a court of law that the violating downloader should have known about the rules that the database producer had set out" (Jansen, 1984, p. 46).

In lieu of or in addition to such a specific policy, many producers rely on the brief "terms and conditions" of use distributed by online vendors. Such statements can go beyond provisions of copyright law as they are included as provisions of the contract between a user and the online vendor. They are not as specific or detailed as formal downloading policies, however.

DIALOG. Following are typical statements excerpted from the DIALOG "Database Supplier Terms and Conditions" effective March 1984 that are sent to every DIALOG user:

COMMERCE BUSINESS DAILY: Customer shall not copy or otherwise reproduce; have reproduced, or willfully allow employees, customers or other parties to copy or otherwise reproduce any portion of the COMMERCE BUSINESS DAILY in machine-readable form without advance written permission from the International Trade Administration ("ITA"), U.S. Department of Commerce.

COMPENDEX and Ei ENGINEERING INDEX: Use or copies of all or part of the COMPENDEX and Ei ENGINEERING INDEX for replacing the database, or the lease, license, or purchase of any publication listed in the Engineering Index catalog is not authorized. The use of materials supplied hereunder or any copies thereof for the purpose of load, resale, rental use, or gift to any third person, organization or corporation is strictly forbidden. No part of COMPENDEX may be copied in machine-readable form for delivery to or made available for the use of any third party.

COMPUTER DATABASE: The Buyer expressly agrees not to reproduce the information retrieved from THE COMPUTER DATABASE in machine-readable, hard copy, or other forms unless advance written permission has been obtained from Management Contents, except that limited reproduction of printed output from the DIALOG system (up to 5 copies) is permitted for distribution within the Buyer's organization only.

DISSERTATION ABSTRACTS ONLINE: This database is copyrighted by the database supplier. Data from this file may not be duplicated, except that reproduction of limited quantities of reasonable portions of the database is permitted for Buyer's internal use but only if Buyer includes a suitable notice of database supplier's copyright in conformity with the 1976 Copyright Law's standards, on all copies. Under no circumstances may copies made under this provision be offered for resale in any media. Copying in machine-readable form is not authorized. Exceptions to these terms are permitted only

with prior written permission from University Microfilms International.

REMARC: No part of the REMARC database may be duplicated in hard copy, microforms, or machine readable form without the prior written authorization of Carrollton Press, Inc., except that limited reproduction of hard copy printed output up to 20 copies is permitted for distribution and use within the user's organization only. Under no circumstances may copies made under this provision be offered for sale or resale.

SCISEARCH AND SOCIAL SCISEARCH: Buyer agrees that the material retrieved from SCISEARCH or SOCIAL SCISEARCH will not be used for commercial resale or sale in any media (electronics, paper, or photographic film) and that the Buyer is licensed to use information derived from the database only for the user of Buyer, Buyer's employees, and/or Buyer's normal constituency, for one-time bibliographies in single-copy form. No part of the materials furnished or data therefrom may be copied in machine-readable form by any user for any purpose without prior agreement with Institute for Scientific Information (ISI).

WASHINGTON POST INDEX: Is copyrighted by Research Publications, Inc. Data from this file may not be duplicated, except that reproduction of limited quantities of reasonable portions of the database is permitted for Buyer's internal use provided Buyer includes a suitable notice or copyright on all copies. Under no circumstances may copies made under this provision be offered for resale or sale in any media. Copying in machine readable form is not authorized. Exceptions to these terms are permitted only with the prior written permission from Research Publications, Inc.

As can be seen from these statements, it is usually best to write for permission before downloading. When a potential downloader writes for permission the request may be handled on a case-by-case basis or, increasingly, the producer has a standard downloading license agreement that the user must sign to be in compliance with the law. Large database producers such as Chemical Abstracts, BIOSIS, Psychological Abstracts, and Excerpta Medica were early leaders with such downloading licenses.

Chemical Abstracts. The Chemical Abstracts policy (formulated in 1983) allows permanent retention and inhouse reuse of downloaded records once the user pays an annual downloading fee. Temporary retention of downloaded records for editing, reformatting, or creation of a search profile for later use is allowable without a downloading license or fee ("Downloading of CAS," 1983; "CAS Extends," 1984).

The permanent storage fees range from $300 ($150 for CA subscribers) to $8,000 ($4,000 for CA subscribers) per year depending on the number of records downloaded. The maximum number permitted is 50,000 records per year (more than the storage capacity of almost any microcomputer).

Chemical Abstracts restricts storage and use of downloaded information to a single site, but remote access to the information is permitted by an organization's divisions or subsidiaries. "Payment of additional fees is required when information is distributed outside a customer's organization or is reproduced in multiple copies of bulletins, bibliographies, SDI services, or other publications" ("Downloading of CAS," 1983).

BIOSIS. The BIOSIS downloading agreement for BIOSIS Previews and Zoological Record Online also allows permanent inhouse retention of downloaded records if a one-time fee per record is paid. Two copies of all downloaded records can be kept permanently (one for security backup) for use at one site only ("BIOSIS Introduces," 1983). A user may download from BIOSIS without signing a downloading agreement provided it is for the purpose of printing once at the user's convenience and the information is not reused or re-searched.

Excerpta Medica. The Excerpta Medica (EMBASE) downloading policy is a restrictive agreement that prohibits permanent storage of downloaded information or creation of inhouse databases. For a $25 fee, EMBASE users are allowed only to download for the purpose of later printing or for "search strategy development." Reformatting, editing, or merging with information from other databases is explicitly prohibited (Jansen, 1984).

Most of the policies require the copyright notice be attached to any resulting printouts. The firms that allow reediting and merging information from their database with that from another database typically require a copyright notice be attached to every record extracted from their database.

Downloading policies attempt to ensure a producer will receive a fair price for use of their data and that the copyright and integrity of their data are protected. Neither the database producer nor the online vendor can tell when a user is downloading. They thus must ultimately rely on the user's honesty or assume that everyone is downloading. Jansen of Elsevier Science Publishers gives a publisher's perspective on the problem. He (1984) says that downloading

> rules should be fair and it must be feasible for the downloader to obey them. On the other hand, the database producer must be careful not to set rules, the violation of which cannot be adequately established. In [Jansen's] opinion, for example, it is difficult to establish how many records have been downloaded. If storage of records is not allowed at all, the moment a record is found in a system, one would know immediately that this rule has been violated. (p. 46)

Policies that are too restrictive, however, run the risk of being ignored by all but the largest companies or the most honest searchers. Liberal policies such as the one of Chemical Abstracts are based on the assumption that it is in both the user's and the database producer's best interests to make extended use of the information while complying with the law and while paying the producer a fair fee. From a searcher's point of view, more restrictive policies such as the Excerpta Medica policy seem to invite non-compliance or use of competitive databases because they severely restrict what can be done legally with the data.

CONCLUSIONS

There is little doubt that the practice of downloading will increase as more online searchers use microcomputers, as microcomputer storage capacities increase, and as more downloading and search software packages enter the market. Database producers are recognizing this fact and are taking a number of steps to either curb downloading or benefit from it. I believe most searchers are willing to pay a reasonable price for the privilege of reformatting or reusing information. Policies or products that facilitate this use, but that are priced so producers can earn necessary revenues, will benefit searchers, vendors, and database producers.

REFERENCES

BIOSIS announces policy on single and repetitive use of BIOSIS previews data (August 1981). *BIOSCENE 10*, 1.

BIOSIS introduces 'Downloading Agreement' for reuse of its data (August 1983). *Database 6*, 7.

CAS extends downloading options (June 1984). *CAS Report 16*.

Casbon, Susan (November 1983). Online searching with a microcomputer—Getting started. *Online 7*, 42-46.

Cuadra Associates completes downloading study (1984). *Online Review 8*, 117.

Downloading: Windfall or pitfall? (February 1984). *Information Today 1*, 1, 4.

Downloading of CAS data now permitted (June 1983). *CAS Report 14*.

Final Report of the National Commission on New Technological Uses of Copyrighted Works (1978). Washington, DC: CONTU.

Gasaway, Laura N. (April 1983). Nonprint works and copyright in special libraries. *Special Libraries 74*, 156-170.

Greguras, Fred M. (1981). Copyright protection of online data bases. In *Online '81 Conference Proceedings*. Weston, CT: Online Inc.

Grotophorst, Clyde W. (September 1984). Another method for editing downloaded files. *Online 8*, 85-93.

Hawkins, Donald T. (1982). To download or not to download online searches. In *Online '82 Conference Proceedings*. Weston, CT: Online Inc.

Inkellis, Barbara (1982). Legal issues of downloading online search results. In *Online '82 Conference Proceedings*. Weston, CT: Online Inc.

Jansen, Arnold A. J. (January 1984). Problems and challenges of downloading for database producers. *The Electronic Library 2*, 41-51.

Maier, Joan M. (October 1979). The three deadly C's—Cost, Copyright, and ac-Counting. *Online 3*, 61-63.

Miller, Jerome K. (Fall 1983). Copyright protection for bibliographic, numeric, factual, and textual databases. *Library Trends 32*, 199-207.

Mortensen, Erik (1984). Downloading: Potentials and restrictions in online searching. In *Online '84 Conference Proceedings*. Weston, CT: Online Inc.

NLM to offer MEDLINE subsets (November 1983). *National Library of Medicine News 38*, 1-2.

Osborne, Larry N. (Summer 1985). Downloading overview. *Journal of Library Administration 6* (2), 13-21.

Spigai, Fran (1983). Downloading: Tempest in a teapot? In *Online '83 Conference Proceedings*. Weston, CT: Online, Inc. Reported in Tenopir, Carol, "The Database Industry Today."

Spigai, Fran (1984). Downloading revisited, 1984: Practices and policies. In *Online '84 Conference Proceedings*. Weston, CT: Online Inc.

Subset license agreement—For domestic recipients of 'Personal Use Subsets' or 'Multiple Use Subsets' (1984). Bethesda, MD: National Library of Medicine.

Swartz, Herbert (January 1985). On-Line databases: The legal dilemma. *Business Computer Systems 4*, 28-29.

Tenopir, Carol (June 1983). Full-text, downloading, and other issues. *Library Journal 108*, 1111-1113.

Tenopir, Carol (February 1, 1984). "The database industry today: Some vendors' perspectives." *Library Journal 109*, 156-157.

United States Code, Supplement V, Title 17 (1981). "General Revision of Copyright Law," Cong. 2d Sess., 19 Oct. 1976. Washington, DC: USGPO.

Wanger, Judith (1983). Downloading: The migration problem of the 1980s? In *Proceedings of the 7th International Online Information Meeting*. Medford, NJ: Learned Information.

Warrick, Thomas S. (July 1984). Large databases, small computers and fast modems—An attorney looks at the legal ramifications of downloading. *Online 8*, 58-70 (July 1984).

Wolfe, Mary (July 1982). Copyright and machine readable databases. *Online 6*, 52-55. ∎

SOFTWARE FOR ONLINE SEARCHING*

Search intermediaries now find it necessary to become experts on evaluating the many microcomputer software packages that are available to aid or enhance the online search process. Whether using a microcomputer for online searching or advising colleagues or end users about their options, searchers need to know about the different types and specific features of the software developed for the online market.

Many libraries and library schools are now sponsoring workshops to inform searchers about online software products. Bill Coons, reference librarian at Cornell University, wrote me about the Cornell library's workshop on online search software. It began with overviews of the advantages of searching with a microcomputer and what is needed to get started. Most of the workshop was devoted to outlining the features of selected software packages. Included were comparisons of 1) general communications packages (e.g., *PC-Talk III* and *Hayes Smartcomm II*); 2) database specific front-end packages (e.g., *Search Helper*); and 3) multisystem front-end packages (e.g., *Pro-Search* and *Sci-Mate*).

At the University of Hawaii Graduate School of Library Studies we have sponsored microcomputer software workshops for librarians and end users. Software packages that we have examined include: 1) general communications packages; 2) front-end packages to access a single online system (e.g., *Search Helper*, *Searchware*, and *In-Search*); and 3) front-end packages to access multiple systems (e.g., *Sci-Mate*, *Pro-Search*). Another category of software that is sometimes overlooked at these workshops is the post processor. Post-processing software allows downloaded records to be formatted or manipulated for future use.

A workshop provides the ideal forum for software comparison and evaluation. Talks by searchers who have experience with the software packages, chances for hands-on experimentation, and lots of time for questions enhance the learning

---

*Reprinted from *Library Journal* Oct. 15, 1985. Copyright © 1985 by Reed Publishing, USA, Div. of Reed Holdings, Inc.

process. The number of software packages increases so rapidly that a series of workshops provides a valuable update for searchers.

For those who can't get to workshops my March 15 column (p. 42-43) provided an overview of searching with a microcomputer and discussion of types of software available. In the October 1, 1984 column (p. 1828-29) I discussed several front-end database access packages, concentrating on *In-Search*, a DIALOG front-end package marketed primarily to novice end user searchers. Since then many new packages have been developed. This column will examine a package in each of three categories: 1) single-system front-end (*Searchware*); 2) a multisystem front-end (*Pro-Search*); and, 3) a post-processor (*Professional Bibliographic System*).

SEARCHWARE

Although the documentation never explicitly states it, *Searchware* is a single system front-end providing access to *DIALOG*. (The company has plans to add other online systems in the future. Like other single-system software, *Searchware* is marketed primarily to the novice searcher who is probably not knowledgeable about online systems or databases.)

Users obtain a *DIALOG* password through the *Searchware* company when they purchase the software. All payments for online time are subsequently made to this company. (*Searchware* documentation refers throughout to accessing the "*Searchware* system" or "*Searchware* databases" with a "*Searchware* password" instead of mentioning the *Searchware* role as an intermediary to *DIALOG*.) This offers the advantage of a single company for both software support and online billing, but places another level between databases and users. It is not an advantageous arrangement for intermediary searchers, but might reduce confusion for occasional end user searchers.

Searchware software is sold in over 50 subject modules, each of which is purchased separately. If you purchased the psychology subject set, for example, the Searchware manual would include short descriptions of each of approximately eight psychology-related *DIALOG* databases. The descriptions are essentially a restatement of the *DIALOG* bluesheets. Additionally, the *Searchware* disk would default to the psychology category of *DIALINDEX* if the user chooses to do a preliminary subject search. The first module sells for $290, with each additional module for $100. Each subject contains approximately 8-12 databases.

There are three levels of searching using *Searchware*. Level 1 provides fill-in screens that first correspond to the AND logic, next to the OR logic and finally to the NOT logic. A searcher is limited to five subject terms on each logic screen and the system allows no flexibility in the way terms are grouped logically. In addition to the subject term screens, Level 1 searchers are prompted for selected nonsubject fields such as authors, language, or date.

Level 2 and Level 3 searching are essentially *DIALOG* native mode searching, with Level 2 searchers entered and stored before log on. Users must input all appropriate *DIALOG* commands, prefixes, suffixes, etc. Eleven pages of instructions in the *Searchware* manual attempt to teach the Level 2 or 3 searcher all they need to know to search.

Although *Searchware* has received positive comments in the microcomputer press, it has some obvious limitations. Communications packages and automatic log on devices can be purchased less expensively. Better documentation and more responsive telephone support are offered by DIALOG directly. More satisfactory front ends are available elsewhere. The appeal of *Searchware*, however, rests with some of its limitations. The very simple Level 1 searches and narrow subject modules offer the end user easy searching for simple topics in a single subject area.

For more information contact: Searchware, 22458 Ventura Blvd., Suite E, Woodland Hills, CA 91364.

PRO-SEARCH

Many searchers are familiar with *In-Search*, Menlo Corporation's front-end package that I reviewed in October 1984. The end user market did not develop as quickly as expected, causing Menlo Corporation to reevaluate their product and their marketing efforts. Accordingly, they replaced *In-Search* with *Pro-Search*, a front-end database access package targeted for intermediary searchers.

Pro-Search is an enhanced version of the impressive but no longer available *In-Search* package. Both provide telecommunications links to *DIALOG* via the major communications networks. Both provide a simplified search interface that leads a user through the steps of database selection, search strategy entry, logging on, and retrieving records. The two packages share several strong features, notably: 1) database descriptions are included in the software; 2) users are led through the search process in a logical step-by-step manner; 3) screen layouts are clear with innovative use of formats and color; and, 4) there are function keys or simple menu choices for many procedures. Database descriptions in the software are useful only if they are kept up to date. A promised update service never materialized with *In-Search*, but is now available on a subscription basis for *Pro-Search*. For $100 per year subscribers receive new database category disks every two months along with any software updates or revisions to the manual.

Pro-Search looks and works basically the same as *In-Search* with some enhancements aimed at the intermediary. The most important enhancement is the ability to access *DIALOG2* and *BRS* via the same simplified search interface. *Pro-Search* provides information on all of the databases that are available on both of these systems. In the database selection step on *Pro-Search* the user first selects a subject. Descriptions of pertinent databases are then displayed, with *DIALOG* and *BRS* databases alphabetically interspersed. The database information provides a handy short version of the *DIALOG Bluesheets* and *BRS Aid Pages*.

At the search strategy step either *DIALOG* or *BRS* operators can be used. *Pro-Search* will translate the in-put to the proper language after log on. A function key activates automatic log on to either *DIALOG* or *BRS*.

Since experienced searchers often prefer to search in native search mode, *Pro-Search* allows native mode searching with automatic log on and simplified downloading. As with many general communications packages, *Pro-Search* allows a search strategy to be entered prior to log on for fast execution once the connection is made to the host system. *Pro-Search* also has stored log on protocols for other online systems. (They must be searched in native mode once log on is complete.) These systems include: *BRS/Afterdark*, *Compuserve*, *Dow Jones News/Retrieval*, *SDC Orbit*, and *Knowledge Index*. Log on protocols for other online services (to a total of 20) can be added.

Another *Pro-Search* feature is an accounting function. *Pro-Search* keeps track of all cost information for each search session and for all sessions conducted over a period of time. For individual search sessions a cover sheet and invoice is generated. The invoice includes information you input about the client and search topic plus a breakdown of all charges for each database searched in that session. In addition, summary reports may be printed by client name, charge code, searcher name, and online service searched.

Pro-Search is available from PBS for $495 plus shipping and handling. (I suggest trying out the trial disk first for $19.95.) If a searcher is always going to search *BRS* and *DIALOG* in native mode, a good general communications package is probably all that is needed and is much less expensive. But, *Pro-Search* is an impressive package for intermediaries if they need help in searching either *DIALOG* or *BRS*, like the time savings provided by function keys and automatic log ons, and will use the online documentation or accounting features.

For more information contact: Personal Bibliographic Software, 412 Longshore, Ann Arbor, MI 48106.

BIBLIO-LINK & PBS

Once a searcher has conducted an online search with a front-end package and downloaded records to the microcomputer disk, a post-processing software package is needed to reformat or manipulate the records. A post processor can merely be a general purpose word processing package or it can be a package developed especially for online searching. Reformatting into a proper bibliographic format is often desirable for researchers, students, and librarians. The *Biblio-Link* and *Professional Bibliographic System* (*PBS*) software is designed just for that purpose.

The two packages are used together. First, *Biblio-Link* takes downloaded records and converts them into a format that is acceptable to the *Professional Bibliographic System* (now called *Pro-Cite*). The searcher provides the communications package or front end to do the searching and downloading. (*Biblio-Link* works with *Pro-Search* and other front-end packages.) It extracts only those fields commonly used in bibliographic citations from records downloaded from DIALOG, BRS, OCLC, RLIN, or MEDLARS. (A separate *Biblio-Link* program is needed for each of these systems.) Consistent field tags needed by *PBS* are added to each record.

Once the records have been extracted, converted, and tagged by *Biblio-Link*, the *PBS* software is used to create bibliographies. An editor feature allows the user to add information, delete unwanted information, or correct typographic errors in each downloaded record. Additional complete records can also be added with the editor.

PBS accepts input for 20 different types of materials including: monographs, journal articles, reports, newspaper articles, dissertations, maps, music scores, computer programs. *PBS* then formats the records into one of several standard bibliographic formats. The formatted bibliography may contain all of the records in a *PBS* file or a subset of records which are selected by an index term search.

Users may choose from among standard formats including: ANSI, *Science* magazine, American Psychological Association, or Modern Language Association. If none of these are acceptable, the user may define his own format. This is done by creating a "punctuation file" to define the spacing, order, labels, and punctuation desired. Bibliographies can thus be created to conform to different journal formats or standards.

Biblio-Link costs $195 with choice of two *Biblio-Links*. *Professional Bibliographic System* (or *Pro-Cite*) is priced at $395 for the IBM-PC version. You will also need a communications package or front-end.

The early versions of *Professional Bibliographic System* are primarily bibliography generators to create nice looking standard printed bibliographies. Newer versions of *Pro-Cite* are also private database software for interactive searching on a microcomputer. Private database packages such as *Sci-Mate*, *INMAGIC*, *SIRE*, and *BRS/SEARCH* are more suited for this purpose. ■

AN INTERFACE FOR SELF-SERVICE SEARCHING*

A stumbling block to end user searching is the lack of a truly easy-to-use and helpful user system interface. It is a difficult problem because a really good interface should incorporate knowledge of the online host, the databases, the search process, and the needs of users. Some librarians are beginning to solve this problem themselves by creating friendly interface programs that allow searching on the major online systems. One of the best I've seen is the self-service database searching

interface that is being developed under a Council on Library Resources grant by William Mischo, Mitsuko Williams, and Linda Smith, all of the University of Illinois at Urbana-Champaign.

The Illinois system helps users develop search strategy offline; selects a BRS, BRS/After Dark, or DIALOG database; automatically inserts appropriate commands and operators; logs on to the host system; executes the search; downloads up

*Reprinted from *Library Journal* Sept. 1, 1988. Copyright © 1988 by Reed Publishing, USA, Div. of Reed Holdings, Inc.

to 20 references; logs off from the host; and links to the University of Illinois online public access catalog (OPAC) to provide local call numbers for journals cited in the articles retrieved.

A TYPICAL SEARCH SESSION

Since development is funded by a grant, all searches are currently recorded for later analysis and all are free of charge to the user. (Regular intermediary searches are billed back to clients.) Users are asked to fill out a questionnaire when the search is completed. There are now sites at Illinois's Engineering Library and the Biology Library. In fall 1988, the Agriculture Library will test the interface and plans are to include the undergraduate library and Beckman Institute library in the near future. Each site's interface is custom-tailored to the subjects and databases most useful to their specialized clientele. Such individualized development is more time-consuming, but allows features to be developed that make the interface truly impressive.

The interface is tied into the Illinois OPAC so a user can search the online catalog or use the remote online searching interface through the same microcomputer. If the menu option "Search for Current Articles in Journals and Magazines" is selected, the user enters the interface program.

Once into the interface, the first screen to appear is a "subject areas" screen. This screen is different in each site because it is designed to reflect the departments and subjects of interest to the primary users of the branch library. Only the undergraduate library and test programs have a generalist subject screen that includes choices, e.g., biology, engineering, education, social sciences, popular magazines, newspaper articles, etc. Asking a user to select a predefined subject area allows the system to select a search database.

For each of the subject areas, a key database was selected by the librarian/programmer. The databases tend to be the major and most obvious choices—e.g., BIOSIS for biology, Compendex or Inspec for engineering, ERIC for education, etc. For subjects without one major database or for multidisciplinary research topics the forced choice of one database may not always be so clear or successful. Institutions without subject-specific branch libraries may need to have two subject screens to narrow down a subject area sufficiently to allow the system to select a database, or develop software enhancements that allow more than one database to be searched for each query.

After choosing a subject area, the user is asked to read two instruction screens. These two screens are the total search instruction and, in most cases, are all that is necessary to conduct a successful search using this system. Two instruction screens are, Mischo believes, the maximum that users will put up with, and the minimum needed to explain the most important searching concepts. As the user progresses through the program the screens provide context-specific information and help. The interface program takes over as much of the mechanics of searching as possible (commands, proximity operators, modification of strategy) so these important parts of searching don't have to be explained to users.

AND WE'RE OFF

After these few preliminaries, users are ready to be led through their search. They are asked to enter a "search title" to help them focus their topic, followed by words representing the most important concept in that topic. For example, for "Microcomputers used in CAD/CAM," the user could enter CAD/CAM as concept one. They are then asked to enter synonyms, alternate spellings, abbreviations, or alternative terms for the first concept. Meaningful examples are given in each version of the interface.

The interface is programmed to supply singulars, plurals, and common alternate endings automatically. A dictionary table of substitution terms allows common synonyms to be searched even if a user does not input them. For example, if a person puts in "corn" in the agriculture interface, the system will automatically search "zea" or "maize" as well. Some thesaurus terms for the databases searched most often can also be incorporated.

For some topics commonly searched at the library site, the program includes prestored term hedges consisting of thesaurus terms. When a user enters one of the hedge "go" words, such as Artificial Intelligence, they are shown a list of common synonyms or related terms for AI from which to select. The terms selected are OR'd together by the system.

CONTROL BY THE INTERFACE

The Boolean OR operator and proximity operators are inserted by the system as needed. BRS stop words and some other misleading words (such as "techniques" or "effects") are ignored. Users can build up to three concept groups that will be ANDed together. When the last concept group is built, the interface logs on to BRS and runs the search. All operations from this point on are controlled by the interface. Users are told what is happening at each stage of the search process, but they never actually see the direct interaction with the online host.

The next thing the user sees is a postings message for each concept and for the final search. Up to 20 citations are downloaded automatically and can be printed locally with call numbers and an explanation of the search attached.

It is what happens unseen by users during the online search that makes the Illinois interface so good. Unlike most of the commercially available front-end programs, this one incorporates the expertise and ideas of experienced online searchers by providing automatic search modification if too few or too many citations are retrieved.

Mischo has attempted to build in "what an online searcher/intermediary would do" to control output. Because he has found that most users enter very specific multiword terms, the system does not insert an adjacency operator between words, but instead uses the BRS WITH (within the same sentence) operator. (On DIALOG this would be the N operator with five or six intervening words.) If fewer than 30 citations are retrieved with the first concept, the searching stops there and the first 20 citations are downloaded.

LIMITING THE SEARCH

Searching is first done on the complete free text. If more than 100 citations are retrieved in total, the search is limited to the title and descriptor fields. If there are still more than 100 citations the Boolean AND between concepts is replaced by the BRS SAME operator (concepts must be found in the same paragraph or same field).

If there are zero postings after concepts are linked, the system will begin to drop concepts. If three concepts are entered by the user, the third concept (and, if necessary, the second concept) will be dropped in an attempt to get something. For some of the databases or subjects, the interface will provide more search modification options such as limiting to English or allowing users to specify unwanted terms or concepts so the system can NOT them out.

INTERESTING STATISTICS

Transaction logs are kept for all searches, questionnaires are distributed to users, and site monitors record information about every search. Together these provide some interesting data about the Illinois project. Between October 12, 1987 and March 31, 1988, over 440 database searches in 214 search sessions were conducted in the Engineering Library. Six databases were available (Inspec, Compendex, Computer Database, Magazine Index, Chemical Abstracts, Current Contents) of which Inspec and Compendex were searched by far the most frequently.

Most of the users like the system and the process of online searching. Over 97 percent had a favorable or very favorable "overall attitude toward the system" and over 88 percent were enthusiastic or very enthusiastic about online searching. Nearly 90 percent were satisfied with their search and over 83 percent indicated that "compared to a printed index, this system is better."

The Engineering Library users are very familiar with keyboards or terminals with over 87 percent indicating that they were experienced or very experienced. It is difficult to determine how much of an effect level of experience had on the 82 percent "successful or very successful" rating on ability to use the system. Results in the undergraduate site may provide a comparison.

INCORPORATING THE RESULTS

Mischo has gained insight into what works and what doesn't in the interface and has incorporated much of this into the system. He has found that a "truncation algorithm is necessary" because people either assume the system can supply singulars and plurals or don't think about them. Other word form variations should be truncated, but sometimes strange results will occur (stemming -ment when someone is searching for cement or -ing from sing.)

The NOT operator is necessary in "a small, but important, number of searches" and should be asked for at the beginning of the search strategy process. Users will enter "very specific multiword phrases" (e.g., fiberglass reinforced epoxy resin) that may appear slightly different in the literature. This makes free-text searching and WITH or NEAR proximity operations necessary.

A limit of 234 characters per concept group "can be of positive benefit" because "users tend to supply nonsignificant or harmful synonyms or related terms if given the opportunity." Users don't seem to have a clear idea of how terms are OR'd together and will enter redundant phrases such as earth metals OR alkaline earth metals.

KEEP ON TESTING

The Illinois system is still under development and testing. The data gathered are helping the developers to refine the interface and to gain insight that will be useful for other librarians who wish to develop or select interfaces for end user searching. Mischo believes "the interface will play a critical role in searching periodical indexes" whether they are available on remote systems, locally mounted on the OPAC, or on local CD-ROMs. The end user should not have to know which of these heterogeneous systems they are accessing and libraries should provide access to all of them through a single central interface.

One important lesson learned is that an interface that can be customized for certain databases and can reflect the subject interests of a group of users can allow more assistance in search strategy, term choice, and search modification. This, of course, complicates the development process. This project is already in its third year and development and testing will continue for at least one more.

Another lesson learned is that many prefer to do their own searches, but computer and sometimes human help is necessary. The system is designed for noncomprehensive searches. The developers assumed that complex or comprehensive searches require a human intermediary. The interface is meant to extend the online catalog by providing access to the journal holdings, not to replace intermediaries.

Mischo is willing to share his programs and ideas with interested librarians. Data analysis is going on now; results will be published in the library literature. Contact: William Mischo, Engineering Lib., Univ. of Illinois, 221 Engineering Hall, 1308 W. Green St., Urbana, IL 61801; 217-333-3576. ∎

4

SOFTWARE FOR
IN-HOUSE DATABASES

As mentioned in Chapter 3, one of the biggest impacts of the microcomputer has been the possibility of creating and maintaining databases in-house. These databases may include information downloaded from an online search, information designed and created locally, or a combination of both. In-house databases for reference use allow librarians to provide access to local collections or to specialized topics of interest to a particular constituency. They reflect the interests and needs at the local level. They allow unlimited searching of customized information without the online meter running or the purchase of large CD-ROM databases, only a fraction of which are of interest to your clientele.

The success of an in-house database depends on many factors. Careful planning, needs analysis, record design, and field specification are important parts of the design process. No amount of careful planning can compensate for inadequate or inappropriate software, because the success and capabilities of an in-house database are ultimately dependent on what the software can or cannot do.

Chapter 4 focuses on in-house database creation, specifically on the process of evaluating and selecting software. This is a topic on which I have written a lot, including a book and several software review articles coauthored with Gerald W. Lundeen. Many of those articles are reviews of specific in-house database software packages and are not included here because I feel the information goes out of date too quickly. (Specific software reviews are included in the complete list of my publications in the Appendix.) Instead, I include articles that describe the process of software selection and provide hints on how to evaluate software. This more general information retains its value much longer.

Still, some of the articles in this chapter mention specific software packages. I have tried to bring information about them up to date. The reader must realize, however, that information about software can never be completely up to date because producers make frequent enhancements, modifications, and price changes. If you are interested in a particular package you will need to get the most up-to-date information from the software producers themselves.

"Identification and Evaluation of Software for Microcomputer-Based In-House Databases" was first published in 1984. It is essentially a literature guide on what was then the still relatively new topic of in-house databases on microcomputers. Although many hundreds of articles on the topic have appeared since then, I decided to include this article because the discussion of decision making and software evaluation is appropriate even though some of the examples of specific packages are not. This article is not a review of packages; instead it summarizes the literature on in-house database design and gives guidelines or sources for identifying and evaluating software. These principles apply long after the software packages on the market change. A second appendix that appeared in the original version gave names and addresses of software packages. This appendix is omitted now because the final article in this chapter includes a more complete and current list of software. This first article has the most complete treatment of the process of selecting software.

The second article, "Evaluation of Library Retrieval Software," was written in 1980. It is not specific to a microcomputer environment; instead the general principles apply to the evaluation process for any retrieval software for any size of in-house database. This is not the exact version that appeared in the *1980 Proceedings of the American Society for Information Science Annual Meeting*. I have replaced the early software evaluation form with a more polished version done for Gerald Lundeen's and my book *Managing Your Information: How to Design and Create a Textual Database on Your Microcomputer* (Neal-Schuman, 1988). The original form has undergone many revisions and changes over the years and I have seen it reprinted or used by others (with and without credit). The exact form is not important, but after teaching people to evaluate software for over a decade I still feel that some kind of software evaluation form helps ensure consistency in the evaluation process.

The final article in the chapter, "Software Options for In-House Bibliographic Databases," categorizes software that can be used to create microcomputer-based databases according to their major functions and characteristics. The software source list at the end has been updated as much as possible to reflect new versions of packages and new addresses or phone numbers of producers.

Admittedly there is some overlap among the articles included in this chapter. They were written over the span of eight years when new packages for in-house databases were coming out every year. The basic needs and principles remained the same (as did some of the software packages); consequently, by necessity there was some repetition. I chose not to eliminate all of the duplication, because the articles reflect a continuum over time. Information about software has been edited, but not information about selection criteria.

IDENTIFICATION AND EVALUATION OF SOFTWARE FOR MICROCOMPUTER-BASED IN-HOUSE DATABASES*

One of the most important aspects of creating an in-house database using a microcomputer is the choice of software. There are an increasing number of software packages available that are appropriate for library databases, but the choice of the one that best meets your needs is not always simple. This paper examines the growing literature on the topic to provide help in the identification of microcomputer software for library database applications and to assist in the evaluation process. An appendix lists selected microcomputer software directories.

INTRODUCTION

In-house online databases, created by a library or information center to meet the special information retrieval needs of its clientele, are becoming increasingly popular. These databases serve many purposes. They can replace print versions of such locally created tools as referral directories, indexes to vertical file materials, or abstracts of literature on a specific topic. They can be indexes to special types of materials or collections (e.g., audiovisuals, engineering drawings); full text or abstracts of internal corporate reports; or a central access system for all of the information resources in the information center. What in-house databases have in common is that they are all created with the library's own unique constituency in mind. The databases are created for a given situation and thus tend to be narrowly focused and very patron-oriented. They offer online retrieval to materials that are sometimes accessible nowhere else; allow easy updating of often rapidly changing information; and provide increased control over all information resources.

Until recently, however, the high costs of hardware made in-house databases out of reach for the small information center. The proliferation of small, powerful, but relatively inexpensive microcomputers since the late 1970s is changing this, and many managers of small libraries or information centers are now creating (or considering) online information retrieval systems for in-house materials.

The creation of an in-house database is not merely a matter of identifying the application and purchasing a microcomputer. Many decisions and plans must be made to create a successful database system, both in conjunction with and independent from the hardware choice. Some of the most important of these decisions relate to software, for poor software can cost information managers and end users more than the cost of the hardware in terms of wasted time, extensive modifications, and frustration. Without good software that is suited to the application, the system will never perform as it should. Appropriate software is so important that many experts urge potential microcomputer users to first shop for software to meet their needs, then purchase hardware that can run this software.[1]

Information managers must decide whether to purchase a prewritten, off-the-shelf software package, lease or purchase a hardware/software turnkey package, write their own programs, or have custom programs written for them. They must be familiar with existing packages in order to see all options open to them. Finally, they must feel comfortable with their ability to evaluate the many choices in order to develop or select the software that best meets their needs.

*Reprinted with permission of the American Library Association. "Identification and Evaluation of Software for Microcomputer-Based In-House Databases" by C. Tenopir, appearing in *Information Technology and Libraries* Mar. 1984; copyright © 1984 by ALA.

Unfortunately, no definitive formula for choice of micro-computer software for in-house databases is possible because software choice is ultimately dependent on each individual situation. The literature on the topic is sparse and uneven in quality, and "most reports deal with isolated techniques and system features."[2] There is a growing body of literature, however, that can provide help in choosing software for the creation of a microcomputer-based in-house database in the information center. This article will review and evaluate that literature, including sections on purchasing versus programming; directories of software; evaluation of software; and sources for software descriptions or reviews. It will not discuss literature that deals only with microcomputer characteristics or choice of hardware, nor will it include most descriptions of specific in-house database applications. Literature from related fields will be included only as it supplements the library literature.

PURCHASE OR PROGRAM

One of the first software decisions that must be made is whether to purchase a prewritten software package, lease or purchase a turnkey system, or create custom programs. Custom-created programs may either be written by the library or data processing department staff or by consultants hired for that purpose.

The debate over whether to purchase or program is not unique to microcomputer systems, but it surfaces repeatedly with microcomputers because they have been sold as "personal computers" that are especially easy to program and because commercially available microcomputer software has the reputation of being poor.

Until very recently, little microcomputer software for library applications was available, so programming in-house may have been the only alternative. As recently as 1980, the fact that there was little software for libraries and information centers was a real problem in the use of microcomputers in libraries. Pratt said in that year, "There does not seem to be anything presently on the market aimed at libraries. Thus it is necessary for libraries to write, or have written, their own programs for their own purposes."[3]

Lundeen noted in 1980 that "much of the applications software being marketed for micros is of mediocre quality, and it is often very poorly documented. The librarian eager to use a micro in a library application will usually have to write (or have written) the software to do the job."[4] Lundeen went on to point out, however, that "the librarian who is contemplating using micros to automate should realize that the programming is not likely to be a trivial task. Software may well cost much more than the system hardware."[5]

Pratt also realized that the complexity of many library applications complicates in-house programming. He believed "it is unlikely that any library would have sufficient in-house capability to develop an adequate system. To have one custom-designed by outside consultants will probably prove more costly than acquiring one of the already available commercial turnkey systems."[6]

In the last year, a growing recognition of the complexity of the in-house database programming task, together with an increase in the number of available software packages and turnkey systems, has led to a swing away from recommending

customized programming. In spite of Rowat's fear that "packages suitable for use in libraries will not be developed by the commercial sector until the library and information market is perceived to be one of sufficient coherence and size to warrant the considerable investment needed,"[7] more and more writers are realizing that "an astonishing number of companies ... are now competing frenetically to anticipate and fulfill all conceivable needs of consumers of software," including libraries.[8] The number of packages suitable for creating in-house databases has grown tremendously in the last year. The introduction of the de facto standard operating system CP/M, together with the availability of standard higher-level languages on microcomputers, has allowed the proliferation of prewritten software packages.[9]

Programs for in-house databases are complex and expensive to develop, making it less advantageous to do in-house development when something good is available commercially. Complicated "total library systems" are compared to home building in *Small Computers in Libraries*.

> These total systems are much too elaborate and complex to consider writing them "in-house," at least for libraries that do not have NLM-style budgets. This is not to imply, as some think, that computer programming "is too complicated for librarians".... It's not that librarians can't write complex programs, it's that doing so is not their job.
>
> You could build your own home, but hardly anybody does. It's simpler, and probably cheaper, to have somebody else build it.[10]

The *Library Systems Newsletter* estimates that programming costs more than 80 percent of the total cost of developing a new system.[11] This article cites another disadvantage of doing your own programming or having it written for you— "the customer pays directly for the developer's mistakes. In contrast, when one purchases a software package from an established firm, one normally gets a working product that has already been installed and which can be investigated before purchase."[12]

Rorvig, in his 1982 book *Microcomputers and Libraries*, takes exception to the trend away from in-house programming when he states that "the best way for librarians to get the software they need is to learn BASIC or other languages and then to program functions for themselves.... In the final analysis librarians will not receive the applications software of greatest benefit to their institutions unless they themselves learn to program microcomputers. This is not as formidable a task as it might first seem."[13] These statements are not in tune with the growing current consensus and were met with an outcry of dissension.

In a review of Rorvig's book, Gordon says that for librarians to write their own application programs is "neither a practical nor financially feasible approach." She points out that "major computer manufacturers ... spend two thirds of their engineering dollars on software development; and typically 30 percent of a large corporation's total data processing budget is spent on software."[14] Clearly, small libraries cannot afford such an investment.

Schuyler advises that the "expertise needed to program a sophisticated application is quite substantial; the time necessary is considerable." He goes on to warn that "information such as this, written with a tone of authority, may set the reader on the wrong path from which it may be time consuming (and therefore costly) to recover."[15]

Even favorable reviews of Rorvig's book by Grosch and by Pratt take exception to his opinion on programming. Grosch advises, "It still is true that a certain class of serious professional users will find that they must do some software development; however many librarians will find an assortment of software to enable them to use their micro as a professional support tool."[16]

Pratt warns:

> Except under unusual circumstances this [writing your own program] is not a good idea. The writing of a fully debugged and operational system to perform any library task is not something to be undertaken without a strong commitment of resources and time. It is difficult to do, especially by inexperienced programmers. Librarians simply do not have the time to become good programmers in addition to their normal duties.[17]

The consensus in the library literature seems to have changed in two years to favor the purchase of existing microcomputer software or turnkey systems rather than developing programs from scratch. This may not always meet every need in all situations, however. Turnkey systems especially allow no local modifications, and the application must be tailored to meet the constraints of the software. A middle ground that combines both options is often desirable.

Modifying an existing software package to meet individual needs may provide the best of both options. Kelley recommends purchase of "modular software" for applications that are "fairly complex and unique." Modular software is defined as a "program that acts as a tool, enabling someone with very limited programming skills to develop useful programs which are somewhat specific to the user's situation."[18] Database management systems (DBMS) are well-known examples of modular software.

The literature contains many descriptions of DBMS software, including examples of libraries or information centers that have adapted different DBMS programs for the creation of in-house databases. The DBMS literature is too extensive to be covered completely in this article, but the adaptation of DBMS for use in libraries is addressed, as DBMS software allows information managers to create customized database systems without having to do extensive programming. There are many commercially available DBMS programs suitable for library/information retrieval applications to varying degrees. Kelley believes a "DBMS program is the most important piece of software one can purchase."[19]

Another, more difficult, way to combine prewritten software and customized programming is to purchase a package written in a known programming language and to write additional routines "to layer over the preprogrammed ones."[20] The problems with this approach are that the information center must then also be responsible for programming and that modification of an existing program may affect other parts of the program in unexpected ways. Plans for any such modifications should be made cautiously.

If prewritten software is the best option for the creation of microcomputer-based in-house databases, how can information managers find out what is available? Vickery and Brooks saw the need for a directory of available software for use in libraries in 1980.[21] Even in January 1982, there was "no easy way of discovering what software was available."[22] Garoogian calls this a "variation on the familiar library problem of bibliographic control."[23] In the last year, several publications have appeared that help to meet this problem.

SOFTWARE SOURCES

Until 1982 there were no microcomputer software directories targeted to library or information applications, although there were directories of microcomputer software applicable to other special interest areas (notably education and business). Several general microcomputer software directories have had to serve the information manager's needs. Myer's 1982 book includes an annotated list of software directories of all types. Garoogian covers sources for identification of software (pre-1982) in her article in the premiere (February) issue of *Software Review*.

Datapro Directory of Microcomputer Software began publication in 1981. In its section on "Data Management and Database Management," it includes information about DBMS, file management, storage and retrieval, and specialized storage and retrieval software packages. *Small Systems Software and Services Sourcebook* describes more than thirteen hundred small-computer software packages. ·*MENU*· *The International Software Directory* (*ISD*) is available online via DIALOG (file 232). It is a combined online file that describes more than thirty thousand commercially available software packages for micro- and minicomputers. Management Information Corporation, Cherry Hill, New Jersey, publishes an annual survey on small business computers, peripherals, and software.

Many other microcomputer software directories include only programs for a specific type of computer or operating system. (See, for example, *The IBM Personal Computer Software Directory*, Farmingham, Mass., International Management Services, second quarter, 1983.)

Database management system software for microcomputers is included in general DBMS directories, notably *A Buyer's Guide to Data Base Management Systems* (Delran, N.J.: Datapro Research Corp.) and *Datamation* magazine's regular DBMS software surveys. Appendix A lists some general microcomputer software sources.

These general directories include more software packages that are inappropriate for library applications than are appropriate. They therefore provide an information glut and can be frustrating to use. Recently published directories that are limited to library applications software are briefly reviewed by Tenopir.[24] These directories are a welcome addition to the field and will be examined more closely here. Publication information for each is given in appendix A.

Online Micro-Software Guide and Directory: 1983-84 includes descriptions of more than 5,700 microcomputer software packages, many of which are database management systems. A chart compares the major features of the most popular DBMS packages, although not enough information is given to allow real evaluation.

Information for each package includes:

- name, address, phone number of company
- contact person
- software name and version and date released
- cost
- applications
- operating environment
- hardware requirements
- documentation (a list and prices but nonevaluative)
- product description (several descriptive sentences)
- where purchased.

The arrangement of the *Online Micro-Software Guide* is alphabetical by company, with indexes by software name and producer. An addendum provides a much-needed index by applications, but an index by operating systems or hardware would be another useful addition.

The arrangement of this directory is straightforward and easy to follow. Four packages are listed on each page with a reduced typescript that keeps the size of the total directory manageable but causes some eyestrain.

A large number of microcomputer software packages are added to the market each month. Supplements to the directory in October 1983 and 1984 include hundreds of these new packages. The microcomputer software market changes so rapidly, however, that a printed publication can never be up-to-date. The *Online Microcomputer Software Guide and Directory* is also available online in a BRS as "File Soft."

A nice feature of this directory is the inclusion of nontechnical articles on various aspects of software use and a bibliography of articles on microcomputer software. These additions make this directory more than just a listing of hundreds of packages.

Micro Software Report: Library Edition (Meckler) came out in July 1982. This directory contains almost three hundred software packages, approximately sixty of which are DBMS. It does not claim to be selective, so it is difficult to explain why there are four hundred fewer packages in it than in the Online, Inc., directory. One explanation is that the Meckler directory is more focused on the library market: the Online directory contains many general-purpose software packages that might be used in information work. Another reason is that information on packages in the Meckler directory was gathered from printed sources, while Online contacted software vendors directly.

Micro Software Report is arranged alphabetically by software-package name with an index by application. Information for each package includes:

- package name
- producer
- description (one to two sentences)
- equipment requirements
- source of reviews if any
- whether or not the review was favorable

- installations (this element is usually missing)
- price
- address.

Citations for reviews is a nice idea that was expanded in the fall of 1983 with the publication of *Microsoftware Evaluations.* (See "Software Description and Reviews," in this article.) No articles or guides to evaluation are included in the directory.

A 1983 edition of *Micro Software Report* (o.p. 1986) includes many new software packages, additional review citations, an index to software by producer, an index to producers, and an index to software by type of equipment. The new edition is better than the first, since the first seems to have suffered from the hurry to get it out. Three pages of addenda and errata arrived with the 1982 edition.

The Online and Meckler directories are limited to microcomputer software for information work, but other directories of library/information software also include some microcomputer software. *Directory of Information Management Software: For Libraries, Information Centers, Records Centers* covers only commercially available software packages for the creation of in-house databases. Detailed information on more than fifty packages includes:

- software name
- address and phone number of vendor
- contact person
- hardware and operating system environment
- capabilities and components of the package
- total price based on several typical library scenarios
- sample installations
- evaluative comments.

The information is more comprehensive than that given in the two microcomputer software directories because the scope of this directory is limited to in-house database software. A hardware index allows ready identification of the microcomputer packages. Additional lists of special application software and general-purpose DBMS suitable for information work include only name of package and address and phone number of vendor.

The 1983 *UNESCO Inventory of Software Packages* (o.p. 1988), contains descriptive and comparative information about many software packages for information work. It is not limited to microcomputer software, nor limited to software for one type of library application, but attempts to be a comprehensive international summary of all software for information work.

Information on software for this directory was solicited from libraries and information centers around the world. Information managers were asked to notify the National Center of Scientific and Technological Information about computer applications in their centers. The information about the software used in their applications was then verified with the software vendors. Locally developed software, as well as commercially available packages, are included.

In addition to these directories, several journals have published listings of library applications software. Results of the second annual survey of the library automation market by J. Matthews in the March 15, 1983, *Library Journal* include a directory of all active systems, including microcomputer systems. The October 1982 *Software Review* includes descriptions of five microcomputer packages for library applications. The July 1982 issue of *Program* profiled several British software packages for in-house databases. *Monitor* surveyed interactive online software in April and May 1982.

Appendix A lists all of these directories and periodicals that will help the information manager identify software packages for the creation of microcomputer-based in-house databases. Other new directories can be expected now that the microcomputer software market is growing so rapidly.

EVALUATION OF SOFTWARE

Software directories allow available packages to be located, but they as yet provide little help in the evaluation of these packages. This is in part because of the lack of critical or evaluative information in the directories, but it is also because, as mentioned earlier, software evaluation is so dependent on individual situations. There is no one best microcomputer software package for every library's in-house database system because "best" will vary with varying needs. However, some general guidelines for software evaluation are applicable to every in-house database.

The literature on evaluation of software for library applications is still sparse, unlike the extensive literature on educational software evaluation. Library and general computing literature does contain enough information to allow formulation of guidelines, however. In many cases, these guidelines are not unique to microcomputer software selection. Many general principles of selection of automated systems or software evaluation for libraries are applicable to evaluation of software for microcomputer-based databases.

The first step in any software evaluation should be analysis of needs and preparation of general specifications. Tenopir advocates the preparation of formal, written specifications whether or not they are required by the parent organization.

> The exercise of identifying the library's needs and determining specifications to meet these needs is the best way to formulate specific questions to be asked, to communicate needs to the vendor, and to ensure that a software package will be able to deliver all the things expected.[25]

She goes on to outline the things that must be included in the specifications. These include both general and specific library and data processing requirements.

Matthews stresses that each information manager must identify and emphasize "my needs" before thinking about purchasing microcomputer software.[26] "These requirements should be written and reviewed by various shareholders in the selection process."[27]

Emard cautions that the "first, and maybe the most important, thing to remember when you set out on your quest for software is to have your applications (or your problems if you like) firmly in mind—and preferably on paper."[28]

Blair echoes these feelings when he advocates that "you sit down with your staff and outline several major needs before reading the computer journals or visiting a computer store."[29] The questions he suggests answering in the initial phase are:

1. Is there any reason to store retrieval from online database searches?

2. Will editing of reports and other documents be attempted?

3. Are there records that need cross-indexing for retrieval via several keys?

4. Would exchanging files with several other companies be advantageous?

5. To what degree would online accounting and budgeting enhance operations?

6. Do statistics and graphs play a significant role in your reporting procedures?

7. Who will be in charge of the application?

General guides to needs analysis and specification writing for library automation projects are also applicable to the purchase of microcomputer software. Matthews' *Choosing an Automated Library System*, Corbin's *Developing Computer-Based Library Systems*, and Boss' *Library Manager's Guide to Automation* are mentioned by Tenopir as some of the sources that can help in this phase.[30]

When the needs assessment is completed and preliminary specifications have been written, it is time to evaluate how individual software packages meet these needs. Suggested evaluation strategy varies in the literature from the extremely simple to an involved process. Because the requirements of software for in-house databases are complex, the prices are usually higher than other microcomputer software, and because so much staff time is involved in implementing a database system, the evaluation of software for in-house databases should not be overly simplified.

Matthews summarizes possible evaluation techniques for choosing any automated library system. He outlines five possible ways to approach evaluation: subjective judgment, cost-only technique, weighted-scoring technique, cost-effectiveness ratio, and least total cost.[31]

Subjective judgment follows no strategy or set procedure and is not recommended. The cost-only technique also should not be used as it considers only which system has the lowest cost and does not draw distinctions based on priorities of system features. Weighted-scoring allows distinction to be made as to the relative importance of different features, but according to Matthews, "This approach suffers because there is no way to establish a meaningful and understandable relative value among the desired items, and, in addition, there is no way to incorporate the system-life costs for each vendor."[32] In an attempt to solve this perceived deficiency, cost-effectiveness ratio divides the total systems cost of each vendor by the sum of the weighted-scoring score. The least total cost technique looks at all present and ongoing costs of each system and assigns a dollar value to each feature, allowing dollar comparison of all components. No one of these evaluation methodologies is clearly the best way to evaluate software packages. Evaluation should incorporate all of them.

Garoogian includes a lengthy discussion on evaluation with many practical examples.[33] Before the product and the vendor are evaluated, she advises examining possible hardware or software constraints. The software must be compatible with the computer and peripherals in use, and possible software constraints such as operating system and programming language must be identified. If these things do not pose a problem in the individual situation, the software characteristics can then be evaluated.

Among the characteristics of the software that should be evaluated are the following:

- How easy is it for users to interact with the program?

- Instruction manuals should allow interaction with the program. If not, will the vendor provide training?

- Do modifications need to be made, and, if so, do they require a programmer?

- Will you receive new versions (releases) of the program as they become available?

- Does the system have expansion capabilities (e.g., modules)?

- Is complete and accurate documentation included?[34]

Evaluation of the vendor is also important. Garoogian recommends answering the following questions about the vendor in the evaluation process:

- How long has the vendor been in the software business?

- Does the vendor maintain a research and development program directed at the constant enhancement of the product you are considering?

- Does the vendor have an active user group?

- Can the vendor provide references for the companies who use the software you contemplate using?

- Can the vendor offer other packages that interface with the one you want?

- Does the vendor provide technical support?

- Can the software be purchased "on approval"?

- Is there a warranty or some sort of maintenance agreement?[35]

Tenopir advises formalizing the evaluation process by using some sort of form or checklist to ensure consistency with the weighted-scoring technique. Major areas that should be examined and rated in the evaluation include:

- vendor or producer

- software constraints and flexibility

- query language

- security

- output capabilities

- input capabilities and procedures

- documentation

- training

- hardware constraints

- costs.

Specific concerns to be considered in the evaluation are discussed under each area.[36]

Datapro Research Corporation includes information on general evaluation of application software in their *Applications Software Solutions*. They too urge use of a standard questionnaire and rating form to ensure consistent evaluation. They break evaluation into a two-stage process—first evaluation on a technique basis, then comparing the "survivors" on a "management basis, including cost, timetable and risk."[37]

Datapro recommends paying close attention in the evaluation to the following considerations:

1. comparison of the capabilities of the package with user requirements;

2. hardware constraints that may affect use of the package;

3. software constraints such as operating system, compiler;

4. throughput timing, ease of installation, ease of operating, clarity of operating instructions;

5. ease-of-use;

6. maintainability (including documentation, programming language);

7. flexibility of the package in meeting changing needs and growth.[38]

Site visits and benchmark tests or demonstrations are emphasized.

Other authors give hints to help with evaluation of microcomputer software without providing the level of detail in Garoogian, Tenopir, and Datapro. Kelley urges evaluators to preview the software if possible, look for reviews in computer magazines, and tap the experience of both vendors and professional colleagues.[39] *MIS Week* advises securing modification rights and paying careful attention to negotiating performance guarantees.[40]

Blair emphasizes the vendor-user relationship. He says to look for such things as the ability to get software updates, a vendor hot line for customer questions, or a company newsletter. He recommends seeing the package run on a hardware configuration identical to yours if possible (with at least a demonstration) and buying a copy of the documentation before buying the software.[41]

Emard stresses building a relationship with the computer store that sells software and evaluating the store just as you would a software package. (This approach will work with general-purpose software, but library-specific packages are generally not sold through the computer stores.) He also discusses at length the importance of documentation, suggesting the following evaluation criteria:

- Is the manual of appreciable length?

- Are there any illustrations and detailed examples?

- Is the documentation organized in a coherent fashion?

- Is there an index?

- Are "cheat sheets" enclosed (i.e., cards that summarize system commands)?

- Is there a glossary?[42]

Boss also stresses the importance of complete documentation, even with inexpensive packages. He concludes that modifications are difficult to make without good documentation, and new employees can be trained more rapidly if the documentation is good.[43]

Matthews gives suggestions to help librarians become wise microcomputer-software shoppers. He advises reading the microcomputer literature, but be sure to insist that all jargon be explained by vendors and ask them to show you how desired features work rather than just asking if it can be done. Reading and comparing vendors' literature and software manuals will also help in the evaluation process.[44]

Dowlin believes that "service is the most important element in selecting a system. This service should not only cover hardware repair and maintenance, but should include software assistance and handholding. It is extremely important to have a reliable, *and interested*, local dealer."[45]

Norris and Marincola's "Guidelines for Developing an Online In-house Database through a Commercial Vendor" are also applicable to evaluation of prewritten software or turnkey systems. Under "Selecting a Vendor," they advise comparing:

- cost

- system/software capability

- support mechanisms

- responsiveness

- organizational features

- customer satisfaction.[46]

All of these authors emphasize the importance of the vendor and the documentation—two things that are often overlooked in practice. They also recognize the importance of the opinions of colleagues and users of the packages. Personal contacts at conferences, user groups, and vendor lists of installations are all essential to the evaluation process.

Other recommended evaluation criteria vary but usually include such things as hardware constraints, how the various features of the software meet your needs, expandability, and the opinions expressed in reviews or by colleagues.

Evaluation is not a simple process. It involves time and rigorous application of consistent criteria. Datapro summarizes the problems with evaluation of applications software:

Package evaluation is hard—each package has hundreds, even thousands of features. No two packages are alike, or even close. Each has its strengths and weaknesses. It becomes mind-boggling to compare packages in a rational way.[47]

Rational evaluation is not impossible, however, and can be done successfully if the proper commitment of time is made. If evaluation seems too difficult or time-consuming, it is also possible to get help in this phase. Hayes emphasizes that the "consultant's advice will be of even greater value than ever before since the array of alternatives will be vastly increased and the complexity of effect upon the library deeper."[48]

There are a growing number of both library and software consultants who can aid in software evaluation. Also, there are now many workshops being offered by SLA, ASIS, graduate library schools, and others on the identification and evaluation of software for in-house databases.

SOFTWARE DESCRIPTIONS AND REVIEWS

Printed descriptions and reviews of specific software packages help in the evaluation process. Several new journals now feature reviews of microcomputer software for in-house databases. (These journals are reviewed by Tenopir and Beisner.)[49] Two periodicals that are dedicated to microcomputers in libraries often contain descriptions and reviews of software. *Small Computers in Libraries* (*SCIL*) (now Meckler) has been published monthly since 1981. It has short software reviews often written by librarians who are using the packages for their own applications. SCIL is up-to-date and easy to read. It is a valuable tool in the evaluation of microcomputer software for library applications. *ACCESS: Microcomputers in Libraries* [now o.p.] is a quarterly journal that includes articles on software and library applications among its longer subject-oriented articles. Unlike SCIL, it publishes programs as well as software reviews.

Other journals include information about software for database and other library applications for all types and sizes of computers. *Library Software Review* (v. 1, no. 1, Feb. 1982) "seeks to provide an overview of software products and the way they can be used in library and educational settings."[50] Software reviews are lengthy and intermixed with substantive articles on all aspects of library and education software management. The two Online, Inc., magazines, *Online* and *Database*, often contain descriptive information about microcomputer software. Online, Inc., is actively expanding its coverage of microcomputer applications. *Library Hi Tech*, first published in the summer of 1983, includes a column on library software.

Some recent monographs include information about specific software packages for microcomputer-based in-house databases. Woods and Pope's *Librarian's Guide to Microcomputer Technology and Applications* has information on all types of library applications of microcomputers, including software used in more than four hundred libraries. It includes users' opinions of commercially available microcomputer software. It is also a good source for identifying locally developed software that a library will share with other libraries.

Proceedings of the International Online Meeting, National Online Meeting, Online Inc. yearly meetings, Aslib conferences, and the American Society for Information Science twice-yearly meetings are other fruitful sources for microcomputer software descriptions. Increasingly, traditional library journals such as *Special Libraries* and *Library Journal* carry descriptions of microcomputer database applications.

A publication from Meckler Publishing is devoted to evaluations of microcomputer software for information work. *Microsoftware Evaluations* is a compendium of evaluations solicited from current users of the software. Sample screen displays and printouts highlight the narrative reviews. This new publication should be of great help in the evaluation process.

Two online databases, SOFT on BRS and DIALOG's Microcomputer Index, help with the location of general microcomputer software reviews that have been published in the microcomputer journal literature. Both cover many microcomputer periodicals.

In addition, there are a growing number of business-oriented services that scan and summarize the microcomputer literature. PrimeStar, for example, offers a monthly printed SDI service that scans most of the micro magazines, in addition to general business sources such as the *Wall Street Journal, Business Week, Fortune*, etc. *Business Systems Update* includes abstracts and citations to articles about microcomputer business systems, general software solutions, specific business solutions, turnkey systems, outside services, specific business topics, hardware news, and systems software. Articles cover all types of special applications on microcomputers, not just business applications.

Microcomputer Software Letter is another of a growing number of new publications aimed at the microcomputers-in-business market. It provides information on new business-oriented software packages, how to modify prewritten programs, and evaluations of different packages for the same application. Like PrimeStar's service, *Microcomputer Software Letter* is a synthesis of longer articles found in the microcomputer and business literature.

CONCLUSION

Microcomputers are allowing even small special libraries and information centers to create in-house databases, but the success of the system is very dependent on the software chosen. Thanks to standardization of operating systems, availability of higher-level languages, and a growing software market, many prewritten or turnkey software packages are now available for microcomputer-based in-house database systems. These programs are complex and often more expensive than other microcomputer software. Identification of all possibilities and careful evaluation are thus important steps. Luckily, there are a growing number of consultants, directories, and reviews that can help with both of these steps.

No publication or consultant, however, can create a magic formula to allow information managers to choose the best microcomputer software package. The various new directories can be used to identify software possibilities, but a clear understanding of each situation together with a written set of specifications are necessary in order to use the tools and to evaluate the software packages. Software choice is ultimately a personal and somewhat subjective process, but there is an increasing number of guidelines and aids that can assist in this important decision-making process.

REFERENCES

[1]Jeff Pemberton, "Should Your Next Terminal Be a Computer?" *Database* 4:4-6 (Sept. 1981); _____, "The Spread of Microcomputers — Fast and Wide," *Database* 5:6-7 (Aug. 1982); John B. Gordon, "Microcomputer Applications in a Corporate Headquarters Staff Environment," in *Online Micro-Software Guide and Directory, 1983-84* (Weston, Conn.: Online, 1983), p. 8-15; John C. Blair, Jr., "Decision Support Systems Software; The Key to Library Microcomputer Operations," in Helen A. Gordon, ed., *Online MicroSoftware Guide and Directory, 1983-84* (Weston, Conn.: Online, 1983), p. 3-7; Joseph R. Matthews, "The Automated Library System Marketplace, 1982: Change and More Change!" *Library Journal* 108:547-53 (Mar. 15, 1983).

[2]Beatrice Marron and Dennis Fife, "Online Systems — Techniques and Services," *Annual Review of Information Science and Technology* 11:169 (1976).

[3]Allan D. Pratt, "The Use of Microcomputers in Libraries," *Journal of Library Automation* 13:13 (Mar. 1980).

[4]Gerald Lundeen, "The Role of Microcomputers in Libraries," *Wilson Library Bulletin* 55:184 (Nov. 1980).

[5]Ibid.

[6]Allan D. Pratt, "Microcomputers as Information Dissemination Tools," in *Communicating Information: Proceedings of the 43rd Annual ASIS Meeting*, V. 17, eds. Allen R. Benenfield and Edward John Kazlauskas (White Plains, N.Y.: Knowledge Industry Publications, 1980), p. 316.

[7]M. J. Rowat, "Microcomputers in Libraries and Information Departments," *Aslib Proceedings* 34:29 (Jan. 1982).

[8]Don R. Swanson, "Miracles, Microcomputers, and Librarians," *Library Journal* 107:1057 (June 1, 1982).

[9]Rhoda Garoogian, "Pre-written Software: Identification, Evaluation, and Selection," *Software Review* 1:12 (Feb. 1982).

[10]"Turnkey Trends," *Small Computers in Libraries* 2:5 (Feb. 1982).

[11]"Software for Micros and Minis," *Library Systems Newsletter* 1:14 (Aug. 1981).

[12]Ibid.

[13]Mark E. Rorvig, *Microcomputers and Libraries: A Guide to Technology, Products and Applications* (White Plains, N.Y.: Knowledge Industry Publications, 1982), p. 41, 101.

[14]Helen A. Gordon, review of *Microcomputers and Libraries*, by Mark E. Rorvig, *Online* 6:44 (May 1982).

[15]Michael R. Schuyler, review of *Microcomputers and Libraries*, by Mark E. Rorvig, *Information Technology and Libraries* 1:308 (Sept. 1982), with a reply from Rorvig: 308-9.

[16]Audrey N. Grosch, review of *Microcomputers and Libraries*, by Mark E. Rorvig, *Special Libraries* 74:102 (Jan. 1983).

[17]Allan D. Pratt, review of *Microcomputers and Libraries*, by Mark E. Rorvig, *Small Computers in Libraries* 2:6 (Feb. 1982).

[18]David Kelley, "Software—What's Available," in Ching-chih Chen and Stacey E. Bressler, eds., *Microcomputers in Libraries* (New York: Neal-Schuman, 1982), p. 66.

[19]Ibid., p. 67.

[20]John C. Blair, Jr., "Micros, Minis and Mainframes ... A Newcomer's Guide to the World of Computers—Especially Micros," *Online* 5:20 (Jan. 1982).

[21]A. Vickery and H. Brooks, "Microcomputer, Liberator or Enslaver," *Proceedings of the Fourth International Online Information Meeting* (Oxford, England: Learned Information, 1980), p. 394.

[22]Rowat, "Microcomputers in Libraries," p. 32.

[23]Garoogian, "Pre-written Software," p. 13.

[24]Carol Tenopir, "Software for In-House Databases: Part I, Software Sources," *Library Journal* 108:639-41 (Apr. 1, 1983).

[25]_____, "Evaluation of Library Retrieval Software," in *Communicating Information: Proceedings of the 43rd ASIS Annual Meeting*, V. 17, eds. Allen R. Benenfield and Edward John Kazlauskas (White Plains, N.Y.: Knowledge Industry Publications, 1980), p. 64.

[26]Joseph R. Matthews, "Introduction to Micros" (talk given at the Online '82 Conference, Oct. 1982).

[27]Matthews, "The Automated Library System Marketplace," p. 550.

[28]Jean-Paul Emard, "Software Hang-Ups and Glitches: Problems to Be Faced and Overcome," *Online* 6:18 (Jan. 1983).

[29]John C. Blair, Jr., "Software Applications Packages and the Role of the Computer Applications Specialist," *Online* 5:65 (Mar. 1982).

[30]Carol Tenopir, "Software for In-House Databases: Part II, Evaluation and Choice," *Library Journal* 108:88 (May 1, 1983).

[31]Joseph R. Matthews, *Choosing an Automated Library System: A Planning Guide* (Chicago: American Library Assn., 1980), p. 49.

[32]Ibid., p. 50.

[33]Garoogian, "Pre-written Software."

[34]Ibid., p. 18-20.

[35]Ibid., p. 20-21.

[36]Tenopir, "Software for In-House Databases: Part II."

[37]*Datapro Applications Software Solutions* (Delran, N.J.: Datapro Research Corp.), p. 106.

[38]Ibid., p. 105-6.

[39]Kelley, "Software," p. 71.

[40]"Step by Step Method for Software Purchasing," *MIS Week* (Oct. 20, 1982).

[41]Blair, "Software Applications Packages," p. 69.

[42]Emard, "Software Hang-Ups and Glitches," p. 20.

[43]Richard W. Boss, "Software Documentation," *Software Review* 1:167 (Oct. 1982).

[44]Matthews, "The Automated Library System Marketplace," p. 550.

[45]Kenneth E. Dowlin, "Micro Mag," *Library Journal* 107:237 (Feb. 1, 1982).

[46]Carole L. Norris and Diana A. Marincola, "Guidelines for Developing an Online In-House Database through a Commercial Vendor," in *Proceedings of the Third National Online Meeting*, eds. Martha E. Williams and Thomas H. Hogan (Medford, N.J.: Learned Information, 1982), p. 437-38.

[47]*Datapro Applications*, p. 103.

[48]Robert M. Hayes, "Consulting in Computer Applications to Libraries," *Library Trends* 28: 396 (Winter 1980).

[49]Tenopir, "Software for In-house Databases: Part I," p. 639-41; Karl Beisner, "Microcomputer Periodicals for Libraries," *American Libraries* 14:46 (Jan. 1983).

[50]Beisner, p. 46.

APPENDIX A.
SOFTWARE SOURCES

Directories Specific to Library/Information Applications

Gordon, Helen, ed. *Online Micro Software Guide and Directory*. Westport, Conn.: Online, Inc., 1983.
Directory and guide to more than seven hundred software packages for all types of information center applications.

Kazlauskas, Edward, ed. *Directory of Information Management Software: For Libraries, Information Centers, Record Centers, 1987/88*. ALA/Pacific Info. $49.
Information on commercially available software for in-house databases.

Nolan, Jeanne, ed. *Micro Software Report: Library Edition*. 2d ed., 1983. Meckler Publishing Co.
Includes descriptions of nearly three hundred microcomputer programs of interest to libraries.

UNESCO Inventory of Software Packages. Tel-Aviv, Israel: National Center of Scientific and Technological Information, 1983. (P.O. Box 20215). (o.p. 1988).
International software directory for information work.

General Directories: A Selected List

Auerbach Software Reports. Auerbach Publishers. 2v. Updated monthly, looseleaf.

A Buyer's Guide to Data Base Management Systems. Delran, N.J.: Datapro Research Corp., 1974- . Updated annually. Selected from *Datapro 70*.

Datamation regularly surveys software packages. Of special interest to information center applications are: May 1982 "Application Software Survey," December 1981 "System Software Survey," and September 1981 "The DBMS Market Is Booming."

Datapro Directory of Microcomputer Software. Delran, N.J.: Datapro Research Corp., 1981- . Updated monthly, looseleaf.

Datapro Directory of Software. Delran, N.J.: Datapro Research Corp., 1975- . Updated monthly, looseleaf.

Datapro 70. Delran, N.J.: Datapro Research Corp. 3v. Updated monthly, looseleaf.
Guide to hardware and software.

ICP Software Directory. Indianapolis, Ind.: International Computer Programs. Semiannual. 5v.

Minicomputer Software Quarterly. Wayland, Mass.: Applied International Management Services. Quarterly.

Small Systems Software and Services Sourcebook. Available from J. Koolish, Information Sources, Inc., 1807 Glenview Rd., Glenview, IL 60025.
Describes thirteen hundred packages.

Available Online

·MENU· International Software Database. DIALOG, file 232.

File Soft, BRS.

Other Useful Sources

The Electronic Library will devote one issue to a directory of mini- and microcomputer software. Learned Information Ltd., Oxford, England.

Library Hi Tech. Pierian Press, Ann Arbor, MI.
Began summer 1983 and includes information on software.

Monitor surveyed interactive online software in April and May 1982. Learned Information, Ltd.

Nolan, Jeanne, ed. *Microsoftware Evaluations*. 4th ed. Meckler Publishing, 1987.
Evaluations of library-oriented microcomputer software by users.

Small Computers in Libraries. Meckler Publishing.

Library Software Review reviews information applications software. Meckler Publishing.

Available Online

File Soft, BRS.

·MENU· The International Software Directory (ISD), DIALOG, file 232.

Microcomputer Index, DIALOG, file 233.

Microcomputer Software and Hardware Guide, DIALOG, file 278. ∎

EVALUATION OF LIBRARY RETRIEVAL SOFTWARE*

INTRODUCTION

In the past two years the number of commercially available software packages for online retrieval systems has greatly increased. In the next few years the number of such packages will continue to grow. Many libraries that formerly would have planned development of an in-house system, or that would not have been able to consider an online retrieval system at all, will now be evaluating these software packages for possible purchase. Librarians who will be responsible for this evaluation may have limited experience in choosing and evaluating software packages. They may be very accomplished users of existing data bases and various automated systems, but many will have never worked directly on software development. Following is criteria for evaluating library retrieval software packages by the librarian with limited computer expertise.

ASSESSING NEEDS

Before any evaluation of specific products can take place, the librarian must evaluate exactly the library's needs. The exercise of identifying the library's needs and determining specifications to meet these needs is the best way to formulate specific questions to be asked, to communicate needs to the vendor, and to ensure that a software package will be able to deliver all the things expected.

Whether formal specifications are required by the parent organization or not, they should be developed as a first step. This step should address both general and specific library requirements and answer the questions listed below.

- Why is a new system desired and needed?

- What old system is present and how will the new system replace or interact with it?

- How will the new system affect other library functions?

- Ideally, what will the new system do? (Be detailed and specific.)

- Do you have special requirements which must be met? (e.g., need for special characters like the ALA print train, MARC compatibility?)

- What things must the system do and what would be nice, but are not required features? (Detail and rank all features.)

- What will the system look like in 1 year? In 5 years? In 10 years?

- Who will be the primary users of the system? Will a librarian serve as an interface or will end users be the primary target?

- Should access be available in one location only, in multiple locations throughout one facility, or in multiple facilities?

- What is the expected size of the database and how fast will it grow?

- What management, personnel, and data processing support will there be for the system?

- What is a reasonable and acceptable price range?

The initial step should also address data processing requirements.

- What hardware is presently available in-house? What is its capacity, its operating systems, its future in the organization?

- Is new hardware necessary or feasible? Would the data processing department prefer to purchase hardware compatible with a company-wide plan or is purchase of a hardware/software package by the library possible?

- What programming languages are currently supported or will be supported in the future?

- Will the data processing staff be involved in this project? What priority will it have with them? Have they worked with the library before?

- Do heavy demands on the computer and shifting priorities pose a threat to the library's use of the in-house hardware and personnel?

Once the needs and requirements of the library have been identified, it is time to identify specific software packages on the market and to evaluate them for the application. Figure 1 outlines and summarizes the general areas of evaluation which are discussed in more detail below. Each software package under consideration is evaluated on a separate form. A score for Poor or Not Avail. is used when a feature is of poor quality or some needed feature is not available with this package. OK or Acceptable is used either to rate a feature which meets the minimum standards or when a feature which is not available is not required for your application. Good is used when features exceed minimum requirements. Evaluative comparisons can then be made, leading to the choice of the most satisfactory package.

*Reprinted from *Communicating Information: Proceedings of the 43rd ASIS Annual Meeting 1980.* Copyright © 1980 by American Society for Information Science.

Name of software _____
Overall Rating _____

	LEVEL OF IMPORTANCE	RATING	SCORE
VENDOR/PRODUCER			
Reputation			
Library knowledge			
Other products			
Users of this product			
Response to this product			
Support services			
Geographic location			
Accessibility by phone			
Your reactions			
SYSTEM OUTPUT			
Display format			
Customizing features			
Printed lists			
Statistical reports			
Tape generation			
SYSTEM INPUT			
Special input			
Variety of input means			
Ease of procedures/commands			
Ident. of new input			
Ease of deletions, adds, changes			
Flexibility of format			
SEARCHING			
Query language			
User formats			
Error messages			
Thesaurus			
All fields searchable			
Distinction among fields			
Logical combinations			
Simple searching			
SECURITY			
Levels of passwords			
Security from alteration			

	LEVEL OF IMPORTANCE	RATING	SCORE
Log on procedures			
Back-up systems			
Usage tracking			
TRAINING			
Online training lessons			
Query language			
Documentation			
Training classes			
Ease of learning			
EQUIPMENT			
Hardware warranty			
Hardware reliability			
Trade-in benefits			
Downtime procedures			
Back-up procedures/features			
Service			
Ongoing costs			
Terminals			
Dial-up access			
Number of terminals			
Response time			
Other peripherals			
OTHER CONSIDERATIONS			
Size capabilities			
Clarity of costs			
Cost comparison with other systems			
Cost comparison with existing system			
TOTAL SCORE			

Fig. 1. Software evaluation form. Updated and taken from: Tenopir, Carol, and Gerald Lundeen. *Managing Your Information: How to Design and Create a Textual Database on Your Microcomputer* (Neal-Schuman, 1988).

VENDOR OR PRODUCER

A basic concern when evaluating a software package is the creator and marketing agency of this package. Questions to be addressed include:

- Does the vendor or producer have a reputation for reliability, responsiveness, and quality?

- Are they primarily a library-focused agency or a general software house? (Libraries have unique requirements of which non-library focused companies are often unaware and communication with them may be more difficult.)

- What other products have they developed? Are these products still in use and can you talk to people who are using them? Do they rate the products and the firm highly?

- How many information centers have purchased their retrieval package? (For a new product this may not be as important if the company rates highly in other areas.) What do these other information centers say about the package? How do their needs and size compare to your application?

- What kind of support services are offered? (e.g., installation on your computer, debugging, conversion services, etc.)

- Are they geographically located so they can be responsive to your questions or problems?

- Are they easy to reach with questions? When you call can someone there answer your questions immediately?

- Do you feel good about the firm and their salespeople? Are they responsive to your questions? Do they try to put things in your own terms? Do they really know the product? Are they familiar with similar products offered by other firms?

SYSTEM OUTPUT

Essential to any system is output—what the user and the library will receive from the system in response to queries. Both online display and printed listing capabilities must be examined with the following guidelines:

- Is the display format easy to understand and read?

- Can the display format be custom tailored? (e.g., full record or specified partial record?)

- Are printed lists and reports available as well as an online display? (e.g., acquisitions lists, thesauri, custom tailored holdings lists)

- Are statistical reports generated when needed? Can other kinds of statistics be generated if needed? (e.g., new titles added, total number of volumes and titles, etc.)

- Can a tape be generated as output? (Can be used for COM catalog.)

SYSTEM INPUT

How information is to be entered into the retrieval system, both as an initial building process and as an ongoing procedure, must be carefully evaluated answering the following questions:

- Can OCLC or MARC tapes be used as input if this is your requirement?

- Can you choose the input means—direct key to disk or key to tape, OCR, etc., and can several methods be used? (You may want to convert existing cataloging using OCR or tapes, but will probably want to enter new information directly at the terminal.)

- Are the procedures for adding new items easy and are commands easy to remember? Does the online format prompt input?

- Are there built-in safeguards which tell you if an input error is made?

- Are newly input items identifiable?

- Can deletions of entire records or partial records be easily made? Additions and changes also?

- Is the user able to specify record structure to meet any specific needs? Are records variable length and is the format free?

SEARCHING

The user must be able to easily locate items in the data base or the system is virtually worthless.

- Is the query language easy to learn and easy to use?

- Is there a beginning user format that explains commands in detail and an experienced user format which bypasses lengthy explanations?

- If improper search language or commands are used does the system respond with intelligible error messages and provide alternative actions?

- Is a thesaurus available online? Available in hard copy?

- Can all fields be searched without specifying fields? Can a distinction be made between fields if desired?

- Can terms be combined in logical AND, OR, NOT combinations?

- Can most users perform a simple search (finding a book by author, title, or a single subject) with no librarian interface?

SECURITY

The security of information in an online catalog must be considered from the following angles:

- Are there different levels of passwords for different classes of users?

- Can the system be used in a search-mode with no password?

- If no passwords are needed by browsers, is the database secure from alteration by unauthorized users? (ie. passwords required to add new information or edit existing information.)

- Is it so difficult to logon that use is prohibitive?

- Are there automatic backup systems for newly added materials? For editing? For the data base as a whole?

- Can usage be tracked?

TRAINING

The level and quality of training available should also be considered before purchase of a system.

- Are online training lessons available?

- Are some training features incorporated into the query language?

- Are sufficient and clear documentation and training manuals available? Are they available for users, librarians, and data processing staffs?

- Are training classes for both the library staff and the data processing staff available? Are these classes available at your facility?

- Can the uninitiated user learn to use the system with online instructions? With short written lessons? Or are detailed lessons needed?

EQUIPMENT

Costs and features of computers, terminals and peripherals vary considerably and must be examined.

- If hardware is to be purchased or leased with the system: is it covered by a sufficient warranty? Is someone in-house familiar with it? What does the literature and your data processing department say about the hardware? Are special facilities required? Will you get a trade-in benefit when better hardware becomes available?

- How will you handle downtime? What is available as a backup and is this backup automatic? Is there a service department that can answer your questions immediately and service personnel who will come on site quickly?

- What are ongoing costs for maintenance and/or lease?

- Are special terminals required? If so, are they readily available and does the cost compare with other terminals?

- Can the system be accessed by dial-up access as well as by terminals directly wired to the system?

- How many terminals can the system support? Can more be added in the future?

- What is the normal response time? How does peak use affect the response time?

- Are peripherals needed now? Can they be added to the system if needed? How will they be billed?

OTHER CONSIDERATIONS

- What size of data base can the system handle? What sizes are operating now and are there any upward limits?

- Are all costs available and relatively steady? Are there hidden costs monthly or yearly?

- Is the total cost competitive and within your projected budget?

- If you have done a cost analysis of your present system, how do these costs compare in 1 year? In 5 years? In 10 years? (Remember your automated system will likely be performing services not now offered and not figured into your existing costs.)

CONCLUSION

Librarians must consider all aspects of a retrieval package before purchase. Discussions with the in-house data processing staff, with users of various systems, and with a variety of vendors is helpful and necessary. The final decision about which system to purchase should be made by evaluating all systems by the same criteria, however. Coupled with an evaluation of the library's needs, this evaluative comparison will provide a framework for a decision. ■

SOFTWARE OPTIONS FOR
IN-HOUSE BIBLIOGRAPHIC DATABASES*

The last time I discussed microcomputer software for the creation of in-house databases (*LJ*, May 1, 1983, p. 885-888), there were only a few packages on the market. Since then, many new packages have appeared, while some older ones have undergone extensive revisions or upgrades.

DATABASE CHARACTERISTICS

It may be tempting to use the least expensive software you can find for an in-house microcomputer database. This usually means a general purpose file manager program or database management system program. Most of these programs were not designed for bibliographic-type files, however, and many impose severe restrictions on the design and searching power. They must be carefully evaluated with the unique characteristics of bibliographic databases (and your particular application) in mind. Characteristics of bibliographic databases not usually found in business or other applications include:

- Composition mostly of alphanumeric character strings rather than numbers needing computations. Even when numbers are included, they are frequently treated as character strings (e.g., volume numbers, pages, etc.).

- Each record tends to have many fields, but the same or similar fields are present in most records in the database.

- Fields are frequently lengthy (titles or abstracts for instance), but the length of each field will vary from one record to the next.

- Some fields have repeating values that must be treated separately but equally (e.g., descriptors, multiple authors). The frequency of repetition is usually unpredictable from one record to the next.

- Many applications require searchable access to most fields.

- Search capabilities are important, e.g., Boolean logic, word proximity, searching on a specified field or fields, and truncation.

- Information usually doesn't change quickly and the number of records will tend to grow continually.

These characteristics have a direct effect on what software is appropriate for a bibliographic database. Software that has been successfully used for bibliographic applications can be divided into two categories which can then be subdivided into different software types.

GENERAL PURPOSE PACKAGES

General purpose software packages are designed to be appropriate for many different applications, and can usually be purchased from local computer stores or mail order distributors, frequently at discounted prices. The producers generally know nothing about bibliographic databases, so it is up to you to evaluate and adapt the packages for your special requirements. General purpose packages include three main types: Data Base Management Systems (DBMS), File Managers, and Text Retrieval Systems.

DBMS

There are many microcomputer DBMS packages on the market, and many of them have severe limitations for bibliographic applications: fixed-length fields with restricted field lengths, the inability to handle more than one value per field, and restrictions on the number of fields or size of records.

The biggest advantage of a DBMS is its ability to use more than one file at a time. Users establish a relationship between files, and link different files together as needed. For example, one file may contain records describing a library collection; another may contain information about each authorized patron of a library. A third "transaction" file might be created by linking parts of the collection file with the patron (borrower) file. If you need such capabilities, the disadvantages of a DBMS program may be less important.

DBMS packages usually come with a programming language and almost always require some programming to make them work for your application. Expect to spend time for development, with the tradeoff that the more powerful DBMS languages allow you the flexibility of programming to meet your needs.

Another advantage for some popular DBMS packages is that there are many easy-to-use books about the packages available. Librarians who have used these packages to create bibliographic databases may even share the programs they have written. Meckler's *Small Computers in Libraries* often reproduces DBMS programs. Library applications programs for one popular DBMS are given in Karl Beiser's *Essential Guide to dBase III+ in Libraries* (Meckler, 1987).

Unlike some other DBMS programs, Revelation (Cosmos, Inc.) accommodates variable-length fields and supports repeating field values. Although it is a complex program, it seems to be ideally suited for bibliographic databases.

File Managers

File managers are distinguished from DBMS packages by their ability to support only one file. Many of them are much

---

less complex to use, due in part to the fact that they are much less powerful. They generally do not offer powerful search capabilities or a variety of report-writing options. They may have severe restrictions on file design issues such as field length, number of fields, and values per field. They are marketed for the general user with fairly simple requirements, such as name/address files. They might work well, however, for simple, small bibliographic files. The investment in money and time is frequently so much less than other types of programs that it may pay to try them out. There are many file managers on the market, all of which need to be evaluated carefully for any bibliographic application.

Text Retrieval Software

Text retrieval software differs from other types of software in that it deals with unstructured text rather than information separated into fields. A common application of text retrieval software is for control of word processing files which are already in machine-readable form. It is not usually used for bibliographic fields which are more highly structured, but it could be used to provide retrieval to files that were created from downloading records from several bibliographic databases on different online vendors. If such files contain several incompatible structures and you do not have the time to edit records for compatibility, a text retrieval package can provide access to entire records.

Text retrieval packages generally offer powerful search capabilities—Boolean logic, truncation, word proximity searching—but because there are no fields, the system must search the entire database for word occurrence and there is no customizing of output.

SPECIAL PURPOSE PACKAGES

None of the general purpose packages were designed specifically for bibliographic databases. It is up to the database designer, therefore, to evaluate the applicability of each package carefully, and frequently to make either programming enhancements or compromises in database design. Packages that have been designed with the unique characteristics of bibliographic databases in mind solve many of these problems.

These packages typically are purchased from their producer or from specialized vendors and they frequently cost more than the general purpose packages. Their markets are smaller, so you will not find how-to-do-it books in the local bookstore, but the library literature and library conference proceedings discuss many of these packages. Special purpose packages include: Information Storage and Retrieval Programs, Library Applications, and Bibliography Generators.

Information Storage and Retrieval Programs (IS&R)

These packages are designed to model the powerful search and retrieval capabilities of the large online systems such as DIALOG or BRS. Although they vary in exact features, most software include Boolean logic, truncation, proximity searching, set building, and some customized output design. There

are few restrictions placed on record or field size, fields are typically of variable length, and repeating values in a field are accommodated.

Almost all of these packages require an IBM PC or compatible. Except for very small databases, a hard disk is recommended (and sometimes required). Like the large commercial vendors, these packages usually create inverted (dictionary) indexes to facilitate speedy searching so the software adds a high overhead to the storage capacity required. Several good information storage and retrieval packages cost less than $1000.

Library Applications

Library applications packages offer less flexibility than IS&R packages, because the field specifications and output features are frequently preset. They are good if you have a standard library file (such as a catalog of books) with requirements that match the programs' capabilities. These often include other library functions such as circulation. Directories can be checked for a complete listing of packages in this category.

Bibliography Generators

Many information storage and retrieval programs can be used to generate bibliographies, but there is an entire category of software that primarily serves this purpose. These packages are not designed to build an online database (though some may be used for small databases); they are designed to be used to create correctly formatted features that can create bibliographies.

Their strength lies in their output features that can create bibliographies formatted according to the rules of different bibliographic styles (e.g., *Chicago Manual*, ANSI format, etc.). Users can often specify their own format as well. Bibliography generators are especially valuable to researchers, but may also be used in a library.

More detail on all these packages, plus a step-by-step guide to building an in-house microcomputer-based textual database, can be found in *Managing Your Information: How to Design and Create a Textual Database on Your Microcomputer*, by Gerald Lundeen and myself (Neal-Schuman, 1988).

SOFTWARE SOURCE LIST

DBMS

dBase III+
Ashton-Tate, 10150 W. Jefferson Blvd., Culver City, CA 90230, 213-204-5570

R:BASE System V
MicroRIM Inc., 3380 146th Place SE, Bellevue, WA 98007, 206-641-6619

Revelation, Advanced Revelation
Cosmos, Inc., 1346 14th Ave., PO Box 1237, Longview, WA 98632, 206-423-0763

File Managers

FYI3000
FYI, Inc., 4202 Spicewood Rd., PO Box 26481, Austin, TX 78755, 512-346-0133

Nutshell, Nutshell Plus
Canterbury International, Ashland Technology Center, 200 Homer Ave., Ashland, MA 01721, 617-881-7404

PFS First Choice
Software Pub. Corp., 1901 Landings Dr., Mt. View, CA 94043, 415-962-8910

Q&A
Symantec Corp., 10201 Torre Ave., Cupertino, CA 95014, 408-253-9600

Savvy
The Savvy Corp., 122 Tulane SE, Albuquerque, NM 87106, 505-265-1273

Text Retrieval Packages

TEXTBANK
Group L Corp., 481 Carlisle Dr., Herndon, VA 22070, 703-471-0030

ZyINDEX
Zylab Corp., 233 E. Erie St., Chicago, IL 60611, 312-642-2201

Information Storage & Retrieval Programs

BRS/Search for Micros
BRS Software Group, 1200 Rte. 7, Latham, NY 12100, 800-833-4707

CAIRS
(no longer serviced in the United States)

Concept Finder
MMIMS, Inc., 566A S. York Rd., Elmhurst, IL 60126, 312-941-0090

INMAGIC
InMagic Inc., 238 Broadway, Cambridge, MA 02139, 617-661-8124

Pro-cite
Personal Bibliographic Software, 412 Longshore, Ann Arbor, MI 48106, 313-996-1580

Sci-Mate Software System
(File Manager/Editor/Searcher)
Inst. for Scientific Info (as of 1989 serviced by Personal Bibliographic Software)

Personal Librarian (formerly SIRE)
Cucumber Info Systems, 5611 Kraft Dr., Rockville, MD 20852, 301-984-3539

STAR
Cuadra Associates, Inc., 2001 Wilshire Blvd., Santa Monica, CA 90403, 213-829-9972

Library Applications

Card Datalog
Data Trek, Inc., 121 W. E St., Encinitas, CA 92024, 619-436-5055

M/Series 10 (formerly InfoQUEST)
Utlas International, 1611 N. Kent St., Arlington, VA 22209 703-525-5940

Mandarin
Media Flex Inc., Box 1107, Champlain, NY 12919, 518-298-2970

Micro Library Systems
Sydney Dataproduction, 11075 Santa Monica Blvd., Los Angeles, CA 90025, 213-479-4621

Ocelot
ABALL Software Inc., 2174 Hamilton St., Regina, Saskatchewan, Canada S4P 2E6, 306-569-2180

Bibliography Generators

Notebook II
Pro/Tem Software, Inc., 2363 Boulevard Circle, Walnut Creek, CA 94595, 800-826-2222

Pro-cite
Personal Bibliographic Software
(see Information Storage & Retrieval Programs)

Reference Manager
Research Information Systems Inc., 1991 Village Park Way, Encinitas, CA 92024, 619-753-3914

Sci-Mate Editor
(see Information Storage & Retrieval Programs)

CHAPTER

5

CD-ROM

From the time CD-ROM databases became commercially available in 1985, they have captured the imagination and favor of librarians. Compact optical disks provide a durable high-density storage medium that allows large portions of databases to be brought into the library. Chapter 5 focuses on the technology, impacts, and products of this newest information medium for locally held databases.

A word about terminology and spelling is in order, because inconsistencies are natural when a technology is new. Although CD-ROM databases are certainly brought "in-house," when I use the term *in-house databases*, I am referring, as in the previous chapter, to databases that are designed, created, and maintained as well as searched within the library. The computer and storage technology used for the in-house database are not significant to the definition.

When I use the phrase *locally held databases* I am referring to published databases or portions of databases that are purchased or leased for local searching. I use the phrase *locally held* to contrast with online remote databases—those that are housed by an online vendor and are accessed via telecommunications lines.

Locally held databases typically are purchased from either the database producer or a third-party vendor. They may be delivered on magnetic media (usually floppy disk or tape for loading onto a local hard disk) or on optical media such as CD-ROM. Such databases on magnetic media are not new; many of the large databases such as Medline or ERIC were available on magnetic tape before online systems were up and running.

In these articles and other library literature you will find the CD referred to by many names. It may be called compact disk (or disc), laser disk (or disc), CD-ROM (or CDROM), or optical digital disk (or disc). Actually, CD-ROMs are one type of optical digital disk, the type that has taken over the locally held database market in libraries for now.

CD-ROM is the newest and now most popular medium for bringing databases into the library. This is so for many reasons. Each CD holds up to 600 megabytes; they are comparatively durable; CD readers are relatively inexpensive and their installation does not require hardware experts; and the yearly price of a database on CD-ROM often compares favorably to the subscription price of a printed index.

The first article in this chapter, "Databases on CD-ROM," defines CD-ROM and provides an overview of their potential and promise. This was written in January of 1986 and describes the products that were available at that early time in the development of CD-ROM databases. Since it was (and is) a new technology, the products and companies are changing rapidly. "CD-ROM in 1986," written at the end of that year, updated the information in the first article. "What's Happening with CD-ROM" is a further update that examines general characteristics of the CD-ROM marketplace in 1988 and reviews some of the many publications devoted to the CD-ROM medium that has been so rapidly embraced in the library world. I suspect the optical disk marketplace will not settle down for many years to come. Taken together, these three articles give an idea of the types of products and potentials offered by CD-ROM.

One of the earliest optical disk products for libraries was Information Access Company's InfoTrac. (It came on a twelve-inch disk originally, not a compact disk.) Many libraries passed out questionnaires to their InfoTrac users and did studies of how it was used in their library. "InfoTrac: A Laser Disc System" does more than describe InfoTrac as it was in 1986; it summarizes several libraries' experiences with and evaluation of end user optical disk searching using the InfoTrac database. Patrons usually loved it; librarians often had mixed emotions. Results of surveys and comments from librarians in several libraries are included in this article.

The last two articles discuss issues that have been generated by CD-ROM. Publishers sometimes seek, and frequently need, guidance from librarians as to what CD-ROM products are most desired by the library marketplace. Meetings with CD-ROM producers and librarians at the 1987 American Library Association annual conference are described in "Publications on CD-ROM: Librarians Can Make a Difference."

"CD-ROM Costs: What Are the Media Tradeoffs" was written for a presentation at the Library and Information Technology Association (LITA) Preconference Institute on Optical Publishing and Libraries at the 1987 annual meeting of the American Library Association. I incorporated parts of it into a *Library Journal* column called "Costs and Benefits of CD-ROM," but I chose to include the longer original version in this collection.

Together I believe these articles provide a sampling of the issues, concerns, and products spawned by the CD-ROM technology. CD-ROM will undoubtedly continue to be one of the big technologies and generate issues in the library database world for years to come.

DATABASES ON CD-ROM*

Databases on CD-ROM (compact disc-read only memory) impacted on the database world in 1986. Several prototype products were exhibited at the July ALA conference, and CD-ROM products attracted the most attention in the exhibits and discussions at the Online '85 meeting in New York in November and at the International Online meeting in London in December. Some recent conferences have been devoted entirely to optical discs of all types, including CD-ROM. Several of the products seen at these meetings are now available for purchase.

WHY COMPACT DISCS

Compact discs are being used by database publishers as a high-density medium for distribution of databases or database subsets (see my column in the May 15, 1985 *LJ*, p. 42). Libraries can subscribe to these CD-ROM databases much as they now do with printed materials. The discs are mailed to subscribers on a quarterly, monthly, or yearly basis for searching on the library's own microcomputer that is equipped with a CD-ROM reader. Some database distributors provide the necessary hardware.

Unlike remote databases that charge for online connect time, locally held databases can be searched as much as desired with no additional charges. A library can budget for databases like other subscriptions. They are ideal for database searching by patrons, eliminating concern for password protection or online charges.

Floppy disk and magnetic tape subsets have been available for several years, but the CD-ROM is expected to replace them because optical (laser) media offer several advantages over the magnetic media.

Optical discs provide high-density storage. One CD-ROM 4.75-inch disc holds 600 megabytes (600,000,000 characters) of storage. According to Digital Equipment Corporation (DEC), that is equivalent to 1600 floppy disks (the capacity of floppy disks varies widely, from only 100K bytes on a single-sided, single-density floppy, to 1.6 megabytes on an IBM/AT floppy and over five megabytes available soon on some systems). The

CD-ROM capacity is equivalent to 200,000 single-spaced pages or 46 days' worth of continuous data transmission at 1200 baud. The entire *Encyclopaedia Britannica* fits on one compact disc.

Optical discs are more durable. Each disc has a protective coating. As an optical medium they are not sensitive to magnetic fields, dust, or fingerprints. A beam of light reads the discs rather than a head in contact with the surface, so discs are expected to last at least ten years.

CD-ROM discs cannot be erased or altered once they are created, a real advantage from a database publisher's standpoint because the integrity of the publication is preserved. "Read Only Memory" means that once a compact disc is mastered at a production facility it cannot be changed. Erasable and Direct Read After Write (DRAW), one-time-write, many-time-read digital discs will be available soon primarily for use as computer storage devices.

All optical digital discs, including CD-ROM, are created by a high-powered laser that burns pits into the disc. The initial mastering of a disc is expensive, but economy is realized by making multiple copies of the master at the production site. To read a compact disc it is inserted into a CD-ROM reader which contains a laser beam that focuses on the disc's tracks. The light beam is reflected differently from the pits than from the unpitted areas. The two states of reflected light correspond to the binary 1s and 0s in digital information. CD reader access speeds are much slower than Winchester disc drives (½ to 2 seconds for CD as compared to 30-50 milliseconds for the Winchester disc drive). Their many other advantages seem to overcome this disadvantage for these applications.

CD-ROMs are favored by many in the database industry over other optical digital technologies because CD readers are relatively inexpensive and are widely available. Major manufacturers are working on a standard CD format, to make it possible to run a variety of discs on the same reader. Not all database producers agree that CD-ROM is the best optical medium. Information Access Company's InfoTrac system (described in my column in *LJ*, May 15, 1985, p. 42) and others use 12-inch optical discs instead of CDs. There have been long delays in getting a CD-ROM mastered.

For further information about CD-ROM technology see: Nancy K. Herther, "CD ROM Technology: A New Era for Information Storage and Retrieval?," *Online*, November 1985, p. 17-28; and Brower Murphy, "CD-ROM and Libraries," *Library Hi Tech*, Consecutive Issue 10, 1985, p. 21-28.

For a description of all optical disc technologies including CD-ROM, see: Information Systems Consultants, Inc. *Videodisc and Optical Digital Disc Technologies and Their Applications in Libraries*. Wash., D.C.: Council on Library Resources, Inc., January 1985.

SilverPlatter

SilverPlatter Information Inc. (a merger of IMLAC Standard Information Systems and International Standard Information Systems) has 16 CD-ROM databases available (*NTIS*, *A-V Online*, *ERIC*, *GPO*, *MEDLINE*, etc.) with seven planned for 1989. According to Chris Pooley, director of marketing and sales in the United States, SilverPlatter is "talking with a host of [other] information providers...."

ERIC will be priced in the "neighborhood" of $3000 to $4000 per year, a yearly subscription to *PsycLIT* will be $5000.

A subscription to all of these includes the full database, *not* a subset. If a single disc for a database gets full, an archival disc will be made. Quarterly updates will continue to replace the current information disc. For example, an archival disc of *ERIC* might contain information from 1966 (when the database began) through 1977. The current disc in this hypothetical example would include information from 1978 to the present.

All of the databases distributed by SilverPlatter use the same hardware configuration. User libraries will need an IBM-PC or compatible with 256K bytes of main memory for each work station desired. A printer is optional, but recommended. SilverPlatter will sell Hitachi CD-ROM readers at a price "under $1000."

The search software was developed by SilverPlatter. It supports Boolean logic, proximity searching, free-text or specified-field searching, and truncation. Function keys are used for commands. Pooley says the software is designed for both expert users and novices. The expert searcher can go directly to the information desired without being "encumbered by [a series of] menu screens"; the novice can use built-in help functions.

The library market is the primary target for these databases. SilverPlatter envisions both librarians and end users using the CD-ROM databases. Because of the wide range of databases available, SilverPlatter is an exciting alternative to online remote-databases searching for academic, public, and school libraries. For more information: Chris Pooley, SilverPlatter Information Inc., 37 Walnut St., Wellesley, MA 02181; (617) 239-0306.

UNIVERSITY MICROFILMS INTERNATIONAL

University Microfilms International (UMI) now has both CD-ROM and 12-inch optical disc databases. Products include *ABI/INFORM*, *Newspaper Abstracts*, *Periodicals Abstracts*, and the *Dissertation Abstracts* databases. Unlike other optical disc products, UMI envisions combining remote and local database searching. An IDS 1000 and business work stations are available. Yearly subscriptions include bimonthly updates.

For more information contact: Christine Ellis Gordon, University Microfilms International, 300 N. Zeeb Rd., Ann Arbor, MI 48106-1346; (313) 761-4700 or (800) 732-0616.

CD-ROM GUIDEBOOK

One indication of the expanding number of CD-ROM applications is the 1987 publication of *Optical Publishing Directory*, a CD-ROM guidebook. Aimed at the library market, the *Directory* lists CD-ROM technology, publications, peripherals, and services. It concentrates on databases and "data products."

For more information contact: Learned Information, 143 Old Marlton Pike, Medford, NJ 08055-8707; (609) 654-6266. ■

CD-ROM in 1986*

Databases on CD-ROM (compact disk-read only memory) were the biggest news in the database industry in 1986. During the year, many new CD products became available, others were announced as forthcoming, and some of the big names in the information industry (e.g., DIALOG and H. W. Wilson) entered the CD marketplace. It was also a year of uncertainty and flux, with Digital Equipment Corporation (DEC) entering the market in the spring only to suspend its database distribution in the fall, prices of CD products changing frequently, and the number of users not yet approaching the projected figures. The professional literature was replete with articles explaining potential benefits of databases on CD-ROM; in addition, several books on the topic were published (see "References").

CD-ROM allows database producers to distribute copies of their databases on a medium that is more durable than magnetic disks and that provides high density capacity (up to 600 megabytes per 4¾-inch disk). Libraries can offer unlimited end-user searching of these locally held databases, because they are priced on a subscription basis rather than on a connect-time basis and because the hardware, software, and database are all under local control rather than being reliant on telecommunications networks.

Although the potential for use of and impact of CD-ROM on libraries, publishers, and the online industry is expected to be profound, most experts predict a coexistence of technologies. CD is expected to be used in libraries with high volume online use of particular databases for retrospective searching by end-users, in libraries that want to budget and pay ahead for searching, and in areas where telecommunications is a problem. Online access is expected to be used for current searches, searches on less-used databases, and searching by libraries that do not want to commit themselves to the upfront subscription costs of laser discs. Print is expected to continue to coexist with online and CD and to continue as most publishers' main revenue source for many years to come.

Because laser discs are a new distribution medium for databases, there are still several unresolved problems. Different products use different software, making it difficult for a library to provide access to all the databases it wants. Laser discs are not yet standardized, so every disc cannot be played on the same disc player peripheral. Investments in multiple microcomputer workstations make start-up costs high for the library. Most laser disc updates are sent monthly, quarterly, or yearly so the information is not usually as current as corresponding online products. Finally, because the industry is so new, it is easy to get confused over who is in the business, what products are offered, and how laser discs will complement or replace online or printed products. This article discusses some of the developments in this area during 1986.

DEC BOWS OUT

The instability of CD-ROM products is demonstrated by the exit of DEC from the CD-ROM database publishing market. DEC had agreements with several large database producers including Engineering Index, NTIS, and Chemical Abstracts to produce and market subsets of their databases on CD-ROM. DEC's ambitious plans at the beginning of 1986 included future development of an entire "library" of CD-ROM databases. Instead, after only six months as database publishers, DEC decided to refocus on their traditional strengths of hardware, software, and services rather than continuing in publishing.

DEC still provides private compact disc production for in-house databases or for publishers who want to market their own databases. They also sell CD-ROM players and search software. For a library this private production service could be a way to distribute the online library catalog to remote sites or it could be used as a backup to the online catalog.

Mary Berger of Engineering Index (EI), one of the database producers affected by DEC's decision, spoke at the 1986 Annual Meeting of the American Society for Information Science. Berger discussed three areas of consideration for database publishers who are contemplating CD-ROM products.

The first area is *financial/business*. EI believed one advantage of CD-ROM over online was that they would maintain more control over their database. In reality, CD-ROM products are usually joint ventures involving, in addition to the database producers, software firms, disc mastering organizations, hardware vendors, and financial backers. Publishers do get more customer data than they do with their online products, but complete control is still not in the publisher's hands. In addition, the price of CD-ROM products must be set with the online, printed, and magnetic tape products in mind so no one customer segment is alienated.

The second area mentioned by Berger is *marketing*. EI first thought that CD-ROM would be a great way to tap new end-user customers, but they found that the existing online customers were most ready to adopt the new technology. Because they are experienced searchers, these existing customers want software with search features and access speeds comparable to online.

Berger's final consideration is *product design*. CD-ROM databases are so new that no one is sure how best to package the information. EI marketed three subsets by topic, a tactic that Berger said seemed to confuse customers. It was difficult for the customers to understand what was on each disc; they would have preferred the entire database divided by publication years.

Other packaging options would be to put partial records from a complete database on a disc (e.g., everything except abstracts), to put more than one database on a disc, or to mix bibliographic information with relevant numeric or full text sources. This last option is "where we ought to be headed" according to Berger, because "we don't want CD-ROM to turn into another microfilm, a convenient storage medium."[1]

NEW PRODUCTS

Although DEC's exit has removed some databases from the market, there seems to be an almost continual offering of new CD-ROM databases. A four-part directory by Bruce Connolly in *Database* and *Online* magazines has attempted to describe and keep current with all of the laser disc databases on the market.[2]

Laser disc databases are now available for many bibliographic sources, including PsycLIT, ERIC, AV-Online, Sociofile, and Excerpta Medica, all from SilverPlatter, Inc.; Aquatic Sciences and Fisheries Abstracts, Life Sciences, and MEDLINE, all from Cambridge Scientific Abstracts; ABI/INFORM and others from UMI/DataCourier; Science Citation Index from ISI; Dissertation Abstracts; Microreviews from Knowledge Access, Inc.; Government Periodicals Index, LegalTrac, InfoTrac, and Magazine Index from Information Access Company (IAC); and Wilson indexes from the H. W. Wilson Company. Source databases include Grolier Electronic Encyclopedia; Poisindex, Drugdex, Emergindex, and Identidex from Micromedex, Inc.; DISCLOSURE; full text of The Wall Street Journal from IAC; Business Research and Marquis Who's Who from Datext, Inc.; EBSCO Serials Directory and Occupational Health and Safety Information from SilverPlatter; and Books in Print and Ulrich's from R. R. Bowker.

Some of the new CD-ROM products that are of the most general interest to libraries are discussed below.

WILSONDISC

At the ALA meeting in January 1987 the H. W. Wilson Company announced the upcoming availability of their CD-ROM WILSONDISC. Twelve of the Wilson indexes are available as separate CD products. Each disc contains retrospective information corresponding to the date the index went online, providing retrospective coverage ranging from early 1981 to December 1984. Index to Legal Periodicals, for example, includes references from August 1981, Readers' Guide to Periodical Literature from January 1983, Education Index from December 1983, and Library Literature from December 1984. Each CD database is updated (and cumulated) quarterly. The annual subscription price ranges from $1,095 to $1,495 per index.

The WILSONDISC search software offers several choices for searchers with different levels of experience. Intermediary searchers may choose to use a replica of the regular WILSONLINE system or "Expert WILSONLINE" commands if they are very experienced. Less experienced searchers might opt to search WILSONDISC with the end-user WILSEARCH software or an even simpler "browse mode" system, where users rely on paging through an alphabetical list of subject headings.

With a modem and a WILSONLINE account, users of the CD-ROM database can use the same microcomputer workstation to dial-up the Wilson mainframe system. A compact disc subscription includes unlimited online searching on the corresponding online database. The subscriber pays only for the telecommunications charges. This enlightened policy will allow great flexibility for intermediaries, as they can immediately and inexpensively update a CD-ROM search with the more current materials that are only available online. The Wilson workstation acts as a combination CD-ROM system, front-end, and online system for a single subscription fee. All of the appropriate hardware and software can be purchased from the H. W. Wilson Company for a price of $4,995 for the complete workstation.

INFOTRAC II

On 15 December 1986 Information Access Company added a CD-ROM product to their twelve-inch laser disc InfoTrac product line. "InfoTrac II" covers Magazine Index citations for the current year and three back years, plus three months of current indexing for The New York Times. Subscriptions to InfoTrac II include a microcomputer workstation with built-in CD-ROM player, a printer, software, and monthly updates. The cost is $4,500 per year.

InfoTrac II search software provides the same simplified searching that comes with the InfoTrac I system. Searching is done by browsing modified LC subject headings; no free text searching or Boolean combinations are allowed.

R. R. BOWKER

R. R. Bowker Company introduced CD-ROM versions of two of their popular reference works this fall. Books in Print (BIP Plus) includes the 1986-1987 records for the entire Books in Print series (including *Books in Print, Subject Guide to Books in Print, Books in Print Supplement, Forthcoming Books,* and *Subject Guide to Forthcoming Books*). In addition, the disc contains names and addresses of publishers.

Ulrich's Plus includes records from the 1986-1987 editions of *Ulrich's International Periodicals Directory, Irregular Serials and Annuals, International Serials Database Update* plus an ISSN index and addresses of periodical publishers.

Both databases will be updated quarterly. Prices for the database with software are $895 for BIP Plus and $395 for Ulrich's Plus.

SILVERPLATTER

SilverPlatter's databases have been available for several months, but prices were revised this fall. An "ERIC CD-ROM starter kit" is available for $1,550 per year. This includes a disc with the three most recent years of ERIC records (including abstracts) which will be updated annually. The starter kit also includes a CD-ROM disc drive and the SilverPlatter retrieval software, which includes such features as Boolean combinations, truncation, and free-text searching. Libraries must have their own IBM PC computer.

Backfiles of ERIC may also be purchased on CD-ROM. Records from 1966 to 1982 for Resources in Education (RIE) are available for $1,500. Current Index to Journals in Education (CIJE) covers 1969-1982 for $750. Both archival sets (three discs) sell for $2,000. New SilverPlatter pricing options are also available for the PsycLIT database from the American Psychological Association. Both a retrospective and current disc, each including citations and abstracts to the journal literature portion of PsycINFO, are available for lease. The retrospective disc covers the period 1974-1982 and now costs $1,495 for the first year of use. Each subsequent year costs $1,195. The current disc (1981-) is updated quarterly for an annual subscription price of $3,500. There are discounts of 10 percent for subscribers to *Psychological Abstracts* in print.

DIALOG ONDISC

DIALOG announced its entry into the CD marketplace at the end of the year. The first database OnDisc is ERIC (since it is in the public domain and, appropriately, was DIALOG's first database online). ERIC OnDisc includes the entire ERIC database from 1966 to the present on a three-disc set for $3,450. The annual fee for the current disc only (1981-) is $1,950. The current disc will be updated quarterly.

The DIALOG OnDisc search software offers two search options. Experienced searchers can search using the standard DIALOG commands or novice searchers can select a simpler menu-driven version. (The OnDisc search software is more attractive than online DIALOG, making use of color and word highlighting.) As with the Wilson disc system, DIALOG OnDisc searches can be saved and uploaded to the full online system for current awareness searching.

DIALOG is planning an entire family of CD databases in the future. Six additional products will be introduced in 1987 aimed at different vertical markets.

STANDARDS

A problem for CD-ROM consumers has been the lack of standardization. The lack of a disc formatting standard means that one cannot simply purchase a CD-ROM player and assume it will work with all discs purchased. Many database producers have gotten into the business of leasing or selling CD-ROM players to ensure compatibility. A proposed ANSI standard for CD-ROM is being voted on by members of the National Information Standards Organization (NISO) in late 1986.

The "High Sierra Group," a group of computer manufacturers, developed this proposed standard. The standard deals with volume and file structures—where information is located on each disc and how that information is addressed by the computer. (Standards for things such as external labeling and bibliographic description may be separate standards developed later.) The European Computer Manufacturers Association has proposed a similar data structure standard to the International Standards Organization, so a compatible United States-international standard for CD-ROM may be forthcoming. Detailed technical explanations of the standard can be found in *CD-ROM Standards: The Book*.[3]

CD-ROM SURVEY

Sociological Abstracts included a questionnaire on CD use in its April 1986 *Note Us* newsletter. Preliminary findings (reported in the October 1986 *Note Us*) showed that 34.5 percent of the respondents felt they would have a CD-ROM search station installed in their facility between 1986 and 1988. Only 23.4 percent felt they would not; the rest either did not know or had no answer.

Respondents were divided on what should be included in a Sociological Abstracts CD-ROM product, but by far the largest number (33.9 percent) favored the entire database from 1963 onwards. The second most popular choice (17 percent) was English-language entries from 1974 onwards. Price was definitely a factor in potential use, with only 0.6 percent indicating they would be likely to subscribe to the CD-ROM product in 1986 or early 1987 if the cost was between $4,000 and $6,000 per year.

CONCLUSION

The Sociological Abstracts survey and observations made by Mary Berger of Engineering Abstracts help to summarize the current state of the CD-ROM database market. Berger's observations included the following:

- The existing online marketplace will be the first to adopt CD-ROM.

- Users need computer literacy because it is more difficult to get the CD-ROM database system up than it is to start online searching.

- Intermediaries will introduce end-users to CD-ROM.

- Database producers have a "long sell" and will not realize quick payoffs. Potential customers need many demonstrations before they are ready to purchase and much hand holding once they purchase the CD-ROM system.

- Training and hotline services are needed for CD-ROM databases just as they are for online.

- CD-ROM products should be different products or be aimed at new users rather than just replicating the online database.

- Software must be up to par in terms of access speeds and search capabilities.[4]

The following are further observations on the CD-ROM market.

- Lower cost products are needed if the CD-ROM potential is to be fully realized.

- Many users want complete databases on CD or segregation by time periods.

- Online will be used to supplement CD use for current information or seldom used databases.

- Users would like database discs to be compatible so they can use the same equipment to access multiple databases.

As it evident from this review, CD-ROM, like all new technologies, remains in its infancy. A review of progress five years from now will likely make 1986 developments look primitive indeed.

NOTES

[1]Mary Berger, "CD-ROM and Optical Publishing" (Paper delivered at the 49th Annual Meeting of the American Society for Information Science, Chicago, 28 September-30 October 1986).

[2]Bruce Connolly, "Laserdisk Directory, Part 1," *Database* 9 (June 1986): 15-26; "Part 2," *Online* 10 (July 1986): 39-49; "Part 3," *Database* 9 (August 1986): 34-39; "Part 4," *Online* 10 (September 1986): 54-58.

[3]Julie B. Schwerin, et al., *CD-ROM Standards: The Book* (Medford, N.J., Learned Information, Inc., 1986).

[4]Berger, "CD-ROM and Optical Publishing."

REFERENCES

Bowers, Richard A. *Optical/Electronic Publishing Directory*. Carmel Valley, Calif.: Information Arts, December 1985- .

Herther, Nancy K. "Access to Information: Optical Disk Solution." *Wilson Library Bulletin* 60 (May 1986): 19-21.

Herther, Nancy K. "CDROM and Information Dissemination: An Update." *Online* 11 (March 1987): 56-64.

Herther, Nancy K. "CDROM Standards Update." *Database* 9 (June 1986): 87-89.

Herther, Nancy K. "CDROM Technology: A New Era for Information Storage and Retrieval?" *Online* 9 (November 1985): 17-28.

Lambert, Steve, and Suzanne Ropiequet, eds. *CD/ROM: The New Papyrus*. Bellevue, Wash.: Microsoft Press, 1986.

McQueen, Judy, and Richard W. Boss. *Videodisc and Optical Digital Disk Technologies and Their Applications in Libraries, 1986 Update*. Chicago: American Library Association, 1986.

Miller, David C. "Running with CD-ROM." *American Libraries* 17 (November 1986): 754-56.

Murphy, Brower. "CD-ROM and Libraries." *Library Hi Tech* 10 (1985): 21-28.

Schwerin, Julie B., et al. *CD-ROM Standards: The Book*. Medford, N.J.: Learned Information, 1986.

Tenopir, Carol. "Databases on CD-ROM." *Library Journal* 111 (1 March 1986): 68-69. ∎

WHAT'S HAPPENING WITH CD-ROM, PART 1*

Since databases on CD-ROM were first introduced in 1985, developments and new products have appeared regularly. As we begin 1989 we can expect a continued increase in the number of databases on CD-ROM and some innovative enhancements to the products. In addition, a growing number of publications about CD-ROM help all of us keep up with what's happening.

DIRECTORIES

The first challenge facing librarians is just to find out what is available on CD-ROM. Several printed directories help with that challenge.

Optical Publishing Directory (3d ed. Ed. by Richard A. Bowers. $45) was published as a paperback by Learned Information (143 Old Marlton Pike, Medford, NJ 08055-8707) in fall 1988 to replace earlier loose-leaf editions. Complete new editions will be published each year with periodic updates available for purchase between editions. Only products that are actually available are listed—no beta tests, demonstrations, or "vaporware" (announcing or selling a product before it actually exists). The 1988 edition shows 196 real products, up from 128 in 1987.

A one-page description of each product makes up the bulk of the volume. Name, address, and phone number are given for each vendor, as well as descriptive information and price. There are indexes by type of database and by broad topic, as well as the standard subject index. Appendixes provide information about optical database producers, vendors, and manufacturers of CD-ROM drives. The glossary is a nice addition.

*Reprinted from *Library Journal* Feb. 1, 1989. Copyright © 1989 by Reed Publishing, USA, Div. of Reed Holdings, Inc.

A competing and very similar directory is published by Meckler (Meckler Corporation, 11 Ferry Lane W., Westport, CT 06880). *CD-ROM in Print: 1988-1989*, edited by Jean-Paul Emard, is the second edition, replacing the first edition edited by Nancy M. Nelson. The cost of the second edition is $37.50, with a ten percent discount if you place a standing order.

The main part of the directory provides an alphabetically arranged description of CD-ROM titles currently "in print." There are more entries than in the Learned Information directory, probably because the Meckler directory does not follow the rigorous criteria that a product must be ready for shipping to be listed.

Entries include who produces the database, who provides the CD-ROM version, a description of the content, technical specifications, and price. Indexes are provided for database producers, CD vendors, titles, CD-ROM players, as well as subjects. A glossary is included.

Another publication that I have found very useful as a CD-ROM directory and sourcebook is Volume 1, No. 1 (Spring 1988) of *Access Faxon*. Although it includes descriptions and prices of only those CD-ROM titles available from Faxon, it describes those over 60 publications in detail and lists well over 200 titles. Also useful are a list of magazines and books about CD-ROM and articles on training the library staff to use CD and choosing CD-ROM hardware.

Access Faxon will be a semi-annual publication priced at $24 per year. A charter subscription rate of $12 is quoted, but I received one copy of the first issue free in the mail. I was given another by a colleague, and picked up several more at the Online '88 Conference, so I suspect interested libraries can find a free copy of the first issue.

MAGAZINES

Several magazines devoted to CD-ROM are good places to find out about new CD-ROM products, technical issues and standards, and how colleagues are implementing CD-ROM access in a library environment. Some are aimed at the librarian market, others have a wider audience in mind.

CD-ROM Review [o.p.] is a mass market quarterly sold on newsstands or available by subscription ($14.95. IDG Communications/Peterborough, 80 Elm Street, Peterborough, NH 03458). Every issue includes a "Discography," a directory of CD-ROM titles that are commercially available. Arrangement is by CD vendor, with all titles from that vendor, prices, and very short descriptions of each title given. The October 1988 issue included over 80 vendors with a total of over 160 titles.

Each issue contains readable, nontechnical articles that review new products or discuss issues in the CD-ROM marketplace. The October 1988 issue, for example, had an article on the *Oxford English Dictionary* on CD-ROM, one on vaporware, and one on voice synthesis for the blind. A most useful feature of this magazine is the many advertisements and new product descriptions.

CD-ROM Librarian, as its name implies, has a much narrower audience. It is published ten times per year by Meckler Corporation for $65 per year. "Optical News" and ads keep librarians up-to-date with new products or enhancements. Articles tend to focus on detailed product reviews and descriptions about specific problems or applications. Knowledge of CD-ROM technology and its use in library settings is assumed.

To illustrate the difference between *CD-ROM Librarian* and *CD-ROM Review*, compare the review of the *Oxford English Dictionary* in the July/August 1988 issue of the former with the October 1988 review in the latter. *CD-ROM Review*'s three-page article (two are text, one is a picture) is titled "CD-ROM Rocks the Ox." The *CD-ROM Librarian*'s version is six pages including tables with the title "*Oxford English Dictionary* on Compact Disc." *CD-ROM Review*'s is almost leisure reading, the *CD-ROM Librarian* article requires concentration (and some motivation). One is not necessarily better than the other (they both reach the same basic conclusion about the *OED* on disc), but they are useful for different audiences and different purposes. If you don't need the technical detail, *CD-ROM Review* has broader appeal and is more consistently readable.

Meckler also publishes *Optical Information Systems* (bi-m. $95) and *Optical Information Systems Update* (18/yr. $227), useful for database producers, educators, and others involved with optical discs.

In spring 1988, Online Inc. spun off a new publication to join *Online* and *Database*. *The Laserdisk Professional* (6/yr. $86. Pemberton Press Inc., 11 Tannery Lane, Weston, CT 06883), aimed at the library/information professional market, has a very practical and focused mission. First-year issues contained articles on such things as: how a university library runs a CD-ROM searching program; reports from OCLC on how their customers use CD-ROM; and evaluation and comparison of CD-ROM products in particular subject areas. Articles are written by librarians and others who are working with CD-ROM products on a regular basis.

The "Laserdisk News" section covers the latest news and products in the field and editorials provide insights into important issues. There are several regular columns covering such things as book reviews, journal article reviews, hardware, software, public access issues, and Canadian viewpoints. Photographs, charts, and tables enhance the visual appeal of *The Laserdisk Professional* without being overused (as sometimes happens in a publication such as *CD-ROM Review*).

MAJOR PRODUCTS AND PRODUCERS

Librarians who as yet have no CD-ROM products in their libraries may wonder about the companies that sell or produce these products and what kind of products are available. Many of the databases are made available by publishers or online vendors that already have a firm foothold in the library market, others come from new names. According to most estimates, there are now over 200 CD-ROM products commercially available from over 100 database producers or CD vendors. Many of the 200 databases are CD-ROM versions of existing online databases (which are in turn online versions of existing print publications).

What type of products are available on CD-ROM? The 1988 edition of *Optical Publishing Directory* shows there is a wide range of topics and types available within the almost 200 commercially available CD-ROM databases. General reference is the largest category at 17 percent. Business, scientific, and education/social science each account for approximately 12 percent, computer science/engineering has ten percent, and medicine has nine percent. Directories, government, law, and library automation each provide about six percent, with the remaining miscellaneous. A majority of the databases are bibliographic or bibliographic with abstracts (41 percent), 28 percent are "reference," 18 percent full text, nine percent statistical, and five percent images or sound.

An article in the November 1988 *Laserdisk Professional* (Paul Travis Nicholls, "Statistical Profile of Currently Available CD-ROM Database Products," p. 38-45) analyzed the content of the 1987 edition of Bowers's *Optical Publishing Directory*. A cursory check of the 1988 edition suggests that the profile is essentially the same, even though it contains more than 50 percent more titles.

The 1987 CD databases were mostly updated quarterly (48 percent) or less often (26 percent). Monthly or bimonthly updates were provided for 18 percent of the databases and weekly, eight percent. Business or general databases were updated most frequently. A trend toward allowing a user to select more frequent updates started in 1988 and will certainly continue in 1989.

In 1987 almost all CD products had a print or online equivalent. About half of the CD-ROM databases were also available both in print and online, an additional 35 percent were available only online. As the CD industry matures, more print publishers will elect to go directly to CD-ROM when they start electronic publishing and many more original publications will be available only on CD-ROM. Innovation in this relatively new medium is really just beginning. Innovation may mean repackaging or combining existing materials, providing new search features, or offering more visual appeal.

Some examples of innovation include: Science Citation Index, Compact Disc Edition from the Institute for Scientific Information (ISI), that offers a unique "related records" search feature; a planned series of products from OCLC that will combine full text from a variety of publications such as *Twayne's United States Authors Series* with relevant portions of the OCLC Online Union Catalog; and the Electronic Anthology of Art from EBook, Inc. and EBSCO that will include electronic pictures of art work in addition to fully searchable text describing the work and the artist.

THIRD-PARTY VENDORS

Just like in the online world, CD-ROM has some database producers that also sell their products directly and some that choose to go through a database vendor. Third-party vendors that make many databases available and are well established in the library marketplace include SilverPlatter, DIALOG Ondisc, OCLC, and EBSCO. (OCLC and EBSCO produce some products as well as vend others.) Major database producers familiar to libraries that have decided to produce and sell their own CD databases include: H. W. Wilson Company, UMI/DataCourier, R. R. Bowker, Institute for Scientific Information, Cambridge Scientific Abstracts, John Wiley & Sons, PAIS, and others.

Librarians are faced with the task of evaluating not only the content of each database offered by each of these companies, but evaluating the search/retrieval software as well. Over 55 different search software packages are in use. The third-party vendors all use proprietary software developed especially for all of their products. One major advantage of selecting several databases through a vendor such as SilverPlatter is that all will use the same search software.

Database producers that elect to produce their own CD products either develop proprietary software or contract to use a CD-ROM software company's software. Nicholls found in 1987 that about one-half of the total number of CD products then available had proprietary software used for a single product only. The rest of the products used one of only seven different software programs: SilverPlatter, Wilson, FindIT, OCLC Search CD450, Lotus, Online Computer Systems, or TMS. The impact on the time of library staff members to evaluate, learn, and teach users the various software interfaces has yet to be measured. ■

INFOTRAC
A Laser Disc System*

Of all the databases on laser disc that are now available, only Information Access Company's *InfoTrac*™ has been used long enough in enough libraries to provide data on customer satisfaction and usage. Nearly 300 libraries now use the *InfoTrac* system, 85 percent of which are academic libraries and 15 percent of which are public libraries. Several libraries have monitored usage or surveyed users.

INFO ON *INFOTRAC*

InfoTrac provides bibliographic records from over 2,000 business, technical, and general interest magazines and newspapers. One 12-inch laser disc contains records from the current year plus retrospective records for three years. A newly available back-file disc contains retrospective information back to 1980.

Subject headings are based on the Library of Congress Subject Headings; there are no abstracts. The full text of many of the articles is available on microfilm with subscriptions to IAC's *Business Collection* and *Magazine Collection*.

Most subscribers to *InfoTrac* elect to lease a complete turnkey system from IAC, which includes from one to five microcomputer workstations and inkjet printers, a laserdisc player, retrieval software, and the monthly updated database on laser disc. Prices per year vary with the hardware

*Reprinted from *Library Journal* Sept. 1, 1986. Copyright © 1986 by Reed Publishing, USA, Div. of Reed Holdings, Inc.

configuration, but a two-workstation system is $12,000 annually. An optional package comes equipped with modem and software to allow connection to online databases and downloading to floppy disk.

USERS' REACTIONS

The opinions and information reported here are taken from surveys and comments from several libraries: Roesch Library, University of Dayton; Hamilton Library, University of Hawaii; Salt Lake County Library System; Colorado State University Libraries; University of California, San Diego Library; Indiana University Libraries; and Meriam Library, California State University, Chico.

All of these libraries report overwhelming user acceptance of *InfoTrac*. Typical comments from various sites include: "It's fantastic, great. I love it!"; "Fast, easy to use"; "I think this *InfoTrac* is fantastic. I hope it'll be here permanently"; "It's fast, easy, and prints the citations needed quickly and quietly. It's great!"; "Please keep it! This is the best. In fact, if possible, get more." And my favorite: "YAHOO!"

Waiting lines at *InfoTrac* workstations developed at several libraries, causing some to impose time limits of between 10 to 30 minutes.

Most academic libraries found that the heaviest (and most enthusiastic) use comes from undergraduates who are using it instead of general printed indexes. A wide majority of undergraduate users in all libraries indicated they found useful references on their topics and that they preferred *InfoTrac* over printed indexes.

Graduate students and faculty users are more often critical of the system. Although a majority in all surveys are positive about *InfoTrac*, these research-oriented users are more likely to question the journal coverage in the system, to complain about the lack of retrospective material, and to ask for similar systems with different subject focus. *InfoTrac* is used as a supplemental tool, not as a complete research tool.

Most librarians agree with this perception. Several librarians commented that the journals indexed in *InfoTrac* make it appropriate for general topic searches and business searches, but most of the journals are not research sources.

The University of Hawaii has placed a cautionary note near the *InfoTrac* terminals. It warns users: "ATTENTION: To achieve a comprehensive search for references please use other appropriate printed subject indexes. Please see the reference librarian for help."

Several librarians indicated they felt uncomfortable with the unquestioning assumption by many students that a computer tool must be comprehensive and of higher quality than a printed index. One librarian commented, "I am torn. Students like *InfoTrac* so much and seem to be pleased with their results. Yet I know what they are *not* getting by relying on this one source."

Still, for most users, what they *do* get is sufficient. Some librarians commented that *InfoTrac* seems to be bringing users into the library who never used the printed sources anyway. A university library director believes "the public relations value of the system overcomes any shortcomings and is well worth the cost."

DOCUMENT DELIVERY

Many users asked that call numbers of the journals be displayed in the *InfoTrac* citations or wished it only indexed the journals held by their library. There seems to be some confusion among users over just what is included in the system. Several users in each library obviously confused it with the library card, COM, or online catalog; others couldn't understand why something found on *InfoTrac* couldn't be found in the library. (IAC says that to master a custom disc that would just contain one library's collection and call numbers would be prohibitively expensive. Perhaps this will be a viable option for large library systems in the future or perhaps the *InfoTrac* data can be linked with a library's journal holdings via the online catalog.)

One faculty member in a university library had bigger plans: "This is great. Now if you can only get the journal article to pop up on the screen." Libraries that use *InfoTrac* in conjunction with IAC's microfilm document collections (about 20 percent of all *InfoTrac* subscribers) report enthusiastic response. Many *InfoTrac* citations contain a microfilm collection access number that correponds to the full text of the article on the *Business Collection* or *Magazine Collection* film.

Stan Workman of the Salt Lake County Library System comments on the use of the microfilm collections in conjunction with *InfoTrac*:

> We are presently operating with a central Periodicals Resource Center at headquarters which is equipped with two *Magazine Indexes*, two *Magazine Collections*, one *Business Index*, one *Business Collection*, and four *InfoTrac* stations. This area is staffed during most of our service hours with clerks who provide service to our branches by receiving requests by telephone from patrons, obtaining articles from these services and sending the article(s) via high-speed telecopiers.
>
> Thus far we have reduced our periodical subscriptions by about 25 titles, eliminating unnecessary duplication with *InfoTrac* and *Magazine Collection* coverage. We are committed to expanding these services to other branches as quickly as budget will allow. Being able to deliver full text on the spot is very gratifying after years of checked out, lost, or mutilated periodicals.

EASE OF USE

Almost all users, even those who have never used computers before, found *InfoTrac* easy to use. Librarians observed that once *InfoTrac* was "discovered" by someone, they would often bring in their friends and teach them how to use it. One academic librarian commented "I think we have overestimated the need for training on this type of system. Minimal written instructions and peer teaching seem to be working fine."

InfoTrac is simple to use. It uses subject heading access and displays records under a subject heading plus subject headings alphabetically near the chosen heading. No Boolean combinations of terms or free-text searching are allowed. Printing desired citations is done by hitting a print key.

This simplicity of searching imposes some limitations, of course. Because terms cannot be combined, complex searches are not possible. There are many subdivisions of subject headings, necessitating entry at the correct alphabetical spot and paging through screens of references or the thesaurus to find the precise subject desired. Librarians note that this is not always realized by users. Users have been observed reading through long lists of citations under broad subject headings to find those few citations exactly on their topic. (They don't seem to mind, however.)

Searching *InfoTrac* is basically the same as searching a printed index, but with the convenience of a printer attached. (This convenience should not be underestimated. It was mentioned many times by users in all surveys.) Some users and librarians point out that serendipity is easier in a printed index. More cross-references are needed in *InfoTrac*, as is better quality control of spelling and subject formats. (Salomon Brothers Inc. is entered in at least eight different ways.)

Most libraries report that *InfoTrac* installation is relatively easy ("especially if you have a systems office"). Start-up and shut-down each day take from between five and ten minutes, but at least one library has elected to leave the system up 24 hours. Most have found the hardware to be reliable if in-house wiring is reliable. There are the occasional users who remove the *InfoTrac* software from the floppy drives and use the computers for word processing, but no libraries report continual problems.

The one equipment inconvenience mentioned by many users of *InfoTrac* is the Hewlett-Packard Thinkjet printers. Although the printers are quiet, problems with paper jams, dirty print heads, and ink cartridges that frequently have to be replaced are annoying to reference librarians.

OTHER PRODUCTS

IAC has added other laser disc databases since the success of the *InfoTrac* system. These other systems use the *InfoTrac* software and are compatible with *InfoTrac* hardware.

A backfile disc of *InfoTrac* takes the citations back to 1980. This first backfile will eventually contain four years of citations, while the current *InfoTrac* system will always include the current and three previous years.

LegalTrac provides indexing to over 800 law journals, newspapers, and other legal publications from 1980 to the present. It is the laser disc equivalent of IAC's *Legal Resources Index* database. *Government Publications Index* includes eight years of *GPO Monthly Catalog*. Updates to both *LegalTrac* and *GPI* are monthly. They may be purchased on the same or separate discs. Also available are *Academic Index*, *National Newspaper Index*, *Health Index*, and *General Periodicals Index*.

CONCLUSION

Any shortcomings of the *InfoTrac* system are not apparent or not important to most users. Users are almost universally enthusiastic about their first encounter with a laser disc system. The system makes library research more interesting and tolerable, and the potential for additional systems with broader subject coverage is exciting to users and librarians alike.

Such in-house laser disc databases provide an attractive alternative or supplement to printed indexes. They also provide a way to introduce end user searching of databases, but with a predictable cost.

FURTHER READING

Beltran, Ann Bristow. "Use of *InfoTrac* in a University Library." *Database*, June 1986, p. 63-66. (Indiana University Libraries).

Earnest, Douglas J. & Jennifer Monath. "User Reaction to a Computerized Periodical Index." *College and Research Library News*, May 1986, p. 315-318. (Colorado State University).

Pease, Barbara & William Post. "*InfoTrac*: a Review of an Optical Disc-Based Public Index." *Serials Review Winter 1985*. (California State University, Chico).

Stephens, Kent. "Laserdisc Technology Enters Mainstream: Easy-to-Use Periodical Index Gets Heavy Use at California University." *American Libraries*, April 1986, p. 252. (California State University, Chico). ■

PUBLICATIONS ON CD-ROM
Librarians Can Make A Difference*

CD-ROM products were featured many times this summer at the annual meetings of the Special Libraries Association and the American Library Association. A full-day special session on "What Is CD-ROM and Why Should We Care?" drew over 500 people at SLA. At ALA, the Technology in Public Libraries Committee of the Public Library Association attracted an even larger audience for their day-long program on the "Implications of CD-ROM for the Public Library." The Library and Information Technology Association held a two-day pre-ALA conference on "Optical Publishing and Libraries: Cheers or Tears?"

In the midst of many overviews of CD-ROM technology and the descriptions of specific products or applications, one recurring theme emerged. Attendees were reminded over and over again that because CD-ROM publishing is still in its infancy, librarians are in a good position to help direct the future development of CD-ROM products. Libraries are often first with a CD-ROM player and are frequently the first market for many CD-ROM publications. Libraries have a large constituency that allows them to test products and a knowledgeable staff to help with evaluation.

CDs AND THE LIBRARY MARKETPLACE

The state of the CD marketplace was presented to special librarians by Nancy Melin Nelson, editor of Meckler's *CD-ROM Librarian* (formerly, *Optical Information Systems Update/Library and Information Center Applications*). She said that approximately half of the CD products currently available are being marketed to the information specialist, a trend that contradicts earlier market projections. The library market is strong because it has a base of installed CD drives and many libraries are eager to try out new information technologies. As of June 1987 there were over 100 different CD products for the library market listed in Meckler's annual publication, *Guide to CD-ROMs in Print*. (Learned Information also publishes an annual directory: *Optical Publishing Directory 1987* by Richard Bowers includes over 80 available products.)

Nelson separated CD products for libraries into four categories. **Cataloging Support** saw the first CD product on the market (*BiblioFile*). There are now over 500 *BiblioFile* installations. Many other library service and supply companies such as EBSCO, Faxon, and OCLC are bringing cataloging back to the local level with CD cataloging support databases. **Online Public Access Catalogs** are more recent applications for CD-ROM technology. CD OPACs can now be created by many firms, e.g., Brodart, Auto-Graphics, and WLN.

Collection Development is gaining rapid acceptance in libraries, notably with *Books in Print Plus* and *Ulrich's Plus* from Bowker and *Lasersearch* from Ingram. The fourth category provides the greatest number of CD products; **Reference**

Support accounts for 80 of the 100 products counted by Nelson. Most of them are CD versions of textual databases that are already online. Since they are already in machine-readable form it is easier to create a new product quickly.

PUBLISHERS RESPONDING TO USERS' NEEDS

New CD publications will not necessarily just be copies of existing online databases. Publishers need to know what types of publications or combinations of publications are wanted. CD publishers are beginning to provide more innovative products in response to users' needs. Microsoft's *Bookshelf* combines ten reference publications on one disc. *Bookshelf* includes the *The American Heritage Dictionary, Bartlett's Familiar Quotations, Roget's Thesaurus,* the *1987 World Almanac and Book of Facts,* the *U.S. Zip Code Directory,* the *Chicago Manual of Style, Business Information Sources, Houghton Mifflin Spelling Verifier and Corrector, Houghton Mifflin Usage Alert,* and a collection of forms and letters. All this for under $300!

Bookshelf is meant to be used in conjunction with a word processing program, allowing an author to verify words or facts, or to add information to a text from one of the source publications. (A copyright notice is automatically transferred and only a limited number of lines of text can be transferred at one time.) Microsoft is planning a *Legal Bookshelf, Medical Bookshelf,* and similar products.

Librarians can probably think of many other useful combinations of publications. Nelson mentioned as one example the need for a combined *Index to Legal Periodicals* and *LEXIS.*

Gary Kindall of KnowledgeSet, the developer of CP/M and co-host of *Computer Chronicles* on PBS, spoke on the future of CD-ROM. He sees the possibilities of interconnecting knowledge as the most exciting future potential of CD-ROM. The random access and high-density storage capabilities allow CD publications to overcome the linear nature of a book. Information within documents can be related by topics, not by artificial page boundaries. Subject associations are built into each document so each user can retrieve related information dynamically as desired.

Text, graphics, sound, and motion will all coexist in future optical publications. The subject links will allow each user to retrieve the information and form of most interest to them. The vision of Vannevar Bush in his classic 1945 article in *Atlantic,* "As We May Think," and Ted Nelson's "Hypertext" of the 1960s may be fulfilled with optical technology. (For a good description of hypertext as it relates to CD-ROM, see T. J. Byers, "Built by Association," *PC World,* April 1987, p. 244-251, one of seven articles in the issue's "CD-ROM Special Report.") Imagination and guidance are needed to create useful and creative new publications.

PRACTICAL ADMINISTRATION POLICIES

In addition to the content of the CDs, publishers and libraries need practical information about administrative aspects of the new technology. Many questions still need to be answered, such as: How frequently should discs be updated? What software features and search techniques work best? What kind of hybrid systems (such as links between online and "ondisc" databases) are desired?

Nelson described a joint project between the nonprofit Alexandria Institute in Boulder, Colorado and Melin-Nelson Associates to put together a group of ten key libraries across the United States that would serve as testing grounds for CD products. These test libraries would help provide information to other libraries about the space needed for CD-ROM publications, staff requirements, and environmental requirements. They would work closely with the publishers to help develop better products and ensure CD is integrated successfully into the library environment.

LIBRARIANS & PRODUCT DEVELOPMENT

The potential important role of librarians in CD product development was mentioned by several speakers at the LITA preconference. Tom Lopez, vice president of the CD-ROM Division of Microsoft, told of some ways libraries and librarians can help in the development stage:

- Serve as Beta test sites and/or set up demonstrations of CD products. Formal and informal user reactions can be communicated to publishers.

- Help design new products by talking to end users to discover what publications are needed on CD-ROM and to help publishers develop better search techniques and better user interfaces.

- Understand cost and space issues to make the best choices and to help other libraries plan for the future.

- Assume a new role in education and distribution of information.

Lopez urged librarians to enter the challenge of creative, innovative CD products. "Technologists will work out the bugs" of the optical medium, he said, but it takes "creative people who will design products that people will enjoy." Value adding in new CD publications will go beyond the indexing and abstracting librarians do today to include specialized indexes for different types of users, cross references across data types (e.g., the telephone directory with an atlas), and the dynamic links of hypertext. Both the contents and the software can add value. Lopez's goal is "to make information retrieval as easy to use as an automatic teller machine."

Ron Dunn, director of Washington operations of the American Chemical Society, emphasized the immediate potential and challenge to librarians at this stage in CD development. He urged librarians to understand the implications of CD in the library in terms of: hardware, space, demand,

security, coexistence of media for different users and different uses, and costs. Publishers haven't always set sensible prices for their CD products, partly because of fear of migration from printed products to discs and partly because they don't really know what is a sensible price. Librarians have already helped send CD prices down by not purchasing products that initially were priced too high.

Librarians can also influence product design. "Don't just accept what's given to you," Dunn challenged, but do let publishers know the types of products you would buy."

LITA distributed a 99-page report on optical publishing prepared by David C. Miller of DCM Associates. *Special Report: Publishers, Libraries, and CD-ROM; Implications of Digital Optical Printing* is $12 per copy prepaid from: LITA/ALA, 50 E. Huron St., Chicago, IL 60611-2729.

TAKING ON THE CHALLENGE

Parke Lightbown, vice president of Utlas, concluded his talk on standards at the PLA workshop with a list of actions that libraries should take now. First of all he urged librarians to "take on the challenge" of assuming a leadership role in the CD publication industry. The market hasn't yet taken off with the public as it will in the near future, so librarians can establish themselves early as leaders and make a difference in the products and prices offered. "Money talks" and if libraries buy right now the "vendors are listening," he said. It means being willing to spend some money now, some on products that might not be used until next year.

Once products are purchased, Lightbown urged librarians to take the time to evaluate them and respond with serious thought. Communicate with publishers in writing about what you like and what you don't like about the products. Tell them about future enhancements or products you would like to see.

Lightbown recommended that libraries only purchase discs that conform to the High Sierra data format standard. This standard is being voted on in 1987 by both NISO (National Information Standards Organization) and ISO (International Standards Organization). Also watch for and contribute to user interface standards. A NISO committee under Charles Hildreth is now working on the issue of a common command language and interface for information retrieval systems. The proliferation of CD-ROM publications makes the problem of many different software interfaces even more evident.

Librarians are also involved in developing a standard for description of the contents of CD publications. Catalogers may already be having nightmares at the thought of ten or more different books placed on one CD-ROM. Other unique cataloging challenges such as parts of several books intermixed with sound and graphics or elimination of the static page reference system (How will an author cite a portion of hypertext?) need to be confronted by the information retrieval community.

The most concrete evidence of a publisher's willingness to listen to librarians occurred at the PLA program. Min Yee, vice president of Microsoft, announced the establishment of a Library Advisory Committee at Microsoft. Committee members will bring their knowledge of what products are needed and will help design products and test programs for Microsoft's expanding CD publishing plans.

As a first step, Yee distributed a questionnaire to attendees that will help tell Microsoft how CDs are presently being used in libraries and how they will be used in the near future. Each respondent is asked to supply a "wish list" of CD-ROM products. The results of the survey are available from Microsoft.

Responses came from 177 public libraries of which 45 percent were currently using CD-ROM. Of those not yet using CD-ROM for public use, over half expect to be by 1990.

Librarians ranked as first choice on the wish lists a variety of products including library catalogs, statistical sources, indexes and local information databases. Second choices included full texts of literature, newspapers, periodicals, biographies, etc. Third choices included ready reference sources such as dictionaries, almanacs, and encyclopedias.

For more information about the survey or the Library Advisory Committee contact: Min Yee, Vice President, Microsoft Press, 16011 NE 36th Way, Redmond, WA 98073-9717.

CD-ROM COSTS
What Are the Media Tradeoffs?*

An increasing number of publications are available on CD-ROM in addition to their print and online versions. Some of them are exact duplicates of the print or online products, others are subsets or enhanced versions. The number of CD-ROM publications is expected to continue to grow as publishers look for a variety of distribution alternatives for their products. Although my presentation focuses on indexing/abstracting publications, many other types of publications such as reference books are now available on CD-ROM.

When the same (or similar) material is available in a variety of formats, librarians must make difficult purchasing decisions. Each medium offers its own unique advantages and

each has its own disadvantages. The advantages must of course be weighed against the costs of each medium in order to make an intelligent decision. The final decision may be to purchase (or continue) only one form of a work or to simultaneously use more than one form.

The focus of my presentation is on the cost side of the cost/benefit equation because the characteristics and advantages of each medium have been discussed by other speakers. Still, it is useful to summarize the advantages and disadvantages of print, online, and CD access to indexing/abstracting information (see Table 1). The relative weight of each advantage will vary from library to library.

Table 1

Advantages and Disadvantages of Print, Online, and CD-ROM

PRINT

ADVANTAGES	DISADVANTAGES
Supports simultaneous users	Uses lots of space
Portable	Limited access points
Patron familiarity	Patrons must copy references
Little or no training time for staff and patrons	Requires physical processing
No equipment required (except furniture)	Each volume must be searched separately
Print is aesthetically pleasing and relatively easy on the eyes	Time consuming for complex research
Easy to browse	
Available at any time	
Older information is available	
Library purchases and owns volumes	

---

*Presented at the 1987 LITA Pre-conference on Optical Publishing and Libraries, American Library Association Annual Meeting, San Francisco, Calif., July 1987.

ONLINE

ADVANTAGES	DISADVANTAGES
Up-to-date	Often recent information only
Little space required	Requires telephone lines
Can use a dumb terminal or a microcomputer	Reliant on telecommunications network and host computer
Pay only for use	The more you use, the more you pay
Multiple access points	Requires training and practice
Many databases (some not available in print or CD) from one source	Access speed is slow
Search many years simultaneously	
Often merges two or more indexes that are separate in print (e.g., *PAIS Bulletin* and *Foreign Language Index*)	
Results printed out or downloaded	

CD-ROM

ADVANTAGES	DISADVANTAGES
Fixed subscription price	Prices relatively high
Patrons like it	Library usually does not own the material
Gives the library a good image	May require switching disks for large databases
Multiple access points	One user per disk (usually)
Search several years simultaneously	Some training still required (software varies)
Available at any time	
Software aimed at end users	

Costs should be estimated and weighed against benefits before a purchasing decision is made. All immediate start-up and ongoing costs for each option should be considered. Although the precise costs are different for each index and in each library, costs can be broken down into the following major categories:

- subscription, purchase, or access price
- physical processing
- intellectual processing
- staff time
- space
- furniture
- equipment
- maintenance and supplies.

SUBSCRIPTION, PURCHASE, OR ACCESS COSTS

Costs of different products may be difficult to compare because each publisher sets its own subscription, purchase, or access policies as well as its own pricing schedule. Several common alternatives for each medium exist, however.

Printed indexes are usually purchased on a subscription basis. Once a volume is purchased it is owned outright by the library. The yearly subscription price typically covers monthly or quarterly update volumes plus a yearly cumulated volume or volumes. If a current subscription is canceled, the library retains all of the previously purchased volumes.

Online is typically on a pay-as-you-go basis. The library pays for the amount of time they are connected to a database and/or for the amount of information accessed. Connect time may be lower if the library commits to a minimum number of connect hours. There may be some start-up fees or monthly minimum fees, but they are usually low.

CD-ROM is typically on a subscription-lease arrangement. Libraries purchase *permission to use* a CD-ROM database, not the disks themselves. Under this arrangement, if a current subscription is canceled, all disks must be returned to the publisher. Thus, libraries will no longer have access to retrospective information on disk if they cancel their current subscription.

Most of the major CD-ROM indexes operate this way, but there are exceptions. When an updated WILSONDISC disk is received by a subscribing library, the library may give the old disk to a branch or another library (but they may not sell it). PAIS will let the library keep the last disk received if the current subscription is canceled. (Nonsubscription reference disks such as the Kirk-Othmer Encyclopedia of Chemical Technology from John Wiley and Sons are often owned outright by the purchasing library.)

Some publishers establish price links between the different versions of their indexes. A subscription to a CD database from WILSONDISC, for example, includes unlimited access to the corresponding online database. This allows users to start a search on the CD database (updated quarterly) then find the most current information on the online database (updated twice a week) for only the cost of the telecommunications access fee. Access to all of the other WILSONLINE databases is allowed with the user's password, but at the standard connect-time rates. Wilson also links their print products to their online product by offering online discounts to subscribers of the corresponding printed index.

Psychological Abstracts offers 10 percent discounts for multiple subscriptions to their CD-ROM product and 10 percent discounts for subscribers to the printed index. Other database producers offer reduced online rates for subscribers to their printed products.

PHYSICAL PROCESSING

Start-up physical processing costs for printed indexes include the costs of shelf markers, setting up a check-in record, and labeling any back issues ordered. (In most cases printed indexes are already being received by the library so this has probably already been done and the decision will be whether to continue an existing subscription.) The physical start-up procedures for online access entail getting the software and/or equipment set up, a process that does not take much time especially if the library has some experience with microcomputers. CD-ROM start-up requires installation of the hardware and software. The time required to set up a CD system ranges from one hour to two days if there are hardware problems.

Ongoing physical processing costs associated with print are the time (and therefore costs) of: checking-in volumes, labeling, claiming (if necessary), targeting volumes for a security system, shelving, and reshelving. The major ongoing processing cost for online is the updating of search aids and manuals. CD-ROM disks may be checked in like printed volumes (so a check-in record must be established). For most CD indexes, the old disks must be returned when updates arrive.

INTELLECTUAL PROCESSING

Intellectual processing costs are typically at start-up when the new material is cataloged. Almost all libraries catalog printed indexes, some catalog CD indexes, hardly any catalog online databases. The cost of cataloging will vary in each library.

STAFF TIME

A more substantial cost factor is that of staff time. Staff time is required to learn to use a product, to use it to find needed information, and to assist patrons in using a product. Printed products require minimal start-up time, CD-ROM products require some orientation and practice, and online searching requires extensive training and practice.

On an ongoing basis, staff time with print and CD products is primarily to assist patron use. Online requires substantially more staff time to do searching for patrons or to assist patrons to do their own searches. Ongoing refresher courses for online intermediaries are recommended.

SPACE, FURNITURE, AND EQUIPMENT

The equipment and furniture required to use a particular medium are related to the amount of space needed by that medium, so these three cost categories will be discussed together. Equipment and furniture are mostly start-up costs, while the cost of space is ongoing.

For printed indexes there is an investment in furniture (including shelving, tables, and chairs), but usually no other equipment is needed. Floorspace requirements can be substantial with printed indexes. (Cohen and Young, of Aaron Cohen Associates [1], estimate 0.1 square feet per volume.) These start-up and ongoing costs vary with the size of the index and with how many older volumes are retained by the library. It should be noted that floorspace requirements for printed volumes usually do not completely disappear when a print subscription is replaced by online or CD. Most online or CD products do not go back as far in time as the printed indexes, which necessitates retention of some older volumes.

Discounting the retention of older printed volumes, online frequently has very low space and furniture costs if searching is done by the librarians in their work areas. End user searching areas require space for terminals or microcomputers, some user aids, and a small work area. (Cohen and Young estimate 40 square feet per workstation.) Phone lines must be available. Start-up equipment costs are of course higher, requiring at least one microcomputer with modem, communications software, and printer (or a terminal). If the microcomputer is located in the librarian's work area it can be used for other things, so the cost is not borne totally by the online service.

CD-ROM has the highest equipment costs of the three media. A typical workstation consists of a microcomputer (frequently requiring a hard-disk drive), a CD-ROM player, and a printer. One workstation typically costs around five thousand dollars. Many libraries will want more than one workstation to minimize patron queues. Furniture required includes a table and chair(s) for each workstation. The table must be large enough to hold all of the equipment with space for user aids and a small work area. With telephone lines, a modem, and appropriate software, the CD-ROM workstation can serve double duty as an online station.

MAINTENANCE/SUPPLIES

Printed indexes require only physical processing supplies (e.g., labels) and preservation costs (e.g., repair or binding) in the way of maintenance and supplies.

Because both online and CD require hardware, there are the costs of hardware maintenance, either on a yearly contractual basis or as needed for repairs. Both also require printer supplies such as paper and ribbons or ink cartridges. The cost of such supplies is not inconsequential, especially when the system is in a public area.

Table 2

Cost Considerations for PAIS, PSYCHOLOGICAL ABSTRACTS, and READERS' GUIDE

	Paper Start-Up	Paper Yearly	Online Start-Up	Online Yearly	CD-ROM Start-Up	CD-ROM Yearly
SUBSCRIPTION*						
PAIS		$295/year (Bulletin) + $495/year (F.L.I.)		$69/hour $10/hour-tele. $0.30/full rec. offline		$1795/year (1972-present) Quarterly updates
PSYCHOLOGICAL ABSTRACTS		$750/year		$55/hour $10/hour-tele. $0.20/full rec. offline		$4995/year (1974-present) 2 disks, Quarterly updates
READERS' GUIDE		$110/year		$40/hour $10/hour-tele.		$1095/year includes online use (1983-present) Quarterly updates
PHYSICAL PROCESSING	Check-in rec. Shelf labels Volume labels	Check-in Labeling Shelving	Hardware and software set-up	Update manuals	Hardware and software set-up	Check-in PAIS and PSYCHOLOGICAL ABSTRACTS: Return old discs READERS' GUIDE: Old disks do not have to be returned
INTELLECTUAL PROCESSING	Cataloging				May catalog	
STAFF TIME		Assist patrons	Training on all appropriate systems READERS' GUIDE: Training on WILSONLINE	Update training Assist end users Do searches	Learn about system	Assist patrons
SPACE	0.1 square foot per volume Work space	0.1 square foot per volume Work space	40 square feet per workstation or less	40 square feet per workstation or less	40 square feet per workstation	40 square feet per workstation
FURNITURE	Shelves Tables Chairs	Additional shelves	Table Chair		Table Chair	
EQUIPMENT			Microcomputer Modem Printer Phone lines	Phone lines	Microcomputer Printer CD-ROM player	
MAINTENANCE	Labels	Labels Preservation	Printer paper Printer ribbon or cartridges	Hardware maintenance Printer supplies	Printer paper Printer ribbon or cartridges	Hardware maintenance

*NOTES: All subscription costs are at the maximum rates with no discounts. PAIS and PSYCHOLOGICAL ABSTRACTS online costs are on the DIALOG system. READERS' GUIDE online costs are on the WILSONLINE system. READERS' GUIDE CD-ROM subscriptions include unlimited online time at $10/hour for telecommunications.

SOURCE OF FUNDS

Where will libraries get the funds for yet another new medium? There are several options being considered in libraries. One option is to cancel subscriptions to the printed equivalents and use these funds for the CD-ROM subscription. One problem with this approach is that the start-up costs still must be borne. Even if the start-up costs are not considered, yearly subscription prices for CD-ROM databases are still typically higher than the price of a subscription to the printed equivalent. (CD subscription prices are expected to come down at some point.) If a current subscription to the printed form of an index were no longer available, many libraries would need to have more than one CD-ROM workstation to accommodate demand. Multiple workstations mean multiple subscription costs, not to mention multiple hardware costs.

A second option is to pay for CD-ROM databases from the materials budget just as for any other subscription. If no increases in the budget are possible, libraries must reexamine their total acquisitions patterns and user needs in order to set new priorities. One problem with this option is that the other items in the materials budget are owned, while most CD products are only leased.

A final option is to charge patrons for use of the CD-ROM database. Most libraries now charge for online access, but very few assess a direct fee for the use of a printed index. CD-ROM costs are different from online costs in that online costs are associated with amount of use and CD costs are not. As with a printed index, the library pays a set price for a CD database subscription, regardless of how much it is subsequently used. Determining a fair and adequate access price would be guesswork at this point. Charging for a database on CD-ROM raises basic philosophical issues beyond the scope of this talk.

Some libraries have funded their first year of CD-ROM access through grants. The grant may cover start-up costs, but when the grant runs out these libraries must face the same cost decisions as other libraries if they are to continue their subscriptions.

CONCLUSION

Some cost comparisons have been published recently and more will undoubtedly appear in the library literature this year and next. A cost model that emphasizes the costs of physical facilities is presented by Cohen and Young [1], library building consultants. They compare costs of paper, online and CD versions of ERIC, Applied Sciences and Fisheries Abstracts, and Excerpta Medica. Alberico [2] looks at Psychological Abstracts. Hatvany [3], Helgerson [4] and others discuss cost comparisons in general.

Most writers conclude that all three media are likely to coexist in libraries. The advantages of each are thought to justify this coexistence, while the cost differences are not sufficiently clear to base a decision on cost alone. Alberico concludes:

> While the library which acquires a CD-ROM database can expect to realize some savings on searching the corresponding online database, it is probably not a good idea to try to justify a CD-ROM subscription on a strictly financial basis. Print, online, and CD-ROM technologies are different enough from one another to make it unlikely that any one will supplant any of the others. All three technologies can and will coexist. Without a doubt, they will have an impact on one another. We hope that CD-ROM will reduce online costs, but it could just as conceivably result in increased online traffic as users become more sophisticated and aware of the advantages offered by online searches.

REFERENCES

[1]Elaine Cohen and Margo Young, "Cost Comparison of Abstracts and Indexes on Paper, CD-ROM, and Online," *Optical Information Systems* (November-December 1986): 485-90.

[2]Ralph Alberico, "Justifying CD-ROM," *Small Computers in Libraries* 7 (February 1987): 18-20.

[3]Bela R. Hatvany, "Criteria for Converting to CD-ROM," *Proceedings of the 1986 National Online Meeting*, Medford, N.J.: Learned Information, 1986, pp. 163-66.

[4]Linda W. Helgerson, "CD-ROM: A Revolution in the Making," *Library Hi-Tech* 4 (No. 2, 1986): 23-27. ■

6

FULL-TEXT DATABASES

When online databases first became available for searching in the early 1970s, almost all were bibliographic. The machine-readable files mounted by DIALOG, National Library of Medicine, and Orbit were by-products of computer typesetting of the massive printed indexes and abstracts such as Index Medicus, Chemical Abstracts, ERIC, NTIS, and BIOSIS.

Most online searching by intermediaries in the library environment is still done on bibliographic databases. Bibliographic databases still have a valuable role in document location, in research, and in making the world's literature known. The fastest growing category of databases today is not bibliographic, however, but full-text.

Full-text databases provide complete textual portions of magazines, newspapers, books, or other materials. They allow every word of a text to be searched and are a step toward solving the perennial problem with bibliographic databases—that of document delivery.

I became interested in full-text databases in the early 1980s when I was a doctoral student at the University of Illinois, Graduate School of Library and Information Science. What especially intrigued me at that time was the contention by some full-text vendors that once documents were available in full-text form, controlled vocabulary indexing and bibliographic databases became obsolete. I studied this contention in a small way in my doctoral dissertation and have been working on related issues ever since.

Several of my shorter articles on full-text databases are reprinted here. I did little editing of these because, although new full-text databases are added all the time, few full-text products change or go away. (Some of the articles that were more out-of-date are not included here. There is a complete listing in the Appendix.)

"Searching Full-Text Databases" describes the major systems that offer a substantial number of full-text databases and their search features. In this article, full-text databases are categorized by the type of information they include, with examples of specific databases for each category. Some uses of full-text and hints for search strategy conclude the article. The search strategy hints are based on the results of studies done by others and on a series of research projects I have undertaken since 1983.

"Newspapers Online" describes how to access online versions of newspapers both in bibliographic and full-text databases. The timely nature of newspapers makes them prime candidates for online full-text and a growing number of online systems provide access to them.

In "Full Text Database Retrieval Performance" I describe much of the full-text research done through 1984. This is a longer article with a more scholarly tone, as it is based on my dissertation research. Although it is a different type of article than the *Library Journal* contributions, I chose to include it because it summarizes the work on searching full-text databases and presents results of my 1983-1984 study that compared controlled vocabulary searching with free text searching on the Harvard Business Review Online file. I found that, on the average, searching the full texts provides much higher recall, but controlled vocabulary searching retrieves some unique relevant documents while offering a less costly, higher precision search technique. The ability to choose either full-text searching or controlled vocabulary searching depending on the situation offers the online searcher the most flexibility.

"Search Strategies for Full Text Databases" brings the review of research up to date as of 1988 and describes a study I conducted in 1988 on the Magazine ASAP full-text database. The study suggests that the best search strategy for full-text is dependent on the purpose of the search and on the writing style of the texts being searched. Full-text databases such as Magazine ASAP that include a variety of materials thus provide a special challenge to searchers.

Full-text databases will continue to be the fastest growing category in the online, and soon, the CD-ROM, database world. To date, use of these databases has not been as high as anticipated, something that will change over time. The look and utility of these databases will also be changing in the near future. As faster transmission speeds and higher magnetic and optical storage densities become available, pictures, graphs, and charts will become an integral part of full-text. Further studies on optimal search techniques and better display formats will help searchers and database producers make better use of full-text online.

SEARCHING FULL-TEXT DATABASES*

Full-text databases are being added almost every month to many of the major commercial online systems. In the last five to six years, the complete texts of many magazines, newspapers, and books have joined full-text legal documents and newswires online. Although these materials are not complete replacements of printed works (they do not yet include graphics and certain parts of printed works, e.g., letters to the editor, advertisements, short news items), full-text databases are attractive alternatives to bibliographic databases or, in some cases, to printed publications.

THE FULL-TEXT SYSTEMS

Some of the major commercial online systems that offer a large number of full-text databases and that are commonly used in U.S. libraries include LEXIS and NEXIS, BRS, DIALOG, STN International (Chemical Abstracts Service Online), VU/TEXT, NEWSNET, and Dow Jones News Retrieval. (Systems less often used in libraries such as CompuServe and The Source have more limited search features and are excluded from this discussion.)

Each of these systems uses some standard search and display features that are also used for searching bibliographic databases and are familiar to all searchers. The major online systems allow every word in the texts to be searched (except stop words) and use inverted index file structures. Standard search techniques include: Boolean operations (typically AND, OR, and NOT), proximity searching (usually adjacent, sometimes within a certain number of words or within the same field), and truncation (most commonly right-hand truncation of either a specified or unspecified number of characters). Typical display features allow the user to specify what fields or combination of fields they wish to see displayed.

Some search and display powers on these systems are especially useful for full-text searching: proximity operators that allow words to be searched in the same grammatical sentence (BRS); proximity operators that allow words to be searched in the same grammatical paragraph (BRS, DIALOG, STN, Dow Jones); proximity operators that allow the user to specify any number of intervening words (DIALOG, LEXIS/NEXIS, STN, NEWSNET, Dow Jones); automatic searching of plurals and singulars (LEXIS/NEXIS, VU/TEXT, BRS);

automatic searching of equivalent words such as British/American spelling or abbreviations (LEXIS/NEXIS, BRS); word frequency counts to sort display output or to help with relevance judging (BRS, STN, VU/TEXT); highlighting of search words (LEXIS/NEXIS, VU/TEXT, STN, DIALOG); and display of only those portions of texts that contain the search terms (LEXIS/NEXIS, BRS, VU/TEXT, STN, DIALOG).

THE SEARCHER'S ARSENAL

These features need to be part of a searcher's arsenal to search full text most effectively. Experienced full-text searchers recommend replacing the Boolean AND to link concepts with the "same paragraph" operator or within approximately 20 words. A study I am now doing on search techniques for full texts of popular magazines suggests that searching within the same paragraph retrieves on the average the best combination of relevant articles without an unwieldy number of false drops. The Boolean AND operator retrieves more documents (both relevant and not) and is useful when there are several concepts in a search, not all of which could be expected to be mentioned in a paragraph or when one or more concepts is imprecise. For example, a search using AND between the concepts morals or ethics AND televangelists retrieved documents that did not use the terms morals or ethics in the same paragraph with the term televangelists, but that discussed specific types of ethical behavior.

Other studies have shown that the more often search terms occur in a document, the more likely that document will be relevant. Systems that provide word occurrence tables (BRS and STN) or allow sorting by number of times words occur (VU/TEXT) offer a good way to deal with the large numbers of documents that are sometimes retrieved in a full-text search. Highlighting and displaying only those portions of the text that contain the search terms further facilitates relevance judging and makes full-text viewing more cost effective.

TYPES OF FULL-TEXT DATABASES

The materials that are available in full-text form on each of these systems varies considerably. Speaking of full-text databases as a single entity may be as fallacious as lumping together all people who search databases for their own use as "end users." The amount of information and type of information available in full-text form varies as much as individual end users' experience, expertise, and needs do. Effective search strategies for each type can be expected to vary also. Types of full-text databases readily available include:

- scholarly or technical journals (the American Chemical Society journals on STN International and BRS);

- popular magazines (widely read, nonscholarly magazines such as those available in Magazine ASAP on BRS, DIALOG, and NEXIS. These can be further subdivided into categories: news [*Time* and *Newsweek*]; business [*Forbes* and Money]; hobby [*Popular Photography* and *Popular Mechanics*]; political/commentary [*New Republic* and *Nation*]; "women's" [*Ladies' Home Journal* and *Redbook*]; entertainment [*Rolling Stone*, *Sports Illustrated*, and *Teen*]; and popular science [*Science* and *Psychology Today*]);

- newsletters (mostly highly specialized, industry-oriented, available on NEWSNET and NEXIS);

- newspapers (dailies or weeklies ranging from the *New York Times* to the *Allentown Morning Call*. Mostly on NEXIS, VU/TEXT, and Dow Jones News Retrieval);

- newswire services (national and international, such as AP, UPI, Reuters, and even Tass, are on NEXIS, NEWSNET, Dow Jones, and DIALOG as well as on services such as CompuServe and The Source);

- reference books (encyclopedias are available on most of these systems. In addition, standard technical reference books such as the *Merck Index*, *Kirk-Othmer*, *Mental Measurements Yearbook*, and several drug handbooks are available on DIALOG, BRS, NEXIS, STN, and Dow Jones);

- directories (the most common type of reference book online is the directory, including *Books in Print*, company directories, *Marquis Who's Who*, the *Official Airlines Guide*, "Peterson's Guides," on various systems including BRS, DIALOG, NEXIS, Dow Jones);

- government documents (including periodicals such as *Code of Federal Regulations*, *Department of State Bulletin*, and *Federal Register* on NEXIS and *Commerce Business Daily* on DIALOG); and

- statutes and court decisions (on LEXIS, WESTLAW, and JURIS).

Some full-text databases are made up of a single publication. Harvard Business Review Online on DIALOG and BRS includes several years of articles from that one journal. *The Academic American Encyclopedia* and most directories contain a single title per file. NEXIS and LEXIS always allow the user to select a single title for searching, forming an ad hoc single title file. Other databases and the grouped library option on NEXIS and LEXIS put several different publications together: McGraw-Hill Publications Online file on DIALOG has over 30 major journals published by McGraw and the Magazine ASAP database includes over 100 popular magazines.

A VARIETY OF STRATEGIES

Search strategy and uses should be expected to vary with the type and amount of information in full text. Searching within the same sentence or paragraph should be a more successful strategy with chemistry journals. Paragraph searching and display on popular-style periodicals can easily give a reader a false picture. For example, a search of "marriage contract" in the same paragraph as "Charles and Diana" might retrieve a recent article in *McCall's* that contained a paragraph that gave details of their marriage contract. Only by reading the next paragraph does the reader learn that in fact there is no contract; the "relevant" paragraph was reporting nonsense.

According to my study of Magazine ASAP, the mixture of types of journals sometimes makes good search strategy difficult. The news magazines cause many false drops even when searching for concepts within five or ten words of each other because articles about political campaigns just list many unrelated concepts discussed in a speech. These strategies are often too restrictive to retrieve more factual, lengthy articles found in magazines such as *Psychology Today* or *Science* where paragraph retrieval works better.

USES OF FULL TEXT

Like bibliographic databases, full-text databases can be used to compile a list of documents on a subject. For this use searching for words in titles or on controlled vocabulary descriptors if available will yield a cost-effective, high-precision search. Searching for concepts within the same paragraph will retrieve many more documents, including some that treat the desired concepts peripherally to the main focus of the article. Searchers need to review titles and preferably KWIC portions of all documents before printing or displaying full texts.

Studies conducted by the American Chemical Society show that if the printed copy of a journal is readily available, users prefer to print out citations or relevant paragraphs and citations and get the complete articles in original form. As document locators full-text databases are not used to replace printed journals; instead they are used to allow enhanced bibliographic-style searching.

On the other hand, full-text databases as document delivery aids allow a known article to be located online and printed out or downloaded on demand. Here the emphasis is not so much on the search capabilities but on the database as a substitute for hard copy.

JUST BROWSING

Full texts as browsing devices have not been cost-effective on systems that have connect-time pricing, but it can be valuable if price does not enter into the picture. Browsing through certain journals whenever they are updated or browsing through articles after a broad subject search will allow users to serendipitously find material of interest just as they do with printed journals.

Search strategies should be broad for browsing—the latest update of a particular journal or a simple subject search. Searching for concepts linked with the Boolean AND operator may work here because studies have shown that although precision is poor with AND searching in full text, many relevant documents are retrieved that are not retrieved by paragraph or word proximity searching. Other studies have shown that people who are searching full-text databases for their own use have a higher tolerance for irrelevant materials than they do when an intermediary does a search for them.

A final, unique use of full-text databases is to retrieve isolated facts or paragraphs in a document. For this purpose searching for concepts within a certain number of words is often the best strategy. This is the real power of full text and has some interesting implications for the way people read texts and perhaps for the way authors write.

A couple of years ago I was giving a speech on full-text databases to a group of authors and publishers. As I explained the advantages of being able to search on every word in the article and then to display only those portions of the article that contained the search terms they stopped me, "You mean that someone can read only the paragraphs or lines that contain the terms searched and then go onto the next document and read only a paragraph or a few lines in that one also?" The idea of paragraph retrieval—of reading isolated portions of text out of context—appalled them. They saw it as a threat to the integrity of writing and to an author's meaning.

Hypertext links between related portions of documents will further facilitate this new kind of reading. Full text online will become even more paragraph retrieval—not document or article retrieval. The searcher and database designer will have powers over reading that most authors have never considered. ■

NEWSPAPERS ONLINE*

The exclusive licensing of the *New York Times Information Bank* databases in 1983 to Mead Data Central for its NEXIS system focused attention on online access to daily newspapers. *The Information Bank* databases are still available as a NEXIS database, but some libraries have been hesitant to become NEXIS customers. Other online search services that provide access to daily newspapers with general circulation are available for library use. Libraries may choose from a variety of search service vendors, to access either bibliographic databases that index newspapers or full text databases with complete newspapers online.

INDEXING AND ABSTRACTING

National Newspaper Index: Indexes of major daily newspapers are available on both DIALOG information services and Orbit. DIALOG's *National Newspaper Index* (*NNI*), produced by Information Access Corporation (IAC), 362 Lakeside Dr., Foster City, CA 94404 includes indexing of the *New York Times*, *Wall Street Journal*, and the *Christian Science Monitor* from 1979 to the present and the *Washington Post* and *Los Angeles Times* from December 1982 (DIALOG file 111).

NNI indexes these five newspapers from the front page to back page, excluding only weather charts, stock market tables, crossword puzzles, and horoscopes. This complete coverage allows for somewhat esoteric newspaper items such as recipes, cartoons, letters to the editor, or movie reviews to be searched and retrieved. With indexing from 1979 and monthly updates, *NNI* is useful for retrospective searches as well as current event searches.

Daily indexing of the five newspapers in *NNI* is available in IAC's *Newsearch* database, DIALOG file 211. (*Newsearch* also includes current indexing of other IAC databases: *Magazine Index*, *Trade and Industry Index*, *Legal Resource Index*, and *Management Contents*.) Indexing of the Western Edition of the *Wall Street Journal*, the *Los Angeles Times*, the *Washington Post*, and the national edition of the *New York Times* is available online within 24 hours; the *Wall Street Journal* Eastern Edition and final Late Edition of the *New York Times* are available later. Different page numbers from different editions are noted in each citation so searches can be limited by the edition available in your library. *Newsearch* contains 15 to 45 days of citations. In the middle of each month they transfer 30 days of citations to *NNI*.

NNI contains no abstracts. Subject searching must be done on article titles, named people, or Library of Congress subject descriptors. *NNI* and *Newsearch* records are brief, so microfilm or hard copies of corresponding editions of indexed newspapers should be available in the library.

NNI is available on Computer Output Microfilm as well as online via DIALOG. *NNI* can also be accessed through a user friendly interface system called Search Helper (available

*Reprinted from *Library Journal* Mar. 1, 1984. Copyright © 1984 by Reed Publishing, USA, Div. of Reed Holdings, Inc.

from IAC) that allows easier searching of the IAC databases including *NNI*. Search Helper uses a microcomputer and software that leads the user through the process of search formulation before automatically logging on the DIALOG. Search Helper can be used by librarians who do not have a lot of DIALOG searching experience or by library patrons for self-searching.

NNI is a timely index to major newspapers and is accessible on DIALOG, the online search system most used by public and academic libraries. The computer output microfilm and Search Helper products are interesting support services, designed to make *NNI* more useful in the public and academic library settings. IAC may soon be offering access to complete newspaper texts. This enhancement will make the *NNI* database more useful, since a major frustration is the need to guide patrons to the complete text of the correction edition of each newspaper.

Newspaper Abstracts: *Newspaper Abstracts*, available on DIALOG (file 603), is from UMI, Inc. (300 North Zeeb Road, Ann Arbor, MI 48106). It contains comprehensive indexing for over 19 major regional, national and international newspapers. Coverage for most of the publications begins in 1984 and updates are made on a weekly basis. Papers indexed are: *American Banker*, *Atlanta Constitution*, selected articles of the *Atlanta Journal*, *Black Newspaper Collection*, *Boston Globe*, *Chicago Tribune*, *Christian Science Monitor*, *Denver Post*, *Detroit News*, (London) *Guardian* and *Guardian Weekly*, *Houston Post*, *Los Angeles Times*, *New Orleans Times-Picayune*, *New York Times*, *Pravda* (English edition), *San Francisco Chronicle*, *Saint Louis Post-Dispatch*, *USA Today*, *Wall Street Journal* (as indexed by Dow Jones), and *Washington Times*. Indexed material includes news, business, finance, economics, editorials, commentaries, letters from and obituaries of prominent people, arts, entertainment, leisure, special series and supplements, and (in all but *The New York Times*) sports.

Also available through DIALOG (file 649) is Information Access Corporation's *Newswire ASAP*. This database provides complete text and indexing of current and retrospective news releases and wire stories from PR Newswire (from January 1985), Kyodo's Japan Economic Newswire (from July 1987), and Reuters Financial Report (from June 1987) with daily updates. PR Newswire provides news releases from over 1000 companies, government agencies, and other organizations on new products and services, quarterly earnings, and business news. Kyodo provides information on Japanese finance, industry, government and high technology as well as companies. Reuters provides international business and financial news and analysis with stories of mergers, trades, commodities, stock markets, and political events.

The Information Bank: The other major online newspaper indexing service is still *The Information Bank*, now available from Mead Data Central as part of the NEXIS system. The professional staff of *The Information Bank* continues to provide indexing and abstracting to create the database that is then updated daily on NEXIS. Unlike *Newspaper Index* or *National Newspaper Index*, abstracts are available on *The Information Bank*. The *New York Times* is covered from 1969 to the present with 10 other newspapers and 39 magazines covered from 1972.

General circulation newspapers indexed and abstracted by *The Information Bank* in addition to the *New York Times*

include the *Atlanta Constitution*, *Chicago Tribune*, *Christian Science Monitor*, *Houston Chronicle*, *Los Angeles Times*, *Miami Herald*, *San Francisco Chronicle*, *Seattle Times*, and the *Washington Post*. The most complete and timely coverage is of the *New York Times* with daily updates of the Late Edition. Coverage and update lag for other items in *The Information Bank* vary.

In my December 15, 1983 column in *LJ* (p. 2310-12), I mentioned the advantages and disadvantages of *The Information Bank* on Nexis versus the old *New York Times Information Bank* search system and *NNI* on DIALOG. Advantages include the inclusion of abstracts, the availability of the full text of current newspapers on the same search system, and the more extensive retrospective coverage. Disadvantages include the selective indexing policy of *The Information Bank* that varies with the newspaper, high costs of the NEXIS system, and the fact that few libraries are NEXIS subscribers.

FULL TEXT SYSTEMS

Indexing and abstracting services solve only part of the access problem, of course. Access to the complete texts of newspapers is available online to libraries through several search systems.

NEXIS: In addition to *The Information Bank*, NEXIS provides the full text of the *New York Times* from June 1980 to the present. Updates are daily with each day's Late Edition of the *New York Times* available within 24-48 hours of publication. Included are all articles, features, columns, editorials, letters, and news stories, with selective inclusion of other items.

Items can be searched by titles, any word in the text of any story, or by assigned controlled vocabulary descriptors. The NEXIS search system is a powerful (comparatively expensive) system with many sophisticated, user-friendly features.

NEXIS also provides access to the text of the *Washington Post* quarterly from 1982 to the present and the *Christian Science Monitor* from 1980 to the present. These do not include assigned subject descriptors.

NEXIS is by now not the only online system for searching newspapers in full text. More regional papers are becoming available on systems that libraries may access if they choose.

Vu/Text: Vu/Text Information Services Inc. (1325 Chestnut St., Philadelphia, PA 19101) offers the full text of several newspapers in addition to the other full text databases such as the *Academic American Encyclopedia*. Although Vu/Text is a wholly owned subsidiary of Knight-Ridder, not only Knight-Ridder papers are included. Newspapers available on Vu/Text as of September 1988 include: the *Washington Post* from April 1983 to the present, the *Philadelphia Inquirer* from 1981 to the present, the *Philadelphia Daily News* from 1978 to the present, the *Herald-Leader* (Lexington, Kentucky) from 1983 to the present, the *Morning Call* (Allentown, Pennsylvania) from 1984 to the present, the *Detroit Free Press* (1982-) and *Miami Herald* (1983-). Over 150 regional publications are available on the Business Dateline in full text.

Updates on Vu/Text are daily, with most newspapers current within 24 hours. Vu/Text provides a keyword field and has a master controlled vocabulary, but each newspaper must decide to assign keywords.

The Vu/Text system allows free text searching on any word in any newspaper article, but it has some search strategy limitations at this time. There is no word proximity capability yet (Vu/Text promises such a feature soon) and parentheses cannot be used with Boolean operators. Symbols substitute for English language Boolean operators. Still, searching on Vu/Text is relatively straightforward and there is a valuable display option allowing stories that contain the most occurrences of search terms to be displayed first. Display can also be limited to only the page containing the search term.

Any standard terminal and modem can be used to search Vu/Text. With no contract for a monthly minimum, subscribers pay for time used plus a monthly maintenance fee of $15. A contract fee of $96 per month minimum usage is available (applied to usage fee). Volume discounts automatically occur after five hours per month at any one rate.

Why would such regional newspapers want to go online with Vu/Text? Donna Willmann of Vu/Text explained that "most newspapers decide to come up because their clipping files are a mess. They are coming up to have an electronic library inhouse for their staff." It is less expensive to come up on a system that is already established and with national marketing it may earn extra revenue to offset costs.

Libraries will have the advantage of being able to offer access to many regional newspapers that they would never have in hard copy. Vu/Text can expand the library's newspaper offerings with low up-front costs.

Info Globe: The *Toronto Globe and Mail* has been online longer than any other newspaper. It is available through the *Info Globe* system, the online information division of the *Globe and Mail* (444 Front Street West, Toronto, Ontario, M5V 2S9). Coverage is from November 14, 1977 to the present and updates are daily, with the online version available on the same day as the printed newspaper. Stock market quotations are available in a separate *Info Globe* database, *Marketscan*.

Controlled vocabulary descriptors are assigned by indexes to aid subject searching, but every word of the complete text can be searched in a free text mode. *Info Globe* is searchable via any standard terminal and modem. U.S. access is through Telenet or Tymnet.

The Dow Jones News/Retrieval Service: For very current, but selective information from the *Wall Street Journal* and *Barron's* from 1979, including stock market quotations, there is still no system comparable to the Dow Jones News/Retrieval Service's Text-Search (P.O. Box 300, Princeton, NJ 08540). News and stock quotes are updated continuously throughout the day, making the system current within minutes or even seconds. Selected articles from the *Wall Street Journal* and *Barron's* are retained back to June 1979 in Text-Search's News Archive. News from *The Wall Street Journal*, *Barron's*, and Dow Jones News Service dating from 90 seconds to 90 days is available in a separate file, the Dow Jones News. Text-Search's *Wall Street Journal* is a full-text file available 6 AM daily.

Dow Jones News/Retrieval is widely used by special libraries that often need very current business information. Of the newspaper databases, it is the most timely but probably of the least general interest.

MORE INFORMATION

Online access to newspapers in their complete text or to indexes or abstracts of newspapers are readily accessible through these systems. More regional newspapers are coming online and choices can now be made by librarians as to what newspapers, systems, and amount of newspaper information will be available through the library.

Although there is information on newspaper databases in many publications, it changes so rapidly that published articles are rarely up-to-date. Current information about any database must come from the database producer or online vendor. ■

FULL TEXT DATABASE
RETRIEVAL PERFORMANCE*

INTRODUCTION

Complete texts of many journals are now available for online searching. Most of these full text databases have been made available on the same or similar search systems that provide access to bibliographic information. The systems use inverted files that retain limited context information (e.g., paragraphs and location of words within paragraphs). The retrieval techniques used are simply those that were developed earlier for bibliographic databases. Retrieval relies on Boolean

logic, word stem searching with truncation, and word proximity specification. Minor adjustments have been made for the display of full text databases, allowing words resulting in retrieval to be displayed in context; but changes have not been made in retrieval techniques. This is due to the reliance on search systems that provide access to many types of databases, all of which are by-products of improved techniques for creating printed publications.

Many producers of full text databases assume that these existing search systems and techniques are suitable for all types

*This research was funded in part by a doctoral dissertation scholarship award from the American Society for Information Science Research Committee and the Institute for Scientific Information. Produced from *Online Review* by permission of Learned Information, Inc., 143 Old Marlton Pike, Medford, NJ 08055.

of databases including full text. Some publishers have added index terms or abstracts to the texts, but more are assuming that the ability to search every word in the text will provide adequate (or improved) retrieval. The study reported here was designed to test these assumptions, by examining whether an extension of available technology to include full text in fact leads to improved retrieval performance. Various measures of that performance are examined. The scope of this study is limited to testing retrieval characteristics of full text databases as they are available today on standard inverted file systems. This retrieval is compared with retrieval from searching fields commonly available in bibliographic databases.

SUMMARY OF RELATED LITERATURE

There is no consensus in the literature about the relative merits of reliance on free text, natural language searching of full text vs. controlled vocabulary enhancement, or searching on the bibliographic fields only. Most of the opinions expressed are based on extensive experience with searching descriptors and free text words in titles or abstracts of bibliographic databases and growing experience with searching full text databases. Only a limited number of research studies have examined full text searching.

A series of studies conducted by the American Chemical Society (ACS) and BRS [1] found that users of the ACS Full Text Journal Article database could locate pertinent articles through the full text that were not retrievable by assigned descriptors because the information of value to the users was peripheral to the main focus of the articles. Inexperienced users found that searching with natural language terms in the full texts was easier than searching with controlled descriptors.

Studies by Hersey et al. of the Smithsonian Science Information Exchange (SSIE) compared retrieval performance from searching subject indexing codes with searching text words in a database of research in progress [2]. The study found that both methods retrieved some unique relevant documents. Full text searches retrieved detail, index code searches retrieved concepts and broad subjects. Recall and precision were both higher for the index code searches.

Stein et al. studied patent literature to compare searching on words from the complete texts with searching on various parts of a patent record [3]. The full text yielded significantly better results than any single surrogate, with summary and description next best. Titles, abstracts, and claims provided the poorest retrieval.

A recent study of epidemiology literature by Cleveland et al. also compared full text search results with the results of searching on various document surrogates [4]. Best results in both recall and precision came from the combination titles/abstracts/references searches. Next best were abstract/references. The full text ranked third in both recall and precision.

Many studies over the years have examined bibliographic databases to compare the results of searching controlled vocabulary terms with free text natural language searching [5-13]. The conclusions of the studies differ as to what part of a document surrogate offers the most complete retrieval, but they agree that no one part achieves complete recall. Comprehensive searches must use more than one method because each part of a document surrogate offers its own unique contribution.

Overlap studies have shown that even if recall and precision are similar for different representations, specific documents retrieved differ [7, 14]. Searches on different representations retrieved different documents, illustrating the unique contribution of each representation.

METHODOLOGY

In order to compare results from searching the full text of journal articles with searching of various parts of a document's surrogate, the same articles must exist in both forms and be available through the same search system. Most of the full text databases available through free text commercially available search systems lack one requisite part. The American Chemical Society journals on BRS contain abstracts, but have no controlled vocabulary descriptors. The ASAP journal databases on Dialog contain controlled vocabulary descriptors but have no abstracts. The many journals and books on Mead Data Central's Nexis system include only the text—no abstracts or descriptors are added. The Harvard Business Review Online, available on both BRS and Dialog, was however, ideally suited as a test database for this study.

Harvard Business Review Online (HBRO) includes the full texts of all Harvard Business Review articles from 1976 to the present. (In addition, bibliographic-only records from 1971-1975 are in HBRO but were excluded from this study.) Abstracts of 100-250 words are added to each article by editors. Indexers add controlled vocabulary terms to represent each article's major subjects, products and services, geographic areas, industry categories, and corporate functions. Together these term lists contain over 3,000 terms of varying levels of specificity.

All searches in this study were conducted on the BRS system. BRS allows all subject related fields to be free text searched. Searches can be limited to any field or to a combination of fields. BRS allows Boolean logic searching, word truncation, and proximity searching. The various proximity features, which allow the searcher to specify where words appear in relation to each other, were especially useful in this study. Proximity searching on BRS can be by word adjacency, within sentences, or within fields or paragraphs. Full text paragraphs correspond to grammatical paragraphs for proximity purposes.

Two display features were added by BRS to ease viewing results from full text database searching. These features are an "occurrence table" and a "print hits" command. The occurrence table gives the paragraph and word position of search terms for each document retrieved. Each phrase that is linked with a proximity operator is counted as one occurrence in the table. Synonyms linked with a Boolean OR operator are counted separately in the occurrence table. (The Boolean AND does not work with the occurrence table feature.) The "print hits" command displays only those paragraphs that have search statement matches.

The search topics used in this study are business-related questions submitted to the online search service of two university search services from 1979 through 1982. It is assumed that these questions are fairly typical of business online search topics because both are large universities that offer undergraduate and graduate degrees in business. Topics from one of the two universities are biased toward labor relations, however, because business searching was done at the Labor and Industrial Relations Branch library rather than the business/economics library. Search topics used in the study are listed in the Appendix.

The researcher conducted all of the searches personally. This has the advantage of eliminating the variable of searcher experience and style. It has the potential disadvantage, however, of the searcher learning the contents of the database as searches are conducted. To guard against possible searcher bias and so the searcher could not learn from previous search results, all search strategies were developed in advance. All results were printed out without being viewed online and search strategies were not changed online for the same reasons. This procedure has the disadvantage of being a somewhat artificial "fast batch" method, and does not fully use the interactive capabilities of the online system. It would have been more difficult to control extraneous variables and searcher bias with a truly interactive procedure or with multiple searchers, however.

A series of four searches was conducted for each question: (1) a search of natural language words or phrases in the text of the article only, (2) a search of natural language words or phrases from the title only, (3) a search of natural language words or phrases from the abstract only, and (4) a search of controlled vocabulary index terms only. Additionally, the combination of results from two through four above was considered in the analysis.

Search strategies used both single words and multi-word phrases (with the adjacency operator) as appropriate to the topic. For the free text fields of titles, abstracts, and full texts the same search strategy was used to allow comparison of results. BRS search features of word adjacency or proximity, Boolean ORs and truncation were used as appropriate for each topic, but in an identical way for each free text search of a single topic. Each free text strategy was translated as intact as possible into controlled vocabulary terms.

Searches on the full text used the paragraph proximity operator rather than the Boolean AND as recommended in the HBRO users' manual. This strategy allowed the occurrence table feature to be used and follows the advice of both BRS and HBRO. When two concepts were searched in a topic this means the text results retrieved articles where the search terms appeared in the same grammatical paragraph, not anywhere throughout the complete text. The results of this study should be interpreted with this in mind.

As each search was conducted the following information was recorded: (1) the total number of documents retrieved by each of the four methods, (2) the accession numbers of the documents retrieved for each method, (3) for documents retrieved from full text searches, where in each text (which paragraph(s) and how many times) the search terms were found.

A panel of three university Business faculty judged the relevance of all retrieved articles from all searches. They did not know which search method or methods resulted in the retrieval when they made their relevance judgements; they were given only each search question and its pool of photocopied articles. Results were tabulated as relevant or not relevant based on the majority decision of the judges.

FINDINGS

Total documents retrieved by the union of the four search methods (full text, abstracts, controlled vocabulary, and titles) range from one to sixty-nine in the thirty-one searches that retrieved documents. (Five topics retrieved no documents.) The bibliographic union is the union of documents retrieved by the abstract, controlled vocabulary and title fields—the combination of fields normally available in a bibliographic-only database. Half of the searches retrieved eleven or fewer documents but, due to several searches with a large number of retrieved documents, there was a mean retrieval of more than twenty-one documents per topic. (See Table 1.) Relevant documents retrieved ranged from zero to twenty-three.

As expected, the full text generally retrieved more total documents than any surrogate field or combination of fields. On the average, as can be extracted from Table 1, full text retrieved 7.4 times more total documents than did abstracts, 5.7 times more than controlled vocabulary, and 3.4 times more than the bibliographic union. Because only one search retrieved a document through the title filed, titles are not considered in the quantitative analysis throughout this study. The bibliographic union in this study is thus the union of abstract results and controlled vocabulary results.

Table 1

Mean of Relevant and Total Documents
Retrieved by Each Search Method

Search method	Mean # of total	Median # of total	Mean # of relevant	Median # of relevant	Range of total	Range of relevant
Union	21.2	11	4.5	2	1-69	0-23
Full text	17.8	9	3.5	2	0-65	0-18
Abstract	2.4	1	1.0	0	0-11	0-04
Controlled vocabulary	3.1	1	1.2	0	0-24	0-15
Bibliographic union*	5.3	3	2.0	1	0-29	0-18

*Excludes titles

Differences in total documents retrieved may be due in part to the greater number of words in the full text, but that does not explain the similarity between the number of total documents retrieved by the abstracts and by the controlled vocabulary. The abstract field contains an average of twenty times more total words than the controlled vocabulary fields, yet abstract searches retrieved an average of 2.4 documents per search and controlled vocabulary searches retrieved an average of 3.1 per search. Unique words were not counted, but the controlled vocabulary can be expected to have a higher proportion of unique words than abstracts.

When relevance is considered, the gap narrows between full text retrieval and abstracts or controlled vocabulary retrieval. Still, more relevant documents are retrieved by full text searches than by any other representation. The presence of the HBR journal article texts allowed relevant documents to be retrieved that would not have been found with any other representation.

Relative recall shows what percentage of the total relevant documents retrieved was retrieved by each representation or by the full text. Recall for an individual search method is the proportion of relevant documents a searcher would retrieve if only searching with that one method.

Table 2 indicates that on an average, for the questions searched in this study in the HBRO database, when searching on the full text alone nearly three-quarters of all relevant documents were retrieved. By themselves, controlled vocabulary or abstract searches each contributed an average of approximately one-quarter to one-fifth of the total relevant documents (28% and 19.3% respectively). The bibliographic union percentage increased to 44.9%.

Table 2

Mean Relative Recall and Precision Ratios (in percents)

	Full text	Abstract	Controlled vocabulary	Bibliographic union
Mean recall	73.9	19.3	28.0	44.9
Mean precision	18.0	35.6	34.0	37.0

On the average over 26% of the total relevant documents retrieved were not retrieved by any one search method or by the bibliographic union. Total reliance on one search method in HBRO precludes a comprehensive search in many cases. In the twenty-three questions in which relevant documents were retrieved, the full text retrieved all the relevant documents in nine questions, the controlled vocabulary retrieved all in three questions, the bibliographic union retrieved all in four questions, and the abstract never retrieved all relevant documents.

As expected, the full text searches had a lower precision ratio than did abstract or controlled vocabulary searches. The search strategies used in this test followed the recommendations in the HBRO's user's manual for increasing relevance in full text searching, yet full text still achieved an average precision ratio of only 18%. This is approximately half the precision of the other two search methods.

In addition to standard measures of recall and precision, the uniqueness of each document retrieved was measured for each search method. Uniqueness measures facilitate the selection of the preferred search method; they also demonstrate clearly the value added by each field in terms of specific relevant documents contributed.

Tables 3, 4 and 5 show the three uniqueness measures used for relevant documents and all documents retrieved. The first asymmetric uniqueness measure AU (Table 3) shows what percentage of a set of documents retrieved by a search method is unique to that method when compared pairwise to another method. The second asymmetric uniqueness measure AU2 (Table 4) shows the contribution of a method to the pooled pairwise retrieved set. Combination uniqueness CU (Table 5) gives the percentage of the total documents retrieved that are contributed by any single method. Formulae for deriving these three uniqueness measures are given in the appropriate tables.

Table 3

Mean Asymmetric Uniqueness Values
(for relevant and total documents retrieved)

Measure	Relevant	Total
AUfa	.808	.925
AUaf	.231	.467
AUfc	.906	.972
AUcf	.712	.772
AUfb	.744	.909
AUbf	.506	.670

f = full text, a = abstract, c = controlled vocabulary, b = bibliographic union

It is calculated by dividing the number of documents retrieved in set i that are not also in set j by the number of documents in set i.

$$AUij = [Ri - Rj] / Ri$$

where '−' is the complement.

Table 4

Mean Second Method Asymmetric Uniqueness Values
(for relevant and total documents retrieved)

Measure	Relevant	Total
AU2fa	.760	.801
AU2af	.054	.135
AU2fc	.717	.807
AU2cf	.217	.169
AU2bf	.261	.258

f = full text, a = abstract, c = controlled vocabulary,
b = bibliographic union

It is calculated by dividing the number of documents retrieved in set i that are not also in set j by the number of documents in the union of the two sets.

$$AU2ij = [Ri - Rj] / [Ri + Rj]$$

where '−' is the complement and + is the union.

Table 5

Mean Combination Uniqueness Values
(for relevant and total documents retrieved)

Measure	Relevant	Total
CUf	.551	.673
CUa	.045	.104
CUc	.216	.154

f = full text, a = abstract, c = controlled vocabulary

It is calculated by dividing the number of documents retrieved in set i that are not also contained in the union of the searches of the other representations by the union of all representations.

$$CUi = [Ri - [Rj + Rk + Rl]] / [Ri + Rj + Rk + Rl]$$

where '−' is the complement and + is the union.

In all instances the full text contributed a higher percent of unique articles than any other search method. These findings are consistent with the recall percentages and suggest a preferred search order. The combination uniqueness figure of .045 for abstracts indicates that 95.5% of the relevant documents could be retrieved without searching the abstract field. Compared to abstracts, controlled vocabulary made a much greater contribution of unique relevant documents in HBRO (21.6%). The relative recall figures for these two fields were reasonably close, yet the abstracts contained a much lower percentage of unique documents than other fields. These

uniqueness figures indicate that of the representations tested in this study, abstracts are of the least value for high recall.

These results also support the relative recall findings by indicating that the full text searched alone would contribute almost three-quarters of the relevant documents (AUfb). To determine if the cost and effort to add the additional access points of abstract and controlled vocabulary are justified by the potential retrieval of the additional 25% of the relevant documents, the increased precision offered by these fields must be considered.

The low precision results of the full text searches cause a high cost per relevant citation and a high level of user effort as they scan many irrelevant items to find relevant ones. An accurate method of predicting relevance would be useful to searchers and could be incorporated into retrieval system design. Two factors that might help to predict relevance in full text databases are: (1) the number of times the search terms appear in the text, and (2) where in the text the search terms appear.

These two factors were examined to see if there is a relationship between relevance and word occurrence patterns. The BRS occurrence table feature allows searchers to view this word placement information online. For relevant documents retrieved by full text, the search terms occurred an average of 8.69 times per document. This compares with only 3.69 times in non-relevant documents.

It would be useful for searching if a threshold for word occurrences could be established, above which there would be a greater assurance of retrieving relevant documents. Table 6 shows the average precision ratios for all questions listed in order of frequency of occurrence. This demonstrates the relationship between word occurrence and precision and can be used as a searching guideline on HBRO. When compared to the overall average precision ratio of 18% for full text this table is especially striking. By using word occurrence numbers as a guide to relevance the searcher can increase the chances of viewing a relevant document.

Table 6

Mean Precision Ratios for Number of Times
Search Words Occur*

# of times words occur	Mean of all precision ratios	# of documents
1-5	12.6%	412
6-10	29.2%	89
11-15	55.0%	20
16-20	66.7%	12
21-25	72.7%	11
Over 25	37.5%	8

*These ratios were derived by pooling all retrieved documents from all search questions by number of times words occurred and computing a precision ratio without regard to individual questions.

Table 7 shows that as the number of paragraphs with search terms increases, the precision ratio generally increases. In documents where search terms occur in only one paragraph, there is almost an 87% chance that the document will not be relevant.

Table 7

Precision Ratios for Number of Paragraphs in Which Search Phrases Occur

# of paragraphs	Precision ratio	# of documents
1	13.4%	417
2	27.9%	68
3	34.5%	29
4	64.3%	14
5	62.5%	8
6	83.3%	6
7	50.0%	2
8	0.0%	3
9	100.0%	1
10	0.0%	1
Over 10	33.3%	3

Another factor that seemed to be an accurate predictor of relevance was joint retrieval by both a full text search method and a controlled vocabulary search (See Table 8). Of those twenty-one items that were retrieved by both methods, fifteen (71%) were relevant, compared to an average precision ratio of 38.1% for controlled vocabulary. Joint retrieval by abstract and full text showed less dramatic results. Approximately 51% (twenty-three of forty-five) were relevant.

Table 8

Relevance of Documents Retrieved by More Than One Search Method

Search methods	# of relevant	# of non-relevant	Precision ratio
Controlled vocabulary/full text	11	3	78.57%
Abstract/full text	19	19	50.00%
Controlled vocabulary/full text/abstract	4	3	57.14%

Full text searching often retrieved many more unique relevant documents than either controlled vocabulary or abstract searching. One frequent contribution of the availability of full text is, thus, an increase in the number of documents retrieved.

An examination of a portion of the relevant documents retrieved only by the full text revealed four major characteristics. These are: (1) level of specificity can better match the question, (2) full text can compensate for deficiencies in the controlled vocabulary, (3) some concepts are implied in the text, (4) full text sometimes uses more synonyms and can thus compensate for incomplete search strategies.

Articles that on the whole are broader in scope than the search request (that include the search topic as only a minor portion of the article) are the major reason for full text-only contributions. The HBRO abstracters and indexers attempt to match the depth or level of specificity of each article taken as a whole. Thus, an article on unionization of professional employees may list the specific professions in the text, but these are not mentioned in the abstract or controlled vocabulary terms. (For documents retrieved only by abstracts this was sometimes the reason for retrieval—the search topic was broad and terms in the abstract were broader than the text terms.) In one question articles on the decline of productivity in the US mentioned many reasons for this decline, including labor unions. The specific reasons are accessible only via the full text where they are listed or mentioned briefly. This variance in the level of specificity was the one major reason for many of the text-only retrievals.

Another contribution of the full text is that it compensates for deficiencies in the controlled vocabulary. Several topics did not have appropriate descriptors for a concept, so narrower or broader terms had to be used. HBR's policy of assigning only five descriptors means that only the major issues in an article are indexed. This, plus the policy of indexing and abstracting at the level of specificity of the article as a whole, results in many full text-only retrievals. All articles retrieved by the full text only seemed to have appropriate index terms within the constraints of the controlled vocabulary and the HBR indexing policy.

Compared to abstracts, full text facilitates retrieval of articles that mention a specific facet of a topic, but that are generally broader in scope than the search question. Full text also retrieved some articles when one facet was assumed but not explicitly mentioned in the abstract. For example, in one question the abstracts of some documents implied that recreational facilities provided to employees to reduce tension are benefits, but the term "benefits" was not explicitly used. In another question the concept of "attitudes" or "feelings" about hard work was implied.

Abstracts sometimes used jargon or a single term for a concept in the text while the full text stated it in several ways. For example, in one question the title and abstract of an article referred to "Mexicans." The text, however, used various synonyms such as "hispanics," "chicanos," "Mexican-Americans," resulting in retrieval. In another question, "hard-to-employ" was the only term used in the abstract of one document to describe unemployed workers. Unemployment caused by layoffs was included in the article but the term "layoff" was found only in the full text.

In only nine of the twenty-three topics that retrieved relevant documents were all documents retrieved by the full text. For the rest of these twenty-three topics the abstract and/or controlled vocabulary were required to achieve comprehensive retrieval. Strengths and contributions of each field were discovered in examining unique documents retrieved by each. As it should, the controlled vocabulary controlled synonyms and language changes over time. The abstract brought together major concepts of an article that may have been discussed separately in the text. It also somewhat standardized language. Each search method made its own contribution and often this contribution depended on the nature of the search question or the individual articles in the database. No one method is complete for every question.

CONCLUSIONS

This study showed that in the Harvard Business Review database no one search method always provides comprehensive retrieval. The presence of the full text often allows articles to be retrieved that could not be found by searching on titles, controlled vocabulary descriptors, or abstracts. These latter two value-added fields did sometimes contribute unique relevant documents, however, and serve to standardize vocabulary and bring concepts together. Full text searching at the paragraph level results in many false drops, with a precision ratio half that of the controlled vocabulary and abstract searches. The number of times search terms appear in a text and the number of paragraphs that contain search terms can be used to improve precision. This kind of information should be available in full text searching. Joint retrieval by full text and controlled vocabulary is another precision aid.

The research on the use and retrieval characteristics of full text databases is just beginning. Although much research on bibliographic databases and the nature of language is pertinent to full text databases, full text has unique characteristics that call for additional research. There are many potential areas for future research that are specifically concerned with full text. Taken together this research will have many uses and impact in the near-term future. It will help search intermediaries develop better search strategies when approaching lengthy full texts, it will assist database producers to decide what value added fields should accompany their texts (if any), and it will provide systems designers with clues as to how to modify existing search systems and design future systems to best meet the needs of users.

ACKNOWLEDGEMENTS

I wish to thank the following people at the University of Illinois at Urbana-Champaign for their advice and helpful criticisms: Dr. Linda C. Smith, Dr. Charles H. Davis, Professor Martha E. Williams, Professor F. W. Lancaster and Dr. Lawrence W. S. Auld.

APPENDIX

Search Topics

* topics that retrieved no documents
** topics that retrieved no relevant documents

*1. I am focusing on the fact that length of service or longevity in a given job situation produces complacency and agreement with the status quo, thus breeding low creativity and risk taking levels among workers.

2. I would like literature on cutback management or the process of transition management or administration.

3. Workaholism, workaholics, attitudes toward hard work.

** 4. Dale Carnegie courses in effective speaking and human development. Business students taking career writing skills course will share in the search for information on their research reports. Their goal is to mount an argument for or against company sponsorship in the 14-week Carnegie course. They would need to read not only Carnegie philosophy but as much as possible on the practical applied aspects of Carnegie speech training. They will need some idea of other confidence-building courses or training circumstances.

** 5. Any occupational stress studies specifically dealing with multi-ethnic situations.

6. US exporting of manufactured goods to Asia.

7. I am trying to develop a psychographic and demographic profile of people who buy newly introduced products long before they become widely popular. According to diffusion theory, these early adopters will differ from the early majority, whom they will influence. The purposes of this study are to find out if there are such differences between the groups; to detail the differences; to be able to design advertising approaches on the basis of those differences.

* 8. The topic I am researching is the turnover and job satisfaction of female accountants.

** 9. Interactive computer-aided decision support service. We are investigating the commercial viability of a service.

10. How do working women cope with time pressures resulting from dual-role responsibilities? What are the health effects of time pressure in general and with respect to sex? What are the health effects of perceived work overload?

*11. Package or group tours and their restrictions.

12. Effect of diet and exercise programs on reduction of absenteeism and increase of productivity among corporate staffs and executives.

13. Scheduling of extended work hours. Computation of productivity and safety in relation to extended work hours.

14. Economics and law of compensation, especially for business or government damage to the environment and to human health. Also interested in mitigation of impact from government projects, for example efforts to not kill fish at dams.

**15. Job searching by dual-career couples.

16. Retraining workers for new jobs as an alternative to layoffs.

*17. Comparative studies of women's participation in the labor force in the US and the USSR.

18. Experience with quality circles in the US.

19. Collective bargaining by women-dominated professions such as social workers, nurses, librarians and teachers.

**20. Trade unions and guest workers (migrants, migrant workers, foreign workers) in Western Europe.

21. Personnel policies for spouses working in the same firm.

22. Impact of collective bargaining on the introduction of new technology.

23. Health education programs in industry.

24. Collective bargaining in colleges and universities.

*25. Social and economic impacts of teacher strikes on the community.

**26. Technical and training assistance from the AFL/CIO and other trade unions in Africa.

27. Minorities in apprenticeship programs in both the public and private sector.

28. Information retrieval systems for office files or personal collections.

**29. Professional women's occupational mobility.

30. Women in labour unions.

31. In-plant recreational facilities.

**32. Employer day-care centers.

33. Anything dealing with the concept of comparable worth.

34. Retirement planning by farmers or ranchers.

35. Productivity in Japan vs. productivity in the US.

36. Productivity with unions vs. productivity in non-union companies.

References

[1] Kay Durkin, et al., "An Experiment to Study the Online Use of a Full-Text Primary Journal Database," in *Proceedings of the 4th International Online Information Meeting*: 9-11 December 1980, London, England, Oxford, England: Learned Information Ltd., 1980, pp. 53-56; Seldon W. Terrant, et al., "The American Chemical Society Online Primary Journal Database," in *Information Interaction: Proceedings of the American Society for Information Science 45th Annual Meeting*: 17-21 October 1982, Columbus, Ohio, White Plains, NY: Knowledge Industry Publications, Inc., 1982, p. 379; Seldon W. Terrant, et al., "ACS Primary Journal Online Database," in *Proceedings of the Fourth National Online Meeting*: 12-14 April 1983, New York, ed. Martha E. Williams and Thomas H. Hogan, Medford, NJ: Learned Information Inc., 1983, p. 551.

[2] David F. Hersey, et al., "Comparison of On-Line Retrieval Using Free Text Words and Scientist Indexing," in *The Information Conscious Society: Proceedings of the American Society for Information Science 33rd Annual Meeting*: 11-15 October 1970, Philadelphia, PA, Washington, DC: ASIS, 1970, pp. 265-268; David F. Hersey, et al., "Free Text Word Retrieval and Scientist Indexing: Performance Profiles and Costs," *Journal of Documentation*, 27, September 1971, pp. 1967-1983.

[3] D. Stein, et al., "Full Text Online Patent Searching: Results of a USPTO Experiment," in *Proceedings of the Online '82 Conference*, 1-3 November 1982, Atlanta, GA, Weston, CT: Online Inc., 1982, pp. 289-294.

[4] Donald B. Cleveland, et al., "Less Than Full-Text Indexing Using a Non-Boolean Searching Model," *Journal of the American Society for Information Science*, 35, January 1984, pp. 19-28.

[5] Gerard Salton, "The Evaluation of Computer-Based Retrieval Systems," in *Automatic Information Organization and Retrieval*, New York, NY, McGraw-Hill, 1968, pp. 280-349.

[6] E. Michael Keen, "The Aberystwyth Index Language Test," *Journal of Documentation*, 29, March 1973, pp. 1-35.

[7] Michael J. McGill, *An Evaluation of Factors Affecting Document Ranking by Information Retrieval Systems*, Syracuse, NY: Syracuse University, 1979.

[8] G. Olive, et al., "Studies to Compare Retrieval Using Titles with That Using Index Terms," *Journal of Documentation* 29, June 1973, pp. 108-191.

[9] Donald W. King, et al., *Comparative Evaluation of the Retrieval Effectiveness of Descriptor and Free Text Search Systems Using CIRCOL*, Rockville, MD: Westat Research Inc., 1972.

[10] Cyril W. Cleverdon, "The Cranfield Tests on Index Language Devices," *Aslib Proceedings*, 19, June 1967, pp. 173-194.

[11] T. M. Aitchinson, et al., *Comparative Evaluation of Index Languages*, part 2, London, England: The Institution of Electrical Engineers, 1970.

[12] F. Wilfrid Lancaster et al., "Evaluating the Effectiveness of an On-Line Natural Language Retrieval System," *Information Storage and Retrieval*, 8, 1972, pp. 223-245.

[13]Karen Markey et al., "An Analysis of Controlled Vocabulary and Free Text Search Statements in Online Searches," *Online Review*, 4, 1980, pp. 225-236.

[14]Jeffrey Katzer, et al., *A Study of the Impact of Representation in Information Retrieval Systems*, Syracuse, NY: Syracuse University, 1982. ∎

SEARCH STRATEGIES FOR FULL TEXT DATABASES*

INTRODUCTION

Since the early 1980's when NEXIS first became available online via the Mead Data Central system, the complete texts of many general interest magazines, journals, and newsletters have been added to the major commercial online search services. Although many more journal titles are still accessible online in bibliographic-only databases, the gap in the ratio of full text coverage to bibliographic is narrowing.

Full text databases online hold great promise for solving document delivery problems, especially as transmission speeds increase and graphic images are added. The capability of searching every word in a complete text impacts retrieval capability and search strategy techniques as well. Full text databases are not yet total replacements for print because most do not include graphics and they often exclude non-article portions of journals (things such as letters-to-the-editor, book reviews, advertisements, etc.). Still, they are a great step forward in document delivery and in enhanced retrieval of information.

RELATED LITERATURE

Advice on how to best search full text databases has come from database producers, online vendors, and experienced searchers [1]. Most recommend avoiding use of the Boolean AND operator to link concepts, searching instead on concepts found within the same grammatical paragraph or within a specified number of words. A study by the author compared retrieval performance of text using words within the same paragraph to retrieval performance of controlled vocabulary descriptors and words from abstracts [2].

A follow-up study showed that the Boolean AND retrieved additional relevant documents, but with lower precision ratios [3]. That study also looked at ways to optimize full text searching through ranking algorithms [4]. These tests all show full text searching achieves high relative recall with low precision. A study in legal texts showed the opposite [5], raising the possibility that different types of literature or different styles of writing (as well as different approaches to search strategy) result in different retrieval performance.

The study reported here extends the author's earlier research to explore results obtained from different strategies for searching full texts of popular magazine literature. Using a database that contains complete texts of many different magazines introduces the variable of writing style and offers the ability to compare results based on type of literature. This study tests the widely held assumption that searching for concepts within a paragraph will yield the best search results by looking at several search techniques.

Any examination of full text search results must explore reasons why users might search text databases. If the primary motivation is the same as for bibliographic retrieval—that is to locate some documents on a given topic, then the measures used to evaluate bibliographic database retrieval performance should be appropriate for full text evaluation. Measures such as precision and recall may not be so appropriate if the purpose for searching full text is to locate a single relevant fact or a bit of information within a larger document. Recall is an inappropriate measure with retrieval of facts. Some recent studies [6-8] have found that end users use full text databases as both document locators and as fact or partial document retrieval tools. End users may be more tolerant of browsing through less relevant or irrelevant documents using KWIC features than when an intermediary does a bibliographic search for them. The present study looks at search strategies for full document retrieval as well as for partial document retrieval.

SYSTEM FEATURES

This study tests full text searching using search features that are available on commercial online systems of today. The major commercial online systems that provide access to full texts typically allow every word in the texts to be searched (except stop words) and employ inverted index file structures. They use some standard search techniques that were developed originally for bibliographic databases. These techniques include: Boolean operations (usually AND, OR, and NOT), proximity searching (typically adjacent, within a specified number of words, within the same field), and truncation (usually right-hand truncation of a specified or unspecified

*Produced from *Proceedings of the 51st Annual Meeting of the American Society for Information Science* by permission of Learned Information, Inc., 143 Old Marlton Pike, Medford, NJ 08055.

length). Other refinements to search techniques were added specifically for full text databases, including proximity searching within the same grammatical sentence or paragraph, display of only the paragraphs that contain search terms, some automatic word standardization (e.g., automatically searching both singular and plural forms of a word, both British and American spellings, both standard abbreviations and their spelled out form) and, less commonly, word frequency information for help with relevance judging.

DESCRIPTION OF THE STUDY

The Magazine ASAP [TM] database on the DIALOG system was used in this study. Magazine ASAP (MASAP) is produced by Information Access Company and provides the full texts of articles, editorials, columns, reviews, product evaluations, and recipes from over 100 popular magazines from 1983 to the present. The magazines vary considerably, including such disparate titles as *Time*, *Popular Science*, *New Republic*, *People*, *PC Week*, *Science*, *Teen*, and *Playboy*. MASAP records include (in addition to the document texts) such things as bibliographic information, controlled vocabulary descriptor terms, and caption headings.

DIALOG search features that are especially useful for full text search and display include:

- proximity operators including: word adjacency (W), within a certain number of words in a specified order (nW), within a certain number of words in either order (nN), and within the same grammatical paragraph (S),

- the ability to specify a field or fields (e.g., text only or title and text) for search and display,

- a Key-Word-In-Context (KWIC) display that displays only those portions of the complete text that contain the search words or phrases.

DIALOG has no word occurrence features (such as sorting of output by number of search words) or automatic word equivalency features.

Eight questions have been searched and analyzed so far for this study on the MASAP databases. Queries came from reference questions posed by undergraduate students at a university library or by members of the public at a public library. (These questions were not originally searched online.) Most are current event topics that were posed to allow students to gather enough relevant information for a term paper or class presentation. Table 1 lists the questions searched to date and the strategies used online.

Each question was searched in several ways in order to test the proximity variations available through DIALOG and to allow comparison of the "SAME" paragraph feature with other search techniques. Each search of the full text looked for words or phrases in the text using the following relationships to link concepts:

1. Boolean AND

2. Within the same grammatical paragraph (the (S) operator on DIALOG)

3. Within 10 words in either order (10N)

4. Within 5 words in either order (5N).

The choice of 10N and 5N between words was arbitrary. Such word proximity features are commonly used with full text searching with the assumption that increasing the number of intervening words will increase recall.

Search terms or phrases used standard features such as the adjacency operator (W) or truncation as appropriate. It was expected that the precision ratio would increase as the word relationships got more specific, and that the (S) operator would yield the best overall balance of recall and precision.

All searches were conducted by the author, an experienced DIALOG searcher. This has the advantage of consistency but the disadvantage of a single searcher's view of strategy. The same words or phrases were used for each of the four search techniques searched for each question. Relevance was judged by the searcher.

Table 1
Queries Searched and Search Strategies

---

1. How do liquor laws affect the liquor industry?

   liquor(w)industry/tx **AND** (laws or legislation)/tx
   (S)
   (10N)
   (5N)

2. Is abortion discussed in sex education programs? Does sex education have any effect on the abortion rate (increase or decrease)?

   sex(w)education/tx **AND** abortion/tx
   (S)
   (10N)
   (5N)

3. How does attitude toward death vary by religion?

   (death or dying)/tx **AND** religio?/tx **AND** (belief? or attitude?)/tx
   (S)   **(S)**
   (10N)   **(10N)**
   (5N)   **(5N)**

4. Is plagiarism in politician's speeches or writings new? Is it common?

   plagiarism/tx **AND** politic?/tx
   (S)
   (10N)
   (5N)

5. How have microcomputers been used with preschool children?

   (microcomputer? or micro(w)computer?/tx) **AND** (preschool? or
   nursery(w)school)/tx   **(S)**
                                             (10N)
                                             (5N)

6. Find me information about the morals or ethics of tv evangelists.

   (((TV **or** t(w)v or television)/tx **AND** evangelis?/tx) **or** televangelis?)/tx
   AND (ethic? or moral?)/tx   **(S)**
   (S)   **(10N)**
   (10N)   **(5N)**
   (5N)

7. I need information on the fishing rights that were granted to the Soviet Union by Pacific nations such as Kiribati and Vanuatu.

   (kiribati or new(w)hebrides **or** vanuatu **or** Pacific)/tx **AND**
   fish?/tx(2n)right?/tx **AND** soviet/tx   **(S)**
                         (S)   **(10N)**
                         (10N)   **(5N)**
                         (5N)

8. Can you get AIDS from mosquitoes?

   (aids or acquired(w)immun?(1w)syndrome)/tx **AND** mosquito?/tx
                                              (S)
                                              (10N)
                                              (5N)

PRELIMINARY RESULTS

Table 2 shows for each question and each search method how many documents were retrieved, how many relevant documents or partially relevant documents were retrieved, relative recall, and precision scores. The four text strategies go from broadest to most narrow and are inclusive—that is the broadest strategy (linking concepts with the Boolean AND) includes all of the documents retrieved by the other methods.

The same paragraph strategy (S) is the next broadest and includes all of the documents retrieved by (10N) or (5N), with the rare exception of when words within 10 or 5 words of each other are in different grammatical paragraphs. By definition the (10N) strategy includes all items retrieved by (5N), which is the most restrictive. Recall would thus be expected to decrease with each technique, while precision would be expected to increase.

Table 2

Documents Retrieved by Search Techniques

QUESTION #	SEARCH STRATEGY	DOCUMENTS RETRIEVED	RELEVENT RETRIEVED			PRECISION	RELATIVE RECALL
			ALL	PART	FALSE		
1	AND	7	3	3	1	86%	67%
	(S)	5	2	2	1	80%	33%
	(10N)	2	1	1	0	100%	33%
	(5N)	1	1	0	0	100%	17%
2	AND	57	3	14	40	30%	
	(S)	22	2	7	13	41%	53%
	(10N)	12	2	2	8	33%	24%
	(5N)	8	0	2	6	25%	12%
3	AND	412*	20	60	332	19%	
	(S)	9	2	3	4	56%	---
	(10N)	1	1	0	0	100%	---
	(5N)	0	0	0	0	---	---
4	AND	30	2	14	14	53%	
	(S)	7	2	4	1	86%	38%
	(10N)	1	0	0	1	0	0
	(5N)	1	0	0	1	0	0
5	AND	25	0	16	9	64%	
	(S)	1	0	0	1	0	0
	(10N)	1	0	0	1	0	0
	(5N)	0	0	0	0	---	0
6	AND	97	11	16	70	28%	
	(S)	12	4	3	5	58%	26%
	(10N)	0	0	0	0	---	0
	(5N)	0	0	0	0	---	0
7	AND	4	2	2	3	57%	
	(S)	2	2	2	0	100%	100%
	(10N)	2	1	1	0	100%	50%
	(5N)	1	1	0	0	100%	25%
8	AND	28	5	11	12	57%	
	(S)	14	5	8	1	93%	81%
	(10N)	10	5	4	1	90%	56%
	(5N)	8	4	3	1	88%	44%

* Relevance judging for question 3 was done by sampling

Recall cannot be measured in this study, but if the broadest strategy (AND) is defined as 100% recall, relative recall can be measured for other techniques.

Precision is difficult to judge with full text because often a single paragraph in a document may have relevant information. Relevance here was judged on a three-value scale: 1) not relevant, 2) part of the document relevant (10 lines or fewer of relevant information), 3) relevant (entire article or more than 10 lines relevant).

As can be seen in Table 3, on the average searching for concepts within the same paragraph offers the best balance of recall and precision for document retrieval. Recall is more than twice that when searching for concepts within 10 words of each other (10N), and precision is slightly better. When full relevant documents are wanted, searching for concepts within the same paragraph appears to be a good strategy. Often the 10N and 5N techniques eliminated relevant documents while retaining some of the false drops. As seen in Table 2, 5N actually had a lower precision score than 10N in some questions and on the average has lower precision and much lower recall than paragraph searching. Reasons will be explored below. As expected, relative recall decreased with each narrower technique.

Table 3

Averages for All Questions

SEARCH TECHNIQUE	TOTAL RETRIEVED	RELEVANT RETRIEVED			PRECISION* RETRIEVED	RELATIVE** RECALL
		ALL	PART	FALSE		
AND	82.9	5.8	17.0	60.0	49.3%	
(S)	9.3	2.4	3.6	3.3	64.3%	52.1%
(10N)	3.6	1.3	1.0	1.4	60.4%	23.3%
(5N)	2.4	.8	.6	1.0	62.6%	14.0%

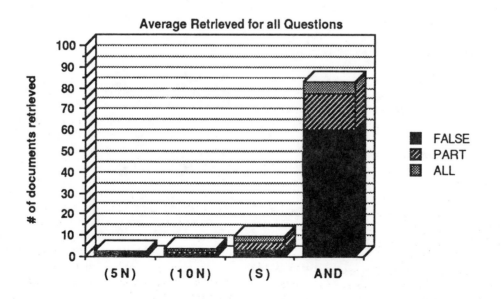

Average Retrieved for all Questions

Although AND retrieved many false drops (for some questions retrieving an unmanageable number of documents), the contributions of using the AND operator with full text should not be discounted. AND contributed on the average many partially relevant documents that were not found by other methods. These documents typically had several sentences relevant to the subject, but words referring to all of the concepts did not appear near each other. For example, a document discussing the current state of the liquor industry did not repeat the terms "liquor industry" in paragraphs discussing laws that affect the industry. Many relevant passages in articles were missed with the other strategies, suggesting that word proximity or paragraph searching may not always be the best methods for fact or partial document retrieval.

EXAMINATION OF DOCUMENTS RETRIEVED

Both relevant and non-relevant documents that were retrieved by each of the search techniques were examined further in an attempt to find patterns for retrieval with each of the techniques.

False Drops

News summary stories resulted in false drops for all of the techniques. These stories listed all of the events of a week or topics addressed in a speech. Similarly, false drops (often within 5 words) occurred in reports of political candidates' positions on various issues. A string of unrelated issues put unrelated topics next to each other, such as a candidate's opposition to: sex education, abortion, and restriction of prayers in schools. These documents were often the only documents retrieved by the 5N technique, resulting in the low precision ratio of 5N in some questions. Perhaps the ability to use this grammatical structure of punctuation in searching would help eliminate false drops.

A mixture of different types of magazines and articles within one full text database seems to pose problems with search strategy since more in-depth relevant articles were retrieved with the same strategies. Some false drops could have been avoided by using the Boolean NOT operator to eliminate non-subject characteristics of a document. As mentioned above, eliminating news stories will increase precision (but will eliminate some relevant documents). Another common source of false drops for all search techniques were book or movie reviews. Allowing searchers to NOT out reviews will eliminate this source of false drops. Foot notes also resulted in some false drops and could be eliminated from searching.

Often the false drops retrieved with full text are attributable to the English language and cannot be readily eliminated by changes in search techniques. For example, a false drop in question #8, AIDS and mosquitoes, carried the sentence "you can't fight attack helicopters piloted by Cubans with band-aids and mosquito nets." A false drop in question #5, microcomputers with preschool children, included the sentence "... warns that the computerization of the home via cable TV, microcomputers, and other interactive systems will enable organizations to construct master profiles of citizens that

make today's data collection seem like nursery school activities." Term frequency occurrence data (not yet available in DIALOG) [2] and ranking algorithms [4] would probably help precision in these cases.

Unique Relevant Documents

As mentioned above, AND contributed many relevant sentences or paragraphs in otherwise irrelevant documents because some concepts were implied or not repeated next to other concepts in the query. In an entire article on AIDS, the very relevant line that "mosquitoes do not carry the disease" does not need to mention AIDS by name. Such partially relevant documents in fact retrieval would probably be eliminated by word frequency algorithms. Fully relevant documents were less frequently uniquely retrieved, but question #6 (televangelists) contributed many with the AND operator. The reason is clear; moral (or immoral) behavior does not always have to be referred to with the terms morals or ethics. Discussions of specific behaviors were relevant, but did not always use the broader terms morals or ethics in the same paragraph as televangelists.

STYLE

The journals themselves might be a predictor of relevance to a certain degree. For example in the question on AIDS, relevant documents came from *Science*, *Science News*, and *Time*. False drops and no relevant documents came from titles such as *Flying*, *Datamation*, *Fortune*, and *Cycle*. Precision ratios could thus be improved if searchers could select a type of literature, maybe in preselected categories. False drops seem to be an inherent danger in this type of mixed literature database, but it provides access to sources that might not be otherwise known.

Average lengths of sentences and paragraphs could be expected to vary with different types of literature and with different titles and should be examined in more detail. This of course will have a direct effect on searching with sentence or paragraph proximity operators.

CONCLUSIONS

This study of full text retrieval in magazine literature raises as many questions as it answers. Some things that are suggested for full text searching are: the search strategy needs to vary with the purpose of the search (fact or document retrieval), writing style of documents makes a difference in retrieval, searchers should be able to make use of this by the ability to exploit grammar, style, and word frequency in search strategies (for example, the paragraph operator offered the best combination of recall and precision).

The general literature is especially interesting because language is imprecise and the styles vary so much. Database producers can aid retrieval by supplying searchable categories for magazine types and article types. Further studies need to examine average paragraph length, average sentence length, and writing styles to better relate these to retrieval capabilities and search strategy formulation.

ACKNOWLEDGEMENTS

The author wishes to thank Information Access Company, DIALOG Information Services, and Veronica Kane Associates for arranging online access time.

REFERENCES

[1]See articles cited in Tenopir, Carol, "Full-Text Databases," *Annual Review of Information Science and Technology* 19 (1984): 215-246.

[2]Tenopir, Carol. "Full Text Database Retrieval Performance," *Online Review* 9 (1985): 149-164.

[3]Ro, Jung Soon. "An Evaluation of the Applicability of Ranking Algorithms to Improving the Effectiveness of Full Text Retrieval. I: On the Effectiveness of Full-Text Retrieval," *Journal of the American Society for Information Science* 39 (March 1988): 73-78.

[4]Ro, Jung Soon. "An Evaluation of the Applicability of Ranking Algorithms to Improve the Effectiveness of Full-Text Retrieval. II: On the Effectiveness of Ranking Algorithms on Full-Text Retrieval," *Journal of the American Society of Information Science* 39 (May 1988): 147-160.

[5]Blair, D. C. and Maron, M. E. "An Evaluation of Retrieval Effectiveness for a Full-Text Document-Retrieval System," *Communications of the ACM* 28 (1985): 289-299.

[6]Durkin, Kay; Egeland, Janet; Garson, Lorrin R.; and Terrant, Seldon W. "An Experiment to Study the Online Use of Full-Text Primary Journal Database." In: *Proceedings of the 4th International Online Information Meeting: 1980 December 9-11*; London, England. Oxford: Learned Information Ltd., 1980. 53-56.

[7]Franklin, J.; Buckingham, M. C. S.; and Westwater, J. "Biomedical Journals in an Online Full Text Database: A Review of Reaction to ESPL." In: *Proceedings of the 7th International Online Information Meeting, 1983 December 6-8*; London, England. Oxford: Learned Information, Ltd., 1983. 407-410.

[8]Garson, Lorrin R. and Cohen, Stanley M. *User's Manual, Primary Journal Database ACS Full Text File*. Washington, DC: American Chemical Society, 1983. 40p. ■

7

EVALUATING DATABASES
AND SYSTEMS

The next three chapters turn to the process of searching and how searchers can improve their search techniques. Part of that process is evaluation—evaluation of databases, evaluation of online systems, and evaluation of searches. Evaluation of databases and systems is covered in Chapter 7; Chapter 8 covers search strategy and evaluation of the search process; Chapter 9 reviews aids such as directories and textbooks that help the professional online searcher do his or her job better.

The number of databases and online systems has increased dramatically every year since the early 1970s. The *Directory of Online Databases* (published by Cuadra/Elsevier) reports an increase in databases from 400 to 3890 (over 900 percent) from 1980 to 1988. During the same period, the number of online systems increased from 59 to 576. With nearly 4000 databases and over 500 online systems publicly available by the late 1980s, intermediaries need to be experts in evaluation in order to select the best databases and the best systems to search. Comparing, contrasting, and critically evaluating are important parts of any searcher's job these days.

The articles in this chapter are a mixed lot. The first two are lengthy reports of research, the final three are shorter, popularized *Library Journal* columns. Two of the columns report on specific evaluation studies, the third offers general guidelines for online system evaluation. Together the articles in this chapter provide both guidance on how to proceed with the evaluation process as well as examples of some actual evaluations.

"Evaluation of Database Coverage: A Comparison of Two Methodologies" compares in a controlled study two different accepted methods of evaluating databases. The purpose of this study is not to present the evaluation; instead it examines methods of how to evaluate. The methodologies can be used to guide the reader's own database evaluation studies.

"Distribution of Citations in Databases in a Multidisciplinary Field" puts one method of evaluation into practice. Looking at the broad subject of emergency management, this research paper shows how the coverage of the topic in databases follows a predictable pattern according to the law of diminishing returns. Such research helps shed light on the process of searching multidisciplinary topics as well as illustrating how citations in databases follow some basic principles of information retrieval.

The third article reports on a less formal study that I did to compare the two major databases that index magazine literature. "General Literature Online: Magazine Index and Readers' Guide" compares these two popular databases, describing their content, availability, pricing, and record structure. Each database has its strengths and weaknesses and it becomes obvious that a variety of factors has to be considered. This type of comparison is made to help searchers choose from among alternative databases.

From evaluation of databases, the chapter next turns to evaluation of systems. "Evaluating Online Systems" provides a list of criteria by which online systems can be evaluated and compared by searchers. With so many online systems in the world today, it is unlikely that information professionals will be able to search even half of the systems. Comparing systems by some systematic criteria will help the inundated professional cope with all of the choices in the online marketplace.

The final article in this chapter compares two online systems. "Library Use of 'The Source' and 'Compu-Serve'" compares these two end user systems and explores ways they might be used in the library environment. It is not a formal evaluation study, because I was especially interested in the personal anecdotes sent to me by users or former users of these systems. Librarians were willing to share with me their candid impressions and experiences with CompuServe and The Source and I included many in this article.

EVALUATION OF DATABASE COVERAGE
A Comparison of Two Methodologies*

1. INTRODUCTION

A variety of methods for evaluating the coverage of bibliographic databases or printed indexes and abstracts has been described in the literature [1, 2, 3]. These methods vary in assumptions, complexity, effort, and results, yet they have rarely been compared with each other. The identification of one inexpensive, relatively easy and reliable method of database coverage evaluation would be of great help to users and searchers who are faced with an ever-increasing number of databases from which to choose.

Two methods commonly recommended for evaluating and comparing database coverage of a specific subject are the "bibliography" method and the "subject profile" method. This report will examine these two methodologies by applying them to the same subject. It will look at the assumptions behind them, the way they are applied, and some of the studies that have used one or the other of them. The findings suggested by both will be analyzed and compared. The differences in time, cost, and results achieved between the two will also be compared, in an attempt to discover if the two methods allow the same conclusions about database coverage to be drawn, and, if so, if one is easier, less costly, or more reliable than the other.

This project was started as part of a contract to develop a model Directory of Databases of pertinence to the Federal Emergency Management Agency. The subject profile technique was employed in that project [4, 5].

2. METHOD A— BIBLIOGRAPHY METHOD

The bibliography method uses specialized bibliographies or review articles in a specific subject area. The citations in them are looked for in databases. A database that contains a larger percentage of these citations is considered to have more extensive coverage of the materials actually used and needed by researchers in the specific field. Citations that have been systematically chosen by a reviewer in the field imply some quality judgement of these articles. Citations chosen by a bibliographer may or may not imply quality judgement. The evaluation literature does not always clearly differentiate between bibliographies and review articles so they are treated interchangeably in this article.

This methodology was first used to evaluate the coverage of printed indexes and was applied often enough to be called the "standard method of estimating the coverage of a given base in relation to a specific topic" by Yska and Martyn [1]. John Martyn has used the bibliography methodology on several occasions to test the coverage of printed indexes [6, 7, 8]. F. W. Lancaster also recommended using this approach for evaluating the National Library of Medicine's recurring bibliographies because "we can obtain a very good idea of coverage by the use of review articles covering various aspects of the broad subject field" and "it is an adequate method of studying coverage and arriving at a meaningful coverage factor" [2]. In his doctoral dissertation, Virgil Diodato provides a comprehensive survey of the studies that have used this method or variations on it to test coverage of printed indexing and abstracting tools [3].

More recently, the bibliography method has been applied to test how the coverage of *databases* matches the citations in subject specific review articles. John Martyn used a comprehensive bibliography on biodeterioration to test and compare the coverage of Science Citation Index, Biological Abstracts, Chemical Abstracts, Medlars, and Food Science and Technology Abstracts on that subject [8]. He measured coverage of the bibliography citations in each database, as well as how most of these citations could be retrieved by a subject search in the file (recall) without retrieving other irrelevant citations (precision). Martyn found that twenty-three percent of the literature of biodeterioration was not covered by any database, a figure that was similar to his earlier studies of printed indexes. He used this study to justify establishment of a Biodeterioration Information Centre that would create a database of the literature.

Pranas Zunde and John M. Gehl obtained a "representative sample" of fire-relevant bibliographies to test the coverage of fire-relevant literature in eleven databases [9]. No one database contained more than 15.6% of the citations in this multi-disciplinary field. Zunde and Gehl analyzed the sample citations and the retrieved citations by document type and concluded "there is a significant discrepancy between, on the one hand, the needs of authors of publications on fire and, on the other, the type of information on fire available in the selected information [sources]" [9]. Researchers showed a preference for reports in their citations, while the primary document type available in databases was journal articles.

Tests such as these using the bibliography method of database evaluation obviously allow a variety of conclusions to be drawn about how databases meet the needs of authors and researchers in specific disciplines. There are some problems with the methodology, however.

For this methodology to be successful, either a comprehensive bibliography must exist for the subject to be tested or sufficient review articles or bibliographies must exist to give an overview of all aspects of the subject. In order to avoid bias, the review articles or bibliographies must not have been compiled from the databases to be tested. It is easy to ensure that the review articles are not selected from the databases to be tested; it is more difficult to ensure they were not used by the author in his compilation.

Another deficiency pointed out by Martyn is that the "bibliography approach necessarily gives a picture of the situation obtaining at some time in the past" [8]. He points out that because of the time required to compile a bibliography the

*Produced from *Online Review* by permission of Learned Information, Inc., 143 Old Marlton Pike, Medford, NJ 08055.

citations included are normally several years older than the bibliography itself.

The bibliography methodology also assumes that compilers of review articles examine the full body of literature on a subject, exercise quality judgement and select those items that are of the most use to researchers in the field. This is a difficult assumption to confirm. If judgement is exercised, some bias by the author is inescapable.

Perhaps the biggest drawback to the bibliography methodology is the amount of time (and, therefore, cost) required. After bibliographies or review articles are located, a minimum of 300-400 randomly selected citations from the articles must each be searched in each database to be tested. This requires many hours of online connect time. Although some of the studies reported in the literature search a printed equivalent rather than the database itself, in most cases this cannot be considered a complete coverage test of the database. Many databases include more citations than their printed equivalents, merge several printed indexes, have different update schedules, or, increasingly, do not even have a printed equivalent.

In spite of these problems, the bibliography method can provide detailed information about how well a database covers the information cited in review articles or bibliographies on specific subjects.

3. METHOD B—SUBJECT PROFILE METHOD

In its simplest form, the subject profile method involves developing a comprehensive profile of terms that together represent a broad overview of the subject to be tested, running this profile on the databases to be tested, and comparing the number of citations retrieved in each database. The database with the most citations on the subject is judged to be the most useful for the subject.

Elaborations on this methodology are possible. If a random sample of retrieved citations from each database is printed, it allows: (1) calculation of the percent of false drops so an adjusted total number can be calculated, (2) analysis of more detailed characteristics of the contents of each database. This more detailed analysis of the type of information available in a database allows better comparisons among databases and more closely approximates the kind of analyses possible with the bibliography method.

The subject profile method is assumed to provide information on a database's coverage of the "core" material in a field. Thus, in contrast to the assumed purpose of the bibliography method, the subject profile method will show which databases contain more information directly on a topic, but will not reflect the peripheral materials used by researchers in the field.

Gerda Yska and John Martyn used the simplified subject profile technique in their analysis of forty-five databases for coverage on environmental topics. The method was chosen because it is "economical of manpower and ... of its equivalent in machine time and [was] able to produce some meaningful [sic] in a very short time" [1]. Terms that collectively represented environmental interests were chosen for searching in databases of potential relevance. "From the user viewpoint, the results provide an indication of the search product to be expected over a number of areas of each base, and indications of the relative specialisations of the bases studied" [1].

This approach was first used by Martha Williams in her development of an automatic Data Base Selector [10, 11]. Williams proposed using an extended subject profile technique that involves printing and analyzing random samples of citations in an analysis of the coverage of databases of potential interest to the Federal Emergency Management Agency (FEMA) [4]. This analysis was completed by Tenopir and Williams under the direction of FEMA [5].

The major advantage of the subject profile methodology is its simplicity and relatively low costs. Once a subject profile is developed, the online costs of running the typical profile of ten to thirty terms and printing a sample of citations are much less than individually checking 300-400 citations. It also removes from consideration any bias on the part of a bibliographer or reviewer.

The major disadvantages of this method are its reliance on subject terms that may vary from database to database due to indexing procedures, the variation of searching techniques among searchers, and the problem of constructing a profile that will balance retrieving the most citations (recall) with retrieving the fewest false drops (precision).

In spite of these problems, the subject profile technique can provide a relatively easy and inexpensive method of measuring and comparing the coverage of databases in a specified subject area.

4. APPLICATION OF THE TWO METHODOLOGIES

The bibliography and subject profile techniques were both applied to the field of volcanology to compare the results obtained with each [12]. The two primary geologic databases, Geological Reference File and GeoArchive, were compared using both methods.

Volcanology includes the study of terrestrial and extraterrestrial volcanic activities and is especially concerned with eruptions of volcanoes, movement or flows of lava, and ash falls.

The Geological Reference File (GeoRef) database provides international coverage of the full range of geological literature. It is produced by the American Geological Institute and is aimed at the professional geoscientist. It corresponds to five printed indexes: *Bibliography and Index of North American Geology*, *Bibliography of Theses in Geology*, *Geophysical Abstracts*, *Bibliography and Index of Geology Exclusive of North America*, and the *Bibliography and Index of Geology*. Forty percent of the GeoRef database citations originate in the United States; approximately eighty percent of its coverage is journal articles. Coverage is from 1961 to the present, with a size (as of March 1982) of approximately 700,000 citations. GeoRef is available through Dialog Information Services, Inc. as file 89 and through System Development Corporation's Orbit System [13, 14, 15].

GeoArchive also provides worldwide coverage of the literature of all of the geosciences, but it includes citations to both the formal and informal literature. GeoArchive is produced by Geosystems (London). Information from journals, magazines, conference proceedings, doctoral dissertations, technical reports, maps and books is included "regardless of quality of substantive contribution" [16]. Coverage is from 1974 to the present, with a size (as of March 1982) of approximately 420,000 citations. GeoArchive is available through Dialog Information Services, Inc. as file 58 [13, 16, 17].

The coverage, characteristics and indexing features of GeoRef and GeoArchive were compared by C. Oppenheim and S. Perryman [18]. Their analysis employed the question array technique (described by Lancaster and Yska). Oppenheim's and Perryman's conclusions could also be compared to the conclusions reached in the two methodologies tested in the present study. This would expand this comparison to include three out of the five methodologies described by Yska and Martyn for evaluation of database coverage.

Method A

Review articles on volcanology were taken from the Science Citation Index Database (Dialog files 34, 94 and 186—SciSearch). They are identified as document type "REV or BIB" in SciSearch, and were combined with the subject terms volcan (o, ism, oes, ology, etc.) or lava or lavas or ash flow(s) or ash fall(s). Twenty-three review articles were retrieved, with publication dates ranging from 1973-81. These twenty-three articles yielded a total citation pool of 2254. The review articles are listed in the Appendix.

Each citation was assigned a consecutive number and a random number table was used to draw slightly over 300 random numbers between 1 and 2254. The 305 unique citations that corresponded to the random numbers were selected as the sample to be checked in the two databases.

Tables 1-3 show the characteristics of the sample citations. It can be seen that nearly sixty-six percent of the literature cited in the review articles is journal articles, almost ninety-seven percent is in English, and seventy-five percent was published after 1967.

Table 1

Type of Material in Random Sample
from Review Articles

Type of Material	Absolute Frequency	Relative Frequency (percent)	Cumulative Frequency (percent)
Journal articles	201	65.9	65.9
Books	23	7.5	73.4
Chapters in books	20	6.6	80.0
Paper in conference proceedings	20	6.6	86.6
Technical reports	15	4.9	91.5
Maps	10	3.3	94.8
USGS papers or reports	6	2.0	96.8
Special publications of societies	6	2.0	98.8
Theses	4	1.3	100.0
Totals	305	100.0	100.0

Table 2

Language of Material in Random Sample
from Review Articles

Language	Absolute Frequency	Relative Frequency (percent)	Cumulative Frequency (percent)
English	295	96.7	96.7
Other	9	3.0	99.7
Unknown	1	.3	100.0
Totals	305	100.0	100.0

Table 3

Dates of Material in Random Sample
from Review Articles

Date	Absolute Frequency	Relative Frequency (percent)	Cumulative Frequency (percent)
1845–1894 (50 years)	1	.3	.3
1895–1944 (50 years)	9	2.7	3.3
1945–1959 (15 years)	12	3.8	7.2
1960–1964 (5 years)	20	6.5	13.8
1965–1969 (5 years)	52	17.1	30.9
1970–1974 (5 years)	87	28.5	59.5
1975	21	6.9	66.4
1976	33	10.8	77.3
1977	25	8.2	85.5
1978	21	6.9	92.4
1979	18	5.9	98.4
1980	5	1.6	100.0
Unknown	1	.3	
Totals	305	100.0	

Every sample citation was checked online in Dialog's version of both the GeoRef and GeoArchive databases. The titles were searched first using Dialog's word adjacency feature, but if a title was not found, author searches were attempted. Each citation that was found was printed in the full format to allow subsequent analysis.

One hundred and eight (35.4%) of the citations were found in both databases. GeoRef contained 225 (73.8%), 117 (38.4% of the total) of which were unique to GeoRef. GeoArchive contained 115 (37.7%) of the citations, seven of which were unique to it (2.3% of the total). Seventy-three (23.9%) of the citations were not found in either database, a figure consistent with coverage figures found in studies done by Martyn.

Tables 4-6 present a breakdown of the citations found in both, neither, or one database by type of document, language of the original article, and year of publication. This breakdown allows certain conclusions about the coverage of each database to be drawn. It can be concluded from the application of the bibliography method that the GeoRef database provides nearly twice the coverage of the volcano literature than does GeoArchive. Seventy-six percent of the literature needed by researchers in the field of volcanology can be found

if both databases are accessed, yet almost seventy-four percent can be found by accessing GeoRef alone.

Both GeoRef and GeoArchive have good (seventy-five percent or better) coverage of the journal articles, conference proceedings, and book chapters cited in review articles, but theses, books and technical reports are less well covered. GeoRef has much better coverage of a variety of materials (maps, government special publications, society reports) than does GeoArchive.

Older materials cannot be found in either database, although GeoRef does include items from the early 1960s forward. Neither database seems to have picked up many materials prior to its announced coverage dates (1961 for GeoRef, 1974 for GeoArchive).

GeoRef seems to be the better source for foreign language materials, but the inclusion of non-English materials in the review articles is so small, that no definitive conclusions about the database's coverage by language can be reached. What can be concluded is that non-English materials are of little interest to compilers of English language review articles.

In terms of number of useful citations, variety of types of materials, and range of dates, the bibliography evaluation method shows GeoRef to be the better database in the field of volcanology.

Table 4

Type of Material from Review Articles Found in One, Both or Neither Databases

Type	Count Row PCT Col. PCT	In Both	In Neither	GeoRef only	GeoArc only	Row total
Journal		74	41	83	3	201
		36.8	20.4	41.3	1.5	65.9
		68.5	56.2	70.9	42.9	
Book		5	11	6	1	23
		21.7	47.8	26.1	4.3	7.5
		4.6	15.1	5.1	14.3	
Chapter in book	11	4	5	0	20	
		55.0	20.0	25.0	0	6.6
		10.2	5.5	4.3	0	
Map	2	2	6	0	10	
		20.0	20.0	60.0	0	3.3
		1.9	2.7	5.1	0	
Conference Proc.		11	3	3	3	20
		55.0	15.0	15.0	15.0	6.6
		10.2	4.1	2.6	42.9	
USGS paper or report		3	0	3	0	6
		50.0	0	50.0	0	2.0
		2.8	0	2.6	0	
Special pubs of societies	0.9	1	1	4	0	6
		16.7	16.7	66.7	0	2.0
		1.4	3.4	0		
Thesis		0	2	2	0	4
		0	50.0	50.0	0	1.3
		0	2.7	1.7	0	
Tech.rept		1	9	5	0	15
		6.7	60.0	33.3	0	4.9
		0.9	12.3	4.3	0	
Column Total		108	73	117	7	305
		35.4	23.9	38.4	2.3	100.0

Table 5

Language of Materials from Review Articles Found in One, Both or Neither Databases

Language	Count Row PCT Col. PCT	In Both	In Neither	GeoRef only	GeoArc only	Row total
	0	0	0	1	0	1
		0	0	100.0	0	.3
		0	0	.9	0	
English		108	67	113	7	295
		36.6	22.7	38.3	2.4	96.7
		100.0	91.8	96.6	100.0	
Other		0	6	3	0	9
		0	66.7	33.3	0	3.0
		0	8.2	2.6	0	
Column total		108	73	117	7	305
		35.4	23.9	38.4	2.3	100.0

Table 6

Date of Material from Review Articles
Found in One, Both or Neither Databases

Year	Count Row PCT Col. PCT	GeoRef In Both 1.	GeoArc In Neither 2.	only 3.	only 4.	Row total
1845–1894		0 0 0	1 100.0 1.4	0 0 .0	0 0 0	1 .3
1895–1944		0 0 0	9 100.0 12.5	0 0 0	0 0 0	9 3.0
1945–1959		0 0 0	11 91.7 15.3	1 8.3 0.9	0 0 0	12 3.9
1960–1964	0	0 55.0 0	11 45.0 15.3	9 0 7.7	0 6.6 0	20
1965–1969		1 1.9 0.9	13 25.0 18.1	37 71.2 31.6	1 1.9 14.3	52 17.1
1970–1974		22 25.3 20.4	17 19.5 23.6	47 54.0 40.2	1 1.1 14.3	87 28.6
1975		15 71.4 13.9	1 4.8 1.4	4 19.0 3.4	1 4.8 14.3	21 6.9
1976		26 78.8 24.1	2 6.1 2.8	4 12.1 3.4	1 3.0 14.3	33 10.9
1977		16 64.0 14.8	5 20.0 6.9	4 16.0 3.4	0 0 0	25 8.2
1978		15 71.4 13.9	1 4.8 1.4	5 23.8 4.3	0 0 0	21 6.9
1979		10 55.6 9.3	1 5.6 1.4	5 27.8 4.3	2 11.1 28.6	18 5.9
1980		3 60.0 2.8	0 0 0	1 20.0 0.9	1 20.0 14.3	5 1.6
	Column Total	108· 35.5	72 23.7	117 38.5	7 2.3	304 100.0

Method B

The other methodology, the subject profile technique, was tested by creating a subject profile of the field of volcanology by combining broad volcanology terms. Volcan(ism, o, oes, ology, etc.) or lava or lavas or ash flow(s) or ash fall(s) was searched on Dialog's GeoRef and GeoArchive databases and a systematic random sample of approximately sixty citations from the retrieved set was printed. A sample size of sixty allows a confidence interval of ninety percent [19].

GeoRef contains 33,028 volcanology citations, while GeoArchive has 10,324 [20]. Because GeoRef contains material from 1961 to the present while GeoArchive contains material only from 1974 to the present, the number of volcano citations per year of coverage was computed. GeoRef contains 1560 citations per year of coverage; GeoArchive has 1251, indicating that GeoRef has an edge in coverage each year as well as in total coverage.

The citations in each database were analyzed to compare document types, date of citations, and languages. Tables 7-9 summarize this comparison of the volcano materials included in GeoRef and GeoArchive.

Table 7

Type of Material Found in Subject
Search of GeoRef and GeoArchive

Type	Count Row PCT Col. PCT	GeoArc	GeoRef	Row Total
Journal article		40 45.5 66.7	48 54.5 72.7	88 69.8
Book		1 50.0 1.7	1 50.0 1.5	2 1.6
Chapter in book		0 0 0	3 4.5 4.5	3 2.4
Map		0 0 0	2 100.0 3.0	2 1.6
Conference Proc.		14 66.7 23.3	7 33.3 10.6	21 16.7
USGS paper or report		2 50.0 3.3	2 50.0 3.0	4 3.2
Special pubs. of societies		2 100.0 3.3	0 0 0	2 1.6
Thesis		1 33.3 1.7	2 66.7 3.0	3 2.4
Tech rept		0 0 0	1 100.0 1.5	1 0.8
Column Total		60 47.6	66 52.4	126 100.0

Table 8

Date of Material Found in Subject Search
of GeoRef and GeoArchive

Year	Count Row PCT Col. PCT	GeoArc	GeoRef	Row Total
1945–1959		0 0 0	2 100.0 3.0	2 1.6
1960–1964		0 0 0	3 100.0 4.5	3 2.4
1965–1969	0	0 22.7 0	15 22.7	15
1970–1974	52.8	19 47.2 31.7	17 28.6 25.8	36
1975	50.0	3 50.0 5.0	3 4.8 4.5	6
1976		5 50.0 8.3	5 50.0 7.6	10 7.9
1977	37.5	3 62.5 5.0	5 6.3 7.6	8
1978	55.6	10 44.4 16.7	8 14.3 12.1	18
1979		4 44.4 6.7	5 55.6 7.6	9 7.1
1980		11 84.6 18.3	2 15.4 3.0	13 10.3
1981		5 83.3 8.3	1 16.7 1.5	6 4.8
	Column Total	60 47.6	66 52.4	126 100.0

Table 9

Language of Material Found in Subject Search
of GeoRef and GeoArchive

Language	Count Row PCT Col. PCT	GeoArc	GeoRef	Row Total
English	1.	44 52.4 73.3	40 47.6 60.6	84 66.7
Other	2.	16 38.1 26.7	26 61.9 39.4	42 33.3
	Column Total	60 47.6	66 52.4	126 100.0

Based on the subject profile evaluation methodology, the GeoRef database appears to have better coverage of the subject of volcanology. It includes three times as many total citations per year of coverage, and has a much more extensive coverage of older materials. Both databases have a similar majority of journal articles (66.7% for GeoArchive, 72.7% for GeoRef), but they have an almost equal spread of coverage of other types of materials. GeoArchive has more Conference Proceedings and GeoRef has a wider variety of types of non-article materials. Nearly forty percent of the citations in GeoRef are in languages other than English, as compared to approximately twenty-seven percent in GeoArchive. (Seventy-nine percent of the GeoArchive database on the whole is English language, while seventy percent of the journal articles in GeoRef are in English). This again illustrates GeoRef's more diverse coverage in this field.

5. COMPARISON OF THE TWO METHODOLOGIES

The two tested methodologies allow similar conclusions to be drawn about the two databases being compared. Each method shows GeoRef to have more coverage of the field of volcanology, with the bibliography method showing GeoRef to have nearly twice the coverage of GeoArchive, and the subject profile method showing GeoRef to have three times the coverage. These conclusions are not startling since GeoRef has 700,000 total citations to GeoArchive's 420,000.

The format of each database is in part responsible for the much larger number of citations found in GeoRef by the subject profile technique. GeoRef includes some abstracts or short descriptions of article coverage, while GeoArchive does not, and GeoRef typically assigns more subject headings to each record. In subject searching it can therefore be concluded that GeoRef will yield a much higher recall. Although it will still be higher than in GeoArchive, known item searching in GeoRef will not be quite as dramatically better. Indexing and database formatting policies have a bigger impact on the subject profile technique (and on subject searching). These

indexing differences also affect how many of the bibliography sample citations would have been retrieved in the subject profile method. Of the 305 citations in the bibliography method random sample, 21.3% contained a subject term somewhere in the citation that would result in its being retrieved by the subject profile method in both databases. 24.3% would have been retrieved in GeoRef only, and 1.3% retrieved in GeoArchive only. A total of 46.9% of the random sample citations are therefore also represented in the subject profile methodology.

The other characteristics measured are also very similar in each method. Both methods showed a similar percentage of journal article coverage (between sixty-seven and seventy-three percent), with GeoRef having a slightly better percent of journal articles in each method. If the other types of materials are considered as a whole, the ratio of journal article coverage to other types of materials is the same in each method. The breakdown by specific types of other materials differed slightly, however. Unfortunately, the numbers represented by each type are too small to draw many conclusions, but it appears that conference proceedings are not cited in proportion to their coverage in the databases and books or chapters in books are cited much more by volcanologists. Both methods show GeoRef to have a slightly wider variety of material types.

The conclusions on English or non-English language coverage in the two databases varies greatly between the two methodologies. The bibliography method sample is 96.7% English language with no non-English materials found in GeoArchive. This methodology allows the erroneous conclusion to be drawn that GeoArchive contains very few foreign language materials. The subject profile technique reveals that 26.7% of GeoArchive citations in volcanology and 39.4% of GeoRef citations in volcanology are in non-English languages.

This finding casts doubts on the representative nature of the citations in review articles. It seems that the compilers of these articles are heavily biased toward English language materials and reliance on this technique would virtually exclude coverage comparisons of the significant body of non-English language material.

Both methods point to the same conclusions regarding dates of materials. GeoRef has many more older citations than does GeoArchive, a fact that is in agreement with their stated coverage. Both methods show that neither database has retrospectively indexed many materials published before their stated starting dates. Over seven percent of the works cited in review articles were published prior to the coverage dates of these databases. Both methodologies suggest that neither database provides access to materials published prior to 1961 and that GeoRef is the preferred database for materials published prior to 1974.

The bibliography method required approximately 6.5 hours of online time (for a cost of approximately $465). In addition, it required the time to locate review articles, photocopy them, compile a random number table, and select the random sample of citations.

The subject profile method required approximately .75 hours of online time (for a cost of approximately $55). In addition, it required the time to develop the subject profile. If a larger sample was taken to allow a ninety-five percent confidence interval, an additional offline printing cost of approximately $100.00 and approximately .5 additional online hours ($35) would be necessary. Obviously, the subject profile technique is much less costly and less time consuming.

6. CONCLUSION

This study has compared two *methodologies* for database evaluation by applying each to one subject. Its purpose is not to compare databases, but to analyze two of the possible methodologies that can then be used to evaluate databases. Test results from the field of volcanology should not be extrapolated to comparisons of other subjects or to GeoRef and GeoArchive on the whole.

The test comparison of databases by amount of coverage, type of materials included, and dates of coverage show virtually the same results using either methodology. Both methods show GeoRef to have significantly more citations in the field of volcanology, a slightly higher percentage of journal articles, and more coverage of older materials. Because the review articles tested cited literature predominantly in English, the bibliography method does not allow fair comparisons of the language coverage in the tested databases.

Is it fair to compare the two methodologies? The two methods do not test exactly the same thing. The bibliography method relies on the assumption that authors of review articles or bibliographies have selected the best and most useful in the field. Applications of this method have often confused the distinction between a review article that could indeed be expected to reflect this judgement and a comprehensive bibliography that covers all literature on a topic, regardless of quality. It is thus difficult to know how much quality selection has occurred in a sample of citations from a sample of review articles or bibliographies. The SciSearch database from which the sample was drawn in this study labels an article a review or bibliography if it contains over a certain number of references.

If quality selection has occurred in the review articles used, application of this method reveals how the coverage of databases reflects the biases or judgements of a certain compiler. Because the needs of practitioners in the field may vary and quality judgement is a subjective thing, use of review

articles eliminates from consideration much of the literature of potential interest on a topic.

The subject profile method is not biased in this way. It tests databases for coverage of all literature on a topic (within the confines of the database selection policy). This method thus eliminates quality judgement from consideration. The subject profile method only tests for literature that contains terms within the subject profile in each database. It can therefore be affected by database indexing policies and includes only literature relevant specifically to the topic being tested. Peripheral literature that may be cited in review articles but is not directly on a topic (e.g. general geology textbooks) is not reflected in the subject profile method.

If the purpose of coverage evaluation is to analyze how one database covers the literature cited by authors of review articles or bibliographies in a given field, the two methodologies cannot be compared. Only the bibliography method will provide information on how much of this literature is contained in a given database.

If the purpose of coverage evaluation is to compare databases to discover which database has more literature on a given subject, the two methodologies can be compared. It appears that either method will allow the same general conclusions to be drawn. Since the subject profile method is so much less costly, it must be considered the preferred method in such a comparison study.

7. SUGGESTIONS FOR FURTHER STUDY

The underlying assumption that compilers of review articles cite the best materials of use in a field is unproven, but is beyond the scope of this project. The wide discrepancy between citing non-English language materials and their proportion in the literature suggests that authors of review articles and bibliographies are biased toward English materials (or that practitioners in the field underuse non-English articles). It would be useful to know if this assumption is correct when evaluating the bibliography method, but would be difficult to test.

Comparisons of coverage evaluation methodologies should be expanded to include more methods using a larger number of databases. Also, comparisons of other types of evaluation techniques would be helpful in identifying the most reliable, but least costly, evaluation method for a given project.

This study is just a beginning to the needed comparisons of database evaluation methodologies. Considering that the literature of database evaluation has been established for a decade, it is time to compare methodologies, test assumptions, and seek the best ways to evaluate database coverage.

8. REFERENCES

[1]Gerda Yska and John Martyn, *Databases Suitable for Users of Environmental Information*. London: Aslib, 1976.

[2]F. W. Lancaster, "The Evaluation of Published Indexes and Abstract Journals," *Bulletin of the Medical Library Association* 59, July 1971, pp. 279-494.

[3]Virgil P. Diodato, *Author Indexing in Mathematics*. Ph.D. dissertation, University of Illinois, 1981, pp. 25-38.

[4]Martha E. Williams, *A Proposal for FEMA Database Requirements Assessment and Resource Directory Model*, University of Illinois, Coordinated Science Laboratory, 1981.

[5]Carol Tenopir and Martha E. Williams, *FEMA Database Requirements Assessment and Resource Directory Model*, Coordinated Science Laboratory Report No. R942, Prepared for the Federal Emergency Management Agency, 1982.

[6]John Martyn and M. Slater, "Tests on Abstracts Journalism" *Journal of Documentation* 20, December 1964, pp. 212-235.

[7]John Martyn, "Tests on Abstracts Journals: Coverage, Overlap and Indexing," *Journal of Documentation* 23, March 1967, pp. 45-70.

[8]John Martyn, *Services to an Interdisciplinary Need-Group from Computerized Secondary Services*, London, Aslib, 1975.

[9]Pranas Zunde and John M. Gehl, "Fire-Relevant Literature and Its Availability," *Information Processing and Management* 12, 1976, pp. 53-61.

[10]Martha Williams, "Feasibility Study for an Automatic Data Base Selector," *Newsidic* 20, Summer 1976, p. 14.

[11]Martha E. Williams and Scott Preece, "Data Base Selector for Network Use: A Feasibility Study," In: *Proceedings of the ASIS Annual Meeting*, White Plains, New York: Knowledge Industry Publications, Inc., fiche no. 10C-13, 1977.

[12]One possible problem resulting from choosing a geologic field should be mentioned, although it is unresolved in this study. Geology tends to be a somewhat static field that probably uses a larger amount of older materials than other sciences. The conclusions drawn from these comparisons may not, therefore, be transferable to more dynamic fields.

[13]Lockheed Dialog Information System, *Guide to Dialog Searching*, Palo Alto, Ca.: Lockheed, 1979.

[14]T. N. Smalley, "GeoRef: A Description of a Database," *Catholic University of America Report LSC B19*, 1977.

[15]Richard D. Walker, "Database Review: GeoRef," *Online*, April 1977, pp. 74-78.

[16]Richard D. Walker, "GeoArchive: A Brief Review," *Online* 2, October 1978, p. 42.

[17]Richard D. Walker, "GeoArchive Online," *Database* 1, December 1978, pp. 35-45.

[18]C. Oppenheim, "GeoRef/GeoArchive," *Database* 3, December 1980, pp. 41-46.

[19]To achieve a confidence interval of 95% a sample size of nearly 300 would be necessary. The cost of printing such a large sample was beyond my means for this project.

[20]As of 20th March 1982.

9. APPENDIX

Review Articles

Cadle, R. D., "A Comparison of Volcanic with Other Fluxes of Atmospheric Trace Gas Constituents," *Reviews of Geophysics and Space Physics* 18, 1980, pp. 746-752.

Cole, J. W. "Structure, Petrology, and Genesis of Cenozoic Volcanism, Taupo Volcanic Zone, New Zealand—A Review," *New Zealand Journal of Geology and Geophysics* 22, 1979, pp. 631-657.

Dittberner, G. J., "Climatic Change—Volcanos, Man-Made Pollution, and Carbon-Dioxide," *IEEE Transactions on Geoscience Electronics* 16, 1978, pp. 50-61.

Ewart, A., "An Outline of Geology and Geochemistry, and Possible Petrogenic Evolution of Volcanic Rocks of Tonga Kermadec New Zealand Island Arc." *Journal of Volcanology and Geothermal Research* 2, 1977, pp. 205-250.

Ferguson, A. K., "Petrological Aspects and Evolution of Leucite Bearing Lavas From Bufumbira, South West Uganda," *Contributions to Mineralogy and Petrology* 50, 1975, pp. 25-46.

Furumoto, A. S., "Status of Research Leading Toward Volcano Energy Utilization," *CRC Critical Reviews in Environmental Control* 6, 1976, pp. 371-402.

Gage, D. R., "Laser Raman Spectrometry for the Determination of Crystalline Silica Polymorphs in Volcanic Ash," *Analytical Chemistry* 53, 1981, pp. 2123-2127.

Greeley, R. "Volcanism on Mars," *Reviews of Geophysics and Space Physics* 19, 1981, pp. 13-41.

Head, J. W. "Lunar Volcanism in Space and Time," *Reviews of Geophysics and Space Physics* 14, 1976, pp. 265-300.

Jarrard, R. D., "Implications of Pacific Island and Seamount Ages for Ages for Origin of Volcanic Chains," *Reviews of Geophysics and Space Physics* 15, 1977, pp. 57-76.

Kay, R. W., "Volcanic Arc Magmas—Implications of a Melting-Mixing Model for Element Recycling in the Crust-Upper Mantle System," *Journal of Geology* 88, 1980, pp. 497-522.

Luhr, J. F., "Colima Volcanic Complex, Mexico," *Contributions to Mineralogy and Petrology* 71, 1980, pp. 343-372.

McBirney, A. R., "Volcanic Evolution of Cascade Range," *Annual Review of Earth and Planetary Sciences* 6, 1978, pp. 437-456.

Miyashiro, A., "Volcanic Rock Series and Tectonic Setting," *Annual Review of Earth and Planetary Science* 3, 1975, pp. 251-269.

Piermatt, R., "Historical Review of Seismic Studies on Structure of Volcanoes," *Annali Di Geofisica* 26, 1973, pp. 525-559.

Pilger, R. H., "Pacific- North- American Plate Interaction and Neogene Volcanism in Costal California," *Tectonophysics* 57, 1979, pp. 189-209.

Sato, H., "Diffusion Coronas Around Quartz Xenocrysts in Andesite and Basalt From Tertiary Volcanic Region in Northeastern Shikoku, Japan," *Contributions to Mineralogy and Petrology* 50, 1975, pp. 49-64.

Simkin, T. "Volcanology," *Reviews of Geophysics and Space Physics* 17, 1979, pp. 872-887.

Solomon, S. C., "Lunar Mascon Basins—Lava Filling, Tectonics, and Evolution of the Lithosphere," *Reviews of Geophysics and Space Physics* 18, 1980, pp. 107-141.

Sugisaki, R., "Chemical Characteristics of Volcanic Rocks—Relation to Plate Movements," *Lithos* 9, 1976, pp. 17-30.

Sun, S. S. "Petrogenesis of Archaean Ultrabasic and Basic Volcanics," *Contributions to Mineralogy and Petrology* 65, 1978, pp. 301-325.

Suppe, J., "Regional Topography, Seismicity, Quaternary Volcanism, and Present-Day Tectonics of Western United States," *American Journal of Science* A275, 1975, p. 397.

Tomblin, J., "Earthquakes, Volcanos and Hurricanes—A Review of Natural Hazards and Vulnerability in the West-Indies," *Ambio* 10, 1981, pp. 340-345.

ACKNOWLEDGEMENTS

This project was based in part on a contract from the United States Federal Emergency Management Agency Contract No. FEMA EMW-1-4058. I wish to thank Martha E. Williams, Professor, College of Engineering, Coordinated Science Laboratory, University of Illinois, and F. W. Lancaster, Professor, Graduate School of Library and Information Science, University of Illinois, for their careful criticism and advice. ∎

DISTRIBUTION OF CITATIONS IN DATABASES IN A MULTIDISCIPLINARY FIELD*

1. INTRODUCTION

As the number of publicly available bibliographic databases continues to grow, it becomes increasingly difficult for a searcher to select the most appropriate databases for any given search topic. The searcher faces the task not only of deciding which databases are of the most potential relevance, but also of deciding how many databases should be searched to get adequate recall of citations.

Recent studies have emphasized the growing realization of the necessity of searching multiple databases and the increasing frustration in choosing appropriate databases. Robert Niehoff, Stan Kwasny, and Michael Wessells of Battelle's Columbus Laboratories summarized this situation in their article that addressed the related problem of vocabulary incompatibilities among databases:

There is growing evidence to suggest that online users perform a significant percentage of searches with multiple databases. Recent articles in the literature emphasize the fact that no single database contains all the relevant literature on a given topic. Users must recognize that perhaps only sixty to seventy percent of the relevant literature on a given topic will be retrievable from a single database, and then only if the "right" database was chosen [1].

This problem is especially difficult for searches in multidisciplinary subjects where there are no subject specialty databases from which to choose. Choosing the "right" database becomes a formidable task when databases from all subject disciplines must be considered. A search in a multidisciplinary

*Produced from *Online Review* with permission of Learned Information, Inc., 143 Old Marlton Pike, Medford, NJ 08055.

field could potentially involve dozens, or perhaps hundreds, of databases, no one of which could be expected to contain anywhere near sixty to seventy percent of the relevant literature.

Some limits on the number of databases searched on any given topic are obviously necessary. Also needed is some guidance on what specific databases potentially contain the most information of relevance in a given subject area. Choice of databases of most potential relevance to a subject is by definition specific to (and different for) each subject area. Estimates of the number of databases that should be searched may be generalizable, however.

Niehoff, Kwasny, and Wessells did not directly address the problem, but they suggested a solution. The sixty to seventy percent figure, mentioned above, "is nothing more than a manifestation of Bradford's law of scatter at the database level instead of the journal level." [1] If it can be demonstrated that database coverage of the literature on a complex multidisciplinary subject is indeed merely a manifestation of Bradford's law, guidelines for the number of databases that would need to be searched to obtain a given percentage of the literature could be established.

This article will examine database coverage in the field of emergency management. It will test if Bradford's law applies to citations in databases in a multidisciplinary field and identify the databases that contain the most citations relevant to emergency management. The report is an extension of a project undertaken for the Federal Emergency Management Agency to create a model Directory of Databases relevant to emergency management [2].

2. DEFINITIONS

Bradford's Law

In 1948, Samuel C. Bradford first published his theory that has become known as Bradford's law of scatter or Bradford's distribution. [3] Bradford applied his ideas to articles in journals in narrow subject areas. Many explanations, elaborations, interpretations, and applications of this law have been published since then that extend its predictive powers to other areas of interest to information specialists.

Simply stated, Bradford's law says that there is a quantitative relation between journals and the articles published in them. It shows that a large percentage of the articles in a narrow subject area are contained in a small percentage of the journals. The so-called "verbal" or theoretical formulation of this law (as opposed to the "graphical" or observational formulation) states:

If scientific journals are arranged in order of decreasing productivity of articles on a given subject, they may be divided into a nucleus of periodicals more particularly devoted to the subject, and several groups or zones containing the same number of articles as the nucleus, where the number of periodicals in the nucleus and succeeding zones will be 1:a:a² ... [3].

M. Carl Drott has restated Bradford's explanation.

He [Bradford] examined all of the journal titles contributing to a bibliography on applied geophysics. Bradford discovered that he could divide the titles into three groups, such that each group of titles contributed about the same number of articles. Starting with the titles which contributed the most articles, he divided the articles into three roughly equal groups:

The first 9 titles contributed 429 articles.

The next 59 titles contributed 499 articles.

The last 258 titles contributed 404 articles.

The value of this arrangement lies in the number of titles it takes for each one-third of the articles. In this case, Bradford discovered a regularity in calculating the number of titles in each of three groups:

9 titles

9 × 5 titles (equals 45 titles)

9 × 5 × 5 titles (equals 225 titles) [4]

This can also be written $9 : 9 \times 5 : 9 \times 5^2$ or, because the size of the core and the multiplier might be different in each case, $1 : a : a^2$.

Unfortunately, Bradford's theoretical expression of the verbal formulation did not precisely mathematically agree with his experimental results or the graphical representation. Discussions of these differences and how they have been resolved over the years can be found in Wilkinson [5], Cline [6], Vickery [7], and Brookes [8]. Detailed consideration of these differences is beyond the scope of this paper.

A commonly agreed upon formulation for testing for a Bradford distribution has been adopted in this paper [4]. This formula is given as:

$$R(n) = k\log(n)$$

where:

$R(n)$ = cumulative total of relevant citations found in the first n databases when all databases are ranked 1,2,3 ... n in order of decreasing productivity

n = cumulative number of databases producing $R(n)$ relevant conditions

k = constant.

Graphical representation is normally drawn on semi-log paper as shown in Fig. 1. Note the deviation from linearity at each end of the plot. These deviations are typical of Bradford plots for journal literature. When there is no deviation from linearity the plot is sometimes referred to as a Zipf distribution [9].

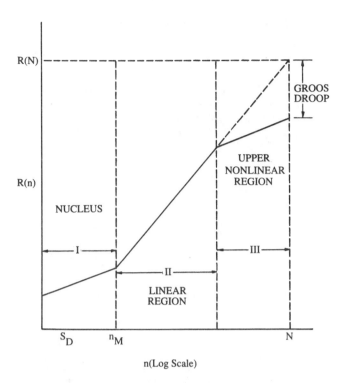

Fig. 1. General forms of Bradford distribution. Source: Cline, Gloria S. "Application of Bradford's Law to Citation Data." *College and Research Libraries* 42 (January 1981): 54.

Although the accepted method of testing Bradford's law is to test articles in journals in a narrow scientific subject, Cline demonstrated it applied to citations in journals in the interdisciplinary field of library science [6]. Bradford's law has also been shown to apply to the items borrowed from a library, the users of a library, contributors to a discussion at a conference, the index terms assigned to documents, and the publication of books by publishers. In fact, B. C. Brookes believes that:

> Bradford's law expresses a very general characteristic of the *physical* aspects of human communication, of its use of the instruments—words, numbers, books, paper, telephone, traffic—which has not yet been generally recognized or exploited in the design of information systems [8].

Bradford's law has thus been shown to be of great interest in a wide variety of practical library and information situations. It can be expected to also be of practical help in deciding how many databases are necessary to be searched in a multidisciplinary field such as emergency management.

Emergency Management

The field of emergency management is concerned with the identification, prediction, and mitigation of, the preparation for, and recovery from large-scale hazards or disasters of all types. Both natural disasters (e.g. storms, earthquakes, volcanic eruptions) and man-made or technological disasters (e.g. nuclear power plant accidents, war, toxic chemical spills) fall within the scope of emergency management.

Many subject disciplines are incorporated in the field. Practitioners potentially have interest in information on a wide variety of topics. For example, in the design of shelters, information about sanitation, food storage, potable water, claustrophobia, etc. may be of interest whether or not it pertains specifically to emergency shelters. Studying structural collapse necessitates at times the entire literature of engineering and, perhaps, medicine. Emergency management interests include very narrow scientific subdisciplines and very broad policy or planning issues.

On the national level, the Federal Emergency Management Agency (FEMA) has emergency management as its primary charge. At the state and local levels, a number of public and private agencies are concerned with the management of all dangers to their citizens.

Emergency management interests thus embrace all disciplines and levels of expertise. Nearly every database is of potential interest. Awareness of the current literature on all aspects of emergency management is important to a wide variety of people and agencies. Bibliographic databases are important sources for awareness of this literature. Assistance in choice of the most useful of these databases and an idea of how many databases are necessary to yield a given percentage of the literature in the field would be helpful to information managers and practitioners.

3. REVIEW OF THE LITERATURE

Recent literature reflects the growing concern with how to choose the optimum number of databases or which specific databases are best for a given topic. This concern is often tied to the growing number of multidisciplinary fields where database choice is not clear-cut and literature may be expected to be widely scattered. Several authors have addressed the issues of multiple-database searches or choice of databases.

Choice of Databases

Choice of the specific databases that will yield the most information on a given topic was the first of these concerns to be addressed. Among the authors addressing the topic, Judith Wanger recognized the problem of selecting the most appropriate databases from among the many available. She believed "the selection of one or more databases that are appropriate for a given information problem actually begins in the analysis of the information problem itself" and that the database selection requires "several different skills and knowledge bases, including a special skill that is not quite definable, but somehow characterizes the expert searcher" [10].

Wanger went on to define principles and skills useful in learning how to select appropriate databases. These principles are based on the classification of databases into levels of potential relevance to a given search problem by four characteristics:

1. Subject/content/topic coverage

2. Source document coverage

3. Time period coverage

4. Searchable and printable data elements of the database [10].

At the time Wanger was writing the only practical ways to classify databases by these characteristics were:

1. trial and error searching

2. review of printed tools

3. take clues from assigned category or classification codes

4. rely on experience, knowledge of the databases, and special analytical skills [10].

Epstein and Angier [11] and Hawkins [12] offered advice on how to conduct successful multiple database searches. Like Wanger, they recognized the need for searching several databases and the problems associated with choosing which databases to search. Hawkins mentioned the several printed database subject guides that were then available as a way to help the choice process. He then moved on to discuss searching strategies. Epstein and Angier used a core list of journals to help choose the most comprehensive databases in psychology and psychiatry. The databases that included coverage of most of the core journals were considered to be the most relevant in the field of behavioral sciences.

Both Epstein and Angier and Hawkins emphasized the special necessity of choosing multiple databases when searching in a multidisciplinary field. Hawkins saw this as an ever increasing problem tied to the changing nature of disciplines:

The last several years have witnessed the emergence of major interdisciplinary fields of science and technology. Examples are energy, materials science, biomedicine, and bioengineering. Traditional boundaries between scientific fields are being broken, and research is becoming more interdisciplinary....

These changes affect the world of online searching as well. As scientific research changes and broadens, searchers must use a more interdisciplinary approach to online searching. The chance that only one database will completely satisfy a search request is becoming smaller [12].

As early as 1975, Martha Williams tested an experimental "database selector" that allowed selection of databases regardless of their vendor, but a commercially available selector has never been developed [13], [14]. Database selection has become somewhat easier in the last few years with the introduction of several cross database tools. Now all major commercial vendors (BRS in 1979, ORBIT in 1978, and Dialog in 1980) offer a master index database that includes indexed terms from all of their databases. These master indexes are useful in helping to locate what databases within one system have the most citations on any given term or combination of terms. These commercial offerings, however, do not help compare and identify databases unless they are on the same

commercial system. Database directories by Williams [15] and by R. Cuadra [16] help in the broad intellectual decisions, but offer no real assistance in the choice of appropriate databases for specific narrow queries.

Evaluation and comparison studies of the coverage of various databases are also helpful in selecting appropriate databases for multi-file searches in a given subject area. The literature of database evaluation is too extensive to review here, but excellent reviews can be found in Diodato [17] and in Yska and Martyn [18].

Number of Databases

Concern with selecting the correct number of databases, especially in multidisciplinary fields, is a more recent and more unusual phenomenon in the literature. Aslib published the results of two studies in the mid-1970s that were of direct pertinence to this concern.

In *Service to an Interdisciplinary Need-Group from Computerized Secondary Services*, John Martyn saw the:

core of the problem is that the twentieth century no longer fits the disciplinary classification of the nineteenth, by which the major abstracting and indexing services are structured. As areas of study become increasingly multidisciplinary, so a growing number of groups and individuals are finding it necessary to use not one but a number of secondary services in order to collect information on their topics of interest [19].

Martyn examined five bibliographic databases ("computerized secondary services") to determine how a group of databases together met the information needs of scientists in the multidisciplinary field of biodeterioration. He found that no single service covered more than sixty percent of the total citations in the field; leading him to conclude "it is necessary to look in a number of services in order to attempt reasonably complete coverage of the topic" [19]. Martyn did not examine enough secondary services to allow him to determine what the number should be in order to retrieve a given percentage of the literature.

Databases Suitable for Users of Environmental Information [18] identified and assessed bibliographic databases that would meet the needs of European users of environmental information. Forty-five databases were evaluated, and the ones that contained the most citations on all aspects of environmental studies were identified.

What is present is a first approximation to guide the user in selecting a small range of bases which have the highest probability of producing material relevant to his interest [18].

Yska and Martyn did not calculate how many of the forty-five databases would need to be searched in order to get a certain number of citations, but this can be readily calculated from their data.

A dissenting view on the issue of multiple database searching was expressed by John Edward Evans [20]. Evans questioned the widespread assumption that multiple database searches are necessary. He examined the databases used in all searches conducted at the University of South Dakota without separating them by search topic or area. Eleven databases accounted for 75.7% of the databases selected in searching; the next eleven databases added only 14.9% of the searches. Twenty-nine databases were needed to achieve 94.7% and a total of fifty-eight databases were used. Based on the results of this study, a policy was implemented to restrict the number of databases used in any given search and to emphasize first the use of the one most likely database from the "top" eleven. Evans concluded:

> there is a relatively small number of databases that are useful in meeting the research needs of an academic search service. There is also the suggestion that the databases whose use was restricted were not entirely germane in the first place and probably should not have been used [20].

The policy decision and conclusions made from this study seem overly broad and are based on the faulty assumption that databases were not used by searchers because they were irrelevant, not because searchers were unaware of their contents. They do not bear directly on the present study, however. Evans' analysis of the number of databases and the number of citations retrieved is of direct interest to this study. In relation to the number of databases necessary to yield a given percentage of the total number of citations, Evans found:

> The analysis indicates that a single database search will retrieve, on the average, 61.0% of the information available. For many researchers this may well be sufficient. Using a second database will usually increase quantitative coverage to 88.3% and three databases, on the average, will retrieve 98% of the information available [20].

Evans' assumption—that the same number of databases in all subject areas, whether multidisciplinary or narrowly scientific, will yield the same percentage of the total literature—is questionable. His conclusions about what will satisfy researchers also seem overly generalized and somewhat naive. The attempt to compute an optimum number of databases to yield a given percent of the literature is pertinent, however, and his data suggest that Bradford's law applies to citations in databases.

Summary of the Literature

The choice of the best and optimum number of databases in online searching is of continuing and growing concern, especially with the proliferation of multidisciplinary fields and the great increase in the number of databases. This concern is reflected in the literature. Much progress has been made in choosing the best databases for a given topic with the creation of master index files, database directories and coverage evaluations. Less progress has been made on the issue of the number of databases, although it is beginning to be studied.

The remaining sections of this paper describe the study conducted to determine if Bradford's law applies to citations in databases in the field of emergency management and to identify the databases with the most citations of relevance to emergency management. Demonstration of a Bradford distribution in databases in the multidisciplinary field of emergency management would allow a calculation of the optimum number of databases to be searched to retrieve a given percentage of the literature.

4. METHODOLOGY

The first step in this project was to learn exactly what the field of emergency management encompasses. This was achieved by talking to various people within the Federal Emergency Management Agency and several local disaster centers. Literature in the field was also reviewed, with special attention paid to references made to useful databases.

Because the field of emergency management includes so many subdisciplines, it was decided that every specific subject could not be comprehensively tested in this project. Instead, the most general aspects of the field were chosen for testing, in the belief that the general interests would be the most multidisciplinary in nature. The following general subjects were selected for searching:

Emergency management

Natural disasters

Man-made disasters

Technological disasters

Assistance, mitigation, operations or preparations for emergencies, disasters or hazards.

These terms were searched using the format and logical relationships appropriate to the online service being searched. Use of such broad terms may bias the study towards those databases with broad, rather than specific, indexing policies, but it was the only practical way to test the nature of the field without searching hundreds of specific subject terms.

Over 750 publicly available databases were reviewed as possible candidates for the study. The primary source for this review was the 1982 edition of *Computer Readable Databases: A Directory and Data Sourcebook* [15]. An initial list of fifty-seven candidate databases was compiled (See Appendix 1). For reasons of economy, this list was narrowed down to the forty databases judged to be of highest potential relevance and available through BRS, Dialog or SDC (See Appendix 2).

The variety of subjects represented by the final forty databases is included in Appendix 2. In addition, types of materials indexed in the databases varies considerably. Primary information types include:

journal articles

government publications

popular magazine articles

books

conference proceedings

research reports

dissertations

research in progress

audiovisual materials

Twenty-two of the databases were searched on BRS, seventeen on Dialog and one on SDC [21]. The same terms were searched in all databases in each system, although the logic and command formulation necessarily differed. A random sample of approximately sixty citations from each database was printed to allow for relevance testing. Relevance was judged by the author to be any citation that was clearly not a false drop. Because no specific query was being tested, a more precise definition of relevance did not apply. The sixty citations allowed a percentage of false drops to be calculated at the 90% confidence level. Differences in databases' indexing policy, multi-meaning of terms in some subject areas, and variations due to different logical formulations across systems were partially compensated for by eliminating obvious false drops. The final number of emergency management related citations per database thus represents only relevant citations.

5. ANALYSIS

Choice of Databases

After the searching and relevance judgement was completed for each of the forty databases, the final number of relevant citations in each was calculated. Fig. 2 presents the databases in ranked order by number of relevant citations.

	Database	Number of citations	Confidence interval
1.	DOE Energy	6089	± 5.7%
2.	NTIS	4401	± 3.9%
3.	SSIE	4317	± 6.7%
4.	GPO Monthly	2460	± 2.0%
5.	Compendex	1852	± 5.5%
6.	Enviroline	1292	± 3.2%
7.	Health Planning	922	± 4.2%
8.	Pollution Abstracts	818	± 3.3%
9.	NCJRS	753	± 7.3%
10.	Safety Science	746	population
11.	ABI/Inform	589	± 7.6%
12.	GeoRef	581	± 3.3%
13.	Inspec	568	± 6.0%
14.	Chemical Abstracts	559	± 3.7%
15.	CAB Abstracts	493	± 8.2%
16.	Medline	485	± 6.9%
17.	Agricola	425	± 6.4%
18.	Excerpta Medica	391	± 7.4%
19.	Frost and Sullivan DM	371	± 5.4%
20.	Energyline	362	± 7.4%
21.	Eric	345	± 7.2%
22.	Aptic	302	± 8.0%
23.	Environmental Bib.	221	± 3.7%
24.	GeoArchive	220	± 2.0%
25.	Oceanic Abstracts	219	± 7.5%
26.	NCMH	207	± 6.9%
27.	Life Sciences	191	± 8.2%
28.	Met/Geo	184	± 4.6%
29.	Magazine Index	154	± 6.8%
30.	PsycInfo	145	± 7.7%
31.	SciSearch	142	± 6.7%
32.	Conference Papers	133	± 6.2%
33.	CRIS/USDA	120	± 7.9%
34.	IH State Publications	110	population
35.	PAIS	94	population
36.	Sociological Abstracts	92	± 7.5%
37.	Biosis	68	population
38.	Comp. Dissertation	55	± 6.5%
39.	Population Bibliography	8	population
40.	EIS	1	population

Fig. 2. Databases ranked by number of relevant citations

This ranking can be used to select those databases that contain the highest total number of citations of interest to the broad areas of emergency management. It should be noted that the ranks could shift slightly where there are small differences among databases because the number of relevant citations in each is an estimate based on a sample.

This ranking does not take into account the wide variety in the number of years included in each database, however, so it does not give any indication of the currency of the citations or density of coverage in any database. In Fig. 3 the databases are re-ranked by the number of emergency management citations per year of coverage. When databases were split into several files, this number represents only the portion searched. Both rankings should be considered when selecting the databases that contain the most information in the field of emergency management.

	Database	Years of coverage	Number of citations
1.	SSIE	5.2	836
2.	DOE Energy	8.2	746
3.	NTIS	7.3	607
4.	GPO Monthly	5.3	464
5.	Compendex	6.2	300
6.	Medline	2.3	208
7.	Excerpta Medica	2.4	162
8.	Safety Science	5.6	134
9.	Enviroline	11.3	115
10.	Health Planning	8.3	112
11.	Inspec	5.2	110
12.	Chemical Abstracts	5.1	110
13.	NCJRS	10.1	75
14.	Frost and Sullivan DM	5.2	72
15.	Pollution Abstracts	12.0	68
16.	SciSearch	2.1	68
17.	Life Sciences	3.0	64
18.	Agricola	7.2	59
19.	ABI/Inform	11.1	53
20.	CAB Abstracts	10.2	49
21.	Energyline	11.1	33
22.	Magazine Index	5.3	29
23.	GeoArchive	8.0	28
24.	GeoRef	21.2	27
25.	Environmental Bib.	8.3	27
26.	Aptic	12.8	24
27.	Eric	16.1	22
28.	Biosis	3.3	21
29.	IH State Publication	5.4	20
30.	Met/Geo	10.1	18
31.	CRIS/USDA	7.1	17
32.	NCMH	13.0	16
33.	Conference Papers	8.8	15
34.	Oceanic Abstracts	18.1	12
35.	PsycInfo	15.0	10
36.	PAIS	10.3	9
37.	Sociological Abs.	23.0	4
38.	Population Bib.	16.1	1
39.	Comp. Dissertation	122.2	1
40.	EIS		1

Fig. 3. Databases ranked by number of relevant citations per year of coverage.

Bradford Distribution

When the total number of citations found in every database is added together, a total relevant citation pool results [22]. With this citation pool and the number of relevant citations in each database, a plot can be drawn to test for a Bradford distribution.

Fig. 4 shows the results of this plot. The straight line is the least-squares fit. The data points fit the line with a correlation coefficient of .995. The plot fits the $R(n) = k\log(n)$ formulation of Bradford's law. It can thus be seen that the linear

portion of a Bradford distribution does apply to databases within the field of emergency management. However, there is not the initial rising curve or concave portion that is characteristic of the usual Bradford nucleus or core. In a typical Bradford distribution, the core deviates from the linear plot due to a higher concentration of relevant citations in the core. In the field of emergency management no deviation from the linear plot is found. This shows that the concentration of citations in the core databases is not as great as might be expected. The general linearity technically makes this curve a Zipf distribution rather than a true Bradford distribution [9].

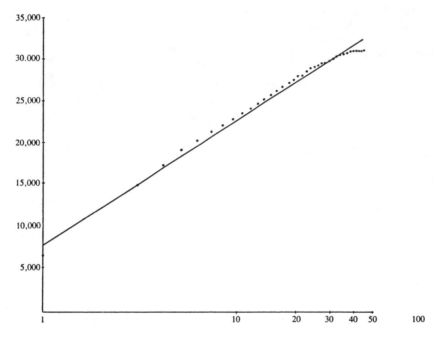

Fig. 4. Semi-log plot of citations in databases.

The number of databases necessary to obtain a given percentage of the literature of emergency management approximates the $1 : a : a^2$ Bradford ratio. Two databases supply approximately one-third of the total relevant citations, 5 (rather than 2×4 or 8) additional databases supply the second one-third, but 2×4^2 or 32 databases supply the final one-third.

Fig. 5 shows a non-logarithmic plot of the data. It illustrates the phenomenon of diminishing returns with the total cumulation growing less and less rapidly with the addition of more databases. Because overlap was not taken into account, the total citation pool does not represent 100% unique citations. It is impossible to know exactly how many of the citations included in the databases with the fewest number of citations are new, unique citations.

Because the Bradford distribution's concentration of citations in the core does not apply to emergency management, no one database will yield a high percentage of the citations in the field. A cumulative frequency calculation (Fig. 6) allows the determination of the number of databases necessary to be searched to obtain a given percentage of the citations. No one database supplies over 19.3% of the total citations [23]. The cut-off in searching could be made at a point that would best satisfy an individual request.

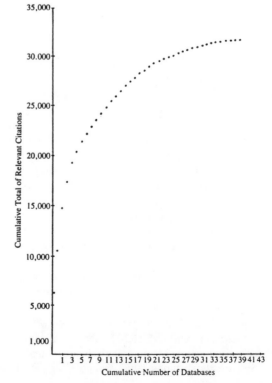

Fig. 5. Number of databases searched for relevant citations.

Some researchers may be satisfied with a 60.7% recall from a search of five databases, others might need a search of the 13-19 databases necessary for 80.6%-89.3% recall. The cost of attempting to achieve 100% recall goes up dramatically as

compared to the recall benefits achieved. Clearly, Evans' blanket policy of limiting most searches to one or two databases would be disastrous in this field.

	Database	Number of citations	Cumulative citations	Cumulative percent
1.	DOE Energy	6089	6089	19.3%
2.	NTIS	4401	10490	33.3%
3.	SSIE	4317	14807	47.0%
4.	GPO Monthly	2460	17267	54.8%
5.	Compendex	1852	19119	60.7%
6.	Enviroline	1292	20411	64.8%
7.	Health Planning	922	21333	67.8%
8.	Pollution	818	22151	70.4%
9.	NCJRS	753	22904	72.7%
10.	Safety Science	746	23650	75.1%
11.	ABI/Inform	589	24239	77.0%
12.	GeoRef	581	24820	78.8%
13.	Inspec	568	25388	80.6%
14.	Chemical Abstracts	559	25947	82.4%
15.	CAB Abstracts	493	26440	84.0%
16.	Medline	485	26925	85.5%
17.	Agricola	425	27350	86.9%
18.	Excerpta Medica	391	27741	88.1%
19.	Frost & Sullivan DM	371	28112	89.3%
20.	Energyline	362	28474	90.4%
21.	Eric	345	28819	91.5%
22.	Aptic	302	29121	92.5%
23.	Environmental Bib.	221	29342	93.2%
24.	GeoArchive	220	29562	93.9%
25.	Oceanic Abstracts	219	29781	94.6%
26.	NCMH	207	29988	95.2%
27.	Life Sciences	191	30179	95.9%
28.	Met/Geo	184	30363	96.4%
29.	Magazine Index	154	30517	96.9%
30.	PsycInfo	145	30662	97.4%
31.	SciSearch	142	30804	97.8%
32.	Conference Papers	133	30937	98.3%
33.	CRIS/USDA	120	31057	98.6%
34.	IH State Pubs.	110	31167	99.0%
35.	PAIS	94	31261	99.3%
36.	Sociological Abstracts	92	31353	99.6%
37.	Biosis	68	31421	99.8%
38.	Comprehensive Diss.	55	31476	99.9%
39.	Population Bib.	8	31484	99.9%
40.	EIS	1	31485	100.0%

Fig. 6. Cumulative citations in databases.

6. CONCLUSIONS AND SUGGESTIONS FOR FURTHER STUDY

Database citations relevant to a multidisciplinary field have been shown to adhere to Bradford's law, or more specifically to follow a Zipf semi-logarithmic plot. Databases can be grouped into three zones, each yielding an equal number of citations, yet each successively containing dramatically more databases.

This phenomenon of diminishing returns might be expected intuitively, but the exact number of databases could not be guessed and has significant practical implications for online searching in multidisciplinary fields. Knowledge of the number of databases necessary to be searched to yield a given percentage of the literature and the individual databases that contain the most citations relevant to emergency management will assist in the search process. It will allow searchers to choose the databases that will yield the most return.

The same methodology should be applied to other multidisciplinary fields to determine if general conclusions drawn from studying one are transferable to others. If it could be demonstrated that multidisciplinary fields have characteristics in common, assistance in choosing the optimum number of databases could be transferable.

Additionally, narrow subjects should be tested on databases to see if Bradford's law of scatter always applies to citations within databases. A comparison of the findings from these subject-specific tests with the tests from multidisciplinary fields could lead to useful conclusions about the nature of scatter of materials in databases.

Overlap of specific citations among databases was not considered in this study because correcting for overlap is more complicated and necessitates a larger sample size. It would be interesting to test if, when overlap is considered, the results would adhere even more closely to the linear plot.

These many aspects of the issues of choice and number of databases require further study. As the number of databases continues to increase, as subject fields become increasingly multidisciplinary, and with the continuing addition of database vendors, these issues will need to be addressed.

7. REFERENCES AND NOTES

[1]Robert Niehoff, Stan Kwasny and Michael Wessells, "Overcoming the Database Vocabulary Barrier—A Solution," *Online*, 3, 4, October 1979, pp. 43-54.

[2]Carol Tenopir and Martha E. Williams, *FEMA Database Requirements Assessment and Resource Directory Model*, Coordinated Science Laboratory Report No. R942, prepared for the Federal Emergency Management Agency, 1982.

[3]S. C. Bradford, *Documentation*. London: Crosby Lockwood, 1948.

[4]M. Carl Drott, "Bradford's Law," *Library Trends*, 30, Summer 1981, pp. 41-52.

[5]Elizabeth Wilkinson, "The Ambiguity of Bradford's Law," *Journal of Documentation*, 28, June 1972, pp. 122-30.

[6]Gloria S. Cline, "Application of Bradford's Law to Citation Data," *College and Research Libraries*, 42, January 1981, pp. 53-61.

[7]B. C. Vickery, "Bradford's Law of Scattering," *Journal of Documentation*, 41, 1948, pp. 198-203.

[8]B. C. Brookes, "Theory of the Bradford Law," *Journal of Documentation*, 33, September 1977, pp. 180-209.

[9]B. C. Brookes, "Numerical Methods of Bibliographic Analysis," *Library Trends*, 22, July 1973, pp. 18-23.

[10]Judith Wanger, "Multiple Database Use," *Online*, 1, 4, October 1977, pp. 35-41.

[11]Barbara A. Epstein and Jennifer J. Angier, "Multi-Database Searching in the Behavioural Sciences, Part 1," *Database*, 3, 3, September 1980, pp. 9-15.

[12]Donald T. Hawkins, "Multiple Database Searching: Techniques and Pitfalls," *Online*, 2, 2, April 1978, pp. 9-15.

[13]Martha E. Williams, "Feasibility Study For an Automatic Database Selector," *Newsidic*, 20, Summer 1976, p. 14.

[14]Martha E. Williams and Scott Preece, "Database Selector For Network Use: A Feasibility Study," In: *Proceedings of the ASIS Annual Meeting*. White Plains, New York: Knowledge Industry Publications, Inc., fiche no. 10C-13, 1977.

[15]Martha E. Williams, *Computer Readable Databases*. White Plains, N.Y.: Knowledge Industry Publications, Inc., 1982, 1516pp.

[16]Ruth Cuadra, ed. *Directory of Online Databases*. Santa Monica, CA.: Cuadra Associates, 1981.

[17]Virgil P. Diodato, *Author Indexing in Mathematics*. Ph.D. dissertation, University of Illinois, 1981.

[18]Gerda Yska and John Martyn, *Databases Suitable for Users of Environmental Information*. London, Aslib, 1976.

[19]John Martyn, *Service to an Interdisciplinary Need-Group From Computerized Secondary Services*. London, Aslib, 1975.

[20]John Edward Evans, "Database Selection in an Academic Library," *Online*, 4, 2, April 1980, pp. 35-43.

[21]Several of the databases are available on more than one of these systems. Databases were generally searched on BRS if possible as a first choice because of lower search costs. Dialog was the second choice.

22Some evidence of specific citations undoubtedly exists in the total numbers, but it was outside the scope of this project to test for citation overlap percentages among databases.

23Because overlap was not calculated, each percentage figure represents the percentage of the total citations retrieved, not the percentage of the unique citations. If overlap was accounted for, each percentage figure would be slightly higher because the total *unique* citation pool would be smaller.

ACKNOWLEDGEMENTS

This project was funded in part by the United States Federal Emergency Management Agency, Contract No. FEMA EMW-1-4058 and in part by a Reese Fund grant from the University of Illinois Graduate School of Library and Information Science. I wish to thank Martha E. Williams, Professor, College of Engineering, Coordinated Science Laboratory, University of Illinois, for her help and advice.

APPENDIX 1: CANDIDATE DATABASES

ABI/Inform
Agricola
Aqualine
American Petroleum Institute (API)
Aptic

Biological Abstracts (Biosis)

CAB Abstracts
Chemical Abstracts (CA Search)
Compendex
Comprehensive Dissertation Index
Conference Papers Index
CRIS/USDA

DOE Energy

Energyline
Enviroline
Environmental Bibliography
Environmental Impact Statements (EIS)
Eric
Excerpta Medica

Frost and Sullivan Defense Market Measures System (DM)

GeoArchive
GeoRef
GPO Monthly Catalog

Health Planning and Administration

IH State Publications
Information Bank
Inspec
Iris
ISMEC

Legal Resources Index
Life Sciences Collection

Magazine Index
Management Contents
Medline
Meteorological and Geoastrophysical Abstracts

National Center for Mental Health (NCMH)
National Criminal Justice Reference Service (NCJRS)
National Newspaper Index
National Technical Information Service (NTIS)
Newsearch
Newspaper Index

Oceanic Abstracts

PAIS
Pestdoc
Pollution Abstracts
Popline
Population Bibliography
Psychological Abstracts (PsycInfo)

Safety Science Abstracts
Science Citation Index (SciSearch)
Social SciSearch
Sociological Abstracts
SSIE Current Research

Toxline
TRIS
Tulsa

Water Resources Abstracts

APPENDIX 2: DATABASES TESTED

Database	Primary subject
ABI/Inform	Business
Agricola	Agriculture
Aptic	Air pollution
Biosis	Biology
CAB Abstracts	Agriculture
Chemical Abstracts	Chemistry
Compendex	Engineering
Comp. Dissertation Index	Multidisciplinary
Conference Papers Index	Multidisciplinary
CRIS/USDA	Agriculture research
DOE Energy	Energy
Energyline	Energy
Enviroline	Environment
Environmental Bibliography	Environment
EIS	Environment
Eric	Education
Excerpta Medica	Medicine
Frost and Sullivan DM	Defense
GeoArchive	Geology
GeoRef	Geology
GPO Monthly	Multidisciplinary
Health Planning	Medicine
IH State Publications	Multidisciplinary
Inspec	Physics, Electronics
Life Sciences	Biology
Magazine Index	Multidisciplinary
Medline	Medicine
Met/Geo	Meteorology
NCMH	Mental Health
NJCRS	Criminology
NTIS	Multidisciplinary
Oceanic Abstracts	Oceanography
PAIS	Social Sciences
Pollution Abstracts	Environment
Population Bibliography	Population
PsycInfo	Psychology
Safety Science Abstracts	Safety
SciSearch	Sciences
Sociological Abstracts	Sociology
SSIE	Multidisciplinary ■

GENERAL LITERATURE ONLINE
Magazine Index and *Readers' Guide**

Two online databases, *Magazine Index* and the *Readers' Guide to Periodical Literature*, are the primary sources for indexing of general interest magazines.

Both *Magazine Index* and *Readers' Guide* index the same type of magazines. They differ, however, in such things as cost, indexing policies, dates of coverage, the number of magazines indexed, and the amount of information in each record. Some of these differences affect search results as well as the decision of which database to search. This column compares the two databases and reports the results of searching the same questions on each.

MAGAZINE INDEX

From its entry into the database market in 1976, *Magazine Index* has dominated online access to indexing of general magazine articles. It consistently shows up in studies of database use as one of the ten most frequently used databases in libraries. From 1976 until late 1985 *Magazine Index* was available exclusively on *DIALOG*. The exclusive contract between DIALOG and *Magazine Index*'s producer, Information Access Company (IAC), was terminated in 1985, so *Magazine Index* and other IAC databases are now available on *BRS*, *DIALOG*, and Mead Data Central's NEXIS. *Magazine Index* is also available on *BRS/After Dark*, *BRS/SEARCH*, *BRS/COLLEAGUE*, and *DIALOG*'s end user search system, *Knowledge Index*.

Magazine Index indexes over 435 magazines from the United States, Canada, and England; it includes all magazines indexed by the *Readers' Guide to Periodical Literature*. The database includes over 2,200,000 articles as of early 1986, covering the period 1959-March 1970 and 1973 to the present. (A retrospective indexing project to fill in this two-year gap in coverage is now on hold, probably not to resume again. Spokespeople at IAC say there has been no great demand for the missing years.)

The records in *Magazine Index* include subject descriptors based on the Library of Congress Subject Headings, with additions and modifications made at the discretion of the IAC indexing department.

Subject retrieval is enhanced in some records by explanatory phrases added to the article title, geographic terms, geographic codes, a named people field, or the inclusion of the text from the captions of graphs, charts, or portraits. Only a very small number of records in the database have abstracts. Abstracts are no longer being added.

Full-text versions of articles from over 82 of the *Magazine Index* journals are searchable in another IAC database, *Magazine ASAP*. These full texts may also be *viewed* (but not searched) in the *Magazine Index* on *DIALOG*.

Though *MI* is updated monthly, current indexing is available daily in the *Newsearch* database. *Newsearch* includes up to 45 days worth of new records that are used for the monthly updates of several IAC databases.

Prices for *Magazine Index* are $90 per connect hour on *DIALOG*, and up to $80 per hour on *BRS* depending on the subscription rate. There is a charge of 20¢ per record printed online and 25¢ per record printed offline on *BRS* and 20¢ online and 40¢ offline on *DIALOG*. *Newsearch* is $120 per hour.

READERS' GUIDE

The *Readers' Guide to Periodical Literature* is the online equivalent of the H. W. Wilson Company's popular printed index. It indexes 186 U.S. and Canadian English-language popular magazines, recommended by the Committee on Wilson Indexes of the American Library Association's Reference and Adult Services Division.

The database includes only records from January 1983 to the present, with approximately 180,000 articles as of early 1986. *Readers' Guide* is updated twice a week with approximately 5200 articles added each month.

RG is available online only via *WILSONLINE*, Wilson's own online system. (*WILSONLINE* also includes all of the other Wilson indexes.) Notable features of the *WILSONLINE* software include the ability to search up to eight files at the same time and automatic switching to a correct controlled vocabulary term when a term is entered that is a "see" reference. The system is relatively easy for intermediaries.

The records in *RG* are brief, including from one to five subject headings from Wilson's own subject authority based on the Library of Congress Subject Headings. Article type codes and explanatory phrases for unclear titles enhance retrieval, but abstracts are not in the file. The information in the database is the same as found in the printed *Readers' Guide*. (Abstracts are available in a separate file, *Readers' Guide Abstracts*, that corresponds to the printed and microfiche *R.G.A.*)

Rates for *RG* are based on a combination of hourly connect-time and offline print charges. Per-hour rates vary from a low of $25 (for subscribers to both the printed index and a subscription of $2400 per year on *WILSONLINE*) to a high of $45 (for those who subscribe to neither the printed nor online versions). Offline prints cost 20¢ per citation with a minimum of $10 for offline printing per search session. There is no charge for online prints.

COMPARISON

To compare results of searching these similar databases, I searched the same six questions on each. After searching I went back to each to try to determine why some things were

---

retrieved on one that were not retrieved on the other. The search questions were those asked at an undergraduate or public library reference desk.

A combination of free-text searching and controlled-vocabulary searching were used as appropriate, although controlled vocabulary was favored when available because most of the requestors wanted just a few highly relevant articles.

SEARCH RESULTS

The first question was a call for information on AIDS in hemophiliacs. Specific relevant subject heading terms exist for both components of this topic in both *RG* and *MI*. There was no overlap in documents retrieved in the two databases, however. Two records were found in *RG*, both from *Science* issues from 1983 and both relevant. They were not retrieved in *MI* because the term "hemophilia" was not assigned.

MI retrieved six articles. Two were about the broader topic HTLV viruses, for which *MI* assigned the term "AIDS" and *RG* did not. The others were retrieved because hemophilia was only discussed as one of many topics in the article and *RG* indexed only the major topics.

Variations in indexing policies resulted in the variations in retrieval. *RG* often did not assign many subject headings, but seemed to index more consistently according to the level of specificity of the documents.

The second question asked was: How have microcomputers been used with preschool children? An obvious database to check here would be *ERIC*, but because many smaller libraries do not have *ERIC* materials in their collections, *MI* or *RG* might be used instead. *RG* retrieved three documents, all relevant, by free-text searching preschool terms and computer(s). (No documents were retrieved with the narrower term microcomputer.) Two of the three were also retrieved in *MI*; the third was not because *MI* did not assign it the term "preschool."

MI has a descriptor "microcomputers" which yielded one citation when linked with the free-text terms for preschool. By broadening the search to computer(s) and preschool(s) an additional six documents were retrieved, three of which were false drops from 1968. One of the relevant documents retrieved by *MI* that was not retrieved by *RG* was found in a journal that is not indexed by *RG*. Another was retrieved because *RG* assigned the narrower subject "video games" rather than "computers." All of the relevant documents were from 1984 or 1985.

Question number three was: How do liquor laws affect the liquor industry? Both *RG* and *MI* had specific relevant subject headings for the two concepts. *RG* retrieved two relevant documents (*Forbes* 1985 and *MacLeans* 1983) and *MI* retrieved a different three relevant documents (*Prevention* 1984, *Boston Magazine* 1981, and *Business Week* 1964). The two documents retrieved by *RG* were not retrieved by *MI* because they were not assigned a subject heading for the liquor laws concept. Of the three retrieved by *MI*, one was too old for *RG*, one was in a journal not covered by *RG*, and one was inexplicably not in the *RG* database even though the magazine (*Prevention*) is indexed by *RG*.

In both databases, a broader search using synonyms for "liquor laws" and "liquor industry" might have been successful.

The next question was a request for information, "anything" on the street drug called Ecstasy (MDMA or MDA). This was the most successful search, retrieving nine documents (all relevant) on *RG*, 13 (12 relevant) on *MI*.

In both *RG* and *MI* there is a controlled term for the drug. If a searcher did not know the drug name before searching, however, by just entering "Ecstasy AND Drug" in each database the controlled term could be found.

Since this is a new topic, the retrospectivity of *MI* did not enter into the results. Seven of the nine hits in *RG* were also retrieved in *MI*. The other two were not in *MI* (*Rolling Stone* December 1985-January 1986 and *Time* June 1985), although they should have been. The same problem occurred in *RG*. A February 1986 article in *Science Digest*, an October 1985 article in *Seventeen*, and an August 1985 article in *Scientific American* were not in the *RG* database. Another two hits in *MI* were in journals not covered by *RG*.

The fifth question asked: What is the role of the Soviet Union in the Philippines? *RG* retrieved no documents with controlled or free-text searches. *MI* has two very specific relevant subject headings "Philippines—Relations with Soviet Union" and "Soviet Union—Relations with Philippines" which were "OR"ed together. One relevant document was retrieved. A broader free-text search retrieved nine documents, all of which were false drops. Most of the false drops occurred because of the *MI* policy to index all pertinent concepts in a document (*RG* limits subjects to five). The Soviet Union and Philippines were found in general foreign policy articles in which both countries were discussed and indexed but were not discussed together.

The sixth and final question was: How does a person's attitude about death and dying differ by their religion? Free-text searches on this topic resulted in many false drops, but controlled terms yielded better results. *RG* had no term for the concept as a whole, providing a "see" reference to the term "death." A narrower term "Cancer Patients/Religious Life" yielded four relevant documents. (Three of these four documents were also retrieved in *RG* by searching death as a subject heading "AND" religion.)

MI had a very specific subject "Death—Moral and Religious Aspects" which was searched in an "OR" relationship with the terms "Death—Attitudes AND Religion?" Of the 34 documents retrieved, 30 were relevant. Eight of the 30 came from the journal *U.S. Catholic*, an additional 12 came from journals such as *Christian Century*, *Christianity Today*, *Christian Herald*, and *National Catholic Report*. The latter two are not indexed in *RG*.

CONCLUSIONS

Because there are no abstracts in either *Readers' Guide* or *Magazine Index* and titles of general articles are often short, controlled-vocabulary searching is the necessary alternative. It is easy and usually retrieved some relevant items. More false drops were retrieved on *MI*, but also frequently additional relevant hits. Sometimes this was because of the retrospective nature of *MI*, more often because of its broader journal coverage.

MI's indexing policy seemed less consistently applied than that of *RG*, making retrieval harder to predict. *RG*'s policy is restrictive, yielding low recall but high precision. In double checking why specific articles were not retrieved, I was surprised to find that both databases sometimes missed articles that should have been included. All of these missed articles were less than eight months old, so it might be explained by backlogs in indexing or indexing priorities. Both also contained many very current records.

It is difficult to choose between *RG* and *MI* for current searches. Both databases yielded unique relevant references, making them complementary rather than duplicative. Both have limited information in their records, and rely on controlled-vocabulary searching. The vocabulary switching feature of *RG* eases such searching in *WILSONLINE*. One deciding factor for many libraries must be cost. *Readers' Guide* is much less expensive. In search situations when a limited number of highly relevant current articles are sought, searching on *RG* can be done very quickly and economically. For retrospectivity, *MI* has no online competition. For comprehensiveness, however, neither is completely adequate. ■

EVALUATING ONLINE SYSTEMS*

A special librarian recently commented to me that the most important skill she was looking for in a person to fill a librarian position is the ability to evaluate online systems. She needs someone who can take the time to find out about all of the likely online systems on the market, compare them by criteria established for her organization, and recommend what systems should be added to her search services. Like many of us, this librarian regularly accesses systems that she feels comfortable searching, but she doesn't have time to study whether others might be as good or even better for the needs of her clientele.

ONLINE SYSTEMS

The importance of these evaluation skills is pointed out by the January 1988 edition of the Cuadra/Elsevier *Directory of Online Databases*, which lists 555 publicly available online services worldwide. This 555 actually represents a slowdown in growth, according to Cuadra Associates. There was a net growth of only 27 new online systems in 1987, which is "only 36 percent of the growth in 1986 and 29 percent of the growth during 1985." For the information professional, 555 systems is still a lot to cope with. Many of the 555 are not of interest to libraries, yet there are dozens of online systems of potential interest in a library setting.

At the 1988 Australian Online Meeting and 1988 National Online Meeting in New York, Martha Williams (University of Illinois-Urbana) presented an overview of online system use by the information center/library market in the United States. She regularly samples 12 percent of this market (550 institutions) by analyzing their online bills. Libraries and information centers are still concentrating their online use on a few systems.

Williams identified 16 systems libraries used, including DIALOG, Mead Data Central (LEXIS/NEXIS), BRS, STN

International, Westlaw, NLM Medlars, Orbit, WILSONLINE, Dow Jones News Retrieval, VU/TEXT, Newsnet, Questel, and The Source. The first seven of these systems account for 98 percent of the use and 97 percent of the expenditures in the library and information center market. DIALOG and Mead Data Central together account for 72 percent of the usage and 80 percent of the expenditures, figures that have held relatively steady since Williams began collecting data in 1982.

EVALUATING DATABASES

For a more detailed discussion of selecting an online system, see Susanne M. Humphrey and Biagio John Melloni's *Databases: a Primer for Retrieving Information by Computer*, Prentice-Hall, 1986. The *number* of databases is an important evaluation criterion if you are trying to meet the needs of the greatest number of people with one system. One reason to use DIALOG, for example, may be because its many databases will give you the greatest variety.

Perhaps more important than just the number is the *uniqueness* of the databases offered. Even if a system does not have a large number of databases, if the ones it does have are available nowhere else, the system is valuable.

Neither number nor uniqueness matters unless the *subjects* of the databases are of interest to your users. What subjects are covered by the individual databases on the system and are there systemwide specializations? Orbit has concentrations in patents and petroleum information. BRS has many education databases available nowhere else.

Different systems are better for different *types* of databases. If you need statistical information you may be better off with a system that specializes in numeric information and provides you with numeric manipulation capabilities. I. P. Sharp offers many numeric databases with a command language that will let you exploit the unique properties of statistical information. DIALOG's Business Connection will calculate reports that cannot be done with the regular DIALOG software. Full-text databases also have particular retrieval and display needs ("Searching Full-Text Databases," *LJ*, May 1, p. 60-61).

Time coverage of databases may be outside of the control of the online system, but often depends on the system. The databases on WILSONLINE mostly go back only to the beginning of the system (generally 1983). The information on NEXIS mostly starts with 1981, when NEXIS began. *Timeliness* refers to how often databases on a system are updated and whether or not a system usually meets its update schedule. Updating ranges from almost instantaneous for stock market quotes to yearly or less for directories or encyclopedias.

How systems help you search different databases will be important to searchers who plan to use many databases. Cross-file consistency makes multifile searching much easier. Medlars and WILSONLINE offer a fair amount of consistency and vocabulary control across databases, DIALOG has very little. Multifile search capabilities vary from allowing only a single file at a time to be searched on Medlars, to user-specified file groupings on systems (DIALOG and Mead).

STRUCTURE

Structure means how the system processes the records to make them searchable. Most of the powerful online systems create secondary inverted indexes that retain field information and word location information so searchers get fast response times even with complex searches using Boolean and proximity operators. Some systems still have no proximity features, making it necessary to "stringsearch" (sequentially scan) the database for free-text phrases, which is extremely limiting. (Medlars requires you to create a 300 or smaller item subject before stringsearching.)

Systems such as The Source and Compuserve do not provide inverted indexes for every word in most of their databases, making it impossible to do the kind of free-text searching possible in the other textual systems.

There are other structural features to look for that impact search capabilities. Can fields be searched separately or all together as the searcher specifies? Can the inverted index be displayed online and can terms be selected directly from the display? To what fields does a subject search default? (If author is included in the default you may get many false drops.) Can individual words in a multiword descriptor be searched?

SEARCH FEATURES

Many of the factors mentioned affect the power of the query language. You might use a prioritized list of desired searching features and match it against a system's capabilities. For textual databases these features should include such things as Boolean operations including nesting, set building, proximity operations, ranging, greater than or less than, truncation, and field specification. For full-text searching, all of the above apply plus searching for words in the same sentence and weighting by number of times search words occur in a document. For numeric databases add statistical manipulation and computations.

INTERFACE/HELP FEATURES

In addition to power, the interface to the query language should be evaluated. A good interface depends on the sophistication and experience of the intended users. For novice or infrequent users is there a menu driven interface? For more frequent users is there a command option? Can either be selected? How easy is the system to learn (from the viewpoint of users)? Are online helps available? Are the error messages meaningful?

OUTPUT FEATURES

Output refers to online display, online printing or downloading, or to offline printing. Are offline prints and online printing both available? How much flexibility does the user have over the formats? Are there system-supplied formats as well as user-designed formats? Are special output formats available, such as label generation (DIALOG) or card catalog output (WILSONLINE)? For full-text files, can you print only those portions of the documents that contain search terms? For numeric databases can you print in columnar or report formats? Can output easily be transferred to a word processing, database, or spreadsheet program for further refinement? Is offline and online sorting available?

SUPPORT

How much does the vendor help and support you? Is there a toll-free number, preferably available as many hours as the system is up? If you call do you get immediate and accurate answers to your questions?

Can you learn to search the systems from the manuals? If your library is expanding the number of online services offered, it is especially important to have good information in the manuals because you may be searching some systems infrequently. Are the manuals regularly updated and is there a fee for this service? Are database summary sheets and other search aids available?

Does the system provide a newsletter on a regular schedule? Is training available in your area? What does it cost? Are any tutorials, computer-assisted instruction, practice files, videotapes, or other learning aids available? NEXIS has a new microcomputer tutorial; DIALOG, WILSONLINE, and BRS have all issued videos in the last year.

Finally, does the system sell any front-end software that makes searching easier? LEXIS/NEXIS, DIALOG, WILSONLINE, Medlars, Dow Jones News Retrieval all have microcomputer software. DIALOG and BRS offer simplified versions of their systems available online.

RELIABILITY/TECHNICAL MATTERS

What is the response time at peak times and at off-peak hours? Of course the most important response time is when you will be doing the most searching, so average times that include responses in the middle of the night are fairly meaningless. Does the software or hardware of the system impose arbitrary limitations on your searching? For example, Medlars allots limited time slices to each user. In complex operations a user will need to respond many times to a time overflow message. Other systems have limits on the number of word variations that can be retrieved in a search. BRS and WILSON-LINE will process only 100 stem variations.

Does the system experience frequent downtime (scheduled or unscheduled)? How will this affect your users and search operations? Are several telecommunications networks supported, so if one goes down you will have an alternate path to the system? What transmission speeds are supported? Are there any special hardware requirements? Mead Data Central used to require their own dedicated terminal; now you can use a microcomputer with Mead's software, but dumb terminals won't work.

COSTS

What is the basis of pricing? Is it based on connect hour, information retrieved, or a combination? Are there minimum usage charges, per month or per year? Are subscriptions required or are they available to reduce costs for high-volume users? Does the price formula seem fair and easy to estimate? Have costs held relatively steady over time?

Williams calculated some average per hour costs on the major systems. Overall, across all systems, libraries spent an average of $122 per hour online in 1986. Per hour costs for individual systems in 1982 and 1986 were:

System	1982	1986
Mead	$150	$141
DIALOG	93	126
Medlars	28	39
BRS	49	69
Orbit	109	130
Westlaw	30	100
STN	122	203

OLDIES AREN'T THE ONLY GOODIES

Multiple system use is made easier with Online Inc.'s *Online International Command Chart*, which presents commands for 15 U.S. systems as well as many Canadian and European systems. If you know one system well it is easy to find how you would do a similar function on another system. (Online Inc., 11 Tannery Lane, Weston, CT 06883; 203-227-8466.) In addition, the multiple system gateways such as EasyNet allow anyone to access many online systems without having individual contracts with the systems or without knowing all of the command languages. Even before really good front-end software that knows dozens or hundreds of systems (and even without a universal common command language), libraries today do not need to limit their online use to one or two "old favorites." ∎

LIBRARY USE OF "THE SOURCE" AND "COMPUSERVE"*

I didn't expect many responses when I asked librarians, twice last year, if they were offering access to either the Source or CompuServe. The two consumer information systems are marketed primarily to home computer users. The lack of enthusiasm for the systems in the responses I did get from librarians was a surprise. Some feel their patrons should access these systems without the library. Others consider the type of information available on the Source and CompuServe to be inappropriate to library use. Still others do not have time to think about adding the consumer information online systems to the many services they now offer.

THE SOURCE & COMPUSERVE: SERVICES

The Source (1616 Anderson Rd., McLean, VA 22102; (800) 572-2070 or (703) 734-7500) is owned by Source Tele-

computing. CompuServe (500 Arlington Centre Blvd., POB 20212, Columbus, OH 43220; (800) 848-8990; (614) 457-8600), is a subsidiary of H.&R. Block. Howard Falk compares the two systems in his "The Source v. CompuServe" (*Online Review*, June 1984, p. 214-224), and describes nine categories of service both offer:

- communication services (electronic mail, bulletin boards, special interest group user conferences, informal communication via "CB" simulator or "chat" features);

- news and publications (newswires, newspaper extracts, limited access to some periodicals);

- business and financial features (daily business news, securities and commodity trading information, investment portfolio management, stock and bond trading information, investment information);

- education features (quizzes on academic subjects, an encyclopedia, college planning information);

- online publication and information (online authorship, access to an information broker);

- personal service features (book ordering, shopping, swapshops and trading, job services);

- travel (airline schedules and booking, restaurant guides, travel planning, information on foreign countries);

- remote computing services (word processing, editing, programming, business applications on system computer);

- entertainment, "other services" to Falk (video games, movie reviews, Hollywood gossip, recipes, sports).

Although they offer basically the same types of services, Falk sees differences in emphasis between the two systems. He feels the Source emphasizes personal information for the at-home user, while CompuServe is oriented to professional and business needs. Both Falk adds, "reach an audience of well-educated and affluent micro/personal computer users," fulfilling their personal consumer and business needs at home. According to Don Picard ("Inside CompuServe," *Link-Up: Communications and the Small Computer*, January 1985, p. 7-11), 60 percent of CompuServe's revenues come from its Business Information Service. Bev Smith ("The Source—Will Its Menu Spell Success?", *Information Today*, June 1984, p. 11-13) says 60 percent of the Source customers use its business offerings, although the communication services are also popular.

The variety of information offered on CompuServe and the Source is almost overwhelming with hundreds of services available through a maze of hierarchical menus. Both find printed subject guides necessary so the user can go directly to specific services.

Librarians used to the research-oriented online systems such as DIALOG, BRS, or ORBIT will find the search capabilities of CompuServe and the Source limited and rather primitive. In most instances, the user selects a number for the service desired or reaches it through a series of subject menus. On CompuServe, once the user has reached the text of the *Academic American Encyclopedia*, for example, the articles must be scanned or read as they would in the printed work. The only access is by the title of each article. On BRS or DIALOG the same encyclopedia can be searched word by word or by any combination of words anywhere in the text. Such sophisticated search and retrieval cannot be done on CompuServe's encyclopedia where the means of access is more like the table of contents of a book, while BRS and DIALOG provide the searching power of a very full index.

The Source does offer some elementary search capabilities in a few databases. In the UPI newswire file, searchers can link as many as three terms with the Boolean "AND" or "OR." In most cases, however, the Source, like CompuServe, offers only simple, menu-driven read or scan capabilities.

Although CompuServe is newer than the Source, Picard says it is growing more rapidly with over 150,000 subscribers as of January 1985, up from only 15,000 in January 1982. Revenues neared $52 million in 1984. The Source, which does not release revenue figures, has 65,000 subscribers.

Both offer inexpensive nonprime time (evening and weekend) rates. CompuServe at $6 per hour for 300 baud access or $12.50 for 1200 baud access and the Source at $8.40 per hour for 300 baud access and $10.80 for 1200 baud and $12 for 9600 baud. Daytime costs go up to $15 per hour 1200 baud access on CompuServe ($12.50 at 300 baud) and $25.80 per hour 1200 baud access on the Source ($21.60 at 300 baud and $27.60 at 9600 baud). Surcharges are added for some databases. Both charge a start-up fee ($39.95 for CompuServe, $49.95 for the Source).

Both can be accessed with the same dumb terminal or microcomputer and 300 or 1200 baud modem that is used for research services such as DIALOG, BRS, or ORBIT and they utilize the same online technologies.

CompuServe and the Source are often called "information utilities" or "videotex" services, but I call them "consumer information systems." "Utility" implies essential services and government regulation. "Videotex" usually means a static, page-oriented, non-ASCII service such as the British "Prestel." Neither term describes CompuServe and the Source, which are distinct from the research-based or "encyclopedic" online services in the type of information they provide, their customers, and their less sophisticated search software.

LIBRARY USE

Although CompuServe and the Source are marketed primarily to home computer owners, I thought more libraries would offer them, since a growing number provide end-user access to DIALOG's Knowledge Index and BRS/After Dark, newer research information services for end-users. I found the opposite trend. Some libraries that once offered the Source or CompuServe have suspended the service.

The Library at Wheaton, a small Christian college in Illinois, is a case in point (see Phillips, Roger, "A Public Access Videotex Library Service," *Online*, September 1982, p. 34-39). The Wheaton librarians had hoped the Source would "ease apprehensive librarians into more complex information retrieval systems such as DIALOG" and provide a "bridge" for library clients to the bibliographic retrieval services. They also wanted to enhance the image of the library as a place to find any type of information service. The UPI national and international news was a prime attraction.

While they charged for intermediary-run DIALOG searches, Wheaton decided to absorb the lower costs of the Source at first. They became one of the heaviest Source users. Jonathan Lauer, former Head of Public Services at Wheaton, tells what happened: "It was with considerable dismay ... given our expectations, that we observed large numbers of students logging-on to games—online football and Adventure and other time and money wasters.... There were times when the library and Source became a mere extension of the College game room. Further, as we later discovered, no number of 'No Games' signs can conquer the insatiable desire to play them when they are available free. And the role of the librarian as policeman is one we reject out of hand....

"National and international news was not what our students wanted. Hometown football scores were much more interesting.... I question whether it is the role of the academic library to underwrite online access to high school sports scores....

"As the semester progressed ... our director had some alarming news. We were spending three to four times what we had budgeted for Source. Student response to the new service had been greater than anticipated. That was good. But the use being made of the system was far more trivial than we had hoped....

"We decided to put a money box next to the terminal and recover our costs. Users were asked to pay for their time at the rate of 10 cents a minute. A funny thing happened. When the service became a cost recovery operation, use plummeted to ground zero. Mighty Wheaton College, one of Source's 50 steadiest customers, dropped out of the running entirely. What our students seemed to be telling us was that when it came from their pockets, 10 cents a minute was too much to pay for games and hometown football scores! This reaction took us all by surprise."

Wheaton suspended student access to the Source. While the students were "more than willing" to pay for DIALOG searches they would not pay for Source consumer information.

Lauer feels that because "the Source and similar systems have been developed for the home computer market ... their place in and adaptability to the academic library remains ... questionable."

Dan Bowell, Head of Public Services at Wheaton, says he has been thinking of exploring the Source again and reexamining its potential value for a small college library. For the last six months, their main source of intermediary searching has shifted from DIALOG to BRS/After Dark because of its bargain rates. Staff intermediaries and two student assistants perform the After Dark searches. Students are charged on a cost-recovery basis.

While a public library might not have the same criteria for the appropriateness of consumer information, Ken Dowlin, Director of Pikes Peak Library District in Colorado Springs, points out another negative consideration from their experience: "the Source requires users to be very familiar with the system, in which case they usually have their own contract. The occasional users do not have much use for it. For all practical purposes, we are no longer promoting this to our users."

The maze of menus and services does not seem to lend itself to casual, occasional users who do not have a specific information need. The most faithful users of CompuServe and the Source spend many hours at home interacting with the systems or use a few specific services regularly.

More libraries maintain accounts with the Source or CompuServe for internal use than for public access. Responses to me suggest that the electronic mail services are, by far, the most popular in libraries. Frequently accounts are maintained to send messages between libraries or between information brokers and library clients.

B. C. Stryck of the Amoco Research Center, Standard Oil Company (Indiana) wrote: "occasionally we use the UPI files on the Source, and we use the bulletin board features once in a while also. Almost all of our usage, however, is with the electronic mail system." They record all online orders on disk transmitted via the Source to their information broker and upload the orders to the order file maintained on the company mainframe computer.

While electronic document ordering via electronic mail can save time and money and could justify the use of such systems in libraries, electronic mail is available from many other sources that have lower costs per transaction and do not charge a start-up fee.

Is there a library place for CompuServe and the Source beyond electronic mail? The low cost of such research end-user systems as BRS/After Dark may be making the Source or CompuServe unnecessary to academic libraries. BRS/After Dark and Knowledge Index provide types of information that may be more appropriate, more in demand, and at reasonable per hour costs.

CompuServe and the Source provide some valuable information services not available on research systems. Airline booking, hotel information, stock quotes, and up-to-date information on the computer industry may interest users of any library. If CompuServe or the Source offered a password feature allowing subscribers to lock out trivial, unwanted services, and those that carry extra premium charges, more libraries might consider offering and subsidizing public use of the systems. Some libraries might target their online marketing efforts to specific services to attract specific users. The Source and CompuServe are easy to use if a user has a specific information service in mind and clear instructions on how to gain access to it.

As more libraries provide public access to online search equipment and users become more aware of libraries as a place for self-service online access to information, more libraries will reexamine the information offerings of these consumer information systems. ■

CHAPTER

8

DATABASE STRUCTURE AND SEARCH STRATEGY

Chapter 8 is about improving searches and search strategy. To be good at searching, the database searcher must have an understanding of how databases are designed and structured, as well as knowledge of each specific system's command languages and search techniques. In spite of over two decades of research into how to improve online systems and the search process, the major online systems of today require training, practice, and often more than a little patience.

Other chapters in this book include information that is helpful in improving search strategy. Many of the articles in Chapter 6, for example, address techniques for improving search strategy with full text databases. Evaluative information in Chapter 7 shows ways to improve strategies for the databases featured. This chapter discusses search strategy from a more universal approach—examining how the structures and characteristics of online systems and databases impact the search process and how knowledge of these can help a searcher.

"Database Design and Management" is a tutorial on how commercial online databases are designed, structured, and implemented online. It approaches databases from the database producer's viewpoint, emphasizing how the decisions producers make affect us as searchers of their products.

Also covered in this first article is how the online vendor processes the databases for searching. Computer processing of databases and the common search features available with the vendor's software can impose limits or provide help with searching. Although the issues and information discussed in "Database Design and Management" are background information rather than direct search strategy hints, understanding how and why something works helps eliminate the "black box" or "inscrutable computer" syndrome and is the first step in building good search strategy.

The second article builds on this information base to look at why some online searches fail, failures that in many cases can be attributed to online systems failing their users. "To Err Is Human: Seven Common Searching Mistakes" was borne from frustration experienced by my beginning online searching students. Simple, seemingly trivial things done wrong have an out-of-proportion impact on a search. With today's online systems it is not enough to have an intellectual grasp of a subject and to develop an appropriate search plan. The most elaborate search strategy can be sabotaged by a forgotten space, a missing letter, or a misplaced keystroke. Perhaps in the future better online systems or front-end software will take care of the formatting tasks and let the searcher take care of only intellectual ones. For now, a part of search strategy and searching diagnostics has to be at the trivial level.

"Searching by Controlled Vocabulary or Free Text?" discusses what might be called a higher level of search strategy development. When to use the controlled vocabulary subject headings and when to rely instead on searching free text through words from titles, abstracts, etc., is a decision faced regularly by searchers of bibliographic databases. Researchers have studied and experienced searchers have offered opinions on this problem. My conclusion as expressed in this article is that there is no easy answer because the decision ultimately depends on many different factors. A good searcher has to weigh the query, the vocabulary, the needs of the user, and the contents of the database to make a decision about the best approach. This decision has to be made anew for every search.

The bottom line on search strategy is that it is still a matter of judgment and experience, mixed with some intuition and innovation. Online searching is an art, not a science.

DATABASE DESIGN AND MANAGEMENT*

Librarians have used online bibliographic database searching for well over a decade. Good searchers are familiar with the content and characteristics of individual databases (such as ERIC or Chemical Abstracts) and with the online system (e.g., DIALOG or BRS) and the commands that are needed to search each database. Searchers must also have an understanding of how databases are created and structured, how they are processed by the online system's computer to enable searching, and what actually happens when a database is searched. This chapter focuses on these issues.

DATABASES

There are many definitions of "database"; in a broad sense, online databases, such as those used by libraries, are merely collections of related information made searchable on computer. These collections are most often related by subject (e.g., information about education or about chemistry); by type of information (e.g., books, dissertations, journal articles); or by issuing agency (e.g., materials created by the U.S. Government Printing Office).

A majority of the databases used in libraries today are bibliographic (also called indexing/abstracting) databases. Bibliographic databases provide citations to literature just as printed indexing tools do. Sometimes abstracts are also available. Bibliographic databases serve as pointers to books, articles, proceedings, research reports, or audiovisual materials; the user must then locate the full document referred to in the bibliographic citations, just as he or she must locate the books in the library after searching the library catalog. Online citations are often called "document surrogates" or "document representations" because they substitute for or describe the actual document.

A typical bibliographic database is composed of between 5,000 to over 1 million individual records, which are surrogates to the corresponding documents. Figure 1 is an example of two records from the ERIC database that are available on the BRS search service. Each record is made up of a series of fields, representing one piece of information describing some particular aspect of a document. The first record in Figure 1 has 14 fields—ERIC accession number, author, title, source, language, issue, ERIC Clearinghouse Code, publication type, availability, year of publication, major descriptors, minor descriptors, identifiers, and abstract. Together these fields provide a surrogate of the original document.

Fields are often divided into subfields, discrete items of information within any given field. In the source field, for example, there are subfields for journal name, volume number, issue number, pagination, and publication date. The major descriptor field in this example has six individual descriptors, each of which can be considered a subfield of the major descriptor field. Subfields may or may not be searchable

online depending on the decision made by the database producer and online vendor.

Subfields may be broken down into data elements, the smallest searchable unit within a database record. Each word in the title, abstract, descriptor, or identifier fields may be a separate data element or keyword when each can be searched individually.

Other types of databases are used less frequently in libraries, but their availability and use are increasing each year. Full-text databases provide complete articles or books online instead of merely a surrogate. In most online systems, the complete document (except graphics) can be searched and retrieved online. Full texts of most U.S. legal statutes, many popular magazines, several encyclopedias, and assorted journals and textbooks are now available online. Figure 2 is an example of a shortened record from Harvard Business Review/Online (HBRO) fulltext database.

Numeric or statistical databases provide different types of numeric data including census data, financial information, economic/labor data, physical or chemical properties, and the like. Some online systems allow this data to be manipulated to create such things as forecasting reports. The nature of the data in numeric databases varies widely, but Figure 3 illustrates a typical type available on the DIALOG system.

Referral (or directory) databases lead the user to a person, company, or product. Telephone "yellow pages" directories, biographical sources, and other referral sources such as software directories, periodical directories, and database directories are now widely available online. Figure 4 contains a referral database illustration.

Most of the databases available in the 1980s are computerized versions of printed works. Beginning in the late 1960s, many publishers of printed indexing and abstracting tools began using computer typesetting to create their print products. Computer typesetting enhanced and expedited the printing process; it also resulted in a computer-readable magnetic tape version of the work. This version, when loaded onto a computer with appropriate searching software, provided a potential source of extra income to the database producer by allowing enhanced search and retrieval and wider distribution of the product.

Many types of publishers now make their products available as online databases. Government agencies, professional societies, large for-profit publishing firms, small entrepreneurial publishers, and academic institutions all create databases.

Typically, databases are leased from publishers by online vendors, such as DIALOG or BRS (also called online systems or hosts), who make the databases available for searching. The vendor has a computer or computers, massive amounts of disk storage, and software for making databases available for searching. The vendors also take responsibility for marketing the services, billing clients, and making arrangements with telecommunications networks that are used by searchers to

(Text continues on p. 135.)

---

*This article will also appear in *Principles and Applications of Information Science for Library Professionals*, John Olsgaard, ed. Chicago: American Library Association, 1989, 52-68. Used with permission.

Sample BRS/ERIC Citations

CIJE Citation
AN EJ229170.
AU MADIKE, FRANCIS V.
TI TEACHER CLASSROOM BEHAVIOR IN-VOLVED IN MICROTEACHING AND STU-DENT ACHIEVEMENT: A REGRESSION STUDY.
SO JOURNAL OF EDUCATIONAL PSYCHOLOGY; V72 N2 P265–74 APR 1980. APR80.
LG EN.
IS CIJDEC80.
CH TM505388.
PT 080; 143.
AV REPRINT: UMI.
YR 80.
MJ ACADEMIC-ACHIEVEMENT. MICROTEACHING. OBSERVATIONAL-LEARNING. SECONDARY-SCHOOL-MATHEMATICS. STUDENT-TEACHERS. TEACHING-SKILLS.
MN ACADEMIC-ABILITY. FOREIGN-COUNTRIES. JUNIOR-HIGH-SCHOOLS. TEACHER-BEHAVIOR. TEACHER-EFFECTIVENESS.
ID NIGERIA.
AB STUDENT TEACHERS GIVEN FIVE WEEKS OF MICROTEACHING, OBSERVATION TRAINING, OR NO PREPARATION, TAUGHT MATHEMATICS TO MALE HIGH SCHOOL STUDENTS IN URBAN, SUBURBAN, OR RURAL NIGERIA. THOSE TEACHERS WHO HAD MICROTEACHING EXPERIENCE DEMONSTRATED GREATER FREQUENCY OF TARGET TEACHING SKILLS, WHILE A COMBINATION OF VARIABLES CON-TRIBUTED TO STUDENT ACHIEVEMENT. (GDC).

RIE Document
AN ED190127.
AU TREU, SIEGFRIED.
IN NATIONAL BUREAU OF STANDARDS (DOC), WASHINGTON, D.C. INST. FOR COM-PUTER SCIENCES AND TECHNOLOGY. (BBB01818).
TI COMPUTER SCIENCE AND TECHNOLOGY: INVESTIGATION OF TECHNOLOGY-BASED IMPROVEMENT OF THE ERIC SYSTEM.
LG EN.

GS U.S. DISTRICT OF COLUMBIA.
SN NATIONAL INST. OF EDUCATION (DHEW), WASHINGTON, D.C. (BBE06621).
IS RIEDEC80.
NO RN: NBSIR-80-2005. CN: NIEIA780015.
CH IR08619.
GV FEDERAL.
PR EDRS PRICE — MF 01/PC 05 PLUS POSTAGE.
PT 142.
LV 1.
NT 122P.
YR 80
MJ COMPUTER-SCIENCE. DATA-PROCESSING. IMPROVEMENT. INFORMATION-SYSTEMS. MICROREPRODUCTION.
MN CHARACTER-RECOGNITION. INFORMATION-DISSEMINATION. INFORMATION-NETWORKS. INFORMATION-STORAGE. INPUT-OUTPUT-DEVICES. MICROFORMS. ONLINE-SYSTEMS. OPTICAL-SCANNERS. TELECOMMUNICATIONS.
ID ERIC.
AB THE RESULTS OF A ONE YEAR STUDY TO IDENTIFY POTENTIAL TECHNOLOGY-BASED IMPROVEMENTS IN THE OPERA-TION, ACCESS, AND UTILIZATION OF THE EDUCATIONAL RESOURCES INFORMA-TION CENTER (ERIC) ARE DESCRIBED. BOTH CURRENT PROBLEM AREAS AND FUTURE POSSIBILITIES ARE CONSIDERED WITH RESPECT TO THE DICHOTOMY: SYSTEM COMPONENTS AND THE TOTAL SYSTEM. EMPHASIS IS ON CHARACTERIZ-ING THE COMPONENT FUNCTIONS OF DATA INPUT AND DATA OUTPUT AS WELL AS THE TOTAL SYSTEM OPERATION IN TERMS OF APPLICABLE CRITERIA (DATA TYPE, VOLUME, PURPOSE, PERFOR-MANCE). TECHNOLOGICAL ALTER-NATIVES ARE THEN DISCUSSED WITH REFERENCE TO THOSE CRITERIA. THE REPORT CONCLUDES WITH A STRUC-TURAL SUMMARY OF OBSERVATIONS, RECOMMENDATIONS, AND SUGGESTIONS FOR FOLLOW-UP STUDIES. A BIBLIOGRAPHY IS ATTACHED. (AUTHOR/RAA).

Fig. 1. Bibliographic records. From BRS System Seminar manual. Used with permission.

AN   856160. 8512.

AU   (1) Salerno-Lynn-M.

IN   (1) Harvard Business Review.

TI   What Happened to the Computer Revolution?.

SO   HARVARD BUSINESS REVIEW. Nov-Dec 1985. p 129.

PT   HBR Article.

NU   ISSN 0017-8012.

DE   Computer-systems. Data-processing. Information-systems. Automation.
      Computer-industry.

MN   General Electric. IBM. American Telephone & Telegraph. Lockheed. Mead. Bibliographic
      Retrieval Service. Dresser Industries. Dresser (France). General Motors. Ford Motor. TRW.
      Wells Fargo Bank. Smith, Harold R. Lewis, Benjamin.

BF   Computers and information systems.

CR   1 OF 9. Martin, James McClure, Carma. Buying Software off the Rack. Harvard Business
      Review. 1983/Nov. p. 32.

      2 OF 9. Rockart, John F. Chief Executives Define Their Own Data Needs. Harvard Business
      Review. 1979/Mar. p. 81.

      3 OF 9. Strassman, Paul. Information Payoff: The Transformation of Work in the Electronic
      Age. NY: Free Press. 1985. p. 45.

      4 OF 9. Skinner, Wickham. Manufacturing: The Formidable Competitive Weapon. NY: John
      Wiley. 1985.

      5 OF 9. Reichardt, Jasia. Robotics: Fact, Fiction, and Prediction. NY: Penguin Books. 1978.

      6 OF 9. Buss, Martin D.J. Penny-Wise Approach to Data Processing. Harvard Business
      Review. 1981/Jul. p. 111.

      7 OF 9. McFarlan, F. Warren McKenny, James L. Corporate Information Systems
      Management. Homewood, IL: Richard D. Irwin. 1983. p. 23.

      8 OF 9. Buss, Martin D.J. Salerno, Lynn M. Common Sense and Computer Security. Harvard
      Business Review. 1984/Mar. p. 112.

      9 OF 9. Atkins, William. Jesse James at the Terminal. Harvard Business Review.
      1985/Jul. p. 82.

AB   Not long ago, the fully automated workplace seemed just around the corner. Now
      computer sales are falling off, most offices get by with word processors, photocopy
      machines, and secretaries. Robots have not replaced workers in factories. Yet the technology
      exists for automating offices and revolutionizing the workplace. Why hasn't it happened?
      The reasons for the slow-down are many. For one thing, managers have not yet learned how
      to incorporate . . .

TX   1 OF 72. Home computer sales are slumping, computer makers continue to fail or to
      withdraw their models, and both the factory and the office of the future remain over the
      horizon. Only a few years ago, the specter of the automated workplace—office and factory—
      caused workers to shudder and social planners to draw up scenarios for retraining and
      reemploying the newly displaced labor force. As late as last year, no respectable
      prognosticator, when asked to estimate the fate of a new computer—based product or
      industry, would come up with a sales figure of less than a billion dollars. This year, caution is
      rampant. Is the computer revolution slowing down?

           2 OF 72. Automating the office does present some obvious . . .

Fig. 2. Fulltext records. From BRS System Seminar manual. Used with permission.

```
File 565:ECONBASE   (Copr. 1988 The WEFA Group)

AUTO RETAIL SALES, NEW IMPORTED CARS, UNITED STATES

    Series Code:   USCARIMP
    Corp Source:   BEA ;   UNPUBLISHED DATA
    Start Date:    JANUARY, 1967 (6701)
    Frequency:     MONTHLY
    Units:         MILLIONS, SEASONALLY ADJUSTED ANNUAL RATE

1988   JAN  3.104     FEB  3.082     MAR  3.005
       APR  3.24
1987   JAN  2.501     FEB  2.99      MAR  2.906
       APR  3.046     MAY  2.959     JUN  3.084
       JUL  3.311     AUG  3.721     SEP  3.757
       OCT  3.343     NOV  3.257     DEC  3.436
1986   JAN  2.948     FEB  2.924     MAR  2.881
       APR  3.167     MAY  3.053     JUN  2.968
       JUL  3.272     AUG  3.334     SEP  3.763
       OCT  3.26      NOV  3.407     DEC  3.841
1985   JAN  2.558     FEB  2.566     MAR  2.347
       APR  2.501     MAY  2.854     JUN  2.801
       JUL  2.917     AUG  2.909     SEP  3.077
         .             .             .          .
         .             .             .          .
         .             .             .          .
1968   JAN   .956     FEB   .995     MAR  1.004
       APR   .966     MAY   .976     JUN  1.002
       JUL  1.024     AUG  1.015     SEP  1.21
       OCT  1.081     NOV  1.058     DEC  1.07
1967   JAN   .629     FEB   .69      MAR   .742
       APR   .748     MAY   .784     JUN   .787
       JUL   .814     AUG   .817     SEP   .803
       OCT   .806     NOV   .852     DEC   .892
```

Fig. 3. Numeric databases. Each record in a numeric database is a table of statistical data, often with text added. From DIALOG System Seminar manual. Used with permission.

```
File 516:D & B - Duns Market Identifiers  (Copr. 1988 D&B)

UNIVERSITY PATENTS INC              Full financials available
1465 POST ROAD EAST
PO BOX 901
WESTPORT, CT  06881


TELEPHONE: 203-255-6044
FAIRFIELD COUNTY        SMSA: 418   (NORWALK,CONN)

BUSINESS: PATENT BUYING, LICENSING & LEASING, MFR CONTACT LENSES

PRIMARY SIC:     6794      PATENT OWNERS/LESSORS
SECONDARY SIC:   3851      OPHTHALMIC GOODS
SECONDARY SIC:   7391      RESEARCH & DVPT LABS
SECONDARY SIC:   7392      MGMT & PUB. RELATIONS
SECONDARY SIC:   0751      LIVESTOCK SVCS X SPEC
SECONDARY SIC:   5199      NONDURABLE GOODS

YEAR STARTED:              1964

                     CURRENT        TREND          BASE
                      YEAR          YEAR           YEAR
                                   (1985)         (1982)

SALES ($):         1,620,000     1,620,000      2,520,000
EMPLOYEES TOTAL:         110            99             25
EMPLOYEES HERE:          20

    SALES GROWTH (%):     - 36
    EMPLOYMENT GROWTH (%): 296

SQUARE FOOTAGE: 12,000   RENTED
NUMBER OF ACCOUNTS: 1,000
BANK: PUTNAM TRUST OF GREENWICH INC
ACCOUNTING FIRM: COOPERS & LYBRAND

THIS IS:

    A HEADQUARTERS LOCATION
    A CORPORATION
    A PUBLIC COMPANY
    A MILLION DOLLAR DIRECTORY COMPANY

DUNS NUMBER:            04-929-4093
HEADQUARTER DUNS:       04-929-4093
CORPORATE FAMILY DUNS:  04-929-4093

CHAIRMAN:          MILES, L. W.   / CHAIRMAN OF THE BOARD
PRESIDENT:         ALPERT, A. S.  / PRESIDENT
VICE PRESIDENT:    KOFFSKY, DAVID  / VICE PRESIDENT
VICE PRESIDENT:    MC PIKE, FRANK R.  / VICE PRESIDENT
SECRETARY:         ROBERT, I. S.  / SECRETARY
MARKETING:         SIEGEL, ROBERT I.  / V P - MARKETING
OPERATIONS:        FRIANT, RAY J. JR. / V P - OPERATIONS
FINANCE:           MCPIKE, FRANK R. JR. / V P - FINANCE
```

Fig. 4. Directory databases. Each record in a directory database gives factual information about companies, organizations, products, etc. From DIALOG System Seminar manual. Used with permission.

access online systems over the telephone lines. Database producers are responsible for the content of their databases, while most online vendors merely take the information as submitted and process it so it can be searched. (In some cases the database "producer" and online "vendor" are the same company. H. W. Wilson Company, for example, both produces and vends its own databases.)

Since the middle to late 1970s, when database searching became widespread, more and more databases have been created expressly for the online market rather than as byproducts of a print technology. Creating a database can be a time-consuming task, even when it is derived from an existing product. The fact that online search tactics differ from manual techniques must be considered when creating an online product. Database producers thus must make a series of decisions as they convert their data to a format acceptable to the online system and as they attempt to make their database the best possible online searching tool.

New database producers (electronic publishers) are faced with the creation of the intellectual work as well as with formatting issues. Database design decisions can be divided into these two major areas: (1) creation (intellectual) decisions, and (2) implementation (software-related or structural) decisions.

CREATION DECISIONS

A librarian searching a database is probably more cognizant of the creation decisions than the implementation decisions. Creation decisions directly affect the quality of the material distributed by the intermediary to clients. Like printed reference sources, databases must be evaluated for content and quality—two things that the database producer has control over.

Creation decisions can be broken down into content decisions, standardization decisions, decisions about value-added fields, and quality control decisions. Together, these decisions will determine how useful and how reliable a database is.

Content of a bibliographic database or a printed index involves decisions on what materials are indexed and to what extent. A publisher of an indexing tool must decide whether to index just journals or just books, or to include materials such as research reports, dissertations, audiovisuals, proceedings, government documents, etc. Sometimes these decisions define the nature of the work (e.g., Conference Proceedings Index or Dissertation Abstracts), but often they become an editorial policy. The type of materials retrieved in a search of course is an important consideration for the intermediary who perhaps must supply the original documents to the end user. The publisher of a printed index decides whether all of the types of materials included in the print version will also be available online. Because of the high cost of printing, some online databases include more records online than in the printed counterparts. It is helpful for the searcher to know by what criteria this selection is based.

Knowing what materials are included in a database does not tell the entire story of content. Index and database producers make a decision about how comprehensively they cover their materials. Very few indexing/abstracting tools include real "cover-to-cover" indexing of journals, for example. Most exclude advertisements, letters to the editor, and other ephemeral materials. Some producers selectively choose articles from a number of journals, while others include all articles from a list of journals. Selection can be based on subject matter, length of the articles, or quality. Many databases concentrate on English language materials only. Figure 5 is an example of some content decisions of one database producer.

Editorial Policy

Our editorial policy is based on three criteria: *inclusiveness*—to abstract the entire range of sociological journals and those in related disciplines irrespective of language of publication; *systematicity*—to abstract fully every core sociological journal and select from related journals those articles directly pertinent to sociology and those written by sociologists; and *continuity*—to abstract journals in chronological sequence of their publication whenever possible.

On the basis of the above criteria, three *types* of journals have been distinguished in the following order of priority:

Type 1— journals published by sociological associations, groups, faculties and institutes, and periodicals containing the term "sociology" in their titles;

Type 2— journals from such related areas as anthropology, economics, education, medicine, community development, philosophy, statistics, political science, etc.; and

Type 3— journals from the humanities and journals of general circulation wherein scholars and laymen publish discussions or criticisms of sociology and sociological topics.

Records consist of approximately

85% journal articles (with abstracts online since 1973);

10% conference papers (1969-1972, citations only, print and online, 1973-1976, print issues only; 1977 forward, citations and abstracts, print and online);

5% books (to 1963, not online).

Fig. 5. Editorial policy of a database producer.

Standardization is an issue that may not be noticed in a printed tool but becomes much more crucial in an online product because online searching is a literal process. That is, computers cannot think or make educated assumptions. The online system's software matches a string of characters that the searcher inputs as a search term. Most software on the major online systems is not sophisticated enough to catch spelling variations (e.g., to recognize the difference between "Labour" and "Labor") or variations in format. In these cases it is to the searcher's advantage to have the contents of the database as standardized as possible. Nonsubject fields that a publisher can control at the creation stage include dates (January 1977 vs. 1/77), places (Chicago, IL vs. Chicago), names (Jones, John B. vs. Jones JB), abbreviations (assoc. vs. association), and spelling. (Some software features aid the searcher dealing with nonstandardized database content. These are discussed below.)

A related content decision is that of value-added fields. Value-added fields include anything added to the basic bibliographic record to aid retrieval or enhance the material retrieved. Typical value-added fields in a bibliographic database include descriptor terms, abstracts, and codes. Codes might represent taxonomic families, subject classification numbers, Standard Industrial Classification codes, etc.

The number and quality of the value-added fields in a particular database often set it apart from other databases in the same subject. These fields provide additional access points to increase the number of documents retrieved. Standardization or control of these fields helps improve precision and recall by imposing a consistent vocabulary on all records in the database.

Quality control impacts the way searchers input search terms and affects the number of citations retrieved. The simplest level of quality control is checking for and correcting typographical errors. If a word in a record is misspelled it will not be retrieved in the normal search process. Some database producers verify the information at input, while others will correct errors reported to them. Since many databases are updated only monthly, there may be quite a lag between when an error is discovered and when it is corrected. Correcting errors can be expensive also.

Other types of quality control are more complex. Eliminating outdated information or verifying the accuracy or quality of the articles indexed are factors that greatly impact the services that are provided. It is more expensive for a database producer to exercise this level of quality control, a fact that may be reflected in the price of the quality database. If information from an online search is inaccurate, is the intermediary (such as a company that produces an initial index), the database producer, or the online vendor responsible? This issue of liability is expected to arise increasingly as there is more reliance on online sources and as intermediaries charge for online searches.

IMPLEMENTATION DECISIONS

File Structures

When the magnetic tape of a database is received by the online vendor from the database producer, the database must be processed (or "loaded") onto the vendor's computer. Each record is stored in accession number order in what is called the linear, sequential, or unit record file. Figure 1 (page 131) could be two records in the linear file of the ERIC database.

If the linear file was the only way records were stored in an online system, searching would be done sequentially by having the computer look at each record in turn (like looking for a particular song on a cassette tape). In a sequential database search, the system would look for a given string of characters, character-by-character through each record in a database. Such sequential scanning is possible (and some software for creating small in-house databases works this way) but it would be very time consuming in a large database. (Imagine searching for the term "library" in the printed ERIC indexes *Resources in Education* and *Current Index to Journals in Education* by starting at the first character in the first record and continuing to scan each of the 500 to 1,000 characters per record in all of the close to a million entries.)

Instead of relying on sequential scanning of the linear file, it is more efficient with today's still limited computer technology to have the computer create a separate file that stores just the searchable data elements from each record with pointers back to the appropriate unit record in the linear file.[1]

In most online systems today, such inverted files (or indexes) are derived from the linear file when the database is loaded by the online vendor. Some systems maintain more than one inverted file—separating the subject-related fields into a default "basic index." Two types of inverted files from the DIALOG system are illustrated in Figures 6 and 7. An inverted file can be thought of as an index to the searchable words or phrases in each record in a database. Each term is extracted automatically from each record and placed in an alphabetically ordered list. Each term in this list contains a numerical pointer to another file that contains information about each term. This information typically includes the accession number of each record that contains the term, the fields where the term is found in each record, and the placement of each term in each field (e.g., the 5th word in the title field in the 500th record).

Inverted file structures greatly speed up searching, because when a user searches for a term, the system goes to the alphabetically arranged inverted file rather than scanning the complete linear file. (This process is somewhat analogous to checking the cover of a record album to decide which band has the desired song, then going directly to that band.) Using the index, the retrieval system first reports the number of records that contain a search term (called "hits" or "postings"). The accession numbers for the records that satisfy a given search request are put into a separate numbered group called a set. Sets are created for each search term or for each search statement entered. Not until the searcher enters a display command does the system use the accession numbers stored in the set to access the linear file records. See Figure 8 for a typical search, and Figure 9 for an example of a print display of a search.

When a database is first made available on an online system, the database producer and online vendor together make certain decisions about the database structure. Individual fields in the records are defined. The fields that are to be searchable are so designated for inclusion in the inverted files. Field tags and subfield delimiters are added to the

(Text continues on p. 141.)

1. DIALOG assigns consecutive ACCESSION NUMBERS to all records received in machine-readable form, creating a LINEAR FILE, where the complete records are stored.

LINEAR FILE

```
30249     (accession number)

Postpurchase   consumer   evaluations,   complaint   actions   and   repurchase
    TI1           TI2          TI3            TI4        TI5             TI7
behavior.
   TI8
Francken, Dick A.
   AU
Journal of Economic Psychology,   1984 Nov Vol 4(3) 273-290
   JN                               PY
Language: ENGLISH  Document Type: JOURNAL ARTICLE
         LA                        DT
Presents a model of postpurchase evaluation processes, which is used as a
  AB1    AB2   AB3       AB5        AB6         AB7         AB8  AB9 AB10 AB11 AB12
theoretical   framework for explaining different kinds of consumer   complaint
   AB13         AB14        AB16         AB17     AB18     AB20       AB21
actions.
  AB22
Descriptors:  CONSUMER   ATTITUDES   (11470);   CONSUMER BEHAVIOR (11480)
              DE1        DE2          DC          DE3      DE4         DC
```

```
30156     (accession number)

Labor   force   participation   of metropolitan,   nonmetropolitan, and farm
 TI1     TI2        TI3              TI5               TI6             TI8
women: A comparative study.
 TI9  TI10    TI11      TI12
Bokemeier, Janet L.; Sachs, Carolyn; Keith, Verna
    AU                   AU              AU
Rural Sociology,   1984 Win Vol 48(4) 515-539
   JN               PY
Language: ENGLISH  Document Type: JOURNAL ARTICLE
         LA                        DT
Examined   data   from 937 metropolitan, 3631   nonfarm-nonmetropolitan, and
   AB1     AB2         AB4           AB5    AB6       AB7            AB8
1231   farm  women  (18-65  yrs of age) from Kentucky to compare personal,
AB10   AB11  AB12   AB13 AB14 AB15   AB17       AB19       AB21      AB22
socioeconomic,   and   family   characteristics and the occupations and
   AB23                AB25          AB26                        AB29
industries of women  in the labor force.
   AB31       AB33 AB34   AB36  AB37
Descriptors:  EMPLOYMENT   STATUS   (17196); HUMAN FEMALES (23450); URBAN
              DE1          DE2       DC        DE3     DE4      DC      DE5
ENVIRONMENTS  (54940);  RURAL  ENVIRONMENTS (45040)
   DE6          DC      DE7       DE8         DC
```

Fig. 6. Inverted index. From DIALOG System Seminar manual. Used with permission.

> 2. DIALOG creates the database's BASIC INDEX, the alphabetical list of subject words (excluding STOP WORDS). Each record is divided into FIELDS (parts), each field is labelled, and the position of each word within a field is noted.

Term	Posting	Term	Posting
a	30249 ·AB2	in	30156 AB34
	30249 AB12	industries	30156 AB31
	30156 TI10	is	30249 AB9
actions	30249 AB22	kentucky	30156 AB19
	30249 TI5	kinds	30249 AB18
age	30156 AB17	labor	30156 AB36
as	30249 AB11		30156 TI1
attitudes	30249 DE2	metropolitan	30156 AB5
behavior	30249 DE4		30156 TI5
	30249 TI8	model	30249 AB3
characteristics	30156 AB26	nonfarm	30156 AB7
comparative	30156 TI11	nonmetropolitan	30156 AB8
compare	30156 AB21		30156 TI6
complaint	30249 AB21	occupations	30156 AB29
	30249 TI4	participation	30156 TI3
consumer	30249 AB20	personal	30156 AB22
	30249 DE1	postpurchase	30249 AB5
	30249 DE3		30249 TI1
	30249 TI2	presents	30249 AB1
consumer attitudes	30249 DE1DE2	processes	30249 AB7
consumer behavior	30249 DE3DE4	repurchase	30249 TI7
data	30156 AB2	rural	30156 DE7
different	30249 AB17	rural environments	30156 DE7DE8
employment	30156 DE1	socioeconomic	30156 AB23
employment status	30156 DE1DE2	status	30156 DE2
environments	30156 DE6	study	30156 TI12
	30156 DE8	theoretical	30249 AB13
evaluation	30249 AB6	urban	30156 DE5
evaluations	30249 TI3	urban environments	30156 DE5DE6
examined	30156 AB1	used	30249 AB10
explaining	30249 AB16	which	30249 AB8
family	30156 AB25	women	30156 AB12
farm	30156 AB11		30156 AB33
	30156 TI8		30156 TI9
females	30156 DE4	yrs	30156 AB15
force	30156 AB37	1231	30156 AB10
	30156 TI2	18	30156 AB13
framework	30249 AB14	3631	30156 AB6
human	30156 DE3	65	30156 AB14
human females	30156 DE3DE4	937	30156 AB4

STOP WORDS		
an	for	the
and	from	to
by	of	with

Fig. 7. Basic inverted index. From DIALOG System Seminar manual. Used with permission.

```
?b 75
        22mar85 12:35:50 User003842
    $0.13     0.005 Hrs File1
    $0.03  Dialnet
    $0.16  Estimated cost this file

File  75:Management Contents - 74-85/Feb
(Copr. 1985 Information Access Co.)

        Set  Items  Description
        ---  -----  -----------
?ss turnover or job?(w)satisfaction or employee?(w)morale?
        S1    1077  TURNOVER
        S2   12532  JOB?
        S3    3219  SATISFACTION
        S4    1779  JOB?(W)SATISFACTION
        S5   16063  EMPLOYEE?
        S6     796  MORALE?
        S7     147  EMPLOYEE?(W)MORALE?
        S8    2820  TURNOVER OR JOB?(W)SATISFACTION OR EMPLOYEE?(W)MORALE?


?ss flextime or flexitime or flexible(w)work?(w)schedule?
        S9      75  FLEXTIME
       S10      40  FLEXITIME
       S11    1715  FLEXIBLE
       S12   22659  WORK?
       S13    1863  SCHEDULE?
       S14      19  FLEXIBLE(W)WORK?(W)SCHEDULE?
       S15     114  FLEXTIME OR FLEXITIME OR FLEXIBLE(W)WORK?(W)SCHEDULE?


?ss s8 and s15
              2820  S8
               114  S15
       S16      30  S8 AND S15
```

Fig. 8. Typical search on the DIALOG system.

```
?t 16/5/1-2

 16/5/1
289478   SPM84D0010
   Effectively Managing Alternative Work Options.
   Olsten, W.
   Supervisory Management, Vol.24, No.4, April 1984, P. 10-15., Journal.
```

Alternative work schedules are popular with employees. For alternative work options to function effectively, the manager must develop specific strategies. Flexible work schedules can result in higher productivity and positive employee morale. The new work styles can be beneficial to the company only when the manager is prepared to handle potential problems. The manager must develop a strategy that includes hiring practices, work plan, performance goals, training program, managerial support, and open communications. There are different systems of alternative work schedules, and a manager must evaluate the appropriate system for his firm.

DESCRIPTORS: Management; Flexible Schedule; Flextime; Work Hours; Strategy; Productivity; Morale; 0605; 0173; 0173; 2427; 0251; 0662; 0240

```
 16/5/2
287779   SPM84B0037
   Taking a Look at Flexitime.
   Morgan, P.I.; Baker, H.K.
   Supervisory Management, Vol.29, No.2, Feb. 1984, P. 37-43., Journal.
```

Many companies are allowing employees to establish alternative work scheduling. The concept of flexitime is encouraged to reduce absenteeism and job turnover, and encourage job satisfaction and productivity. Flexitime originated in Munich, Germany in 1967. An experiment related to flex-time is the compressed forty-hour work week. The organization receives the benefits of employee satisfaction and effectiveness from flexitime. Employees derive personal benefits from flexitime. Flexitime should only be adapted when a correct implementation procedure is followed, and when it is determined that the concept is advantageous to the organization.

DESCRIPTORS: Flextime; Work Hours; Work Week; Absenteeism; Turnover; Job Satisfaction; Employee; Productivity; Organization; Implementation; Benefits; 0173; 2427; 2431; 0058; 0429; 0221; 0958; 0662; 0576; 1641; 1057

Fig. 9. Print display of a search.

records. The field tags differentiate between fields for the inverted file creation program and tell where one field ends and the next begins. Subfield delimiters tell the programs where one subfield ends and the next begins.

One of the most important decisions at this stage is how each field or subfield will be processed for the inverted indexes. Each field will be machine "indexed" ("parsed") by some specified criteria. Parsing is the process of identifying how each record, field, subfield, and data element will be separated and making entries in the inverted index for each separate part. How a field is parsed is important because it greatly affects how the words or terms in a record can be searched.

There are three parsing options available for a database. A different option can be chosen for each field in a database if desired.

"Word parsing" (word indexing) is the approach used for many subject-related fields in many databases. A word is usually defined as any string of letters or numbers that is bounded by blank spaces or punctuation marks. To parse a word-indexed field, the system creates a separate entry in the inverted index each time a word is encountered. Thus, the title *Developing Computer-Based Library Systems* would have five separate alphabetically arranged entries in the inverted index: BASED, COMPUTER, DEVELOPING, LIBRARY, and SYSTEMS.

Most online systems have a list of trivial words ("stop words") that are not included in the inverted indexes. Stop words typically include prepositions such as "of" and "with," articles such as "an" and "the," and conjunctions such as "and," "or," and "but" (although the number of words designated as stop words varies among the online systems).

When the computer creates the inverted index, it checks the stop word list and does not make an entry for any word on the list. Thus, the title *In Search of Excellence* would have only two entries in the inverted index of most systems: EXCELLENCE and SEARCH.

Many systems retain word placement information about the stop words, however, so the system would note that "excellence" was the fourth word in the title of this record and "search" was the second word. The significance of this placement information will be discussed later.

Word parsing is the approach typically chosen for non-controlled fields such as title, abstract, and full text. It means that the word-parsed field can be searched by every nontrivial word that it contains.

"Phrase parsing" (phrase indexing) is usually used for controlled fields where a human indexer has indicated that the words in a phrase go together as a "bound" phrase. Phrase-parsed entries in the inverted indexes include all spaces and punctuation. The computer software can detect where one phrase ends and another begins because the index terms have been marked with a special delimiter.

The author field is often phrase parsed. In Figure 1 the author, "Madike, Francis V.," would generate only one entry in the inverted index. That entry would be exactly as the phrase was entered in the database: MADIKE, FRANCIS V., including all spaces and punctuation.

Phrase parsing keeps bound terms together, but it greatly impacts searching. The entire phrase must be searched in order to retrieve the record. Thus, in a search for this author the user must know to input "Madike, Francis V." exactly as shown

(Madike comma space Francis space V period). Neither Madike nor Francis alone would retrieve this record. Most systems have search features that aid searching phrase-parsed fields. These are discussed below.

"Combination-parsed" fields ("double-posted") are both word and phrase parsed. Bound phrases are kept together, but they are also separated at spaces and punctuation. This approach is typically used in the descriptor or identifier fields where there are bound ("precoordinated") phrases but where individual words are also meaningful.

Double posting is nice for the user because it retains the intellectual decision involved in creating a bound descriptor, yet it allows individual words to be searched when a user may not know the correct form of a bound term.

The first record in Figure 1 has the major descriptors: ACADEMIC-ACHIEVEMENT; MICROTEACHING; OBSERVATIONAL-LEARNING; SECONDARY-SCHOOL-MATHEMATICS; STUDENT-TEACHERS; and TEACHING-SKILLS. Here the semicolon (;) indicates to the system where one bound descriptor subfield ends. For these six descriptors the system would make seventeen separate entries in the inverted index if the field were both phrase and word parsed. The entries would be:

ACADEMIC
ACHIEVEMENT
ACADEMIC-ACHIEVEMENT
LEARNING
MATHEMATICS
MICROTEACHING
OBSERVATIONAL
OBSERVATIONAL-LEARNING
SCHOOL
SECONDARY
SECONDARY-SCHOOL-MATHEMATICS
SKILLS
STUDENT
STUDENT-TEACHERS
TEACHERS
TEACHING
TEACHING-SKILLS

Combination parsing, as you can see, allows the most flexibility for the searcher but also creates the longest inverted index that uses the most space in the computer.

IMPLICATIONS FOR SEARCHING

As mentioned earlier, implementation decisions have a direct impact on how a database can be searched. Word-indexed fields can be searched on individual words, phrase-indexed fields on complete phrases only, and a field that is indexed by a combination can be searched by either words or complete phrases.

Online systems usually have several searching features that provide more flexibility in searching fields regardless of how they are parsed. These features include: truncation, the ability to view the inverted index online, proximity searching, Boolean logic, and the ability to specify a particular field.

Most online systems allow the searcher to use word stem "truncation" search for all terms or phrases that begin with the same character stem. The stem is usually indicated to the system by a special truncation symbol. Thus, putting a truncation symbol after the stem "librar" will find entries in the inverted index under LIBRARY, LIBRARIES, LIBRARIAN-SHIP, LIBRARY AUTOMATION, etc. The truncation symbol varies with the system. It is variously designated as a #, ?, :, $, etc.

Truncation is especially valuable for phrase-indexed fields because it will allow a searcher to retrieve records without knowing the complete phrase. Searching for the author LANCASTER$ will retrieve all records that include any records that contain an author with the last number of Lancaster. The searcher does not have to enter the spacing, punctuation, or initials exactly right because they all come after the truncation symbol. This search might, however, result in some "false drops" (irrelevant records) because it will retrieve all authors with the last name Lancaster.

Most major online systems allow the user to view parts of the alphabetic inverted index online. By looking at the inverted index, the searcher can see what words or phrases are available for searching, see the many term variations that occur especially in uncontrolled fields, and find the exact phrase and format that must be entered to search a phrase-indexed field. This can help eliminate false drops caused by truncation.

An especially powerful feature for searching word-indexed fields is "proximity searching," available on many online systems. Proximity searching allows a searcher to "post-coordinate" phrases from word-indexed fields such as titles or abstracts. This is possible because of the positional information that is recorded by the online system at the time the inverted index is created. The positional information indicates the field and where in the field each term occurs. A user can ask, for example, for the word "library" right next to the word "automation" in any word indexed or double posted field. The system will use the positional information to reconstruct the phrase even though each word is entered separately in the inverted index.

Proximity features vary among systems. Some typical capabilities include the ability to specify: words adjacent to each other (as illustrated above), words with a specified number of intervening words, words in the same sentence, words in the same paragraph or field.

Boolean logic searching is another form of postcoordination but it works at the document level rather than at the field level. The main Boolean operators are AND, OR, and NOT. They allow words or phrases from any fields in a document to be linked together by the searcher. AND designates that both terms must be present in the same record, OR designates that either term may be present, and NOT excludes records that have a specified term. Boolean logic searching is facilitated by the existence of the inverted index. All logical operations are performed using the information in the inverted index.

Some online systems provide some help with inconsistent word forms by providing look-up tables for common equivalencies. Although not widely available, this includes equivalency tables for British and American spelling variations, Chinese Romanization schemes, corporate source acronyms and complete forms, and common abbreviations (e.g., Nov. for November). Currently, all of these are available only on Mead Data Central's systems such as LEXIS and NEXIS.

When a user enters one form or another of the look-up table terms the system will automatically check all documents for either form of the term. On Mead Data Central's systems it is done without informing the user ("transparently" to the user).

Other online systems (notably H. W. Wilson's WILSON-LINE) provide automatic look-ups and searching for controlled vocabulary descriptors. If an incorrect form of a descriptor is entered the system will automatically search for the correct descriptor instead. In the case of WILSONLINE, the system informs the user of the extended search.

Such automatic look-up (termed "mapping") takes part of the burden of search strategy from the searcher. It aids the database producer as well, by substituting for the costly practice of standardization at input.

A final common system search feature that is made possible by the database design and construction conventions discussed in this chapter is the ability to specify particular fields for searching. Most online systems allow the searcher to limit a search to a particular field or fields. This ability speeds searching time and reduces the number of false drops. A search of WHITE$ on only the author field, for example, will eliminate entries with subject words such as "whitewash," "whitewalls," etc. Searching AUTOMATION only as a descriptor or title word will avoid retrieving records where the term was used just in passing in an abstract or full text. Field specification thus allows more precision in searching. It can also be used in some systems in the printing of search results. A searcher can choose which fields in the database records to print, making the final printout a more customized product.

SUMMARY

Database design involves two levels of decision making: creation (intellectual) decisions and implementation (structural) decisions. Creation decisions are made by the database producer and include content, standardization, value-added fields, and quality control decisions. They vary widely among database producers. Implementation decisions are in part dependent on the software of the online system that makes the database available for searching. Implementation decisions include identifying the fields in each record and deciding how each field will be parsed (entered into the system's inverted indexes).

Both creation and implementation decisions impact searching. The quality and amount of information retrieved are in part dependent on creation issues. Search conventions in online system software (e.g., truncation, viewing the inverted index, word proximity, Boolean logic, term mapping, and field specification) together with the implementation decisions have a direct effect on the success of an online search.

REFERENCES

[1]Specially designed computer hardware is being developed for rapid scanning of computer files, thus making possible search and retrieval of large databases without the need of inverted indexes. Although early versions of these "database machines" are now available, they are not yet widely used.

FURTHER READING

Chen, Ching-chih, and Peter Hernon. *Numeric Databases.* Ablex, 1984.

Fenichel, Carol H. "Process of Searching Online Bibliographic Databases: A Review of Research." *Library Research* 2: 107-127 (Summer 1980).

Mintz, Anne. "Online Databases and Liability." *Library Journal* 110:38-43 (September 15, 1985).

"Numeric Databases." *Drexel Library Quarterly* 18 (Summer-Fall 1982). Has 12 papers on the topic.

Palmer, Roger C. *Online Reference and Information Retrieval.* Littleton, Colo.: Libraries Unlimited, Inc., 1983. 2nd ed., 1986.

Tenopir, Carol. "Databases: Catching Up and Keeping Up." *Library Journal* 109:180-182 (February 1983). (Lists recommended textbooks and articles written in 1982 and before.)

_____. "Full-Text Databases." In Martha E. Williams, ed. *Annual Review of Information Science and Technology.* 19th ed., 215-246. Washington, D.C.: American Society for Information Science, 1984.

Williams, Martha E. "Electronic Databases." *Science* 228: 445-456 (April 26, 1985). ∎

TO ERR IS HUMAN
Seven Common Searching Mistakes*

Learning to do online searching is in most cases not particularly difficult, but it involves memorizing a query language and sometimes learning to think in new patterns. Most of the commercial bibliographic systems are designed for knowledgeable searchers and offer little or no online help for the novice. In my semester-long classes and shorter continuing education classes for working librarians, I have noticed that beginning searchers seem to make the same errors and have the same problems year after year. Many of these problems are not terribly serious and all are mastered with practice, but I have collected them through the years in the hope that we can learn something about how search systems could be improved and, less seriously, to let beginning searchers know they are not alone! Because the majority of my classes spend the most time on DIALOG, many of my examples come from that system. Other systems would provide an equal number but slightly different array of problems. I apologize to DIALOG in advance.

LOGICAL ERRORS

Boolean logic is not intuitive to most people. Even if they learned Venn Diagramming and set theory in grade school, most people don't translate it to the real world until they must do it for online searching. Beginning searchers struggle with ANDs and ORs as they learn to ignore the English-language logical flaw that says when a patron asks for information on raising goats AND sheep, in Boolean terms he really means raising goats OR sheep. No matter how good some students get at doing Venn diagrams on paper, they always seem at least once to use AND when they should use OR.

The capability of using parentheses for nested logic both helps and hurts the situation. When parentheses should be included and are left off, the system still will yield a result, erroneous as it may be. It takes a while for most students to identify why they seem to have so many false drops when they enter "Education OR training AND online reference services" in the ERIC database.

Some new searchers go overboard and decide they had better insert parentheses whenever there may be a chance they would be needed. Computers AND libraries thus gets searched as (Computers) AND (Libraries), just for safety sake. Luckily, this doesn't adversely affect search results in most systems, although it causes a few extra key strokes.

TO SPACE OR
NOT TO SPACE

Probably because our widely-used online search systems began with limited features and have added on capabilities as time goes by, there is much inconsistency in how to enter certain commands. When a space is needed and when it is not seems to be a source of frustration for nearly every beginning searcher.

In DIALOG, it is possible to enter Type 1/5/1-2 with a space after the type command or Type1/5/1-2 without the space, but SelectStepsgoatsorsheep with no spaces is disastrous. Goats OR sheep has to be entered with spaces before and after the Boolean OR in any of the major systems, but if you are working with set numbers, 10R2 with no spaces will work just fine, sometimes. In DIALOG, Combine 10R2 without spaces works (combine is one of those old-fashioned commands from an earlier era), but it must be SS S1 OR S2 with spaces to achieve the same results with a different command.

There is some consolation to students. In most cases, it works to say "when in doubt put a space"; it is much worse to not include one that is required.

A ONE OR A SET NUMBER?

In the example above from DIALOG, an S must be used to designate a previous set number when using the Select or Select Steps commands (SS S1 AND S2). Without the S, the system will free-text search for the literal number 1 anywhere in the basic index. When using the combine command, however, since it can only be used for set numbers and not for text searching, no S is needed (C 1 AND 2). Students often get puzzling results such as citations on 1,2-dichlorobenzene when they really wanted Set 1 and Set 2.

In BRS, on the other hand, a set number is assumed whenever a number is entered. If you want to search for a literal number, it must be enclosed in quotes. This causes the opposite problem of combining previous sets 1 and 2 when you really wanted citations on 1,2-dichlorobenzene.

KEYBOARDING PROBLEMS

Speaking of numbers, l980 and 1980 may look alike to a typist, but not to a computer. There are times when it is a disadvantage to be a good typist, especially one who has trained on a typewriter without a one or zero key. (The IBM "library" typing element leaves these off as I recall.) Even experienced searchers who had this habit ingrained early in their schooling find themselves automatically going for the "el" key at times.

The opposite problem—no previous typing skills—is much more common these days. How it hurts library school educators to tell students that they really need to know how to type to be efficient online searchers! Painfully slow input, spelling errors due to pressing incorrect keys, or even simplifying their search strategy for fear of having to type too many terms, plague some new searchers.

IGNORING DATABASE DIFFERENCES

Experienced searchers know that exactly the same search strategy will rarely work on two different databases. Presence or absence of abstracts, length of abstracts if present, presence or absence of controlled indexing, depth of controlled indexing if present, reliance on subject category or other codes, and differences caused by variation in the terminology of different subjects—all these can affect search strategies and results. A search strategy that relies on free-text searching in the ABI/INFORM database with its lengthy abstracts will yield quite different results in a database such as Magazine Index that has broad subject headings and no abstracts.

New searchers often feel more comfortable sticking with one method of searching that they have found to work in one database—regardless of the other databases searched. Some learn to rely on free-text searching with liberal use of truncation and synonyms; others favor thesaurus terms exclusively. It takes a while to learn the best mixture of these techniques and requires database-specific knowledge to be truly expert. It

seems illogical that databases should vary so much and many of us at first don't want to acknowledge that fact.

TOO MUCH FAITH IN THE COMPUTER

Since any results seem impressive when searchers do their first online search, perhaps many do not think to analyze how the results could have been better. Developing a critical eye and re-examining search strategy to determine if there could be more citations or should be fewer are skills that seem to come with experience. I've noticed when training end-users especially, the tendency at first is to accept the computer's word that there is no information on a subject, rather than to examine their search strategy for flaws.

Our bibliographic online systems offer little help in refining strategy since the choice of terms, use of controlled vocabularies, and deciding on the appropriate number of synonyms is entirely up to the searcher. On most of the bibliographic systems, there is no automatic online help if a searcher forgets to input both plurals and singulars, forgets to truncate, or doesn't remember to account for variant spellings or variant forms of words. The online Expand, Root, or Neighbor commands or the possibility of truncation still must be initiated by the searcher in most systems.

WHAT SYSTEM AM I ON?

Almost anyone who knows more than one system's query language gets confused at times. Not only do you have to remember that it is "Expand" in DIALOG, "Root" in BRS, and "Neighbor" in Medline or Orbit, but different database structures, punctuation conventions, and hierarchy of logical operations have to be remembered. The system mode can also be confusing when searching multiple systems—DIALOG is always in command mode and requires a command before you enter a search term; ORBIT always defaults to search mode; and BRS is usually in search mode, except when it is in print mode.

It is easier to learn to search a second or third or fourth system because the patterns of thought are basically the same. Remembering specifics can be confusing at times, however, and is just plain annoying.

SOLUTIONS

The thing that strikes me most about all of these common mistakes or problems is that they have been recognized as problems for years. Experimental systems that solve almost all of them have been or are now in operation. It does take time for research to be translated into commercial systems, but perhaps in the not too distant future most of these problems will disappear.

Logical errors are being focused on again as end-users begin to search more. Ongoing research has led to the development of effective non-Boolean search systems or systems that automatically translate a searcher's natural language request into a Boolean expression. Other studies are examining the differences in language and terminology between subjects.

Automatic thesauri or systems that automatically search for synonyms are being developed.

Some commercial systems have partially solved some of the common problems. NEXIS and LEXIS will automatically search some word variants and common acronyms without the searcher requesting it. Function keys are used to circumvent commands. BRS/After Dark developed their menu driven systems for the same reason. Commercially available "front-end" systems such as the Institute for Scientific Information's Sci-Mate, solve the differences in query languages by translating input into the query language of choice.

Continuing research and developments may cause all of these problems to be solved in the next few years, as systems take on more of the power and responsibility for search strategy and error checking, and as front-end systems solve the problems of inconsistency in and among query languages. Online systems have changed as technology and experience change, but they have had no real plan. Major changes are coming soon to alleviate some of the burden of strategy from the searcher. My students and I are anxiously awaiting that day! Then we will have other problems to report.

I wish to thank my fall 1983 students for suggesting this column, and all of my students of the last six years for contributing to it.

SEARCHING BY CONTROLLED VOCABULARY OR FREE TEXT?*

One of the most common mistakes made by new online searchers who are *not* librarians is to rely completely on free-text, natural-language search strategies. One of the most common mistakes made by new online searchers who *are* librarians is to go to the opposite extreme and use only controlled vocabulary descriptor searching. Even experienced searchers often wonder when it is best to use free-text techniques and when it may be best to use descriptors. Unfortunately, there is no clear-cut or easy answer. After examining the results of over 20 years of research studies and looking at search strategies from searchers of all levels of experience, the only answer I can give to the free-text vs. controlled vocabulary dilemma is *it depends*. It depends on: 1) the database; 2) the vocabulary itself and the indexing policies that dictate how it is applied; 3) the topic to be searched; and 4) the requester.

THE DATABASE

Many databases don't even have controlled vocabulary indexing, but the bibliographic databases used most frequently in libraries almost always do. According to research conducted by Martha E. Williams (and summarized in my column, "The Database Industry Today: Some Vendors' Perspectives," *LJ*, February 1, 1984, p. 156-157), the most frequently used databases in libraries are (in alphabetical order):

- ABI/INFORM
- BIOSIS
- CA Search (Chemical Abstracts)
- COMPENDEX (Computerized Engineering Index)
- ERIC
- Magazine Index
- Medline
- NTIS
- PTS (Predicasts) files
- PsycInfo (Psychological Abstracts)

All of these have a descriptor field that includes terms selected from some sort of controlled vocabulary or vocabularies.

Many of these databases use an extensive and carefully created thesaurus with a reputation for quality beyond the single database. For example, COMPENDEX uses "SHE" (Subject Headings for Engineering), ERIC uses "Thesaurus of ERIC Descriptors," Medline uses the excellent "MESH" (Medical Subject Headings), and PsycInfo uses "Thesaurus of Psychological Index Terms." ABI/INFORM developed a thesaurus and added controlled descriptors at the suggestion of users.

The other databases have controlled vocabularies that are typically used with less confidence or ease. Magazine Index has created a "Subject Guide to IAC" that uses modified and extended Library of Congress Subject Headings. NTIS records are indexed by one of several different thesauri depending on the subject and agency from which the document originated. CA Search uses a drug name authority and "Headings Lists" and Index Guides in place of standard thesaurus. BIOSIS relies heavily on codes and classification numbers that aid searching, but require training to use effectively. Predicasts has a company name thesaurus and a subject term listing.

MORE THAN ONE WAY

Although all of these databases have a descriptor field, the other fields available for free-text searching vary. Title words may always be searched, but only some databases have abstracts. Other fields such as captions or notes may serve as a short abstract-like text, but without the intellectual decision making that goes into the writing of an abstract.

The usefulness of titles for searching varies according to the subject matter of the database. Technical and research articles typically have longer and more meaningful titles than the popular articles found in a database such as Magazine Index. Short or ambiguous titles might be enhanced by the indexers (as Magazine Index does) but the titles are still usually shorter and less informative.

The meaningfulness of individual words in titles, abstracts, or other free-text subject-related fields varies with the subject matter. The level of ambiguity in language and the number of synonyms per concept have been shown to be subject dependent. Usually words in a so-called "hard" or "concrete" discipline (e.g., engineering or physics) are less ambiguous. Words in softer ("abstract") disciplines (e.g., philosophy or sociology) may be less meaningful. In soft disciplines the searcher must do a more careful job of complete synonym development in the search strategy. Studies have shown that a combination of title words and abstract words provide the most comprehensive (highest recall) free-text searches in all types of bibliographic databases.

The trade-off with the increased recall offered by abstracts is a corresponding increase in the number of false drops. If long abstracts are present and the database is large (over 500,000 records or so), abstract words can retrieve an unmanageable number of documents with an unacceptable number of false drops. Controlled vocabulary searching should be considered instead. Unless a search needs to be comprehensive, the best strategy in most large databases in this situation is probably a compromise of searching both title words and descriptors (and identifiers if they are available). Identifiers are used in some databases to add new subject terms or to control subject-related proper nouns.

THE VOCABULARY

Not all controlled vocabularies are created equal. Before relying on a database's descriptors, the searcher should have a good feel for the quality and limitations of the individual controlled vocabulary and the policies that dictate how it is applied.

Most of the databases that use controlled vocabulary descriptors use a thesaurus from which indexers select appropriate terms. Thesauri offer searchers many advantages: control of synonyms, control of variant word-forms (e.g., singulars or plurals), control of homographs, and hierarchical term relationships that facilitate search strategy development.

Other databases may use only a term authority list. Such a list merely documents accepted word forms with references from unused forms. Unlike a thesaurus, there is no hierarchical arrangement of Broader Terms, Narrower Terms, and Related Terms to help the searcher (and indexer) with word and concept selection.

Ideally, a thesaurus takes much of the burden of synonym development and concept building from the searcher. Unfortunately this promise may not always be fully realized.

THE IDEAL THESAURUS

A thesaurus must be sufficiently specific to allow topics to be defined narrowly. Assigning the term "BIOLOGICAL METHODS" to an article on gene splicing (as one database did) offers little chance of precision. Free-text searching of titles and abstracts works better in this case.

On the other hand, if a broad concept needs to be searched, a good controlled vocabulary will facilitate this. Searching for articles on folk tales of any Southeast Asian country, for example, is much easier in a database where the controlled vocabulary takes care of the country concept by assigning a broad overall category of Southeast Asian nations in addition to the specific country names. At least the printed thesaurus should list all of the nations within a broader region so a searcher need not consult an atlas to prepare a search. MESH goes one step further by assigning classification codes to terms and allowing these codes to be searched at any level. For example, a search on the truncated code number for steroids will retrieve all of the steroid categories and specific steroids.

A thesaurus must be as up-to-date as possible or the database should have an identifier field where new topics may be added. "Latchkey Children" was an identifier in ERIC before it recently became a descriptor. Like "Downloading" and "Burnout," latchkey children is a very specific concept with an exact meaning.

A thesaurus should have enough cross references and broad, narrow, or related terms to allow a searcher to find all descriptors that pertain. Scope notes should appear in at least the printed version to clear up ambiguous terms. A "connectedness" ratio has been suggested as a way to evaluate a thesaurus. Connectedness is the ratio of terms linked with at least one other term to the total number of terms in the thesaurus. A connectedness figure of two to five has been recommended by researchers.

The ability to view the thesaurus online is helpful for search strategy development. Unfortunately, the capability to invoke a thesaurus automatically while searching online is rare. (Notable exception: WILSONLINE.)

THE IMPACT OF INDEXING

In addition to thesaurus quality, the database's policy on indexing affects the success of controlled vocabulary searches. Who is doing the indexing will have a big impact as well. H. W. Wilson's experienced professional indexing staff has a reputation for quality. Other databases may have volunteer indexers or indexers spread out over such a wide geographic area that it is difficult to be consistent. Research has shown that in most databases there is little inter-indexer consistency. Finding all possible descriptors for a topic or using free text in conjunction with descriptors may thus be necessary.

Policies on the number of terms assigned will directly affect search results. If a database limits the number (e.g., "assign no more than five descriptors per document"), then only major topics of an article (or the topics seen by the indexer to be most important) will be covered. Relevant documents may be lost. On the other hand, assigning too many terms may negate the precision value offered by controlled vocabulary. The separation into major and minor descriptors (as ERIC does) can be a great help.

THE TOPIC

If one facet of a topic is very broad, using a descriptor term for this facet may be the best strategy. For example, in a search on gymnastic and tumbling programs in primary grades, the controlled term "Primary Education" will not only limit the number of citations retrieved, it will shorten response time considerably. Gymnastics and tumbling are easily free text searched and give better results when they are. A search in PsycInfo that includes the facet of personality factors, or a search in COMPENDEX with one facet of testing or design, will do the same.

If all facets in a search are of equal importance and likely to retrieve sets of equivalent size, controlled vocabulary may not be as important. Graffiti on the subway system, for example, is easily searched free text and retrieves a greater number of relevant items than descriptor terms in Magazine Index.

Controlled vocabulary is frequently useless for new ideas or jargon. If your topic is a current one (e.g., "designer drugs"), free text may be the only effective way to get relevant documents.

THE REQUESTER

If the requester wants a "few good ones" (a high-precision, low-recall search) and there are descriptors that match their topic, then descriptor searching is usually the best bet. Controlled vocabulary searching has been shown to be the most cost-effective search method, allowing retrieval of a small set of precise items at a lost cost per relevant record retrieved. Premenstrual Syndrome and (Migraine/de or headache/de) in the current Medline file on DIALOG will retrieve approximately a dozen highly relevant documents at a minimal cost.

If a more comprehensive search is needed, however, research has shown that controlled vocabulary searching alone is usually inadequate. Indexing policies, limitations of the vocabulary, and the nature of the English language all make it difficult to be comprehensive with descriptors. (Unfortunately, research has shown it is difficult to achieve complete recall even with free-text strategies.)

SUMMARY

No one search method is the best in every database, for every topic, or for every requester. The ability to use a combination of controlled vocabulary and free-text techniques or change strategies online is the mark of a good searcher. Like so much else in online searching, the ability to judge which strategy is best comes with experience and intuition. Although research provides some possible answers, search strategy is not a science. Ultimately, it all depends on the searcher. ∎

CHAPTER
9
USER AIDS

A database searcher relies on a variety of printed, online, and audiovisual tools to help with the search process. These tools range from textbooks that cover the basics of searching, to videotapes or computer programs that teach how to search a particular system, to magazines that explore issues and trends in database searching. Few libraries or searchers can purchase all of them, but there are some that are particularly helpful.

All of the articles in Chapter 9 review search tools, but this chapter is not meant to be an exhaustive list of all the search aids available on the market. Most of the articles discuss selected products or titles within categories, such as directories or training materials. Because new tools come out all of the time and old ones get out of date, I have made extensive revisions to several of the articles in this chapter. In the first article, I have tried to get the information as up to date as possible, as of fall 1988. The reader is advised to check with the publishers mentioned in these articles for their latest editions or publications.

"Keeping Up with Databases" was written especially for this book. It replaces two 1983 *Library Journal* columns ("Databases: Catching Up and Keeping Up" and "More Publications about Databases") that were too outdated to include here. The new version included here covers some of the publications mentioned in 1983, but brings the information up to date and adds new tools that have appeared in the last five years. It is an annotated selected bibliography of the books, magazines, conference proceedings, and other publications that I think are especially useful for database searchers. I have indicated when a publication is reviewed in more depth in another article.

"Learning How to Search" reviews printed, audiovisual, and computer tools that teach people how to search. Some of the sources teach how to search just one online system (these are often produced by the online system itself), others take a broader view and discuss online search methods in general. I have added selected titles that have come out since the original 1987 publication date.

The next two columns review the many directories of databases that are available in print and sometimes online. "Database Directories: In Print and Now Online" and "Database Directories: The Rest" form a two-part review article of these useful tools. The database directory is now a standard reference book that every library should have, whether or not they offer online search services. The variety of directories to choose from is shown in the over thirty directories mentioned in the two articles that were available as of 1985.

The final article discusses printed and online tools designed to help the searcher decide which database or databases to search. "Database Selection Tools" reviews three types of selection aids: directories, online dictionary files, and automatic database selection. The tools range from familiar printed sources to sophisticated "expert system"-like online aids. The help is either at the broad subject level ("which databases cover the subject area this search falls into?") or at the individual search level ("which databases will have the most information on this particular search topic?"). The article discusses the strengths and weaknesses of each type of tool and tells about some of the most widely available products for each type.

All of the tools mentioned in this chapter serve as aids to the online searcher. None of them, however, substitutes for online practice and experience as a way to improve search skills. They help the searcher make decisions and to search better; they do not replace the searcher.

KEEPING UP WITH DATABASES
A Selected Bibliography*

Reference librarians and other professional database searchers know that learning how to search and even conducting searches regularly do not by themselves make good searchers. Database searchers need to keep current on a wide variety of changes, developments, and issues in order to be effective users of databases. How does the searcher keep up with new databases, online systems, and CD-ROM and other optical products; changes and enhancements to familiar online systems or databases; and issues such as downloading, end user searching, and government interest in limiting access to certain information by designating it as "sensitive but unclassified"? Time and effort are required. Some strategies and selected materials for keeping up are given below.

I have separated the tools for keeping up with databases into nine categories, similar to the categories I used in my first *Library Journal* column, "Databases: Catching Up and Keeping Up" (February 1, 1983). Selected titles are given for each of the following categories of tools: 1) textbooks, 2) other useful monographs, 3) bibliographies, 4) periodicals, 5) directories, 6) professional groups, 7) conferences, 8) audiovisuals, 9) computer-assisted learning.

TEXTBOOKS

**Borgman, Christine L., and others. *Effective Online Searching: A Basic Text*. New York: M. Dekker, 1984.
Especially good treatments of searchers and search strategy. Some portions are out of date.

Chen, Ching-chih, and Susanna Schweizer. *Online Bibliographic Searching: A Learning Manual*. New York: Neal-Schuman, 1981.
This book is now too out of date to be used in its entirety (much of the specific information cannot be used, especially the hardware information and the section that provides the online "answers" to the old DIALOG workbook), but the basic discussions of online systems and databases are still some of the clearest elementary explanations. A new edition would be nice.

**Fenichel, Carol H., and Thomas Hogan. *Online Searching: A Primer*, 2nd ed. Medford, N.J.: Learned Information, 1984.
Easy-to-read basic introduction to online systems and databases for the intermediary searcher. Third edition expected in 1989.

**Harter, Stephen P. *Online Information Retrieval: Concepts, Principles, and Techniques*. Orlando, Fla.: Academic Press, 1986.
Includes basic information as well as more advanced discussions of evaluation and information retrieval research. Excellent.

**Humphrey, Susanne M., and Biagio John Melloni. *Databases: A Primer for Retrieving Information by Computer*. Englewood Cliffs, N.J.: Prentice Hall, 1986.
Good treatment of database structure and search features that transcends any one system. Includes information on user-friendly systems and artificial intelligence.

**Li, Tze-Chung. *An Introduction to Online Searching*. Westport, Conn.: Greenwood Press, 1985.
Brief introductory material with lengthy treatments of search commands and features of DIALOG, BRS, ORBIT, and selected end user systems.

**Palmer, Roger. *Online Reference and Information Retrieval*, 2nd ed. Littleton, Colo.: Libraries Unlimited, 1987.
Includes good explanations of how databases are structured and processed by online systems for searching. Tutorial on several major online systems.

Vigil, Peter J. *Online Retrieval: Analysis and Strategy*. New York: John Wiley and Sons, 1988.
In-depth discussions of search strategy for beginning or experienced searchers. Describes major online vendors and basic commands. Includes chapters on front-end software and expert systems.

OTHER USEFUL MONOGRAPHS

Alberico, Ralph. *Microcomputers for the Online Searcher*. Westport, Conn.: Meckler, 1987.
In-depth discussion of hardware and software, including details of specific products. Assumes knowledge of online searching.

Armstrong, C. J., and J. A. Large, eds. *Manual of Online Search Strategies*. Boston: G. K. Hall and Co., 1988.
Compendium of recommended search strategies for specific databases by subject.

Benson, James, and Bella Hass Weinberg, eds. *Downloading/Uploading Online Databases and Catalogs*. Ann Arbor, Mich.: Pierian Press, 1985.
Proceedings of the Congress for Librarians on Downloading and Uploading, Jamaica, N.Y., February 1985.

Benson, James, and Bella Hass Weinberg, eds. *Gateway Software and Natural Language Interfaces: Options for Online Searching*. Ann Arbor, Mich.: Pierian Press, 1988.
Reviews of specific products with some introductory text.

---

*Written November 1988.
**Reviewed in more depth in later articles.

Glossbrenner, Alfred. *How to Look It Up Online*. New York: St. Martin's Press, 1987.

Easy-to-read and entertaining beginning text aimed at end users. Describes many online services and where to find different types of information.

Hoover, Ryan. *Executive's Guide to Online Information Services*. KIPI, 1984; John Wiley, 1986. Distributed by the Association of Records Managers and Administrators, 4200 Somerset, Suite 215, Prairie Village, KS 66208.

Appeals to a wide audience, aimed at decision makers.

Katz, William. *Introduction to Reference Work*, 5th ed. New York: McGraw-Hill, 1987.

Describes databases as reference sources, with good introductory coverage of issues relating to online searching of interest to reference librarians.

Newlin, Barbara. *Answers Online: Your Guide to Informational Data Bases*, Berkeley, Calif.: Osborne/McGraw-Hill, 1985.

Describes databases by types of literature. Basic online search techniques for end users.

BIBLIOGRAPHIES

Batt, Fred. *Online Searching for End Users: An Information Sourcebook*. Phoenix, Ariz.: Oryx Press, 1988.

Selected annotated bibliography and an analysis of the library literature about end user searching.

Hawkins, Donald T. *Online Information Retrieval Bibliography, 1964-1982*. Westport, Conn.: Learned Information, 1982.

Hawkins, Donald T. *Online Information Retrieval Bibliography, 1983-1986*. Westport, Conn.: Learned Information, 1986.

Hawkins, Donald T. "Online Information Retrieval Bibliography" updates published as supplements to *Online Review*, August issues.

Library Hi Tech Bibliography series. Contact Pierian Press (P.O. Box 1808, Ann Arbor, MI 48106) for topics. 1988- .

PERIODICALS

CD-ROM Librarian (Formerly called *Optical Information Systems Update: Library and Information Center Applications*). Meckler Publishing, 11 Ferry Lane West, Westport, CT 06880. Ten issues per year.

News and short articles for librarians who offer (or want to offer) database services on CD-ROM.

Database. Online, Inc., 11 Tannery Lane, Weston, CT 06883. Six times per year.

A spin-off and now companion to *Online*. Includes many database and software reviews.

Database Searcher. (Formerly *Database End User*). Meckler Corp., 11 Ferry Lane West, Westport, CT 06880. Monthly.

News and short articles for the database professional. Lively writing style and focus. Editor, Barbara Quint.

The Electronic Library. Learned Information, Inc., 143 Old Marlton Pike, Medford, NJ 08055. Six times per year.

Worldwide focus on all aspects of library automation. (Editor is in Europe.)

Information Today. Learned Information, Inc., 143 Old Marlton Pike, Medford, NJ 08055. Eleven times per year.

A newspaper format, full of the latest news from the database industry. National and international.

Laserdisk Professional. Pemberton Press, Inc., 11 Tannery Lane, Weston, CT 06883. Six times per year.

The latest spin-off (1988) from *Online*, this one is devoted to optical disk databases, especially CD-ROM.

Library Hi-Tech. Pierian Press, P.O. Box 1808, Ann Arbor, MI 48106. Quarterly.

New technologies and applications for libraries. Includes information about online and CD-ROM databases as well as all aspects of library automation.

Library Hi-Tech News. Pierian Press, P.O. Box 1808, Ann Arbor, MI 48106. Eleven times per year.

Monitors information and literature on all aspects of automation in libraries.

Library Journal. R. R. Bowker Co., 249 W. 17th St., New York 10011. Twice a month.

Includes a regular column about databases.

Online. Online, Inc., 11 Tannery Lane, Weston, CT 06883. Six times per year.

For over a decade the best all-around magazine devoted to databases and aimed at information professionals. Practical and up to date with many articles from librarians.

Online Review. Learned Information, Inc., 143 Old Marlton Pike, Medford, NJ 08055. Bimonthly.

Worldwide focus on databases, written by and for information professionals. Often includes research articles.

RQ. Reference and Adult Services Division, American Library Association, 50 E. Huron St., Chicago, IL 60611. Quarterly.

Includes reviews of new databases in the "Sources" section plus some articles on database issues or how reference librarians are using databases.

Wilson Library Bulletin. H. W. Wilson Co., 950 University Ave., Bronx, NY 10452. Ten times per year.

Includes regular columns "Microcomputing" about new products and "Connect Time" about databases.

DIRECTORIES

(For a complete listing see the articles "Database Directories: In Print and Now Online" and "Database Directories: The Rest," in this chapter. Listed here are the major directories used by intermediaries.)

Directory of Online Databases. New York: Cuadra/Elsevier. Quarterly. Online on BRS and Data-Star.

Hall, James L., and Marjorie J. Brown. *Online Bibliographic Databases: An International Directory*, 4th ed. Aslib, 1986. Distributed by Gale Research, Detroit, MI.

"Online Review Database Directory Comparative Price Guide." February and August issues of *Online Review.*

Williams, Martha E., ed. *Computer Readable Databases: A Directory and Data Sourcebook.* Online as file 230 on DIALOG. Updated and published by Gale Research, Detroit, MI. 1988- .

PROFESSIONAL GROUPS

Machine Assisted Reference Service section (MARS), Reference and Adult Services Division, American Library Association, 50 E. Huron St., Chicago, IL 60611.

Online Section, Division of Information Technology, Special Libraries Association, 1700 18th St. NW, Washington, DC 20009.

Online users groups are located in many areas. For information and the groups near you see: "Circuit News," a column in *Online*, by Margaret Bell Hentz, National Online Circuit Chairperson. Discontinued in 1989.

Several special-interest groups, American Society for Information Science, 1424 Sixteenth St. NW, Washington, DC 20036.

CONFERENCES

In addition to the national meetings of the American Library Association, Special Libraries Association, American Society for Information Science, and other professional societies, special conferences dedicated solely to issues in database searching are held regularly. Even if you cannot attend these conferences, their published proceedings are valuable sources for keeping up with the latest developments in online searching and finding out what other libraries are doing. Additionally, many online vendors hold annual users' meetings to help users stay current with changes on the systems. Many local and regional meetings are announced in the publications of the professional organizations mentioned above.

National Online Meeting. Yearly: New York, in April or May. Contact: Thomas H. Hogan, National Online Meeting, Learned Information, Inc., 143 Old Marlton Pike, Medford, NJ 08055. Proceedings available from the same address.

International Online Information Meeting. Yearly: London, in December. Contact: Learned Information, Ltd., Woodside, Hinksey Hill, Oxford, OX1 5AU, England. Proceedings available from the same address.

Online meeting. Yearly: October. Locations vary throughout the United States. Contact: Online, Inc., 11 Tannery Lane, Weston, CT 06883.

Australian Online Meeting. Yearly: January. Locations vary in Australia. Contact: Library Association of Australia, 376 Jones St., Ultimo, New South Wales 2007.

Small Computers in Libraries Conference. Annual. Contact: Nancy Melin Nelson, ed., Meckler Publishing, 11 Ferry Lane West, Westport, CT 06880.

AUDIOVISUAL AIDS

"BRS/Search Service Video Training Course." 3 parts. BRS Information Technologies, 1200 Route 7, Latham, NY 12110. 1986. Videotape.

"Going Online: An Introduction to the World of Online Information." Learned Information, Inc., 143 Old Marlton Pike, Medford, NJ 08055. 1986. Videotape.

"Going Online for Business Inforamtion." Learned Information, Inc., 143 Old Marlton Pike, Medford, NJ 08055. 1988. Videotape.

"Graffiti on a Database." Learned Information, Inc., 143 Old Marlton Pike, Medford, NJ 08055. 1983. Slide/tape.

"How to Use Wilsondisc: The Browse Search Mode." H. W. Wilson Co., 950 University Ave., Bronx, NY 10452. 1988. Videotape.

"Online Searching: An Introduction to Wilsonline." H. W. Wilson Co., 950 University Ave., Bronx, NY 10452. 1986. Videotape.

COMPUTER-ASSISTED LEARNING

Computer-Assisted Learning (CAI) is the latest training technique to be introduced to online searching. Surprisingly, few CAI programs are yet available; to learn computer searching still requires book media. Mentioned below are some programs that are now available, either through private organizations or the online vendor. Canned introductions on floppy disk that do not include tutorial material are excluded from this list.

DIALTWIG.
This is a DIALOG emulation program developed at the Graduate School of Library and Information Science, Brigham Young University, Provo, Utah. You may create your own databases by downloading records or inputting from scratch.

TRAINER:DIALOG. Caruso Associates Inc., 440 2nd St., California, PA 15419.

Originally developed at the University of Pittsburgh, School of Library and Information Science.

"Learning NEXIS." Mead Data Central, 1987.

"STN Mentor: STN Express Overview." American Chemical Society, 1987. ■

LEARNING HOW TO SEARCH*

Most intermediaries learn how to search by attending a vendor's training course or by taking a class in a library school. In addition, some libraries offer in-house training classes where experienced searchers teach their colleagues (see my column, May 1, 1984, p. 870-871).

Even with formal opportunities available, there are still several alternatives for learning about online searching. Textbooks, videotapes, and computer-assisted instruction programs have been designed either for beginning searchers or for searchers with some experience who wish to sharpen existing online skills. Some of these will train you to conduct searches on a particular vendor's system; others will just expose you to the concepts and issues of online searching by an intermediary.

READ ALL ABOUT IT

The many good textbooks published in the late 1970s and early 1980s are now mostly out-of-date. Luckily, the last three years have seen a new crop of texts for intermediary searchers, plus updated editions of some old ones. The various texts do not completely duplicate each other; each book has different areas of emphasis and different strengths. Most of the texts do not attempt to train the reader in the command language of any one system; instead they instruct in the basic concepts, jargon, and issues of online searching. They can be used in conjunction with online practice by following system tutorials or with the help of a colleague.

Online Searching: A Primer by Carol H. Fenichel and Thomas H. Hogan (Learned Information, 2d ed., 1984) is a concise, basic introduction to online searching by intermediaries. Because it assumes no prior knowledge of online searching, this text is most appropriate for the student or librarian who is not yet searching. They can use it together with online training or by itself to provide a beginning-level understanding of the field.

The strongest chapters in *Online Searching* cover management issues and the reference interview process which are of continuing importance and are fairly time-insensitive. On the other hand, some of the specific information in the chapters on databases and vendors and in the 20+ pages of appendixes is already out-of-date. Material added for the second edition discusses the role of the microcomputer. The chapter on the future mentions videodisc, but in 1984 CD-ROM was not yet an issue.

As its name implies, *Effective Online Searching: A Basic Text*, by Christine L. Borgman and others (Dekker, 1984), covers the basics, but its emphasis is on the person doing the searching and on search strategy development.

The sections on characteristics of good searchers, search strategy, the reference process, vocabulary control, and search evaluation are the strongest. Examples from DIALOG, BRS, and ORBIT searches are given, but the text does not attempt to instruct in the commands of any one system. Human-system and searcher-client interactions are stressed throughout, with the mechanics of searching given only for illustration.

Though published in 1984, almost all the items in the footnotes and bibliography of *Effective Online Searching* are from 1981 or earlier. There is no mention of microcomputers in the hardware section, so management issues resulting from their use (e.g., downloading) are missing. The best use of this text is for intermediaries who want help in refining search strategy skills or interviewing techniques. This information does not go quickly out-of-date.

An Introduction to Online Searching by Tze-Chung Li (Greenwood, 1985) takes a different approach by devoting two-thirds of the book to system-specific search features and commands and attempting to teach readers how to search.

The first 85 pages introduce databases, systems, managing an online service, and the reference interview. Microcomputers are treated in a later chapter. Most of the remainder of the book is made up of chapters on specific commands for DIALOG, BRS, and ORBIT. One chapter summarizes the similarities and differences of these systems' search features. Another summarizes the search features of the end user systems CompuServe, the Source, and Dow Jones. (This book is unique among the texts aimed primarily at intermediaries in its treatment of such systems.)

The advantage of Li's approach is that the reader may be able to learn how to search a particular system or systems without using another source; the disadvantage is that the system features change frequently. Although changes usually supplement rather than replace older search commands, some of the specific system search features will be different than those in this text, and new features will have been added. The individual system manuals will still be needed for detailed information as well as for up-to-date information.

Databases: A Primer for Retrieving Information by Computer by Susanne M. Humphrey and Biagio John Melloni (Prentice-Hall, 1986) takes the opposite tack by discussing

*Reprinted from *Library Journal* June 15, 1987. Copyright © 1987 by Reed Publishing, USA, Div. of Reed Holdings, Inc.

principles and features of online searching with as little mention of specific systems as possible. The book's audience is also broader than the other texts mentioned here, being "written for professionals and students of information science," but also "intended for anyone who feels the need for a basic understanding of retrieving information by computer."

Databases is a handsome book, clearly written, and includes many cartoons and illustrations. Its strengths lie in the discussions of how databases are constructed and the many possible search features. Unlike the other books mentioned, it has sections on user friendliness and artificial intelligence. A chapter on selecting a vendor contains useful information for beginners or experienced searchers.

Sometimes the discussions get too removed from working online systems, however. The section on Boolean operators, for example, includes many "nonstandard" operators such as XOR and NAND, which may confuse the novice. *Databases* is particularly recommended for potential producers of databases or for searchers who want to know more about how system design features influence their searching.

Online Information Retrieval: Concepts, Principles, and Techniques by Stephen P. Harter (Academic, 1986) transcends the features or commands of any one system. It emphasizes evaluation and search strategy and is perhaps best used by someone who knows how to search.

This book combines the broader principles and research of information storage and retrieval with that of online searching. Although it provides introductory material on systems and databases and managing an intermediary service, its particular strengths are in evaluation of databases or systems, characteristics of searchers, and search strategy. Numeric, directory, and full-text databases are treated as well as bibliographic.

The many exercises ("Problems") at the end of each chapter are especially helpful and the bibliographies are extensive. Like *Databases*, readers will find that *Online Information Retrieval* stretches their knowledge of databases and online searching. It will provide a challenge for even experienced searchers.

WATCH ALL ABOUT IT

The videotape *Online Searching: An Introduction to Wilsonline* (H. W. Wilson, 1986) is aimed at the main audience of the Wilsonline system, the librarian. This narrowly defined target audience allows it to assume familiarity with Wilson printed indexes and to use library jargon without further definitions. The "good old card catalog format" is referred to at one point. The narrow audience also allows the videotape to use a folksy, one-librarian-talking-to-another format. Watching this video is like having an in-house meeting (but without time for questions or coffee). Viewers are reminded at the beginning and the end of the program that Wilson's primary considerations are the quality of indexing and timeliness of access. This program uses no fancy graphics or gimmicks. Sometimes the closeups of screen displays are cramped or fuzzy, but the overall quality is good.

This program cannot be used by itself to learn how to search Wilsonline, but it can be used to gain some familiarity with system features and databases. Some basic search instruction is given (e.g., the use of Boolean operators), but the tape

must be used in conjunction with the Wilson tutorial booklet and online practice time.

The BRS training video, on the other hand, is intended to teach viewers "how to conduct an online search on the BRS system." To do this it will use several parts, each of which comes with a workbook. Viewers are asked to turn off the tape at several places throughout the program to complete exercises in the workbooks. When they complete the tapes and workbook exercises they should be able to search BRS online.

The BRS program has a more ambitious purpose than the Wilson tape. In addition to teaching viewers to search, the audience of the BRS tape is less narrowly defined. It attempts to serve anyone who wants to learn to search, calling for a more serious and careful approach.

Each BRS videotape begins with a list of things that will be learned in that tape. Definitions of terms are always included, because a librarian audience is not assumed. The corresponding workbooks are structured to follow along with the tape. How-to instruction is interwoven with background information on databases and how databases are made searchable on BRS. Exact command syntax is emphasized, with each command highlighted in letters on the screen after an online demonstration. Graphics, online searches, and a variety of other images are used with a voice-over technique rather than the chatty approach of the Wilson tape.

The BRS program appears to be well thought out and thorough. Part 1 covers basic systems features from logging on to searching, printing, and logging off. Part 2 gets into some fairly advanced search strategy and refinement procedures. If it is used slowly in conjunction with the workbook exercises and interspersed with online practice, the BRS videotape should be able to teach people how to search. Part 3 covers multifile searching, full-text and advanced work on controlled vocabulary and non-subject searching.

Learned Information Inc. offers 2 general introductory videos that provide information about online searching. *Going Online: An Introduction to the World of Online Information* does not feature any one online system, nor attempt to teach commands. It illustrates what online searching is and can do by using examples from several online systems and showing different potential users. It covers things such as gateway systems as well as online systems such as DIALOG.

Going Online is an excellent program to introduce viewers to the world of online searching. It cannot be used to teach how to search, but that is not its intent. *Going Online for Business Information* uses several databases to introduce online searching benefits to businesses.

LEARNING BY COMPUTING

The missing element from textbooks or videotapes is actual controlled interactive practice. Logging on the systems for all practice can get expensive. For years some library schools have used system emulators with in-house databases to allow unlimited online practice. Microcomputer versions of some of these are now available for purchase.

Brigham Young University's program called *DIALTWIG* emulates the *DIALOG2* software. It is available for MS-DOS systems and comes with two sample databases or users can build their own. Users must devise their own training program. For more information contact Keith Sterling, Graduate School of Library and Information Science, Brigham Young University, Provo, UT 84602.

TRAINER:DIALOG is an MS-DOS computer-assisted instruction program from Caruso Associates Inc. Through a combination of text, exercises, and online practice *TRAINER* teaches people how to conduct DIALOG searches. It can be used in a group environment with supervision by an experienced searcher or for self-instruction. *TRAINER* is meant to be used by a large group (such as end users in a special library)

that needs to search on a particular database. The current version focuses on the electronic Power Research Institute database using DIALOG commands. Other versions may be made available as needed.

TRAINER is an excellent idea for in-house training efforts. It has been developed by people knowledgeable in education for online searching. Contact Elaine Caruso, Caruso Assocs., Inc., 440 2d St., California, PA 15419. ∎

DATABASE DIRECTORIES
In Print and Now Online*

Since the publication of the first database directory in 1976 (edited by Martha E. Williams and Sandra Rouse and published by the American Society for Information Science), printed directories have been the major formal source for finding out what databases are available on a particular topic. Other than a searcher's experience, these printed reference works have continued to be the main way searchers find out what databases are available from a variety of online vendors. (Online search aids such as DIALOG's *DIALINDEX*, BRS/*CROSS*, or SDC's *Database Index* include only those databases available on their respective systems.)

Recently several developments have brought database directories into the spotlight again. These developments include: a new version of an established directory for information professionals, an additional directory for professional searchers, an increase in the number of directories aimed at end user or subject target audiences, and, the most exciting development, online access to the three most complete directories.

This month's column concentrates on the three directories that are aimed at information professionals, available in new up-to-date printed editions, and are all now also available online.

WILLIAMS DIRECTORY

Computer-Readable Databases: A Directory and Data Sourcebook (Martha E. Williams, editor-in-chief) is a comprehensive compendium of all types of databases. Many librarians are familiar with the earlier one-volume editions of this work that focused on word-oriented databases (bibliographic, full text, directory, etc.). The 1985 edition was published by ALA in two volumes (now o.p.).

One volume contains listings for databases in science, technology, and medicine; the second volume includes business, law, humanities, and social sciences. Together, the two volumes describe over 2800 databases. Only publicly available

databases in computer-readable form are included (most, but not all, are online). General interest databases (e.g., magazines, newspapers, biographical information) are placed in the second volume. Multidisciplinary databases that contain material of interest to users of either volume are placed in both volumes "so that each volume is a complete and separate entity." Although page numbers run consecutively through the text in the two volumes, each volume includes the complete set of indexes. This increases the directory's size, but is a handy feature for users.

Computer-Readable Databases is a massive work that provides a wealth of information on each database. For each database the following basic information is listed: name of database, including acronym, former name, and former acronym; producer; frequency of updates; time span covered by most materials in the database; approximate number of items in the database as of December 1984; average number of items added each year; corresponding print products if any; language of the database; and organizations (vendors) that make the database available online. Some database entries contain additional basic information about batch availability, licensing of the database tapes, geographic coverage, sources of the data, or special features.

In addition to basic information, there is a one- or two-paragraph description of the subject matter and scope of each database. Indexing, coding, or classification used in the database are listed also, as are basic record structures for bibliographic databases. Finally, most entries for word-oriented databases mention what user aids are available.

Four indexes make up the last 286 pages of each volume. The Name Index refers to all current and former names as well as acronyms. The thorough Subject Index includes 36 broad controlled categories as well as over 500 noncontrolled keywords taken from the database descriptions. The Producer Index lists names and addresses of the producers of all of the databases in the directory. Each entry gives the names of all databases produced by that agency. The Processor Index gives names and addresses of all vendors of the databases in the

---

*Reprinted from *Library Journal* Aug. 1985. Copyright © 1985 by Reed Publishing, USA, Div. of Reed Holdings, Inc.

directory, along with an alphabetical list of databases they make available. (The DIALOG Information Services Inc. entry goes on for four and one-half columns.)

Computer-Readable Databases has the broadest scope of the database directories. It contains batch as well as online, international as well as U.S., foreign language as well as English, and numeric as well as word-oriented databases. It is also the largest in terms of sheer size and number of pages.

Online Version

This directory, now produced by Gale, is on DIALOG as Database of Databases, file 230 ($48 a connect hour). Updates are irregular. Producer addresses will not be in the online version. The lengthy, descriptive Subject Matter and Scope field will be especially useful for online free-searching.

CUADRA DIRECTORY

The second oldest comprehensive database directory for online professionals has been continuously issued on a subscription basis since 1979. *Directory of Online Databases*, published by Cuadra/Elsevier, is issued quarterly; price, $150/ year. Twice a year a complete master volume is issued. In between complete volumes, subscribers receive a supplement that fits in the back of the master volume.

The July 1988 issue includes entries for over 3000 "reference" (bibliographic or referral) or "source" databases (numeric, textual-numeric, full text, software) made available by 576 online services around the world. Only databases that are publicly available online through a telecommunications network are included, but emphasis is worldwide.

Like the other directories, the Cuadra directory has a main section that is arranged alphabetically by database name. Concise information for each database includes: name of database; type (reference or source and specific type, e.g., bibliographic); one or more broad subject terms from a controlled list; producer; online vendors; conditions for gaining access to the database (e.g., subscription required); narrative description of the content, including subject, coverage, scope, and printed equivalents; language; geographic coverage; time span; and update frequency.

A second section lists names, addresses, phone numbers, telex, FAX and E-mail numbers for headquarters of database producers, online vendors, and gateways.

The third section is composed of six indexes. There is a conventional Subject Index, a Producer Index that lists all databases created by each producer, and an Online Service/ Gateway Index that lists all databases available via a vendor. Unique to this directory is a Telecommunications Index listing all the telecommunications networks that can be used to access each online service vendor. The fifth is a Master Index that lists all databases, producers, gateways, and online vendors and refers back to the appropriate Producer or Online Service Index.

Because it is quarterly, *Directory of Online Databases* is the most continuously up-to-date of the printed database directories. Until the online availability of directories, this was as up-to-date as you could get for database directory information.

Online Version

This directory too will soon be online, via "several online vendors" to be announced by Cuadra Associates this summer. Updates will be twice a year "at a minimum." Producer and vendor addresses will be part of the online record, with a print option on most systems to get the addresses only if they are desired.

In addition to the online databases, Cuadra Associates leases a machine-readable version of the entire directory for mounting on an organization's computer for in-house use.

KIPI-ASIS DIRECTORY

The newest comprehensive directory, and the first to go online, is the *Data Base Directory*, 1988, published by Knowledge Industry Publications, Inc. in cooperation with the American Society for Information Science. The first edition was issued in the fall of 1984. Plans are for future editions to be issued twice a year.

One issue of the directory plus a six-month subscription to the monthly newsletter *Data Base Alert* costs $120. A yearly subscription, including two issues of the directory and 12 issues of *Data Base Alert*, is $215.

Like the other two directories, *Data Base Directory* includes information on all types of textual, bibliographic, referral, and numeric databases on all subjects. The first edition especially concentrates on those databases available online in the United States and/or Canada. Selected foreign databases are included, the new edition promising to contain many more European entries. Approximately 2100 total databases will be included in the new edition.

The printed directory begins with an index to alternate and preferred names for databases (including acronyms and former names). The database listing follows, arranged alphabetically by the preferred name of each database. Information about each database includes: database name including alternate name, former name, acronym; up to six subject headings supplied by the database producer; a short narrative summary of the content and scope; corresponding printed sources; availability of enhanced subject access through subject headings, classification, etc.; name of the producer and special services provided; database "data" including file size, update frequency, approximate number of records added each year, inclusive dates, database type, and types of documents covered in the database; online vendor and price information for each; original data sources; language; restrictions and conditions of availability; telecommunications networks; and search aids available.

The pricing information often includes database charges plus the average price of a "typical" search. This is the only one of the three directories to include this information.

Data Base Directory has three indexes. The Vendor Index gives the name and address of each online vendor plus a list of databases available through that vendor. The Producer Index does the same for all database producers. Finally, the Subject Index provides broad subject access to the databases (although it lists only the database names and not the directory page numbers where the databases can be found).

Online Version

Online access through Knowledge Industry Publication's own in-house computer system has been available since late 1984 for a fee of $60 per hour. Of more use to most searchers is the BRS version, available online since June 1985. File *KIPD* (*Knowledge Industry Publication Database*) on BRS has a royalty rate of $50 per hour. The online file is essentially the same as the printed directory's database listing with producer addresses included as a separate data paragraph. The file will be updated monthly. Magnetic tapes of the entire directory are also available for lease from Knowledge Industry.

CONCLUSION

Online versions of these three comprehensive database directories promise new uses for their valuable information.

Searchers can not only discover what databases are available on a subject or from a producer, they can gather more complex information by using the powers of Boolean logic and free text searching. The narrative database descriptions contained in each directory combined with the shorter controlled fields offer many searching possibilities.

Both the print and online versions of these three directories are valuable tools for online searchers, and the new up-to-date versions provide an almost overwhelming amount of information on databases and systems worldwide. These three directories are the best, most complete, and now the most versatile database tools of the nearly 30 database directories on the market. Next month's column will discuss some of the other printed database directories currently available. ∎

DATABASE DIRECTORIES
The Rest

A look through *Books in Print* or at the computer books counter of any major bookstore will reveal a growing number of database directories. There are now over 30 of these directories, which range from one-subject specialty directories, to guides and directories of popular databases for the home computer user, to comprehensive directories for online professionals.

In last month's column I concentrated on the three comprehensive directories that are now all available online through major online search services (Williams, *Computer-Readable Databases*; Cuadra Associates Inc., *Directory of Online Databases*; and *Data Base Directory*). Online and in print these directories are the most complete and best resources for the information professional.

This month's column will look at some of the other database directories on the market. At the end of the column is a list of selected database directories.

THE GALE *ENCYCLOPEDIA*

The 1985-86 edition of the well-known *Encyclopedia of Information Systems and Services* provides a valuable and up-to-date reference work for databases, although it is not strictly a database directory. The *Encyclopedia* includes descriptive information about all types of "information providers"— organizations that provide computer-readable information. Included are libraries, database producers, online vendors, consultants, associations, etc.

Unlike most comprehensive database directories, the *Encyclopedia* is arranged by the organization that produces

the information, rather than by the database name. Still, each database produced by the same organization is described separately under the producer's name. This work is the most valuable if you know a database name or producer and want to find out more information about them.

The new sixth edition is divided into an international volume and a United States volume. Together they include information on approximately 3600 databases. After the main producer entry there are separate entries for each database created by that producer. These entries contain full descriptive information about the database.

Several of the *Encyclopedia*'s 27 indexes are of special interest to database users. The "Computer-Readable Data Bases Index" lists names and acronyms of databases and is essential if this work is to be used as a database directory. The "Subject Index" includes general and specific subject listings for all entries in the *Encyclopedia*, including databases. (There is no way to tell databases apart from organizations in the subject index, however.) A "Data Base Producers and Publishers Index" puts all 2200 producers together. An "Online Services/ Telecommunications Networks Index" lists nearly 400 online vendors and time-sharing systems.

Although the *Encyclopedia* is not meant to be primarily a database directory as are the others described here, its value to online searchers should not be overlooked.

DATAPRO DIRECTORIES

Datapro Research Corporation publishes two database directories—the well-known *Datapro Directory of Online*

Services and the newer *Datapro Complete Guide to Dial-Up Databases*. The latter is merely a one-volume extract of portions of the two-volume *Directory*. No one needs both works (and for what you get for the price it is questionable whether anyone needs either).

The two-volume *Directory* includes a monthly update service, something that is not available for the one-volume *Complete Guide*. The *Directory* costs $449 for the two master volumes and one year of updates, with a second year renewal price of $394. The *Complete Guide* is $145.

Both works include descriptions of over 1400 publicly available databases. Database profiles are arranged alphabetically in the main section with detailed information about each database.

In addition to the database information and subject index to it, there are indepth profiles of 15 online vendors. Of the over 400 vendors listed in the Cuadra directory the choice of these 15 seems curious. BRS, DIALOG, and Mead Data Central are all included, but NLM, SDC Orbit, and Westlaw are not. OCLC is profiled. UTLAS, WLN, and RLIN are not. Other vendors of interest to libraries that are omitted include Pergamon InfoLine, VU-TEXT, WILSONLINE, and ESA. According to Datapro, vendors were chosen by "editorial discretion."

Other sections in both directories include tutorials on the use of microcomputers for online searching and comparative summaries of microcomputer communications software and modems. Unique to the Datapro publications is a section that reports the results of a Datapro survey of online users who were asked to rank the major online vendors. The information is interesting but may be of limited use as it includes only user's *opinions* of typical system response time, system dependability (up-time), adequacy of documentation, and overall satisfaction.

The main strength of the Datapro *Directory* is its loose-leaf updating, not available for the *Complete Guide*. The software and modem comparisons and microcomputer tutorials are valuable, but available in more depth elsewhere. (See the bibliography in my March 15 column.) The database and vendor information are handled better by the database directories produced by the experts in the online field.

OTHER COMPREHENSIVE DIRECTORIES

Hall and Brown's *Online Bibliographic Directory* is the third edition of a directory published by Aslib. The editors have chosen not to attempt complete comprehensiveness, instead they state the purpose is to provide information on the "principal" English-language online bibliographic databases. All patents databases are omitted, but criteria for other exclusions is not always so clear.

The information included about each database in the directory is complete, including access charges and a reproduction of a typical record, in addition to the usual descriptive information. Other databases are mentioned in the general index.

Although not recommended as a substitute for a more up-to-date and truly comprehensive directory, this work is valuable for its introductory figures on the database industry, its

extensive bibliography, and the complete treatment given approximately 180 selected databases.

Directory of Online Information Resources, published twice a year, is a directory that includes only "the most popular" databases available in the United States and Canada. Once again, criteria for inclusion of the approximately 600 databases in the 1982 edition is not always clear.

Information about each database is less complete than in *Online Bibliographic Databases*, but includes price as well as descriptive information. Indexes give vendor and producer addresses and all databases created by a producer or available on a vendor's system. The main advantage of this directory is its price of $18.50 for one edition or $48 for a two-year subscription (four editions).

END USER DIRECTORIES

"End User Directories" is somewhat of a misnomer since many of the so-called comprehensive directories are used by end users as well and the specialty directories are often marketed to end users. The distinction is made here to differentiate those directories that are sold primarily as inexpensive trade books for a general home computer audience. They concentrate on databases and online services of wide appeal and interest.

Three of the best bargains in this genre are Howitt and Weinberger's *Inc. Magazine's Databasics*, Newlin's *Answers Online*, and Davies and Edlehart's *Omni Online Database Directory*. Each briefly describes commercially available databases, is arranged by subject, and includes additional information that describes databases, online services, and how they might be used.

The Newlin book is the best choice for the total novice. It clearly defines types of databases, online services, and how to get started doing online searching. Editorial comments ranking the databases provide useful distinctions for the novice and seem fair.

Davies and Edlehart is recommended because it starts with useful tutorial information, provides "user's comments" on the databases included, has a vendor directory with addresses and the databases provided by that vendor, and includes a subject index. The information about selected vendors is too limited to be really useful, however.

Inc. Magazine's Databasics is an excellent book but is more limited in its scope. Approximately 100 databases of interest especially to the business community were selected for detailed coverage. The definition of "of interest" to the business community is broad, however, including news, demographics, science and technology, energy and the environment, computers and electronics, and patents and trademarks in addition to business databases.

The information on the 100 databases is detailed, including sample records and things not found in other directories (e.g., a list of journals covered in a database). Other sections provide information on online vendors, information brokers, modems, software, terminals, and selected reference sources. Clear definitions of databases and online services make this a valuable end user tool.

SPECIALTY DIRECTORIES

Subject specialists and information professionals are finding that subsets of database directories are often more useful tools than comprehensive directories when their searching is limited to a particular subject area. In response to this need there is an increasing number of subject specialty directories. These are often in trade book form, such as the Cuadra Associates plans to make subject specialty subsets of their directory available on floppy disks.

The scope and intended audience of these directories varies. They are of use primarily if you need information on databases in a particular subject. The list of specialty directories at the end of this column is not comprehensive because many specialty directories are available only on a limited basis and most are of less general interest.

SELECTED DATABASE DIRECTORIES

Comprehensive Directories

Data Base Directory 1987-1988. White Plains, NY: Knowledge Industry Publications, Inc. in association with the American Society for Information Science, twice yearly.

Datapro Complete Guide to Dial-Up Databases. Delran, NJ: Datapro Research Corporation, yearly. $145. Extracted from directory below.

Datapro Directory of On-Line Services. 2 vols. Delran, NJ: Datapro Research Corporation, monthly updates. $449 including first year of updates, $394 renewal.

Directory of Online Databases. New York, NY: Cuadra/Elsevier, quarterly.

Directory of Online Information Resources. Kensington, MD: CSG Press, twice yearly. $18.50 plus $1.50 handling for one issue; 2-year subscription (4 vols.) $48.

Encyclopedia of Information Systems and Services. 9th ed. 3 vols. Detroit: Gale Research Company.

EUSIDIC: Database Guide. Medford, NJ: Learned Information, 1983. $50.

Hall, James L. & Marjorie J. Brown, eds. *Online Bibliographic Databases.* 4th ed. London, England: Aslib. Distributed in the U.S. and Canada by Gale Research Company.

Information Industry Market Place: An International Directory of Information Products and Services. 5th ed. New York: R. R. Bowker Co., 1984. $49.95.

North American Online Directory. New York: R. R. Bowker, 1987.

Williams, Martha E. & Lawrence Lannom & Carolyn G. Robins, eds. *Computer-Readable Databases: A Directory and Data Sourcebook.* 2 vols. Detroit: Gale, 4th ed.

Directories for End Users

Cane, Mike. *The Computer Phone Book: Directory of Online Systems.* New York: Plume, 1985.

Davies, Owen & Mike Edlehart. *Omni Online Database Directory 1985.* rev. ed. New York: Collier, 1985. $13.95.

Guide to Online Databases. Boca Raton, FL: Newsletter Management Corporation, 1983, n.p.

Howitt, Doran & Marvin J. Weinberger. *Inc. Magazine's Databasics: Your Guide to Online Business Information.* New York: Garland, 1984.

Lambert, Steve. *Online: A Guide to America's Leading Information Services.* Bellvue, WA: Microsoft Press, 1985. $19.95.

Lesko, Matthew. *The Computer Data and Database Source Book.* New York: Avon, 1984. (Low quality paper.) $14.95.

Newlin, Barbara. *Answers Online: Your Guide to Informational Data Bases.* Berkeley, CA: Osborne-McGraw, 1984. $16.95.

Radford, Fred C. *Database Finding Aid.* Byron Center, MI: Alert Consultants, 1984. Print $19.95, diskettes $49.95.

Shafritz, Jay M. & Louis Alexander. *The Reston Directory of Online Data Bases.* Reston, VA: Reston, 1984.

Specialty Directories

Burk, Cornelius F., Jr. *Geoscience Numeric and Bibliographic Data.* Glenside, Australia: Mineral Foundation, 1981. $30.

Chung, Catherine, ed. *Directory of Periodicals Online: Indexed, Abstracted and Full-Text.* 3 vols. Washington, DC: Federal Document Retrieval, 1986. Vol. 1: News, Law and Business, Vol. 2: Medicine and Social Science, in press. Vol. 3: Science and Technology, in press.

Directory of United Nations Data-Bases and Information Systems. Geneva: Inter-Organization Board for Information Systems, 1985, distributed by Unipub.

Federal Data Base Finder. Chevy Chase, MD: Information USA, 1984. $95.

Harfax Directory of Industry Data Sources: The United States and Canada. 2d ed. 3 vols. Cambridge, MA: Ballinger, 1982. $225.

Fischer, Barbara, ed. *Libraries, Information Centers and Databases in Science and Technology: A World Guide.* New York: K. G. Saur, 1985. 2nd ed.

Harfax Directory of Industry Data Sources: Western Europe. 2 vols. Cambridge, MA: Ballinger, 1983. $125.

International Directory of Data Bases Relating to Companies. New York: Unipub, 1979. $13.

Mayros, Van & D. Michael Werner. *Databases for Business: Profiles and Applications.* Radnor, PA: Chilton Book Co., 1982. $19.95.

R & D Database Handbook: A Worldwide Guide to Key Scientific and Technical Databases. Ft. Lee, NJ: Technical Insights Inc., 1984. $292.

Schmid, Alex P. *Political Terrorism: A Research Guide to Concepts, Theories, Data Bases, and Literature.* New Brunswick, NJ: Transaction Books, 1988. 2nd ed.

Williams, Martha E., ed. *Directory of Agricultural Databases*, 1985. Contact Professor Martha E. Williams, Coordinated Science Laboratory, University of Illinois, Urbana. ■

DATABASE SELECTION TOOLS*

Which database should I search to answer this question or for that patron? Is more than one database necessary or appropriate? Which database will give the most unique relevant citations? What databases include a particular journal or several journals of interest? Online searchers face such questions every day. The answer too often ends up being "the database or databases I am accustomed to searching or feel most comfortable with." Studies have shown that online intermediaries search the same handful of databases over and over again. Is it because this handful of databases contains the best and most relevant information or is it because database selection techniques are based mainly on intuition and custom? The answer is most probably some of both.

Although there are no precise answers to any of these questions, there are some tools to help make database selection less reliant on intuition alone: 1) database or periodical directories, 2) online dictionary files, and 3) automatic database selection.

DIRECTORIES

I reviewed database directories available in print and online in two previous columns (*LJ*, August 1985, p. 64-65 and September 15, 1985, p. 56-57). The most popular of the database directories is still the quarterly *Directory of Online Databases* published by Cuadra/Elsevier. This (or a similar directory) should be available in every library that offers online search services.

A database directory gives basic facts about thousands of databases available on hundreds of online systems. With their subject indexes in the print versions and free-text searching in the online versions, they provide a broad subject approach to database selection. They are a good first step for locating potential databases in a subject area you may not be familiar with or do not search regularly. They keep searchers aware of

new databases and databases on online systems they don't use much.

Another type of directory, probably less familiar to searchers, approaches database selection by periodical title. Two such directories are *Directory of Periodicals Online: Indexed, Abstracted, and Full-Text, News, Law and Business* (3d ed. edited by Maria S. Sims, Federal Document Retrieval, Inc., 1987, $125) and *Books and Periodicals Online: A Guide to Publication Contents of Business and Legal Databases* (edited by Nuchine S. Nobari, Learned Information, 1987, $125).

Directory of Periodicals Online

An annual publication, each edition of the *Directory of Periodicals Online* is meant to replace the last. The 1987 edition includes over 7700 periodical titles that are available in over 200 different databases through 125 different online vendors.

The main part of the directory is an alphabetical listing of periodical titles. Brief information is given for each periodical, including: full title, former or alternate title, name of publisher, ISSN, frequency of publication, subjects, name of database(s) that cover the periodical. Cross references are provided from former titles to current titles.

Section 2 provides "Database Online Availability" information. For each database referred to in Part 1, Part 2 gives more information on how to access it online. Information includes: the database name, producer, timespan, update frequency, whether it is a full-text, abstract, or citation database, and the vendors that offer it. Section 3 is a subject index and Section 4 gives addresses for all online vendors that are included in the directory.

To use the directory you would first check Section 1 to see what databases include the periodical you are interested in.

Next a check of Section 2 for each of the databases you found will show what online services have the databases. Information in Section 2 varies in detail and completeness, ranging from a listing with timespans of every single publication indexed in a database to just a mention of the online services that carry a database with no further information on individual periodicals. No information is given on how much of a particular periodical is covered by a database.

It is a big task to compile a directory of this sort. The editors explain that complete information was not always available, but sometimes the omissions in Section 1 seem as if they could be taken care of with better editing. Some entries leave out what databases carry the periodicals; in some entries the periodical title heading itself is left off; there are duplicate entries for some titles and sometimes the duplicates list different databases; and subject indexing is inconsistent (*TMA Leaf Bulletin* has the subject heading "Tobacco"; the *TMA Leaf Bulletin Summary* has the subject heading "Tobacco Industry and Trade").

Books and Periodicals Online

Books and Periodicals Online includes over 6800 periodical titles that are available in publicly available source, numeric, bibliographic, or full-text databases. First available in fall 1987, an update included in the purchase price is planned for 1988. (The promise in the book's introduction of twice-a-year updates will not be fulfilled.) Like the *Directory of Periodicals Online*, the information in this volume was verified with database producers. The introductory material describes in detail the fairly rigorous verification process.

The main section of *Books and Periodicals Online* is the alphabetic title index. For each periodical the following information is given: present title, country of publication, former title, publisher, database, producer of the database, scope of coverage in the database, start date of coverage in the database, names of vendors that carry the database.

Each entry is for one journal title and one database. If a journal is covered in more than one database there is a separate entry for each. *Harvard Business Review*, for example, has 12 entries in the alphabetical listing: ABI/INFORM, Accountants, AMI, F&S Indexes, FINIS, HBR/ONLINE (full-text version), INFOBK, Insurance Abstracts, Magazine Index, Management Contents, NEXIS, and Trade and Industry Index.

The disadvantage of this policy is that it adds space to the directory and some information is repeated. The main advantage is that the many differences in coverage among databases can be clearly seen. Inclusion policies of database producers are given under each periodical title.

In addition to the alphabetical listing, there are a publishers' name and address listing, a list of producers and vendors' names and addresses, and a listing of databases including all of the journals they cover and the vendors that make them available.

ONLINE DICTIONARY FILES

Database and periodical directories provide broad approaches to database selection, but neither helps a searcher decide what database would be best for a specific topic or question. In the mid-1970s Martha E. Williams, director of the Information Retrieval Research Laboratory at the University of Illinois, experimented with a Database Selector that merged the dictionary (inverted) subject indexes of several different bibliographic databases. Searchers would enter their queries in the selector to see which databases had the greatest number of postings on their search terms.

The Database Selector idea was later implemented by several of the major online systems. Orbit's Database Index, Dialog's DIALINDEX, and BRS's file CROSS each contain the inverted indexes of all of the databases on the respective systems. No actual records are in the files, only the terms and posting information that will allow searchers to select databases for searching that have the most postings for a query. Unlike other database selection tools, these online files only cover one system's databases, but for that one system they allow database selection at the specific query level.

Database Index, DIALINDEX, or CROSS offer a relatively inexpensive way to narrow down a search to the databases that have the most records on the topic. They allow a searcher to prioritize database selection by number of postings and remind searchers to try files that may not otherwise be searched. On most systems, searches can be saved in these files for subsequent running in the databases with the most postings.

Online dictionary files have some limitations. Their help is quantitative only—they provide no information about quality or appropriateness of the databases. They still rely on human judgment to select the best files for a particular patron or query. Overlap is not considered, so a searcher does not know which of the databases that have the most postings on a topic will provide the greatest number of unique hits. Although the costs are modest for these files, there are connect time charges for using them.

AUTOMATIC DATABASE SELECTION

Automatic database selection is not yet common, but is becoming an important component of gateway systems. Because gateways offer end user searching of databases from several different online systems, the person searching cannot always be expected to know what databases are even available, much less are appropriate. The EasyNet gateway system (called INFOMASTER and Einstein) selects a database for a user after the user chooses from among a series of subject-related and format-related menu choices. EasyNet's database selection is at the broad topic level, not the individual query level, because database selection is made before the searcher enters his or her actual search.

Chengren Hu, a doctoral student at the University of Illinois, recently evaluated automatic database selection on the INFOMASTER version of EasyNet ("An Evaluation of a Gateway System for Automated Online Database Selection," *Proceedings of the Ninth National Online Meeting, New York, May 10-12, 1988*, Learned Information, 1988, p. 107-114). Students at the Graduate School of Library and Information Science used INFOMASTER to search questions given them by Hu. The system selected the database to search after students selected from among menu choices about the subject of their query. Hu then asked experienced online searchers to select databases for the same queries.

Hu found that "INFOMASTER could select databases as well as human intermediaries when the gateway user properly selected the subject area of a particular query."

The major technique for "automated database selection" by INFOMASTER is through narrowing down the subject selections for a particular query using menu choice by the human searcher, then, selecting a database seemingly at random from among a group of databases for the queries falling in a particular subject field.

The machine does not replace human judgment; instead the searcher's interpretation and then choice of subject area from the menu is the most important factor in database selection by INFOMASTER. For queries where broad subject categorization is not so obvious, INFOMASTER does not perform as well. Although it could be called semi-automatic database selection, the gateway still relies heavily on how human beings judge where a query fits into a subject area. When several databases cover a broad topic, the final choice of one by INFOMASTER seems to be based on some other indefinable criteria programmed into the system. Hu speculates that the other criteria might be economic—certain databases produced by certain database producers seem to be favored by the EasyNet system creators.

FUTURE AIDS

The limitations of all database selection aids and Hu's research suggest future directions for database selection aids. The best automatic aids must combine general subject help with information relating to the specific query. Machine-aided subject categorization and quantitative word frequency analysis should be combined with such qualitative factors as a human expert's opinions about databases or the ability of the machine to "learn" from its users regarding previous choices.

In the future, expert systems techniques should follow improvements in database selection tools. For now, searchers must rely on their own experience, expertise (and intuition) plus a variety of print and online aids. ■

CHAPTER

10

THE DATABASE INDUSTRY
Past, Present, and Future

The final chapter of this book looks at the database and online industry—as it was several years ago, as it is today, and as it is predicted to be in the near-term future. Many of these articles are opinion pieces; they reflect my own opinions or they report on other experts' opinions as expressed at professional conferences.

I have made very few revisions to the articles in this chapter. I wanted to retain the flavor of the time they were written, including at times some predictions that were wrong; therefore I resisted the urge to revise my (or others') predictions or insights regarding the volatile database industry.

"Five Years into the Past ... Five Years into the Future" was written for the Online Northwest '88 conference that happened to coincide with the fifth-year anniversary of my *Library Journal* column. I published it as the fiftieth column I had written for *Library Journal*. It is a look back into database searching as it was five years before (1983) and a projection of what will be the important issues and shaping forces in database searching five years ahead (1993). I chose five trends to highlight: quality control, in-house databases, changes in the way databases look, pricing policies, and changes in the database marketplace. Perhaps by the time you are reading this I will already have been proven correct on some and incorrect on others of my predictions. In 1993 I will go back and read this one to see how close I came!

I chose to put "The Online Future at ASIS" next, because it was written in 1983—the five years into the past of the first article. It is reporting on other people's opinions, the opinions of many of the industry leaders who spoke at the American Society for Information Science's 1983 mid-year meeting in Lexington, Kentucky. I think you will agree that their vision of the future of online searching was essentially accurate, although they did not anticipate certain developments such as CD-ROM. They predicted increasing costs with different pricing algorithms, increased end user searching, continued changes in the database industry, a reexamination of online education, increased telecommunications speed, and improvements in post-processing software. All of these have occurred to one degree or another and are still changing.

Additional reports of industry leaders' predictions and perceptions are included in the next two articles: "The Database Industry Today: Some Vendors' Perspectives" and "Change or Crisis in the Database Industry?" These were written in 1984 and 1986 respectively, so together with the first two articles form a continuum of the status of the database industry from 1983 on through the future. The articles examine the impact on database producers and online vendors of such phenomena as downloading, domination by a few vendors and databases, international buyouts, end user markets, gateways, full-text databases, and optical disks, through the eyes of some of the foremost leaders in the information industry.

Two of the issues mentioned at various times in the first four articles are pricing and quality of databases. These important issues are discussed more in depth in the next two articles. "Is Connect-Time Pricing Obsolete?" is actually the second column I wrote on pricing policies. In 1984 the column "Pricing Policies" appeared in *Library Journal*, prompted by fairly drastic changes in the pricing policies of the National Library of Medicine's MEDLARS system and Mead Data Central's NEXIS and LEXIS systems. Subsequent changes made the 1984 column out-of-date, so I have chosen to reprint here only the 1988 column. It updates some of the 1984 information and discusses the broader issue of connect time pricing and its impacts on searchers, searching, and database producers.

I think it is fitting that Chapter 10 and the entire book closes with my 1987 *Library Journal* column on "Quality Control." Quality of databases, online systems, and searchers is one of the most important issues in the past, present, and future of database searching. It is not a jazzy issue or a time-sensitive one so it does not generate as much interest as technological issues. Some information professionals feel very strongly about the quality of the product they are turning over to a client, but at the same time feel powerless to do much to improve significantly the products and services they access. I keep predicting quality control will be a "hot topic" with database searchers, but other issues keep getting more attention. It is an issue that will not go away and is not getting any better. Placing this column last symbolizes my feeling that without good databases, good systems, and good search techniques, the other issues in database searching are moot.

FIVE YEARS INTO THE PAST ... FIVE YEARS INTO THE FUTURE*

(Based on a presentation for the Online Northwest '88 conference in Corvallis, Oregon.)

This column marks a personal milestone. It is my 50th Online Databases column for *LJ*. A lot has happened in the online world since February 1983 when my first column appeared. I chose this time to reflect on the things that have changed over the last five years (and some things that haven't). I have selected five issues or trends that I feel will have the most impact on database searching for the next five years.

First, a look back. In 1983 a majority of searchers were still using dumb terminals, although most had plans to switch to micros. A majority were still searching at 300 baud, but the impact of 1200 baud was being felt; 2400 baud was not yet available for access to any of the major online vendors.

Dialog's Knowledge Index and BRS's After Dark end user services had just started and we were waiting to see if anyone would use them and how they might impact library services. Although "end user" was a buzzword, the majority of online accounts were still held by libraries. CD-ROM databases did not exist.

ISSUE #1: QUALITY CONTROL

Almost every year for the last five years I have predicted that quality of databases will be a hot topic sometime in the next few years. Why do I still think so? This kind of issue takes a back seat to the excitement of new technologies. When online was new all we really wanted to talk about were the many positive exciting possibilities. The same happened when CD-ROM databases were first introduced. That is natural and appropriate, but as a technology matures, and perhaps as we mature as searchers, there is more time to focus on what we're getting and what we're giving, that is, on the quality of the product we are accessing and passing on to clients.

We need to be more actively concerned with such things as: what criteria are used to select and gather information; the quality of indexing vocabularies and how they are applied; time lags with indexing; and the quality of the input process. All affect the success of retrieval as well as the product we deliver and all affect our capability and reputation as information providers. Any technology is a means to an end; the

end must be the provision of accurate and appropriate information.

ISSUE #2: MORE IN-HOUSE DATABASES

CDs as in-house databases will unquestionably increase in numbers and in amount of use in libraries. There are a few limitations with CDs, however. Until this year, CD databases supported only a single user and are still very limited. The disc must be mastered so it is not easy to update or to add custom enhancements to purchased databases. Other formats for in-house databases will have a big impact on libraries in the years to come.

Last October BRS announced their BRS Onsite—the leasing of major databases to be housed locally at a library. That idea is certainly not new. Before online access was possible and long before BRS existed, a library could lease magnetic tapes of several major indexes for loading onto their local computer. The main difference is that BRS provides the software and support for these local databases and the system can be linked into a local area network (LAN) or into the library's online public access catalog (OPAC).

What is already happening in large academic and special libraries is the merging of access to external databases with access to the internal library collection. This blurring of lines between OPACs (traditionally developed out of tech services) and external database access (traditionally grown out of public or reference services) will continue at an accelerated pace and will have major effects in the library. This merger will impact traditional staffing within the library, cataloging practices and assumptions, and OPAC design, as well as users' perceptions of the library and its collections.

The logical extension of access to the library catalog and to more bibliographic databases through the central library system is the capability of accessing complete texts of selected materials. Many full-text databases are of course available online now, but as yet they have not been made a significant part of in-house systems. Limits on computer storage capacity is one reason; unwillingness on the part of publishers or vendors to lease tapes of full texts is another. But these problems are being solved, so look for more incorporation of full texts into local database systems.

Full texts are good if the information is already in machine-readable form and if they don't contain many graphics. For other materials (those that are used less often, are older, or contain lots of graphics) telefacsimile links with in-house databases may be the best alternative. Telefacsimile is making a comeback in libraries because the machinery is so much better and so much less costly than it was a few years ago.

ISSUE #3: CHANGES IN DATABASE VISUALS

All of this leads directly into the third issue – changes in the way databases look. This year Dialog has introduced pictures into the Trademarkscan database, and it certainly won't be the only one to do so.

Full-text databases of today are not really complete texts nor are they substitutes for print because they exclude photos, graphs, drawings, etc. The trademark images are the first step in the increased availability of graphics in online databases.

The addition of graphics to full-text databases will require better hardware and better software on the part of the searcher. We will need to budget for better monitors, higher disk storage capacities, better printers, and faster modems.

Graphics won't be the only change in the way databases look in the next five years. New designs are being developed now that will change some of the products we are accessing. Everyone has heard of hypertext by now, the linking of documents or different portions of texts to allow related ideas or documents to be retrieved. Hypertext databases are under development now and will allow us to get away from the linear view of text.

ISSUE #4: PRICING POLICIES

Like so many of these issues, CD-ROM databases have been a catalyst for the fourth trend. Lots of us like the idea of unlimited access to a database for a single yearly fee. It enables libraries to offer more end user searching, prepare budgets in advance, and use database searching for teaching purposes.

Librarians are beginning to ask: Why not the option of flat-fee pricing for online databases? And except for heavy users of one database, a high flat fee for one database isn't economical, so why not flat-fee access to a group of databases or an entire online service?

At the Online '87 meeting this past October in Anaheim, California, Telebase Systems (the EasyNet people) previewed something called the Answer Machine, discussed in my column "Is Connect-Time Pricing Obsolete?" (*LJ*, March 1, p. 48-49). The idea of the Answer Machine will be to provide unlimited access to any of the hundreds of databases and many online vendors that can be accessed through the EasyNet gateway. A library will pay a flat yearly fee, set the Answer Machine out in the public area and turn people loose on it. It allows the librarian to select an alternative payment scheme for online access. This is a trend that I think is very positive.

The changes in pricing policies will not be all positive in the next five years. Vendors and database producers are beginning to look for ways to recover revenues lost from our searching at higher transmission speeds, using software that allows us to upload portions of the search strategy, and our downloading of more records. Libraries that do not search at faster speeds or that do not do lots of uploading or downloading in many cases will be penalized financially.

ISSUE #5: MARKET CHANGES

Finally, the fifth trend that will be important for the next five years is changes in the database marketplace. The change that is close to our hearts is the end of the domination of the library market in the database industry. This has been coming for a long time, but has taken much longer than originally predicted. In some ways you may be saying "it was nice while it lasted," but there will also be some positive effects.

The first is that the library market has been pretty well saturated for the last few years. As the total user base for online services grows with more end users, we do have the possibility of lower prices or at least more low price options such as Knowledge Index and BRS/After Dark.

Another positive impact that is just beginning to be realized is the development of more and perhaps better or more varied and innovative products. Also perhaps we will finally see better search software, although I think the development will be at the microcomputer front end level rather than at the online vendor level.

One impact is the increased access to bibliographic citations of other nations' literature. Many major U.S. databases have claimed to cover "the world's literature" on a topic while excluding large parts of the world, notably some Eastern European countries, Asia, and the Pacific. One effect on libraries will be the increased need for translations and the challenges of getting source documents. As serial budgets are being cut, it is unlikely that more foreign journals will be added to U.S. libraries. Better cooperative arrangements and ILL services will be needed.

THINGS THAT WON'T HAPPEN

What would I like to see in five years that I don't think I will?

1. Vastly improved command languages or a common command language. The major vendors will continue to make enhancements and changes but these are mostly technical or minor and cosmetic. They do not profoundly improve the way we can search and retrieve information. As I mentioned earlier, the real developments in software will come at the microcomputer and CD level, although true "computer intermediary" expert systems will take longer than five years.

2. Prices coming down dramatically for the major databases or major vendors. There will be different pricing options, but on the whole, for the average user on standard systems, the prices will not go down and will likely go up.

3. A significant increase in quality of the large databases. (I said we needed to be concerned about it for the next five years, I didn't say anyone would listen to us yet.)

On a more positive note, there are some things I'm glad we are not likely to see in the next five years.

1. The abandonment of controlled vocabulary indexing as more full text becomes available. The unique contribution and role of each will be recognized. Some full-text vendors have been predicting for at least five years that full text online renders indexing obsolete. Recent research shows that is not so. Controlled vocabulary indexing can offer cost-effective, high-precision searching. The development of experimental expert systems has placed a renewed focus on controlled vocabularies as knowledge bases.

2. An end to the intermediary searcher. Many end users, even if they can do it themselves, don't always want to and after they've done a few searches may realize that sometimes a professional can do it better. End users and intermediaries will continue to coexist.

The information professional is in an excellent position to influence and direct many of the coming changes in databases and database services. We are the ones with the longest tradition and most experience with the current products. We contribute a broad vision, encompassing a spectrum of many databases, many technologies, and many users. We need to be actively involved in designing products for the future because the changes will affect all of us. If we don't, there are others who are less qualified or who have different interests who will direct the future of the database industry. ∎

THE ONLINE FUTURE AT ASIS*

The 12th Mid-Year Meeting of the American Society for Information Science was held in Lexington, Kentucky during May. Under the theme "The Online Age—Assessment/Directions," the sessions concentrated on a variety of issues pertaining to the present and future of online searching. Topics addressed in the technical sessions included: management of online information systems, online systems design, education and training of online personnel, library applications of online systems, the role of the end user, specialized online systems, numeric databases, online public access catalogs, evaluation of online systems, and specialized databases. ASIS mid-year meetings are planned and organized by a local committee. The Lexington meeting was cosponsored by the University of Kentucky College of Library and Information Science and the Southern Ohio Chapter of ASIS. Trudi Bellardo of the University of Kentucky served as chairperson.

The opening keynote session and panel discussion at conference end touched on many of the issues that were in evidence at the technical sessions and brought them into focus and context. The keynote address by Charles Bourne of DIALOG on "Issues and Challenges for the Online Industry" and the final panel of experts chaired by W. David Penniman of OCLC, together served to put the issues of the "Online Age in Perspective." Panel members included Donald Hawkins, Bell Labs; Mary Berger, Cuadra Associates; H. Boyle, Chemical Abstracts; and Donald King, King Research. These two sessions highlighted the major issues in online searching that we will all be most concerned with in the next few years. Several of these issues were covered in a bit more depth in my June 1 column (*LJ*, p. 1111-13), and others will be examined more carefully in future columns. This column will summarize

several of those issues and their potential impact on the near future. Nontechnical issues that grow out of technical innovations and changes are seldom given as much attention as they warrant. The experts seem to agree that the issues in the following list are of growing importance:

INCREASING COSTS

The currently changing financial aspects of online searching will continue to change. Because of royalty increases by the database producers, the cost of searching will continue to increase. Bourne pointed out that there is a five percent erosion rate of hard copy subscriptions regardless of online availability, but many database producers fear that the five percent rate will climb with more widespread availability of the online versions of their products. A fallacy in this, according to Bourne, is that since many libraries operate with fixed budgets, when money allocated for online searching is depleted, they simply do not search anymore. (The fallacy in this fallacy is, of course, that many libraries pass on higher charges to their patrons through online searching fees.)

There will be a shift from the current methods of charging based on online connect time to output pricing. The user will be charged more for information taken from a database (through online types, downloading, and offline prints) than for online connect time. With faster terminal speeds and downloading, database producers will be forced to find new ways to get revenues, and output pricing is a fair alternative. Online services may also find it necessary to charge differential connect time rates based on different access speeds. DIALOG can now be processed through dialup at 4800 baud, and 1200 baud terminals are becoming widespread through the telecommunications networks. Differential connect time rates together with output pricing will provide both the database producers and the online service vendors a more equitable pricing structure. This structure is now used with many numeric databases where the information content of each record is much higher than on bibliographic databases.

Bourne also predicted an increase in the number of databases charging monthly minimums and start-up fees, but pervasive changes in pricing structures will take five to ten years because there are many long-term license agreements. Large scale changes cannot happen overnight.

END USER SEARCHING

End user searching will continue to increase, but intermediaries will not disappear. Boyle said that in the larger industrial organization the role of information specialists is becoming more important, not less. When end users are trained to do their own searching, their respect for intermediaries goes up and they begin to treat the information specialist as a co-professional.

Boyle also mentioned that end user searching is coming along very slowly, because in a research group one or two people who enjoy searching become local information specialists who do searching for the others. Herb White, Indiana University, commented from the audience that the number of people interested in doing their own searching has been consistently overestimated. Most people would rather delegate than do a search themselves. King also believes intermediaries won't be a thing of the past, because many people will still want to delegate their searches.

Currently, over 100,000 people do online searches for other people. This number is not likely to decrease. Of DIALOG's current customers, 95 percent are professional intermediaries. Although DIALOG is beginning to tap the market for end user searches, the dimensions of that market are still largely unknown. Intermediaries should not be afraid of end user searching because there is room for all levels of searching. Simple searches to find some information quickly should often more properly be done by the end user, while the more complex and comprehensive searches can be better done by an experienced intermediary.

INDUSTRY CHANGES

There will be changes in the size and organization of the online service industry. More database producers are becoming online services. Companies and organizations such as Pergamon, Chemical Abstracts, and the Institute for Scientific Information (ISI) now offer access to their databases through their own search software and computer facilities. This growth is tempered somewhat by the highly competitive nature of the industry, resulting in the discontinuation of other online services such as the New York Times Information Service. The variety of vendors and producers with healthy competition is a sign of a mature industry, according to Hawkins.

It has been said that the online industry is recession-proof. Bourne said that this is probably because some industries, such as medicine, are recession-proof, so increases and declines in online use balance out. (The growth experienced by the online industry has been stable and constant, not explosive.) The acquisitions of online services and databases by publishers and continued competition will mean continued change in the online industry, while overall growth is maintained. Berger said that there are currently approximately 240 online services, 800 database producers, and 1600 databases.

ONLINE EDUCATION

Online education and training will be reexamined and changed in the near future. Bourne reminded the audience that most online training is being done by the online industry, not the schools. DIALOG trains more people in one month than all the schools in the world do in one year. Several people in the audience questioned the comparability in depth or quality of the different levels of training. The questions of "education" vs. "training" and the kinds of education and/or training for online searching required now and needed in the future must be addressed.

Boyle listed four aspects of education in online searching that must always be present: 1) subject knowledge, 2) understanding of database content, 3) an understanding of what the online vendor did to the data when it was loaded onto the online system, and 4) search system mechanics. Although all four are important to the ability to do a good search, Boyle believes that there has been too much emphasis on search system mechanics in most education or training programs. Merely training someone on the mechanics of searching (or masking the mechanics with front-end software) will not make a good searcher.

As the roles of intermediaries change, more attention will have to be paid to the quality of the data in systems and to comparisons of the quality among databases, according to King. This has important implications for effective online education. King also emphasized the need for subject knowledge in online searching, but Anthony Debons of the University of Pittsburgh reminded the panel that general practitioners and subject specialists are both needed in online searching as they are in medicine.

Education and training of the end users of the data will be another important issue in the near future. King said that educating end users in online searching and databases is more important than training them in the skills of searching, while Boyle said that active training of end users makes the role of the information professional more important. White disagreed with many of the panel's comments on end user training by challenging the assumption that the training of end users should be a goal of our profession. The goal of librarianship is to serve users, he said, not to train them to do something they would rather have us do for them.

SOFTWARE & TELECOMMUNICATIONS

Developments in software and technology will have great impact on online searching in the next few years. Telecommunications will improve, and faster transmission rates will become commonplace. Bourne reported that between 1980 and 1982 there was an increase of eight percent in the number of records printed online, reflecting increased use of 1200 baud terminals rather than widespread downloading.

Downloading is a big issue, however, and was mentioned by all panel members. Martha Williams has called 1982 the year of the microcomputer in online searching, but its full impact is just beginning to be felt. As micros become common in libraries, downloading, front-end processing, and post-processing of information will increase. (Some specific software for these functions was discussed in my June 1 *LJ* column, p. 1111-13.)

Post-processing and a form of downloading may also be done in the near future without a microcomputer. DIALOG is introducing a new feature that will allow numeric data to be reformatted after a search. The ability to "tag" records of interest on a particular database through the search service has been suggested by searchers as a possible alternative to local storing of these records. We may see many of these kinds of changes in the next few years if they seem to be financially viable.

Many other technological innovations were mentioned at the ASIS 1983 Mid-Year Meeting, but they were not the focus of these sessions. The meeting was only one of several held in 1983 that were dedicated to online searching. Its emphasis on many of the nontechnical issues made it especially valuable. As technology causes changes in online searching, these other issues must also be addressed. ∎

THE DATABASE INDUSTRY TODAY
Some Vendors' Perspectives*

"Two vendors—Mead Data Central with textual services from LEXIS and NEXIS and DIALOG Information services ...—account for 81.81 percent of the revenue and 68.56 percent of the usage" in the online searching business, according to the new *Information Market Indicators* report from Professor Martha E. Williams' company, InfoMetrics, Inc. The first research-based extensive audit of online database searching, the report provides a view of the business that before now could only be guessed at.

Indicators will be issued quarterly for a (substantial) subscription fee. It is compiled by examining and analyzing the bills for publicly-available online search services of a statistically valid sample of 12 percent of the users of bibliographic and textual databases. Information about the revenues, use, and growth of databases and online search services has been derived from these bills and projected across the industry. The report is full of a variety of statistics that are probably of most direct use to present and potential database vendors, but are fascinating to almost anyone associated with online searching.

Some other examples of these facts and figures, in addition to the NEXIS/DIALOG statistics, include:

1. Fifteen online vendors are sharing in the over $129 million per year that is spent by U.S. information centers or libraries on textual or bibliographic online database access.

2. These 15 vendors collectively offer nearly 250 unique databases supplied by 151 producers.

3. Six of the 15 vendors—Mead Data Central; DIALOG Information Service; National Library of Medicine; BRS; SDC; and New York Times, still in business in the period covered by this first issue—account for 98 percent of the revenue and 96.5 percent of the use.

4. Just as a few online vendors dominate the market, only three database producers—Mead Data Central, Chemical Abstracts Service, and National Library of Medicine—account for 50 percent of the revenue and 55.47 percent of the use.

5. Each of these big three database producers has one of its databases dominating the business. LEXIS from Mead Data Central, MEDLINE from NLM, and CA Search from Chemical Abstracts Service together account for 44.15 percent of the revenue and 50.29 percent of the use.

6. Other databases that are heavily used included BIOSIS, Auto-Cite from Mead Data Central, Westlaw, Compendex, ERIC, and ABI/INFORM.

According to an InfoMetrics press release, these figures "prove that only a handful of database producers and vendors account for most of the industry's business." That is interesting, although not surprising. The next few years should determine whether the many small databases and online search services can survive. The Williams' quarterly reports will be eagerly read by many database producers and online vendors to see how the competition is faring and to see how they compare with similar databases for services.

IIA DOWNLOADING STUDY

The Downloading Subcommittee of the Information Industry Association (IIA) has just completed a survey of online search vendors and database producers as part of a planned position paper on downloading. Fran Spigai of Database Services in Los Altos, California presented the results of

*Reprinted from *Library Journal* Feb. 1, 1984. Copyright © 1984 by Reed Publishing, USA, Div. of Reed Holdings, Inc.

this survey at the October Online '83 meeting and the November IIA meeting. She also summarized other recent downloading surveys.

Spigai described downloading as a "potential phenomenon" now in a transitional state. Little downloading has occurred as yet, but vendors expect much to take place in 1984. Three factors are seen as leading to an increase in downloading:

1. Higher access speeds to online databases. Twelve hundred baud is now widely used and soon speeds of up to 9600 baud will be available. Downloading of great numbers of citations will become cost effective at such high transmission rates if current connect hour pricing schemes remain in effect.

2. Storage. In the past, online searching used dumb terminals. In 1982, microcomputers with floppy discs began to become more common in libraries; in 1983, hard disc drives with high storage capacity began to be used; in 1984, much larger storage capacities, shared databases using local area networks, and more use of microcomputers in all types of libraries will make storage of databases more common.

3. Software. Although standard communications software for microcomputers has been around since the late 1970s, it has not been geared specifically to online searching applications. In 1982, the first software aimed at this specific function appeared. By 1983, packages with more sophisticated capabilities (e.g., Sci-Mate from Institute for Scientific Information) became available. More advanced enhancements and integrated software that will combine word processing with downloading are expected in 1984. It will become easier to create local databases by downloading subsets of commercial databases and customizing the information to meet the individual library's needs.

These three anticipated factors have caused many database vendors to begin to reexamine their pricing policies and their opinions of, or policies for, downloading. In 1982, policies were virtually nonexistent. User requests to download were determined on a case-by-case basis. By 1983, several database producers began to formulate policies. The IIA survey indicated that by 1984 downloading policies will be prevalent, but will still be evolving and changing.

Downloading policies must be flexible enough to cover the different levels of data reuse. Spigai listed five possible uses, including: single use for local printing; reuse, stored locally for future retrieval; multiple copies within an organization; resale of multiple copies; and reformatting or changing records to meet local needs (adding information to records, etc.). "Downusing" rather than merely downloading is of most concern to vendors.

These different levels of use affect database vendor revenues in different ways. The Association of Information and Dissemination Centers (ASIDIC), which has been working on downloading issues since 1981, recommends a multi-tiered pricing system for different levels of use. They believe that reuse or repackaging is acceptable if it is paid for. Fees should be based on the use to which the records are put rather than

just the number of records output. Payment, however, must be simple, with a single user, single use as the default. A special downloading format may be one way to control payment.

A survey for the Special Libraries Association polled online searchers to determine the extent of downloading. Of 90 user responses, 80 percent felt downloading should be allowed, but approximately 50 percent did not have the equipment to do it. Twenty percent are currently using microcomputers, with another 10 percent planning on acquiring them in the near future. Over 50 percent of these did not reuse database information.

A survey by Cuadra Associates looked at users and online database service suppliers with an emphasis on pricing to help database producers establish downloading policies. The results of this survey were not yet published at the time of this writing.

The IIA survey was sent only to online vendors and database producers to discover their current policies, plans, and opinions. Twenty-five questions were asked. More than half of the respondents indicated that their organization had received inquiries in the last 12 months requesting permission to both download and reuse records. A quarter of the respondents had not received requests for either downloading or reuse, while the remaining approximately 22 percent had received requests for one or the other. Nearly 75 percent of the requestors were going to use the information in-house only, rather than for commercial resale.

A slight majority of the producers believe that eventually downloading will have a positive effect on revenues, while approximately 25 percent feel it will have a negative effect, and 25 percent feel it will have no effect. Most producers believe that downloading is not now widespread, but they feel there will be a definite increase in 1984. When this increase happens, it will be difficult to control, however, as nearly 70 percent of the respondents indicated that they believe online vendors cannot control downloading. Only half feel vendors can even monitor downloading. (Federal legislation to control it is not seen as the answer, however, with 75 percent of respondents nixing that idea.)

Although we may be tired of hearing about downloading and some online vendors, database producers, and users feel it is an overrated nonissue, searchers will feel its effects in 1984. These effects will be positive — greater reuse of records, in-house customized databases on special topics, better reformatting; and negative — increased regulation, fluctuating and inconsistent policies, changes in pricing schemes. Negative or positive, the IIA survey shows that some changes are sure to come.

ONLINE TO PRINT MIGRATION?

An ironic announcement in a supposed era of increased dependence on electronic information is Gale Research Company's news about the availability of the Management Contents database in printed form. Up to now, Management Contents has only been available online; the new print version is called *Business Publications Index and Abstracts*.

The subject/author index portion is issued monthly with quarterly and annual cumulations. The numerically arranged abstracts are issued monthly. Subscriptions are $250 per year for the Index portion, $250 per year for the abstracts, and cumulations cost extra.

Gale claims that the printed index "will enhance your use of the online material by: allowing you to browse the print version at your own pace to plan an effective online search strategy; serving as a source for patrons who do not have access to terminals; providing an additional resource when your terminals are in use; and letting you make simple lookups and searches without incurring online charges or make photocopies of citations and abstracts without paying print charges."

Perhaps Gale understands the real synergy between printed reference tools and online tools, but my first reaction was to think that this represents a big step backwards. In reality, it shows we are not nearly as close to a real online age as we sometimes believe. For the foreseeable future, reference librarians will need to continue to determine when to buy printed indexes and abstracts, when to rely solely on online versions, and, if they have access to both, when to use one or the other. Will we see "migration" from online sources to printed ones? If some small database producers do not do better in the online market, we may have no choice. ■

CHANGE OR CRISIS
IN THE DATABASE INDUSTRY?*

A potential "mid-life crisis" in the database industry was referred to by Judy Wanger of Cuadra Associates, in a speech at the 1985 annual meeting of the American Society for Information Science, held in October. She explained that a mid-life crisis is a period in life "when a person engages in considerable introspection" with thoughts full of self-doubts. A person may question what he has achieved in life or what potential for achievement remains.

Contributing to this crisis in the database industry are the changing nature of databases, online vendors, and their markets, and such issues as: downloading, full-text databases, and optical discs.

At the same conference, Bill Marovitz, president of BRS, spoke of other profound changes in the industry. He believes that databases, publishers, online vendors, and users of databases are all changing. All of these factors together are creating, if not a crisis, at least a time of great transition and many changes. This month's column summarizes these two speeches.

DATABASE CHANGES

Even though the failure of some databases has received attention in the last year, the Cuadra Associates *Directory of Online Databases* has shown a consistent 30-40 percent annual growth rate in the number of databases since the first issue of the directory in 1979. By the end of 1985, there were over 3000 publicly available databases in the world, up from only 400 listed in the first directory.

The subject areas of business/finance and science/technology continue to dominate the database offerings, but more databases are becoming available in arts/humanities and information systems/services. Many of the new databases are non-U.S. publications. Governments are sponsoring new databases, even in subjects such as performing arts and literature. Business and financial data are now available for every region of the world, with detailed data on all industrialized nations.

One potential for crisis comes with the number of small databases now in the marketplace. It is questionable whether most small databases can be profitable or whether they will be driven out by the larger databases. Martha E. Williams' database industry report, *Information Market Indicators* (see my column of February 1, 1984, p. 156) showed that the vast majority of use and revenues is concentrated in a very small number of databases.

To succeed and prosper, small databases will need to reduce their costs, offer unique information of exceptional value, and earn a reputation for high quality. Another option for success mentioned by Wanger is for several small databases that have complementary information to merge or form a joint venture. This will help to reduce costs and will help in marketing.

Whatever option is chosen by the small database producer, there is bound to be some change in the availability of small databases in the near future. Some small databases will fail. Others have been purchased by large international companies, a trend that will continue, according to Marovitz. More manufacturing firms will enter the information industry and traditional print publishers will become more involved in electronic publishing.

ONLINE SERVICES

This same trend of international buyouts and participation in information products and services by noninformation firms is happening to online services. Marovitz pointed out that company acquisitions are driven by economic considerations, as are the future plans of the online service once it has been acquired. For example, an online service is not always used to maximum capacity if its marketplace is limited to only a few time zones. As a result, there is an increasing emphasis on worldwide marketing and service.

*Reprinted from *Library Journal* Apr. 1, 1986. Copyright © 1986 by Reed Publishing, USA, Div. of Reed Holdings, Inc.

Mergers or joint ventures by different kinds of companies will become increasingly common in the information industry, says Marovitz. For example, Sears and IBM are collaborating on a home-videotex project. BRS has a joint venture with Saunders Publishing Company to provide electronic versions of Saunders' publications for the medical community. BRS has recently acquired CLSI. CLSI circulation and online catalog systems are common in public libraries, a marketplace that has room for growth in the online-searching area. BRS hopes to tap this market by offering access to BRS through CLSI terminals.

The number of online vendors has increased almost as dramatically as the number of databases. From only 59 vendors worldwide in the 1979 Cuadra *Directory*, there are now over 440. Data from *Information Market Indicators*, however, shows that only a few vendors dominate in terms of usage and profits. DIALOG and Mead Data Central together account for approximately 70 percent of the use and 80 percent of the revenues in the library/institutional marketplace. When faced with an overwhelming number of databases and services, users react by concentrating their searching on a select few. Wanger blames this on a "crisis of overload."

Some online vendors will fail. Others will succeed because they reflect the growing internationalization of the industry. Many of the new services are in non-U.S. countries, including European, Middle Eastern, and Asian nations. The U.S. now accounts for only 63 percent of the online services, down from almost 77 percent in 1982.

NEW MARKETS

Both Marovitz and Wanger emphasized another reason why some services will succeed and prosper: the targeting of new, specific vertical markets.

The marketplace must continue to grow if a majority of the new databases and services are to survive. Except for some room for growth in public and school libraries, the library market is pretty much saturated. This traditional market will continue to be served and continue to increase its number of connect hours, but there is limited room for expansion in the numbers of library installations.

Because of the proliferation of the personal computer, both Marovitz and Wanger believe the end user professional at home or in the office provides the real potential for growth. A recent survey showed that 17 percent of CEOs in Fortune 500 companies use an external source of electronic information at least weekly. This is not as encouraging as it seems, however, since Wanger quoted a major online vendor as saying that the "need-to-know" market is saturated. The "nice-to-know" market must be attracted. Some services may seek the help of the information professional in tapping hard-to-reach end user markets.

According to Marovitz, the online products and services for end user professionals must be targeted to specific vertical niches. Products that serve unique groups, such as medical professionals, will be the most profitable. Marketing thrusts will thus be away from the general and be focused on specific needs. Special products will be developed to appeal to each target group. BRS, for example, has a goal to have between 80 and 90 percent of the world's medical literature online by 1987. This service to the medical profession includes the appropriate

bibliographic databases already on *BRS*, plus new materials such as full texts of textbooks and journals.

Marovitz says he wants people to identify with one BRS product as if it were their own. He is aiming for brand-name loyalty and wants "people to deal with us as if they are dealing with Tide" (the detergent).

GATEWAYS

New end user markets and the overload felt by intermediaries are leading to another change in the industry. Gateways (secondary online services) offer a single point of entry to many online services. They connect users to a variety of services and databases. Some work transparently to the user; some go to the system or database that a user requests.

Wanger sees such gateways as an indication of the maturing of the database industry. They will bring in new users who might not know about specific services. They may help the small, high-quality database thrive by providing more users, without requiring expensive marketing. They may help new online vendors survive by bringing in new users and by cutting startup and marketing costs.

DOWNLOADING

Downloading is now a fact of online life. As more searchers use microcomputers for searching, the downloading of search results for editing or building inhouse databases becomes an accepted way to enhance services. Wanger feels that although downloading "has come and gone" as a major crisis, it still poses a threat to some database producers.

Most publishers realize that downloading is happening and will continue to happen; many have responded with reasonable written policies and online type charges that provide pricing per item. There is no evidence they have been hurt by downloading.

Some publishers and vendors are more vulnerable to downloading than others, however. Numeric databases are especially vulnerable because it is easy to identify a desired subset of numeric data, download it, then manipulate it locally. Many numeric database vendors rely on profits from users manipulating data on the vendor's system. Textual databases are less vulnerable because of the high cost to store large amounts of textual information locally and because data manipulation is not the source of revenue. According to Wanger, downloading remains a threat to the industry, but models for coping with it now exist.

FULL-TEXT DATABASES

Full-text databases are marketable products, as shown by the BRS medical products and the continued success of *LEXIS*. They are being accepted and used by searchers. The predominance of full text may be farther off than has been predicted, however, because of the unresolved issues of copyright, creation costs, standards, and packaging.

Wanger believes that full-text databases pose many unanswered questions that are indicative of a mid-life crisis in the industry. Still to be resolved are issues such as how full-text databases will complement (or replace) secondary sources; are controlled vocabularies useful in full-text databases; are recall and precision important to users of full text? So far it appears that end users of full-text databases have more tolerance for false drops than search professionals ever imagined.

OPTICAL DISCS

One of the "most important events to provoke crisis," in Wanger's view, is the publishing of databases on optical discs (see my column of March 1, 1986, p. 68). Marovitz sees it as "a turning point" for distribution of information.

Digital optical discs, either 4.75-inch CD-ROM or 12-inch discs, allow users to search a database without accessing the remote online systems such as *DIALOG* or *BRS*. Like a subscription to a printed work, a subscriber to an optical disc database pays a set fee for unlimited use.

Several issues in regards to optical-disc databases are as yet unresolved. There are as yet no standards for hardware or software. Marovitz speculated about how online services such as BRS might profit from databases on disc. Instead of each publisher issuing its own discs with its own search system, online services might make arrangements with several publishers to provide many databases on disc. These databases would then be accessible with the same search software. The vendor role is maintained but with a new technology.

Marovitz also wondered how distribution of discs will occur. Will customers go through bookstores, record stores, computer stores, a "discount house of discs," or continue to purchase directly from vendors and publishers? Online services might still be used for current information at a premium price, while discs may become the less expensive alternative for accessing older information.

OPTIONS

There are many options for delivery of information products, options that can coexist now and in the future. Wanger summarized the four main ones and the advantages of each.

1. Remote online services offer many advantages. A user can search on demand, pay only for what is used, retrieve timely information, and not have to store large amounts of information locally.

2. Downloading for reuse with local software can save money and is useful when the same base of information is needed repeatedly.

3. Databases or groups of databases sold on optical discs may allow publishers to deal directly with their users. They also allow users to search large, locally held databases repeatedly at no additional charge.

4. Print still offers advantages such as ease of use, relatively low cost, no hardware required, and permanence for static information.

Many information delivery forms, producers, and vendors can coexist and prosper. New media and new companies can provide the opportunity for change, not the calamity of crisis. ∎

IS CONNECT-TIME PRICING OBSOLETE?*

Intermediary searchers are accustomed to connect-time pricing. We have developed search strategies and honed input skills to get the most value for our connect hour. We have learned to estimate how much a given search on a given database is likely to cost. Connect time is easy to calculate and easy to explain to patrons. On the other hand, connect time is not always easy to predict, it is difficult to budget, and it favors searchers who can get into and out of an online system as quickly as possible.

Most of the major online systems used in libraries have kept connect-time pricing as the standard pricing scheme for over 15 years. Although there may be minor variations, in general all databases available through one vendor have been priced according to the same algorithm. Other factors in the online world and the way we search have changed in these 15 years, however.

In the fall of 1987 Chemical Abstracts announced that they will begin to move away from connect-time pricing for their databases. This controversial plan by a major database producer, together with the changes over the last few years in the way we do searches, is causing intermediaries, database producers, and online vendors to look again at connect-time pricing policies and alternatives.

TRANSMISSION SPEEDS

One major change in the last few years is the increase in transmission speeds. When online searching began everyone searched at 110 bps or 300 bps. Today with 1200 bps common and 2400 bps available for some systems, searchers can conduct more complex searches and display more records in a

---

*Reprinted from *Library Journal* Mar. 1, 1988. Copyright © 1988 by Reed Publishing, USA, Div. of Reed Holdings, Inc.

shorter time online. Searching at the faster speeds with connect-time-based pricing is obviously more cost effective, especially for printing or downloading large numbers of records. Systems like the Source, CompuServe, and Dow Jones News/Retrieval charge more per hour for faster transmission speeds, but systems like DIALOG and BRS still do not. With 9600 bps access to the major online systems predicted for the near future, some differentiation in pricing depending on speed of access is likely. A single connect-time price penalizes either the searcher who does not have high-speed equipment or the database producer when searchers connect at higher speeds.

DOWNLOADING

Higher transmission speeds encourage practices like downloading when a searcher is using a microcomputer instead of a dumb terminal. A majority of online intermediaries now use microcomputers. Hard disk drives with storage capacities of ten to 50 megabytes are widely available at a relatively low cost. Downloading is simple when you combine inexpensive storage devices with the widely available software packages that offer downloading as a standard function.

Downloading has already had an impact on connect-time pricing. Since the early to mid-1980s most of the databases on the major connect-time systems have added charges for each record viewed online. As I mentioned in an earlier column, "Pricing Policies" (LJ, July 1984, p. 1300-01), one of the reasons these online viewing charges started was because no one can tell when a user is downloading or when they are just printing or viewing records online. Database producers wanted to make sure they would be compensated (at least in part) for records that were downloaded, stored, and reused locally for no additional connect-time charge. Partial records that are used just for search strategy development (such as titles and descriptors) usually may be viewed online for no record charge. Per record charges compensate data providers for the information retrieved rather than for how slow a searcher types or the speed of their modem.

UPLOADING

Widespread use of front-end software allows searchers to formulate and store a search strategy before logging on. After the user formulates and enters the search offline, the software automatically logs the user on to the host system and quickly uploads the search strategy to the host computer. The only typing time online is to make modifications to the initial search strategy.

Connect-time prices have steadily and regularly gone up, partly to compensate for our more efficient techniques and technologies. An experienced searcher with the proper tools (hardware, software, modem) can minimize the online charges for even complex searches. From the searcher's point of view, this is simply good strategy. From the database producer's or online vendor's point of view, this may be revenue lost.

The National Library of Medicine (MEDLARS) and Mead Data Central (LEXIS and NEXIS) are two major online producers that drastically revised their pricing policies several years ago. Each uses connect time as only a small component of their pricing scheme. In late 1983, NLM lowered its connect-hour price while adding a charge for the "amount of work" required by its computer for a given search, and charging for characters transmitted. According to NLM spokesmen, this was done not to increase its fees, but "to charge users more equitably" by charging more for more complex searches and for information retrieved.

Mead Data Central changed in 1984 from a pricing scheme based on amount of computer work, which was criticized as being too complex, to a scheme based mainly on the files accessed. For most of its customers, MDC charges for each publication accessed as a new search, for online or offline printing, plus a small connect-time charge. Federal government agencies are billed on straight connect-time pricing, however. Early in 1988 they simplified the new scheme to eliminate a controversial $3 charge for each modification to a search.

CHEMICAL ABSTRACTS SERVICE

Changes in pricing policies can be met with suspicion or even outrage. In the fall of 1987, the Chemical Abstracts Service announced its intention to move away from connect-time pricing. It met with criticism because this move affects not only its own online service (STN International), but the CAS databases that are offered online on other vendor's systems. Since the Chemical Abstracts databases are relied on by so many searchers and there is no real substitute for the files, online systems such as BRS, DIALOG, ORBIT, QUESTEL, and the others offering CA files may have no choice but to set up different pricing policies as requested.

The new CAS pricing scheme will be phased in gradually. In 1988 there are several components:

- 10¢ for each text-search term. Truncated terms or multiword terms will be charged as single terms;

- $20 for each molecular structure or substructure in a search statement;

- a 1¢ extraction fee for each CAS record extracted from a file to be used as a search term (for example CA Registry Numbers that are extracted from dictionary files and transported to bibliographic files) or for subsequent analysis;

- a 5¢ use charge for partial records "displayed in such a way that they can be linked to specific answers in an answer set." Partial records such as titles and index terms traditionally have been displayable for free to allow search strategy development. CAS believes "some searchers use the free display to identify a subset of answers to be printed or display, circumventing print or display charges for the remainder of the answer set." [My translation: We aren't paying for all of our false drops.] CAS will allow such partial records for free if they are displayed by the online vendor in random order and are unnumbered so a searcher can't use the display to decide which records to print;

- the same connect-time fees as in 1987 (resulting in an overall price increase in 1988 of at least ten percent). The plan is to gradually reduce connect fees as other fees are increased.

Two other policies will directly impact search strategy building. CAS will enforce a policy of charging for information about the CAS files that is found in the inverted index only, search strategy files such as DIALOG's DIALINDEX or BRS's CROS. CAS is also considering a "query import" fee, possibly to begin in 1989. The query import would charge users a fee each time they input a search strategy in a non-CAS file, save it, and then run it in a CAS file. In 1988, online vendors will be required to provide statistics to CAS on how often this practice occurs.

Some online vendors are unhappy about all of the new record keeping and programming required for just one database producer. They must report to CAS all search terms or structures entered. They must be able to keep track of queries imported from other files. They must be able to provide randomized, unnumbered output or charge for previously free record displays.

Vendors can choose whether to charge users directly under the new CAS requirements or to increase connect-time rates in the hopes of covering the new charges that they must pay to CAS. Either way vendors are required to report complete use statistics to CAS or lose the valuable CAS files. Some vendors are concerned about a database producer imposing such special requirements, some of which indirectly impact other files.

Online searchers are concerned about the higher overall costs. Equitable or not, searchers have built their strategy development around connect-based pricing and, if implemented by the vendors, the new CAS pricing policy will require changes in search strategies for the most cost-effective searching of CAS files. Multifile searching, using tools such as DIALINDEX or CROSS, and saving searches will be especially affected.

FLAT-FEE PRICING

A different pricing alternative that is attractive to frequent searchers or to libraries that offer end user services is flat-fee pricing. CD-ROM with its unlimited searching of a database for a single fee may be a catalyst of change in online pricing policies.

CD-ROM's flat-fee yearly subscription price is attractive for several reasons. Without the connect-time meter running, searchers of CD-ROM don't need to be experienced searchers, they can try out different strategies, be more relaxed about searching, and do more browsing through a database. Flat-fee pricing encourages learning and casual use of a system. Librarians know what their yearly cost will be and often can more easily incorporate the charges into a budget request.

Flat-fee pricing as offered with CD-ROM is advantageous to a library if a limited number of databases are each used a lot. Libraries that need access to many different databases will find they still must rely on online searching. Flat-fee pricing at the online system level rather than at the single database level has appeal to many online searchers.

Telebase System's "Answer Machine" may be one response to flat-fee pricing. The Answer Machine, now in beta site testing, is a microcomputer workstation with modem that connects to the EasyNet gateway service. Through EasyNet, library patrons can search on over 900 databases from over a dozen different online systems. The Answer Machine will offer the full powers of EasyNet, including an online "reference interview" to help the system select an appropriate database and online vendor for the search; automatic logon and execution of the search that is entered by the patron; and online interactive SOS help service from EasyNet search experts (the human kind).

For a fixed yearly fee, libraries that subscribe to the Answer Machine service would be able to offer end users unlimited online searching. That fee has not yet been set, but Richard Kollin of Telebase Systems, Inc. anticipates it will be "somewhere around $14,000-$18,000 per year." For large public, academic, or maybe even school libraries, the fixed-fee pricing will encourage unlimited use of hundreds of databases by end users. Flat-fee pricing options from other online systems are being requested by libraries that wish to budget a lump sum for online searching.

The CAS pricing changes are a direct reaction by a huge database producer to searchers' use of new technologies and search techniques that take advantage of connect-time pricing. Can the database producer's need to get increased online revenues be reconciled with the searcher's need to get the most information for the money? CAS is not the first and is not likely to be the last to try to wean us away from connect-time pricing. Perhaps searchers can have more input into alternatives next time. ∎

QUALITY CONTROL*

Each year there is one topic that stands out as *the* hot topic in the online world. In 1986 it was unquestionably CD-ROM. Exciting new technologies tend to take our attention away from the continuing, day-to-day issues and problems in searching. Intermediaries are concerned with more than the technology of online; more and more we are concerned about the quality of the product delivered via the technology. The issue of quality control, while not so glamorous as new technologies, continues to resurface as a serious concern.

Quality control is actually not a single issue, but involves several categories:

- quality of the database itself;
- quality of the sources that are used to create the database;
- quality of the telecommunications link;
- quality of the online vendor; or
- quality of the online searchers and the service they provide as intermediaries.

DATABASE QUALITY

Quality of the database itself, the most visible category, takes several forms:

- efficacy of error checking when the database is created—Good error checking will eliminate typographical errors, duplicate records with different accession numbers, and the same accession number used for more than one record. Although seemingly trivial, typographical errors can result in relevant records being missed, and, at the least, create a shoddy-looking product. Duplicate records result in a direct cost to the user now that most databases charge for each record retrieved.

- correct and consistent record description—In a high-quality database, the same fields always are used to mean the same thing, formatting of information in fields is consistent, and all citation information is correct. Inconsistent contents in fields impairs online retrieval; incorrect or inconsistent citation information impedes retrieval of complete documents.

- correct and consistent subject indexing—The use of a well-developed, cross-referenced, controlled vocabulary by qualified indexers will make subject index terms a more meaningful and useful retrieval tool. Searchers can plan strategy before going online and have more confidence in their search results. Indexing can never be 100 percent consistent, but spot checking and a policy of concern by the database producer can make it as good as possible.

- timely updating—Though timeliness is sometimes in conflict with quality indexing, database producers should at least be truthful and consistent about their updating schedule.

ACCURACY OF INFORMATION

More pernicious and more difficult to detect is poor quality of the information that is used to create a database. Database quality has been tested in court several times recently. The *Greenmoss Builders v. Dun and Bradstreet* case went all the way to the Supreme Court in 1984-85. Dun and Bradstreet used a teenager to gather primary information from the U.S. Federal Bankruptcy Court for input into their Business Information Report database. The student mistakenly reported that Greenmoss had declared bankruptcy, when in fact one of their one-time employees had declared personal bankruptcy. Greenmoss was able to show actual damages as a result of the dissemination of the erroneous information. They were also awarded punitive damages, even though Dun and Bradstreet argued that the error was not made maliciously. "Simple negligence" was enough because the matter was not judged to be of "public concern."

In 1986 the Supreme Court let stand a ruling that the Jeppesen-Sanderson chart-making subsidiary of Times Mirror was liable in a 1973 plane crash that happened because a Jeppesen-Sanderson chart erroneously depicted the flight approach into an Alaskan airport. Though the chart was based on information supplied by the FAA, Jeppesen-Sanderson was judged to be liable because under "strict liability" a company that makes a defective product is liable whether or not there is negligence.

Recently the families of a group of Massachusetts lobstermen were awarded a settlement of $1.25 million. Trusting a National Weather Service report of fair weather, the lobster fleet had put out to sea but an unexpected storm came up and the men drowned. The government was found to be liable.

Intermediaries are at the mercy of the information integrity of the databases they search. If an intermediary passes on incorrect information to a patron, are you or your institution morally or legally liable for any damages that may result? "Information malpractice" (an issue raised by Anne Mintz in *LJ*) is likely to become more of a concern for searchers and database producers in the future. Some database producers are beginning to print disclaimers about the accuracy of the information in their products, but few information intermediaries do so.

Data quality is not expected to get better soon. Dun and Bradstreet now sends information to be included about a company to that company for comment or correction, but many database producers resist such quality assurance procedures because they fear online users will not be willing to pay higher online fees to offset the extra expense or put up with resultant time lags. Jean-Paul Emard of Meckler Publishing

---

warns with the "cutback in government funding for data collection and research, the quality of data gathering is going to diminish. It portends to open up a Pandora's box of dirty data."

QUALITY OF SOURCES

A related issue is the quality of the source materials cited. A searcher is not likely to be sued over the retrieval of poorly written articles or trivia in an online search, but poor-quality articles do clutter up searches on today's huge databases.

Most users do not want comprehensive searches that retrieve hundreds of articles; some users do. Database producers risk the onus of censorship if they begin to eliminate journals or articles based on nebulous quality criteria. The Institute for Scientific Information (ISI) was once sued by the publishers of the *Scanning Electron Microscopy* journal, who claimed that ISI violated antitrust laws by not including their journal in ISI's *Current Contents*.

Clear inclusion criteria and publication of a list of sources included is one way many database producers help the intermediary to judge quality. Indexing that differentiates major and minor topics is of some use. A field with an intellectual quality decision or comment (some databases assign letter grades to reviews) may be a necessary feature in the future, though it makes most producers understandably nervous. One premise of ISI's citation indexes is that the number of times an article is cited reflects on its importance to a topic. Other such nontraditional retrieval aids may be needed.

TELECOMMUNICATIONS QUALITY

Poor quality in a telecommunications link can be irritating, but is more difficult to solve because it is more difficult to pinpoint. Quality of local telephone lines varies tremendously, the amount of traffic varies at each node, and the link made with an online vendor is different each time. DIALOG has attempted to provide better (and less expensive) service by creating their own telecommunications network. Experienced searchers get around poor telecommunications quality with tricks: searching at less popular times, hanging up and redialing to get a new line, and switching from one network to another.

The New England Online User's Group (NENON) has collected telecommunications trouble reports from its members since 1982. Complaints include noisy lines that cause garbled characters, disconnections in the midst of a search, and slow response time. Searchers are asked to record the specific complaint plus the date, time of day, network and vendor names, and port number. NENON batches the reports and forwards them to the appropriate network or vendor.

VENDOR QUALITY

Vendor quality depends on the telecommunications link, but goes beyond that. Other factors include:

- timely and consistently followed update schedules;
- adequate computer power to provide good response time even at peak periods;
- documentation that is kept up-to-date on a regular basis and is routinely checked for accuracy;
- knowledgeable personnel on trouble phone lines;
- consistent system response to input;
- meaningful error messages; and
- software that helps rather than hinders the searcher.

Barbara Quint, editor of *Database Searcher* (formerly *Database Enduser*), is planning to give awards to online vendors who "don't beat up on searchers." In her November 1986 editorial she calls for searchers to submit instances of "errors" that they make repeatedly (such as missing retrieval due to inconsistent use of singulars and plurals). Correcting these kinds of repetitious errors is a natural "job for a machine," not human searchers. Quint says, "A poor search is a mutual problem," between the vendor and the searcher. Search software should help searchers find the information they are looking for and help them get out of trouble. Few vendors have software that succeeds at this because "software hasn't substantially changed for 15 years." It's time vendors "listen to searchers" or "searchers must remember to shop around."

QUALITY OF SEARCHERS

Finally, quality depends on the online searchers themselves and the services they provide. Marcia Dellenbach of the Chicago Public Library addressed this issue at the Online '86 meeting in Chicago in November.

Chicago Public measures the quality of their search service by asking patrons about their satisfaction (about 80-90 percent are satisfied) and by looking at the printouts waiting to be picked up by patrons, to "judge whether or not the question has been answered, if the most appropriate databases were used, and if the strategy used makes sense."

In order to maintain a high quality search service, Chicago Public emphasizes continued training for and communications among searchers. It budgets for vendor, database, and in-house training classes. Vendor and database material is conscientiously updated and distributed to all searchers. Regular meetings allow new features and strategies to be shared. Administrative support and constant reevaluation of the search service are other trails followed.

The attempt to develop a professional searcher's code of ethics also addresses the issues of searcher quality. A proposed code includes ethical guidelines for such things as maintaining awareness of new information sources, making an unbiased selection of databases, and keeping search skills updated.

ACTION

The Quality Assurance Committee of the New England Online User's Group is encouraging searchers from all over the country to record instances of poor quality on the database, telecommunications, or vendor levels and forward them to

NENON, which will send them to the appropriate agencies. A copy of their Trouble Report form is available on the NENON electronic bulletin board on DIALOG's DIALMAIL. Contact Mary Chitty, Quality Assurance Committee, NENON, Inc., P.O. Box 753, Cambridge, MA 02238; 617-732-2813. Other online user's groups are urged to initiate similar campaigns. Perhaps the most effective tactic, however, is to select those databases and online systems that meet our own standards for quality.

BIBLIOGRAPHY

Dellenbach, Marcia, "Quality Control and Effective In-House Procedures for Online Managers," *Online '86 Conference Proceedings*, Online, Inc., 1986, p. 52-56.

Mintz, Anne P., "Information Practice and Malpractice," *LJ*, September 15, 1985, p. 38-43.

Mintz, Anne P., "Information Practice and Malpractice ... Do We Need Malpractice Insurance?" *Online*, July 1984, p. 20-26.

Pemberton, Jeff, "The Dark Side of Online Information— Dirty Data," *Database*, December 1983, p. 6-7.

Shaver, Donna B., Nancy S. Hewison, & Leslie W. Wykoff, "Ethics for Online Intermediaries," *Special Libraries*, Fall 1985, p. 238-245. ∎

APPENDIX
Complete List of Publications by Carol Tenopir
through 1988

1. BOOKS OF ORIGINAL SCHOLARSHIP

Carol Tenopir and Gerald Lundeen. *Managing Your Information: How to Design and Create a Textual Database on Your Microcomputer*. New York: Neal-Schuman, 1988.

2. CHAPTERS IN BOOKS

"Database Design and Management." In *Principles and Applications of Information Science for Library Professionals*, John Olsgaard, ed. Chicago: American Library Association, 1989. Pp. 52-68.

Carol Tenopir and Gerald Lundeen. "Sci-Mate Software System." In *Front-End Software*, Bella Weinberg and James Benson, eds. Ann Arbor, MI: Pierian Press, 1988. Pp. 61-66.

"CD-ROM in 1986." In *Library and Information Science Annual*. Littleton, CO: Libraries Unlimited, 1987. Pp. 21-25.

"Full Text Databases." In *Annual Review of Information Science and Technology*, Martha E. Williams, ed. White Plains, NY: Knowledge Industry Publications, Inc., 1984. Pp. 215-46.

3. EDITED VOLUMES

Pamela Cibbarelli, Carol Tenopir, and Edward J. Kazlauskas, eds. *Directory of Information Management Software*. Studio City, CA: Pacific Information Inc., 1983. Distributed by the American Library Association. 133p.

4. ARTICLES IN INTERNATIONAL OR NATIONAL REFEREED JOURNALS

Carol Tenopir and Gerald Lundeen. "Software Choices for In-House Databases." *Database* 12 (June 1988): 34-42.

"Online Education in Schools of Library and Information Science." *Online* 11 (January 1987): 65-66.

Gerald Lundeen and Carol Tenopir. "Microcomputer Software for In-House Databases ... Four Top Packages Under $2000." *Online* 9 (September 1985): 30-38.

"Online Searching With a Microcomputer: Downloading Issues." *Microcomputers for Information Management* 2 (June 1985): 77-89.

"Full Text Database Retrieval Performance." *Online Review* 9 (April 1985): 149-64.

"Information Science Education in the United States: Characteristics and Curricula." *Education for Information* 3 (March 1985): 3-28.

"Searching Harvard Business Review Online ... Lessons in Full Text Searching." *Online* 9 (March 1985): 71-81.

"Characteristics of Corporations That Founded Libraries: 1910-1921." *Special Libraries* 76 (Winter 1985): 43-52.

Gerald Lundeen and Carol Tenopir. "Microcomputer-Based Library Catalog Software." *Microcomputers for Information Management* 1 (September 1984): 215-28.

Carol Tenopir and Miles Jackson. "Telecommunication and Publishing in the South Pacific." *Electronic Publishing Review* 4 (September 1984): 189-200.

"Identification and Evaluation of Software for Microcomputer-Based In-House Databases." *Information Technology and Libraries* 3 (March 1984): 21-34. Reprinted in *Managing Online Reference*, Ethel Auster, ed. New York: Neal-Schuman, 1986. Pp. 50-69.

"Distribution of Citations in Databases in a Multidisciplinary Field." *Online Review* 6 (October 1982): 399-419.

"Evaluation of Database Coverage: A Comparison of Two Methodologies." *Online Review* 6 (October 1982): 423-41. Reprinted in *Managing Online Reference*, Ethel Auster, ed. New York: Neal-Schuman, 1986.

"An In-House Training Program for Online Searchers." *Online* 6 (May 1982): 20-26.

Carol Tenopir and Margaret Johnson. "OCLC Card Receipts." *Journal of Library Automation* 13 (June 1980): 136-38.

Carol Tenopir and Pamela Cibbarelli. "A Retrieval System for Engineering Drawings." *Special Libraries* 70 (February 1979): 91-96.

5. ARTICLES IN *LIBRARY JOURNAL*, "ONLINE DATABASES" COLUMN

"Database Selection Tools." 113 (November 1, 1988): 52-53.

"Decision Making by Reference Librarians." 113 (October 1, 1988): 66-67.

"An Interface for Self-Service Searching." 113 (September 1, 1988): 142-43.

"Evaluating Online Systems." 113 (June 1, 1988): 86-87.

"Searching Full-Text Databases." 113 (May 1, 1988): 60-61.

"Five Years Into the Past ... Five Years Into the Future." 113 (April 1, 1988): 62-63.

"Is Connect Time Pricing Obsolete?" 113 (March 1, 1988): 48-49.

"Other Ways to Access DIALOG." 113 (February 1, 1988): 44-45.

"Searching by Free Text or Controlled Vocabulary?" 112 (November 1987): 58-59.

"Publications on CD-ROM: Librarians Can Make a Difference." 112 (September 15, 1987): 62-63.

"Costs and Benefits of CD-ROM." 112 (September 1, 1987): 156-57.

"Learning How to Search." 112 (June 15, 1987): 54-55.

"Software For In-House Databases." 112 (May 15, 1987): 54-55.

"Reference Services From OCLC." 112 (April 15, 1987): 58-59.

"What Makes a Good Online Searcher?" 112 (March 15, 1987): 62-63.

"Quality Control." 112 (February 15, 1987): 124-25.

"CD-ROM Update." 111 (December 1986): 70-71.

"The EasyNet Gateway." 111 (November 1, 1986): 48-49.

"Why Don't More People Use Databases?" 111 (October 1, 1986): 68-69.

"InfoTrac: A Laser Disc System." 111 (September 1, 1986): 168-69.

"Four Options for End User Searching." 111 (July 1986): 56-57.

"What's New With WILSONLINE." 111 (June 1, 1986): 98-99.

"General Literature Online: Magazine Index and Readers' Guide." 111 (May 1, 1986): 92-93.

"Crisis or Change in the Database Industry?" 111 (April 1, 1986): 46-47.

"Databases on CD/ROM." 111 (March 1, 1986): 68-69.

"Online Searching in School Libraries." 111 (February 1, 1986): 60-61.

"Full Text and Bibliographic Databases." 110 (November 15, 1985): 62-63.

"Software for Online Searching." 110 (October 15, 1985): 52-53.

"Database Directories: The Rest." 110 (September 15, 1985): 56-57.

"Database Directories: In Print and Now Online." 110 (August 1985): 64-65.

"Systems for End Users: Are There End Users for the Systems?" 110 (June 15, 1985): 40-41.

"Database Subsets." 110 (May 15, 1985): 42-43.

"Library Use of the Source and CompuServe." 110 (April 15, 1985): 58-59.

"Online Searching With a Microcomputer." 110 (March 15, 1985): 42-43.

"Online Professionals." 110 (February 15, 1985): 122-23.

"Conferences for Online Professionals." 110 (January 1985): 62-63.

"Online Searching in the Popular Literature." 109 (December 1984): 2242-43.

"'Other' Bibliographic Systems." 109 (November 1, 1984): 2008-9.

"Database Access Software." 109 (October 1, 1984): 1828-29.

"H. W. Wilson: Online At Last." 109 (September 1, 1984): 1616-17.

"Pricing Policies." 109 (July 1984): 1300-1301.

"IAC's Document Delivery and More." 109 (June 1, 1984): 1104-5.

"In-House Training and Staff Development." 109 (May 1, 1984): 870-71.

"To Err Is Human: Seven Common Searching Mistakes." 109 (April 1, 1984): 635-36.

"Newspapers Online." 109 (March 1, 1984): 452-53.

"The Database Industry Today: Some Vendors' Perspectives." 109 (February 1, 1984): 156-57.

"Online '83 in Chicago." 108 (December 15, 1983): 2310-12.

"More Publications about Databases." 108 (November 15, 1983): 2140-41.

"Online Information in the Health Sciences." 108 (October 15, 1983): 1932-33.

"The Online Future at ASIS." 108 (July 1983): 1332-33.

"Full-Text, Downloading, and Other Issues." 108 (June 1, 1983): 1111-13.

"In-House Databases II: Evaluating and Choosing Software." 108 (May 1, 1983): 885-88.

"In-House Databases I: Software Sources." 108 (April 1, 1983): 639-41.

"DIALOG's Knowledge Index and BRS/After Dark: Database Searching on Personal Computers." 108 (March 1, 1983): 471-74.

"Databases: Catching Up and Keeping Up." 108 (February 1, 1983): 180-81.

6. ARTICLES IN OTHER PERIODICALS

"Student Online Data Base Searching: Part II." *Computing Teacher* 13 (May 1986): 39-40, 57.

"Student Online Data Base Searching: Part I." *Computing Teacher* 13 (April 1986): 18-19.

"The Library Connection: From Folders to Floppies." *Update: Computers in Medicine* 2 (July/August 1984): 27-31.

"The Information Professional in 25 Years." In *Information and Special Libraries in 2009: Informed Speculations.* Chicago: Special Libraries Association, Illinois Chapter, 1984. P. 25.

7. BOOK REVIEWS IN REFEREED JOURNALS

Review of *Information Online 86, Proceedings of the First Australian Information Conference.* (Sydney: Library Association of Australia, 1986.) In *Journal of the American Society for Information Science* 39 (January 1988): 25.

Review of *Online Information Retrieval* by Stephen Harter. (New York: Academic Press, 1986.) In *Information Processing and Management* 23 (No. 4, 1987): 383.

Review of *Information Technology in the Library/Information School Curriculum*, Chris Armstrong and Stella Keenan, eds. (London: Gower, 1985.) In *Journal of Education for Library and Information Science* 27 (Fall 1986): 126-28.

Review of *A Study of User Adaptation to an Interactive Information Retrieval System* by Charles T. Meadow. In *Library and Information Science Research* 6 (July/September 1984): 341-42.

8. INTERNAL REPORTS AND OTHER UNPUBLISHED WORKS

Carol Tenopir and Martha E. Williams. *FEMA Database Requirements Assessment and Resource Directory Model.* Final Report for the Federal Emergency Management Agency, FEMA EMW-1-4058. May 1982. 123p.

9. PUBLISHED CONFERENCE PROCEEDINGS

"Users and Uses of Full Text Databases." In *Proceedings of the 12th International Online Information Meeting, December 1988, London, England.* Oxford, England: Learned Information, Ltd., 1988. 7p. In press.

"Search Strategies for Full Text Databases." In *Proceedings of the American Society for Information Science Annual Meeting, October 1988, Atlanta.* Medford, NJ: Learned Information, 1988. 9p.

"Managing Text: Software Choices for Textual Databases." In *Proceedings of the Online '88 Conference, October 1988, New York.* Weston, CT: Online, Inc., 1988. Pp. 143-47.

Keiko Ikushima and Carol Tenopir. "Coverage of Japanese Scientific and Technical Periodicals in Major English Language Databases." In *Proceedings of the National Online Meeting, New York, May 1988.* Medford, NJ: Learned Information, 1988.

"End User Search Systems: A Comparison." In *Proceedings of the Online '83 Conference, Chicago, October 1983.* Weston, CT: Online, Inc., 1983. Pp. 280-85.

"Contributions of Value Added Fields and Full Text Searching in Full Text Databases." In *Proceedings of the National Online Meeting, New York, April 27-May 3, 1985*. Medford, NJ: Learned Information, 1985. Pp. 463-70.

Carol Tenopir and Barbara Bird. "Introducing Online Search Services Using Videotape." In *The Information Community: An Alliance for Progress, Proceedings of the American Society for Information Science Annual Meeting* 18 (October 1981): 189-91.

"Evaluation of Library Retrieval Software." In *Communicating Information, Proceedings of the American Society for Information Science Annual Meeting* 17 (October 1980): 64-67.

"Realistically Reassessing the Cost and Functions of Special Libraries." Presented at the Special Libraries Association Annual Meeting, June 1979. 22p. ERIC Fiche ED194088.

"Intracorporate Networks." In *Proceedings of the American Society for Information Science Mid-Year Meeting* (May 1979). Microfiche.

Pamela Cibbarelli, Carol Tenopir, and Retha Z. Ott. "LIBNOTES—A Laboratory Notebook Retrieval System." In *The Information Age in Perspective, Proceedings of the American Society for Information Science Annual Meeting* 15 (November 1978): 67-69.

Carol Tenopir and Pamela Cibbarelli. "A Retrieval System for Engineering Drawings." Presented at the Special Libraries Association Annual Meeting, June 1978. 11p. ERIC Fiche ED167168.

"An Environmental Library System." Presented at the Special Libraries Association Annual Meeting, June 1978. 23p. ERIC Fiche ED165737.

"Total Information Centers." In *Proceedings of the Annual Meeting of the American Society for Information Science Mid-Year Meeting* (May 1978). 12p. ERIC Fiche ED165738.

10. PUBLISHED ABSTRACTS

"Online." Section in *Writings on Scholarly Communication: A Selected Annotated Bibliography for Librarians, Publishers, and Scholars in the Humanities*. Washington, DC: American Council of Learned Societies, Office of Scholarly Communication and Technology, 1987.

INDEX

ABI/INFORM. *See* University Microfilms International

Abstracts (free text searching), 145-47
    combined with title searching, 146
    compared with controlled vocabulary searching, 145-47
    full text and bibliographic field searching compared, 84-90
    impact of writing style, 89, 146

Adjacency operator. *See* Proximity searching

American Chemical Society, search studies, 81, 85. *See also* Chemical Abstracts

American Library Association (ALA), 5, 10, 11, 15, 28
    ALANET, 28
    Machine Assisted Reference Service, 152
    national meetings, 62, 65, 72, 153

American Society for Information Science (ASIS), 5
    national meetings, 64, 151, 165, 167, 169
    special interest groups, 151

AND operator (full text searching). *See also* Boolean logic operations
    compared with paragraph proximity and word adjacency, 80, 92-97
    limitations in full text searching, 82
    value in partial document retrieval, 80, 82, 97

Answer Machine. *See* EasyNet

ASIS. *See* American Society for Information Science

Association of Information and Dissemination Centers (ASIDIC), downloading issues, 168

Authority lists. *See* Controlled vocabulary

Automatic database selection. *See* Database selection

AV-Online, 24

Baud rates, 29, 31, 33, 171-72

Biblio-Link, 40

BiblioFile, 72

Bibliographic database. *See* Database, bibliographic

Bibliographic union, defined, 86. *See also* Retrieval performance

BIOSIS, 24, 37, 41, 145, 167

Boolean logic operations, 22, 23, 25, 27, 39, 41, 56, 63, 80, 125, 142-43. *See also* AND operator; NOT operator; OR operator

Bound phrases. *See* Parsing

Bowker, R. R., reference works on CD-ROM, 65

Bradford's Law of Scatter
    database applications, 111-21
    defined, 112-13

BRS. *See also* Online systems
    BRS/AFTER DARK, 10, 15, 16, 22-23, 40, 41, 122, 125, 126, 127, 145
        compared with Knowledge Index, 24-26
        searching, 25-26
    BRS/COLLEAGUE, 122
    BRS Educator, 21
    BRS Instructor, 21
    BRS Onsite, 163
    BRS/SEARCH, 122
    CROSS Index, 25, 160
    display features, 80, 85
    educational use, 21
    electronic mail, 6
    File Soft, 47, 51
    library use, 124-26
    online market statistics, 6, 167
    search features, 41, 80, 85-86, 144
    search methods study, 85, 115
    training video, 153

CA Search. *See* Chemical Abstracts

CAI. *See* Computer Assisted Instruction

CD-ROM, 9-11, 61-78
    advantages, 61-62, 171
    coexistence with online and print, 9-11, 64, 73, 74-78, 171
    costs, 64, 74-78
    directories, 65, 67-68
    hardware, 62-63, 76-77
    history, 62, 64
    in-house databases, 163
    librarians' influence, 72-74
    market survey, 66-67
    products and producers, 64-66, 67-69
    standardization, 64, 66, 73, 171
    12-inch discs, 62
    vendors, 64-66, 69. *See also* Infotrac; DIALOG Ondisc; Microsoft, etc.

Chemical Abstracts, 36-37, 80, 100, 145, 166, 167, 171, 172-73

Combination parsing. *See* Parsing

Command language (database searching), 39, 56, 63, 125
    compared with menu-driven interface, 25-26, 125
    need for standardization, 17, 143-44, 145, 164

Commerce Business Daily, downloading provisions, 34

Communications software. *See* Software, communications

This index was prepared by Dr. Tenopir's indexing and abstracting class at University of Hawaii School of Library and Information Studies Spring 1989. The following are names of the participants:

James Adamson   Wallace Grant

Ah Win   Aung Gyi

Nancy Allerston   Keiko Hassler

Mary Bailey   Soon Young Kim

Patricia Butson   Christine Orrall

Nand Dayal   Fred Roecker